Palgrave Law Masters

Family Law

Palgrave Law Masters

Series Editor: **Marise Cremona**

Family Law

Third Edition

Kate Standley

Law series editor: Marise Cremona
*Professor of European Commercial Law Centre for
Commercial Law Studies, Queen Mary, University of London*

palgrave

First published 2001 by
PALGRAVE
Houndmills, Basingstoke, Hampshire RG21 6XS and
175 Fifth Avenue, New York, N. Y. 10010
Companies and representatives throughout the world

PALGRAVE is the new global academic imprint of
St. Martin's Press LLC Scholarly and Reference Division and
Palgrave Publishers Ltd (formerly Macmillan Press Ltd).

ISBN 0–333–94942–0

This book is printed on paper suitable for recycling and made from fully managed and sustained forest sources.

A catalogue record for this book is available from the British Library.

10   9   8   7   6   5   4   3   2
10   09   08   07   06   05   04   03   02   01

Printed and bound in Great Britain by
Creative Print & Design (Wales), Ebbw Vale

V

Contents

Part III   FAMILY PROPERTY

Preface

Family law continues to develop at a rapid pace. New statutes, new policies, and a constant spate of case-law continue to challenge and to instruct. Keeping abreast of developments remains an exciting but difficult task.

Since the second edition there have been important new developments. Of particular significance has been the implementation of the Human Rights Act 1998, which will have an important impact on family law. Also significant has been the Government's decision not to introduce the proposed reforms of divorce law laid down in Part II of the Family Law Act 1996, despite the general consensus that the reform of divorce is long overdue. Other important changes to family law have included the introduction of new ancillary relief rules in the wake of the Woolf reforms of civil procedure, and the introduction of pension splitting on divorce.

There has continued to be a constant spate of family law cases. Since the last edition there have been important case-law developments, in particular the case of *White* v. *White*, in which the House of Lords considered how the court should exercise its powers in ancillary relief cases on divorce. There have also been important cases on the interpretation of the domestic violence provisions in Part IV of the Family Law Act 1996, the statutory 'threshold' requirements for care orders under the Children Act 1989, and on the defence of acquiescence in the Hague Convention on Child Abduction.

In addition to changes which have already occurred, important changes are due to come into force in the future. Thus, radical changes to the law on child support are proposed, and so are changes to the law on parental responsibility, and adoption.

Because of the expanding girth of family law, particularly the human rights perspective, and the need to cover the many and varied past and future changes, I have had to cut out some material in order to accommodate new developments. Thus the sections on bankruptcy and undue influence and the family home have gone from this edition to allow for other legal developments.

Despite all the changes, the aim of the book remains the same as that stated in the Preface to the first edition, namely to provide an up-to-date, clear and succinct account of family law. I hope it continues to do this. I realise that some readers might prefer a more discursive approach throughout the whole book, but the aim of the book is to give a good grounding in family law, and to whet the appetite and provide the basis for further study and further thought.

For this reason, I have included lists of suggested reading and useful website addresses at the ends of chapters.

I must once again express my gratitude to John, my husband and best friend, for his constant support and encouragement, and also for his preparation of the indexes of statutes and cases.

Finally, I have decided to dedicate this edition to my family law students, past and present. Teaching them all has been a challenging and enriching experience, and also a great deal of fun. I hope that they have enjoyed learning family law as much as I have enjoyed teaching it.

I have endeavoured to state the law as at February 2001.

Kate Standley

Table of Cases

Table of Statutes

Table of Conventions

Table of Rules

Table of Regulations

Part I

Family Law – An Introduction

1 Family Law Today

1.1 Family Law: Changes and Trends

Family law is an area of law where there have been major developments, and where further important changes are due to take place. The last decade, in particular, has witnessed major changes. Of particular importance was the Children Act 1989 which came into force in October 1991, making fundamental and far-reaching changes to the civil law relating to children. In April 1993 a new system of child support was introduced by the Child Support Act 1991, which removed child maintenance in most cases from the courts into the Child Support Agency. Radical changes were also made to the law relating to domestic violence and occupation of the family home by Part IV of the Family Law Act 1996. During the 1990s there was also widespread criticism of the unsatisfactory state of divorce law and a radically reformed new divorce law was expected to come into force in the year 2000. However, in June 1999 the Lord Chancellor, Lord Irvine, unexpectedly announced that implementation of the reforms was to be postponed indefinitely, and in December 2000 he announced that the reforms would not come into force at all. Despite this, there is still almost universal agreement that the introduction of a truly 'no fault' divorce is long overdue, so that reform in some form or another is likely to take place eventually. However, despite the problem of finding a workable new divorce law, there have been important changes in respect of pensions on divorce. Furthermore, in June 2000 a new procedure for dealing with ancillary relief applications on divorce was introduced. A major new development has been the Human Rights Act 1998 which came into force in October 2000, and which has interwoven the European Convention for the Protection of Human Rights and Fundamental Freedoms 1950 into the fabric of English law (see 1.5 below).

Important changes to family law are due to be implemented in the near future. Thus, changes to child support are due to come into force in 2001 to make the process simpler, faster and easier to understand. The law on parental responsibility is also about to be changed to allow unmarried fathers whose names are registered on their child's birth certificate to have 'automatic' parental responsibility. In some areas of family law, changes are not proposed but there has been considerable discussion and debate. There is widespread concern, in particular, about the distribution of property on the breakdown of cohabitation relationships. While reform is not imminent, it is likely that reform will eventually take place. There has also been discussion about the way in which the court exercises its powers to distribute property on divorce.

Other issues such as the legal representation of children and the reform of adoption law are also the subject of discussion. A White Paper on adoption was published at the end of the year 2000. Cost, delay and lack of co-ordination in the family law system are frequently also cause for concern.

In addition to the changes to the law, there have been important developments in the way in which family disputes, particularly divorce disputes, are handled. It has been increasingly realised that adversarial litigation is not an ideal way to solve family disputes. Not only is it expensive, but it increases hostility between the parties which can have an adverse effect on them and their children. For this reason mediation, an alternative form of dispute resolution to that of going to court, has been increasingly promoted (see 1.3 below).

Reforms of the law have brought about important ideological changes. There have been changes in terminology, for example, which have created a change of culture, particularly in the area of child law (see Bainham, 1998). Thus, instead of parental 'rights', we now have parental 'responsibility'. Instead of 'custody', the emphasis is on the residence of the child. Instead of 'access' there is 'contact'. The Children Act 1989 in particular introduced changes of ideology, for instance, a new policy of 'non-intervention', a greater emphasis on children's voices being heard, and the importance of inter-agency co-operation and working in partnership with parents. The law has also witnessed a shift from adult and parental interests towards children's interests. Parents and the State have legal and social responsibilities for children regardless of whether their parents are married or cohabiting. There has also been a greater recognition that children have rights, although some would say that this recognition has not gone far enough. Thus, there are those who advocate that children should have a greater say in legal proceedings, and there has been dissatisfaction with the Government's half-hearted attempt to protect children from physical punishment by their parents.

Another trend in family law is its increasing international dimension. Not only do courts in England and Wales have to deal with such matters as the recognition of foreign marriages and divorces and applications for ancillary relief after a foreign divorce, but it has been increasingly realised that some family matters must be governed not by national law but by international conventions. Thus, there are, for instance, conventions governing child abduction, inter-country adoption, the protection of minors and the reciprocal enforcement of maintenance. The European Convention for the Protection of Human Rights and Fundamental Freedoms has added a further international dimension. The United Nations Convention on the Rights of the Child 1989 is also an important convention which exists to encourage countries to promote and uphold the rights of children. Although there is no court to enforce this Convention, the UN Committee on the Rights of the Child, set up under the Convention, monitors its implementation in Member States and makes recommendations and suggestions to governments about areas of the law needing reform. European Community law has also had some impact on family law in respect of the free movement rights of family members and their rights to social security benefits (see, for example, *Hughes* v. *Chief Adjudication Officer* [1993] 1 FLR 791 and *R* v. *Immigration Appeal Tribunal ex Parte Secretary of State for the Home Department* [1993] 1 FLR 798, and Woods, 1999). The international dimension also has an impact on family law reform. For instance, when the Law Commission was discussing reform of divorce in England and Wales, it made a close study of divorce law in other countries. Recognition of same-sex marriages and 50:50 splits of matrimonial assets on divorce exist in some countries, and the possibility of such developments taking place in the UK has been mooted.

In addition to legal developments, there have been important demographic and social changes. Cohabitation is increasing. Marriage is on the decline. Divorce is common (there are more than 140 000 divorces each year). Increasing numbers of families are lone-parent families (23 per cent of families in the UK, according to *Eurostat*, 1998). More children are being born outside marriage. There are also increasing numbers of elderly persons. These demographic and social changes impact both on family law and on Government policy. Indeed social changes are happening so rapidly that it is difficult for policy-makers to keep up with them (see the report, *Family Change, A Guide to the Issues*, published by the Family Policy Studies Centre, www.fpsc.org.uk).

The Government is committed to ensuring that the family is supported. Lord Irvine, the Lord Chancellor, at the UK Family Law Conference, London, June 1999, opened his speech with the following words (www.open.gov.uk/lcd/speeches/1999):

'Family life is the foundation on which our communities, our society, and our country are built. Families are central to the Government's vision of a secure, just and inclusive society. It is vital that we develop and maintain effective policies to support family life. The Government knows it bears a weighty responsibility to get family policy right first time – it is too important, too central to people's lives, for us to risk rushing headlong into change for change's sake, legislating in haste and repenting at leisure.'

In 1998 the Home Office published a Consultation Paper, *Supporting Families*, in which it was also stated that '[F]amily life is the foundation on which our communities, our society and our country are built' (Foreword, p.2). The Consultation Paper made several proposals, including the introduction of various programmes to support the family, such as the National Family and Parenting Institute, the Sure Start programme and early years' initiatives. 'Parentline', a telephone helpline service to families needing practical advice on the problems they face, has also been established. Jack Straw, the Home

Secretary, in *Supporting Families* (at p.4), identified three principles upon which Government policy on the family is based: first, that children's interests must be paramount; secondly, that children need stability and security; and thirdly, that, wherever possible, Government should offer support to all parents so that they can better support their children. The Government stressed, however, that it should be wary about intervening in areas of private life, and should also recognise just how much families have changed (paras. 4 and 5, p.4). Nonetheless, the Government stressed a preference for recognising family life based on marriage.

In its proposals for supporting families, the Government said that attention should be concentrated on the following five areas, as these were areas where Government action could make a difference (p.5, *Supporting Families*):

- 'ensuring that all parents have access to the advice and support they need, improving services and strengthening the ways in which the wider family and communities support and nurture family life;
- improving family prosperity, reducing child poverty, and ensuring that the tax and benefit system properly acknowledges the costs of bringing up children;
- making it easier for parents to spend more time with their children by helping families to balance work and home;
- strengthening marriage and reducing the risks of family breakdown;
- tackling the more serious problems of family life, including domestic violence and school-age pregnancy.'

1.2   The Function, Scope and Nature of Family Law

One way of understanding family law is to consider what functions it performs. Family law can be described as having the following functions: defining and altering status; providing physical protection and economic support; and providing mechanisms for adjusting and dividing property. These functions may overlap. Thus, when a couple divorce, the decree of divorce alters their status, but they may also need to take steps to ensure that their property interests are adjusted and that they and their children have financial support. Defining the functions of family law also provides a set of criteria or goals against which the success or failure of the law can be judged, in order to help assess whether reform is needed. Thus, for instance, the law governing the property rights of cohabitants could be considered in the context of the protective, supportive and adjustive functions of family law to establish whether the law needs reforming. Another way of considering family law is to ask what its objectives should be. Lawson (1999) suggests as possible objectives the support of marriage and the family, the minimising of conflict on relationship breakdown, the protection of children, listening to children's wishes, avoiding delay, and doing all these things as efficiently and cheaply as possible.

However, whether family law adequately performs these functions and satisfies its objectives also depends on how far the boundaries of family law should extend. In other words, it depends on its scope.

The scope of family law depends partly on whether the word 'family' is given a wide or a narrow definition. There are different ways of defining a family. It may be defined as members of the same household, or as a group of people related by blood, or as a group of parents and children. In some cultures the extended family is important, but in the UK the word 'family' usually refers to the nuclear or immediate family. The 'family', however, has no legal personality as such in English law. Instead, statutes give rights and remedies to individual family members (spouses, parents, guardians and children). Although most family law cases are concerned with the nuclear family (father, mother and children), not with the extended family (grandparents, aunts, uncles and cousins), other family members and persons outside the immediate family can apply to the courts. Thus persons other than parents can apply for orders under the Children Act 1989, although they often need the court's permission to do so, and the law on domestic violence now provides remedies for persons other than married couples, cohabitants and their children.

Family law has increasingly made provision for cohabiting couples, but largely only for cohabitants living in heterosexual partnerships equivalent to the relationship of husband and wife. However, it has been argued that the law should give more rights and remedies to gay and lesbian partners. Bailey-Harris (1999), for example, has argued in favour of a 'robust interpretation of the Human Rights Act by the judiciary in this country to ensure that lesbians and gay men enjoy the right to respect for family life from a position of equality with heterosexual women and men' (p.560).

English law has given some recognition to homosexual cohabitants, but it is of a limited kind. Thus, in *Fitzpatrick* v. *Sterling Housing Association Ltd* [1999] 2 FLR 1027, the question was whether Mr Fitzpatrick who had lived with his male partner in a stable and long-lasting relationship should be entitled on his partner's death to succeed to a protected tenancy under the Rent Act 1977. The House of Lords held by a majority of 3 to 2 that he was entitled to succeed to the tenancy as the word 'family' in para. 3(1) of Sched. 1 to the Act could be interpreted flexibly to include the same-sex partner of the tenant's family. It was held that the word 'family' involved a relationship where there was a degree of mutual interdependence, the sharing of lives, caring and love, commitment and support. On the facts, Mr Fitzpatrick had been a member of the deceased's 'family' and was therefore entitled to succeed to the tenancy. Despite finding in Mr Fitzpatrick's favour, however, the House of Lords was unwilling to interpret 'living with the original tenant as his or her wife or husband' (in para. 2(2)) to include a homosexual partnership. It also stressed that its decision was strictly limited to the interpretation of the Rent Act, and that it was not a case which gave homosexuals rights more generally.

Nonetheless, the decision does provide judicial recognition that the family can mean more than the 'traditional' family. Indeed, Ward LJ in the Court of Appeal in *Fitzpatrick* said that the family should be defined in terms of its functions rather than in terms of its structures or components. His Lordship said that its functions could be 'procreative, sexual, social, economic, and emotional,' but that this list was not exhaustive. His Lordship stated that not all families functioned in the same way.

Despite finding in favour of Mr Fitzpatrick, the decision nevertheless shows the reluctance of the English courts to give same-sex cohabitants the same legal recognition as heterosexual cohabitants. In some countries, however, same-sex partners have been given legal rights similar to those possessed by married couples. In The Netherlands and France, for example, homosexual partners can enter into registered partnerships and thereby acquire legal rights and obligations similar to those possessed by heterosexual partners, and in New South Wales, Australia, the term '*de facto*' spouses includes cohabiting same-sex couples. Although there are no proposals to introduce registered partnerships in this country, the courts have been increasingly willing to recognise the family rights of homosexual partners. Thus, for example, lesbian couples have been allowed to adopt children and to have children live with them on family breakdown. Furthermore, in a recent case which received considerable media coverage, two gay men were allowed to keep the twins they had acquired by means of a surrogacy arrangement entered into with an agency in the USA.

We have established that family law is largely concerned with the rights and duties of the immediate family and the remedies available to it, but how far do the boundaries of the subject extend? As the family, and consequently family law, does not exist in a vacuum, family law inevitably interacts with other areas of the law, such as contract, trusts, tort, criminal law and administrative law. Certain specialised areas of law also affect families, in particular tax law, labour law, education law, housing law and social welfare law. Traditionally, however, family law does not cover all these areas but is confined to marriage, divorce, cohabitation and related financial and property issues, including some of the law relating to children. Thus, family law is not concerned with all the law affecting families, but concentrates instead on the creation and removal of status (marriage, divorce, parenthood), on the legal consequences flowing from the creation and removal of status, and on protection for family members. Family law also extends into the area of child law, so that adoption and local authority powers and duties in respect of children are included. New developments in human reproductive technology and surrogacy are also included. Masson (1997, at 178) encapsulates some of the distinguishing characteristics of the family justice system:

'The family justice system impacts on most people through the control over divorce, the reordering of legal relationships, the consequent reallocation of property, and the enforcement of obligations to provide financial support. It is concerned not only with private relationships between adults and between adults and children, but also with the relationship between families and the State through public law, child protection proceedings, and the workings of the Child Support Agency (CSA). At its centre are the family courts, but much of what is found in court orders is the result of lawyer negotiation or family mediation, or a combination of the two.'

One of the distinguishing characteristics of family law is its discretionary nature. Judges often have to conduct difficult balancing exercises. This is particularly true in private law children's cases and in disputes between divorcing couples about property and finance. Because of the complexity of family life, the courts must inevitably possess considerable discretion, and in fact earlier cases do not always create strict precedents as they do in other branches of the law. However, while discretion has the great advantage of flexibility, discretion can have disadvantages (see Schneider, 1993). It can, for instance, create unpredictability and arbitrariness. Different judges may come to different conclusions in similar cases. Unpredictability, uncertainty and the fact that different courts reached markedly different decisions on similar facts was one of the Government's justifications for moving child maintenance from the courts into the Child Support Agency. More recently, there has been concern about the discretionary nature of ancillary relief proceedings and a presumption of a 50/50 split was proposed in order to introduce certainty into the system. The proposal has, however, been rejected, at least for the time being.

The discretionary nature of family law governs the way in which appeals are dealt with by the courts. Because of the discretionary nature of family law there may be several reasonable solutions to a family dispute, and for this reason the appeal courts are unwilling to overturn decisions made by the lower courts unless the decision is wrong in law or is outside a band of reasonable decisions and therefore plainly wrong (see *G* v. *G (Minors)(Custody Appeal)* [1985] 1 WLR 647). This rule should be borne in mind when considering an appeal.

1.3 The Importance of Mediation and Settlement

Most family disputes arising in private family law, that is between private individuals, are settled by agreement and negotiation with or without the assistance of lawyers. In fact, despite the number of reported cases, most cases do not go to court, and, even if they do, are often settled at the door of the court. Most family lawyers work within a conciliatory framework. Many family law solicitors are members of the Solicitors' Family Law Association (SFLA) which aims to encourage the amicable resolution of family disputes. It has a Code of Practice (now in its fourth edition) which governs the way in which solicitors who subscribe to the Code must practise. The Family Law Bar Association has similar aims.

Mediation has been increasingly used, and increasingly promoted, as a better way to settle family disputes than going to court, particularly for separating and divorcing couples in respect of some or all of the issues arising from relationship breakdown. Not only does mediation provide a means of avoiding the cost, expense, trauma, uncertainty and delay of litigation, but it helps improve communication between the parties and reduces hostility, conflict and bitterness. Mediation can also empower the parties, thereby making them better able to deal with disputes arising in the future, for instance in respect of their continuing parental responsibilities.

What is 'mediation'? In practical terms it involves both parties sitting down with a neutral arbitrator whose task is to help them identify issues in dispute and discover how to resolve them by reaching agreement. The aim of the process is not for the mediator to impose a solution on the parties but for the parties themselves to explore the possibility of reaching agreement. The process is confidential and non-coercive. If mediation about property and finance on divorce is successful, then the agreement made by the parties can be incorporated into a court order known as a consent order, a document prepared by the parties' lawyers which is subsequently endorsed by the court (see 9.8).

Mediation techniques were originally developed for settling disputes about children, where 'conciliation' was the term used, and which was provided by both in-court and out-of-court schemes. However, it was increasingly realised that conciliation techniques were extremely valuable for settling the whole spectrum of issues arising on divorce, not just disputes about children. Hence similar techniques were used to help settle disputes about property and finance, and the term 'mediation' came to be used. Mediation techniques therefore aim to settle disputes arising on divorce, not just about children but also about finance and property. The importance of mediation in the context of divorce is evidenced by the fact that the Solicitors' Family Law Association (SFLA) Mediation Committee and the UK College of Mediators have recently produced a financial disclosure document based on the court Form E but adapted for mediation purposes (the form can be downloaded from the UK College of Mediators' website – details at the end of this chapter).

Mediation in the UK is performed by three main types of organisation: by the court welfare service whose staff are trained social workers; by independent agencies; and by law firms. The court welfare service's role is centred on helping couples settle disputes about residence and contact issues in respect of children on family breakdown, although property and financial issues are often entangled in discussion (see the research by Greatbatch and Dingwall,

1999). The role of the independent agencies, like that of the court welfare service, originally focused on disputes about children, but since about the mid-1990s they have offered a comprehensive mediation service dealing with all issues arising on relationship breakdown. As far as law firms are concerned, some employ mediators to work alongside them, but some solicitors (and barristers) are lawyer–mediators, because where comprehensive mediation is required it is better if the mediator also possesses a knowledge of the law. Under the new ancillary relief scheme (see 9.2), the district judge also effectively acts as a mediator in the Financial Dispute Resolution (FDR) appointment.

While there is generally widespread support for mediation, it has also been the subject of concern. One concern originally voiced was that there was no clear idea about what the process really involved, as there was considerable diversity of practice. However, with the creation of the UK College of Family Mediators, practice has now been standardised. The College has a Code of Practice, a disciplinary Code and a Complaints Procedure. Another concern has been that agreements reached by mediation might not always be those of the parties but might have been imposed by the mediator, or imposed by the party in the stronger bargaining position. Some commentators have been concerned that removing disputes from the court might create 'lawyerless justice' and might even threaten the rule of law. Another concern has centred on the problem of domestic violence and mediation. Greatbatch and Dingwall (1999) have examined how allegations of domestic violence are handled in mediation sessions, and have found (see pp.174–5) that the assumptions on which mediation is based (namely the peaceful resolution of disputes in a reasonable and rational matter) are fatally undermined when domestic violence has occurred in the parties' relationship.

Mediation was set to play a greater role under reforms of divorce law (see 7.5) which were due to come into force in the year 2000 under Part II of the Family Law Act 1996, but which were indefinitely postponed in June 1999 and eventually abolished in December 2000. However, although these reforms will not now be implemented, the Government remains fully committed to supporting mediation for divorcing couples. The Lord Chancellor, Lord Irvine, in a speech given at the Fourth European Conference on Family Law organised by the Council of Europe and held in Strasbourg in October 1998, stated that the British Government wished mediation 'to become a central element in the culture of dispute resolution – a culture which will become less and less about gaining advantages over, and "scoring points" off, an ex-partner and more about making sensible arrangements for the future.' In a speech at the UK Family Law Conference, London, in June 1999, Lord Irvine said that the 'rolling out of publicly funded mediation' under Part III of the Family Law Act 1996 would continue. (Lord Irvine's speeches are available on the Lord Chancellor's Department's website – details at the end of this chapter.)

1.4   The Courts Administering Family Law

There is no special family court in England and Wales. Family cases are heard
in the Family Division of the High Court, in county courts, and in magistrates'
family proceedings courts. Some proceedings are heard in any of these courts,
but some must be heard in a particular court. Thus, for example, divorce proceedings are heard in specially designated county courts called 'divorce
county courts', and child abduction and other cases with an international
dimension are heard in the High Court. Children Act 1989 cases, and applications for non-molestation and occupation orders under Part IV of the Family
Law Act 1996 can be heard by magistrates' family proceedings courts, county
courts or the High Court. Contentious probate cases (cases where a will is disputed) are heard in the Chancery Division of the High Court. Non-contentious
probate matters are dealt with by the Family Division of the High Court (e.g.
granting letters of administration to a person to enable him or her to deal with
the estate where there is no will).

Magistrates' Family Proceedings Courts

Cases in the magistrates' family proceedings courts are heard by lay and
stipendiary magistrates specially trained in family work who are assisted by
the clerk of the court. Magistrates can make private law orders (e.g. orders for
financial provision and orders in respect of domestic violence) although they
have a more limited jurisdiction than the superior courts. They can make
adoption orders concurrently with county courts and the High Court. Private
law cases under the Children Act 1989 can be heard in the family proceedings
court (e.g. for a s.8 order or parental responsibility order), except where they
involve divorce. Public law cases under the Children Act must start in the
magistrates' family proceedings court, but can be transferred up to the county
court or High Court. Complex or urgent cases can, however, be transferred
from the magistrates' to a county court or the High Court, where there is a
need to consolidate proceedings.

County Courts

County courts deal with most family law matters. Most county courts are designated 'divorce county courts', which have jurisdiction to grant decrees of
divorce, nullity and judicial separation, and hear applications for ancillary
relief. Injunctions relating to domestic violence can be granted by county
courts, as can s.17 applications under the Married Women's Property Act
1882. County courts also have jurisdiction to make declarations in respect of

beneficial ownership of property. Under the Children (Allocation of Proceedings) Order 1991, certain county courts are designated as care centres and family hearing centres for hearing Children Act 1989 proceedings, and are staffed by specially qualified judges. The county court also has a limited jurisdiction to deal with wardship matters, but these are usually dealt with by the High Court. Difficult, lengthy or serious public law or private law cases can be transferred from the county court to the High Court. (Private law cases are those brought by private individuals, generally in the context of divorce or separation. Public law cases are those brought by local authorities and include matters such as care, supervision and emergency protection orders.)

The Family Division of the High Court

The Family Division of the High Court hears wardship cases, child abduction cases under the Hague and European Conventions, and appeals and cases transferred from family hearing centres or magistrates' family proceedings courts under the Children Act 1989. Private law proceedings in the county court can be transferred to the High Court and from the High Court to the county court depending on the complexity, difficulty or gravity of the case (ss.38 and 39 Matrimonial and Family Proceedings Act 1984). The Family Division of the High Court consists of the President (the Rt Hon Dame Elizabeth Butler-Sloss) and 16 High Court judges. (For an interesting account of the work of the Family Division by a former High Court judge, see Hale, 1999.)

Court Personnel

Special personnel assist the courts in proceedings involving children. Court welfare officers and guardians *ad litem* provide social work expertise and support in private and public law children proceedings respectively. Their function is to investigate the child's circumstances and report to and advise the court. The court welfare functions are provided by: the probation service; the children's branch of the Official Solicitors' Department; and local authority guardian *ad litem* and reporting officer services. However, because the system has been criticised for lacking integration, in July 1999 the Government announced the introduction of a new service, the 'Children and Family Court Advisory and Support Service' (CAFCASS), amalgamating the services provided by court welfare officers, guardians *ad litem*, reporting officers and the children's branch of the Official Solicitor's office (see the Consultation Paper, *Support Services in Family Proceedings: Future Organisation of Court Welfare Services*, HMSO, 1998). The Criminal Justice and Court Services Bill has introduced CAFCASS. Clause 12 of the Bill provides that the central functions of this non-departmental public body, which is accountable to the Lord Chancellor, are to: (i) safeguard and promote the welfare of children; (ii) give advice to any court about any application made to it in such proceedings; (iii) make provision for children to be represented in such proceedings; and (iv) provide information, advice and other support for children and their families. This new service is due to come into operation in April 2001.

1.5   Family Law and the Human Rights Act 1998

The Human Rights Act 1998 came into force in October 2000, as a result of changes proposed by the Government in its White Paper, *Rights Brought Home: The Human Rights Bill* (1998, Cm 3782). The effect of the Act is to weave the European Convention for the Protection of Human Rights and Fundamental Freedoms into the fabric of English law. The Act makes Convention rights directly enforceable in the UK. The Act will have an impact on family law.

A major effect of the Act is to impose new obligations on courts and public authorities. Under the Act, English courts when deciding a question which has arisen in connection with a Convention right must 'take into account' the judgments, decisions and opinions of the European Court of Human Rights, the opinions of the Commission on the merits of an application or on its admissibility, and decisions of the Committee of Ministers (s.2). Furthermore, primary and subordinate legislation, so far as possible to do so, 'must be read and given effect in a way which is compatible with the Convention rights' (s.3). Where the House of Lords, the Privy Council, the Court of Appeal or the High Court determines that a legislative provision is not compatible with a Convention right, it may make a 'declaration of incompatibility' to that effect (s.4). Public authorities must also ensure that they comply with the European Convention, for the Act makes it unlawful for a public authority to act in a way which is incompatible with a Convention right (s.6). As courts are 'public authorities' for the purpose of the Act, they too must act in a way which is compatible with the Convention. Any person who is the victim of an unlawful act (or proposed act) of a public authority may bring court proceedings against the authority or rely on the Convention right concerned in any other legal proceedings (s.7). In such proceedings, the court can grant such relief or remedy, or make such order, within its powers as it considers just and appropriate, including awards of damages in civil proceedings (s.8).

Before the Act came into force, an applicant who wished to challenge the UK Government under the European Convention would have to bring a complaint to the European Commission of Human Rights in Strasbourg, and, if the complaint was declared admissible, then it would go in most cases to the European Court of Human Rights. A complainant could only do this, however, if he or she had exhausted all the available remedies in the UK. A successful claim against the UK before the European Court has several consequences. First, it can result in the UK government being ordered to pay a successful applicant compensation in the form of damages. Secondly, it obliges the UK to amend existing law or introduce new law to conform with the judgment of the European Court; and thirdly, it creates a body of jurisprudence which creates precedents for future cases. Despite the implementation of the Human Rights Act 1998, it still remains open to a person to take a complaint to Strasbourg, provided remedies in the UK have been exhausted.

It must be stressed that the Human Rights Act does not directly introduce the Convention into UK law. Decisions of the European Commission and Court of Human Rights are not binding on the UK courts: they must merely be 'taken into account' (s.2). Primary and secondary legislation must be read and given effect to in a way that is compatible with the Convention, but only 'as far as possible to do so' (s.3). Furthermore, as the Convention is regarded as 'a living instrument ... which must be interpreted in the light of present day conditions' (*Tyrer* v. *UK* (1979–80) 2 EHRR 1, para. 31), the European Court does not follow the strict rule of precedent. Similarly, the UK courts are not bound by previous decisions of the European Court. For this reason the UK courts will 'be able to build up a new body of case-law which takes into account Convention rights' (para. 2.8 of the White Paper).

The article of the European Convention which is most pertinent to family law is art. 8 which provides as follows:

'1. Everyone has the right to respect for his private and family life, his home and his correspondence.
2. There shall be no interference by a public authority with the exercise of this right except such as is in accordance with the law and is necessary in a democratic society in the interests of national security, public safety or the economic well-being of the country, for the protection of disorder or crime, for the protection of health or morals, or for the protection of the rights and freedoms of others.'

Article 8 places the State under a positive obligation to ensure that the rights enshrined in art. 8 are respected. Other articles which are likely to be invoked in family law cases are: art. 3 (right not to be subjected to torture and inhuman and degrading treatment); art. 6 (right to a fair trial); art. 12 (right to marry and found a family); art. 13 (right to an effective remedy); and art. 14 (right not to be discriminated against).

Prior to the implementation of the Human Rights Act, family law cases had been brought under the convention in a wide range of different circumstances. These are referred to where relevant throughout the chapters which follow, but the following list gives some examples of the sorts of situations in family law where claims have been brought:

- by transsexuals arguing that the UK's failure to allow them to change their sex on their birth certificates and to marry in their newly acquired sex was a breach of arts. 8 and 12 (see, for example, *Rees* v. *UK*; *Cossey* v. *UK*; *Sheffield and Horsham* v. *UK* at 2.2);
- by children and parents arguing that corporal punishment of children was a breach of art. 3 (see, for example, *A* v. *United Kingdom (Human Rights: Punishment of Child)* [1998] 2 FLR 959; *Campbell* v. *Cosans* (1982) 4 EHRR 293);
- by a wife arguing that entry by her husband to move property from their former matrimonial home constituted a breach of art. 8 by the police (see *McLeod* v. *UK* [1998] 2 FLR 1048);
- by parents prior to the Children Act 1989 alleging that the process by which their children had been taken into care was a breach of art. 8 because they had been insufficiently involved in the decision-making process (*W* v. *UK* (1987) Series A, No 121);
- by parents alleging the process by which a Scottish local authority had taken their child into care was a breach of art. 8, as they were denied access to documents at the 'children's hearing' (*McMichael* v. *UK* (1995) 20 EHRR 25);
- by a father arguing that the State's failure to promote contact between him and his daughter, who was living with her grandparents after her mother's death, constituted a breach of art. 8 (*Hokkanen* v. *Finland* [1996] 1 FLR 289);
- by a natural father who was not married to the mother alleging that the UK was in breach of art. 14 as he was discriminated against, because, unlike the mother, he had no automatic parental rights in his child (*McMichael* v. *UK*, see above).

Some claims under the Convention have not been successful because the European Commission or Court of Human Rights has recognised a wide 'margin of appreciation' in the State's decision-making process. In other words, it has recognised that different Member States have a band of reasonable discretion in which they are permitted to exercise their powers while remaining in compliance with the Convention. Whether the 'margin of appreciation' principle will be used by the UK courts under the 1998 Act is not yet clear, but the UK courts are likely to use the principle of 'proportionality', which requires that any action or inaction must be proportionate to the legitimate aim pursued.

Although the European Convention on Human Rights does not make express provision for children (it was drawn up to protect the rights of adults), children are entitled to the same rights as adults under the Convention. Herring (1999) has pointed to a possible tension between the welfare principle in the Children Act

1989 and the rights of family members under the Convention, and believes that 'in the light of the Human Rights Act and the centrality of the welfare principle in the Children Act, the courts are going to be forced to develop some kind of synthesis between the two approaches if at all possible' (p.224). He considers that an approach based purely on rights or on welfare is unsatisfactory and advocates instead the use of a relationship-based welfare principle, which requires the court to 'ascertain what would be the best set of relationships between the parents and child' (p.235). Fortin (1998) believes that the 'Strasbourg jurisprudence may not always augur well for British children,' and is in favour of a child-centred inter-pretation of the Convention, as it would be 'unfortunate in the extreme if such a change heralded an increased willingness to allow parents to pursue their own rights under the Convention at the expense of those of their children' (p.56).

It is difficult to predict the likely impact of the Human Rights Act on family law. However, one view expressed by Kingscote (1998 at p.201) is that, as UK legislation and case-law, particularly the law relating to children, already recognise the importance of individuals' rights to respect for family life, the Act is unlikely to result in any great changes to domestic law. What is clear, however, is that family lawyers will have to make sure they are familiar with the Convention and its case-law. Family law cases are also likely to last longer because human rights' arguments will be increasingly used. In fact human rights' arguments are already being used. In *In Re F (Minors)(Care Proceedings: Contact)*, 22 June 2000 *The Times*, where a human rights' argument was used in a contact in care case, Wall J said that he would be disappointed if the Convention were to be routinely paraded in such cases as a make-weight ground of appeal, or if there were in every case to be extensive citation of authorities from the European Court of Human Rights, particularly where reliance was placed on cases pre-dating the Children Act 1989. Thus, while the Human Rights Act will quite clearly present family lawyers with new chal-lenges and a rights-based framework in which to approach family cases, we will have to see what scope will be accorded to human rights' arguments in family cases. It is unlikely, however, that the courts will allow the floodgates of human rights to be opened. The more likely approach is that the courts will decide that English family law principles are sufficiently fair and just on their own to govern the case in question.

Summary

1 Family law has witnessed considerable changes. Major changes were introduced by the Children Act 1989 and the Child Support Acts 1991 and 1995. There have been recent changes to the law on pensions on divorce, and procedural changes in respect of ancillary relief on divorce. However, the proposed new divorce law has now been abolished. New child support provision is proposed, and also changes to give some unmarried fathers 'automatic' parental responsibility. An important

change has been the implementation of the European Convention on the Protection of Human Rights by the Human Rights Act 1998.

2 Family law has also witnessed changes in terminology, which have created ideological changes in some areas. Of particular importance has been the change from parental rights to parental responsibilities, and also a growing recognition of parenthood as the primary status rather than marriage and cohabitation.

3 Family law has witnessed an increasing international dimension, and there have been important demographic and social changes, in particular the decline of marriage and the rise of cohabitation.

4 One way of looking at family law is in terms of the functions it performs. Family law can be described as having the following functions: defining and altering status; providing physical and economic protection or support; and providing mechanisms for adjusting and dividing property.

5 There is no definition of the 'family' in family law, but family law is increasingly concerned not just with the family based on marriage but families based on cohabitation and also single-parent families. The courts have also given some (but not much) recognition to homosexual and lesbian relationships.

6 Because of its human element and the infinite variety of family circumstances, family law cases are usually decided by applying flexible discretionary rules. Courts have considerable discretion. Each case tends to turn on its own facts, and there are relatively few fixed principles, particularly in the area of child law. Furthermore, earlier cases do not generally create strict precedents as they do in other areas of the law.

7 The settlement of family cases by mediation and negotiation is encouraged in order to avoid cases going to court. In private family law matters, litigation is usually a matter of last resort. Mediation and negotiation are increasingly encouraged in ancillary relief cases on divorce.

8 There is no family court in England and Wales. Family cases are heard in magistrates' family proceedings courts, county courts and the Family Division of the High Court.

9 The Children and Family Courts Advisory and Support Service (CAFCASS) has been established to co-ordinate the various court support services.

10 The Human Rights Act 1998 came into force in October 2000. The effect of the Act is to weave the European Convention for the Protection of Human Rights and Fundamental Freedoms into the fabric of English law. It is likely to make an impact on family law, but to what extent is unclear. Of particular importance for family law are art. 8 (right to family life), art. 12 (right to marry and found a family) and art. 4 (right not to suffer inhuman and degrading treatment).

11 The Government is committed to supporting the family, and Government policy always has the family in mind.

Further Reading and References

Bailey-Harris, 'Third Stonewall Lecture – Lesbian and gay family values and the law' [1999] Fam Law 560.

Bainham, 'Changing families and changing concepts – Reforming the language of family law' [1998] CFLQ 1.

Barton, 'The homosexual in the family' [1996] Fam Law 626.

Bissett-Johnson and Barton, 'The similarities and differences in Scottish and English family law in dealing with changing family patterns' (1999) JSWFL 1.

Broberg, 'The registered partnership for same sex couples in Denmark' [1996] CFLQ 149.

Cretney and The Rt Hon Dame Elizabeth Butler-Sloss (eds), *Family Law – Essays for the New Millennium*, Family Law, 2000.
Davis, 'Monitoring publicly funded mediation' [1999] Fam Law 625.
Dewar, 'The normal chaos of family law' (1998) 61 MLR 467.
Eekelaar, 'A jurisdiction in search of a mission: family proceedings in England and Wales' (1994) 57 MLR 839.
Eekelaar and Nhlapo (eds), *The Changing Family,* Hart Publishing, 1998.
Fortin, *Children's Rights and the Developing Law*, Butterworths, 1998.
Fortin, 'Rights brought home for children' (1999) 62 MLR 350.
Fortin, 'The HRA's impact on litigation involving children and their families' [1999] CFLQ 237.
Fricker, His Honour Judge, 'Family law is different' [1995] Fam Law 306.
Fricker, 'Mediation: the way forward' [1999] Fam Law 826.
Glennon, '*Fitzpatrick* v. *Sterling Housing Association Ltd* – An endorsement of the functional family?' (2000) *International Journal of Law, Policy and the Family* 226.
Greatbatch and Dingwall, 'The marginalization of domestic violence in divorce mediation' (1999) IJLF 174.
Hale, The Rt Hon Mrs Justice, 'The view from Court 45' [1999] CFLQ 377.
Harris, 'The aims of the family justice system' [1996] Fam Law 714.
Herring, 'The Human Rights Act and the welfare principle in family law – conflicting or complementary?' [1999] CFLQ 223.
Kaganas and Piper, 'Domestic violence and divorce mediation' (1994) JSWFL 265.
Katz, Eekelaar and Maclean (eds), *Cross Currents: Family Law and Policy in the US and England*, Oxford University Press, 2000.
Kingscote, 'Incorporation of the European Convention on Human Rights' [1998] Fam Law 195.
Lawson, 'Reflections on the family justice system' [1999] Fam Law 203.
Lewis, 'The problem of lone-mother families in twentieth-century Britain' [1998] JSWFL 251.
Masson, 'Family justice studies – New directions and developments' [1997] Fam Law 178.
Pascall, 'UK family policy in the 1990s: The case of new labour and lone parents' (1999) *International Journal of Law, Policy and the Family* 258.
Piper, 'How do you define a family lawyer?' (1999) 19 *Legal Studies* 93.
Richards, 'Family mediation is for real' [1999] Fam Law 115.
Richards, 'How is mediation different from counselling, advising and arbitrating?' [1999] Fam Law 173.
Schneider, 'The tension between rules and discretion in family law: A report and reflection' [1993] 27 Fam LQ 229.
Silva and Smart (eds), *The New Family*, Sage Publications, 1999.
Swindells, Neaves, Kushner and Skilbeck, *Family Law and the Human Rights Act 1998*, Family Law, 1999.
Wasoff and Dey, *Family Policy*, The Gildredge Press, 2000.
Woods, 'Family Rights in the EU – Disadvantaging the disadvantaged?' [1999] CFLQ 17.

Websites

Government Services

Acts of the UK Parliament: www.hmso.gov.uk/acts.htm
Department of Health (circulars, subject index, publications, press releases and research and development): www.doh.gov.uk/

Department of Social Security (includes information on child support, etc.): www.dss.gov.uk/
Her Majesty's Stationery Office (full texts or summaries of Acts of Parliaments (since 1996) and Statutory Instruments): www.official-documents.co.uk/
Home Office (press releases, publications, subject index including Acts of Parliament, Bills, research): www.homeofffice.gov.uk/
House of Lords' Debates (*Hansard*): www.parliament.the-stationery-office.co.uk/pa/ld/ldhansrd.htm
Law Commission: www.lawcom.gov.uk/
Lord Chancellor's Department (press notices, the courts, consultation papers, reform on family matters, speeches, research, publications, statutes, human rights and related sites): www.open.gov.uk/lcd/
Official Solicitor (including the Child Abduction Unit, with information and guidance about child abduction): www.offsol.demon.co.uk/
United Kingdom Parliament (information and publications, including Bills before Parliament, and House of Lords' judgments since November 1996): www.parliament.uk/

Courts and Law Reports

Beagle (European Court of Human Rights' website, with summaries and extracts from European Human Rights' cases, and links to judgments): www.beagle.org.uk
British and Irish Legal Information Institute (free access to legislation and to cases heard by the High Court, Court of Appeal and House of Lords since 1996): www.bailii.org/
The Court Service (executive agency of the Lord Chancellor's Department which includes details about the court, practice directions, county courts' geographical jurisdiction, judgments of the Court of Appeal and High Court, and details about tribunals, including the Office of the Social Security and Child Support Commissioners): www.courtservice.gov.uk/
Europa (European Union website, which includes information, case-law etc.): europa.eu.int/index.htm
European Court of Human Rights (information, pending cases, judgments, decisions, basic texts, press releases, text of European Convention on Human Rights): www.dhcour.coe.fr/
House of Lords (judicial business, including texts of opinions): www.parliament.the-stationery-office.co.uk/
Incorporated Council of Law Reporting (daily law notes, free headnotes and summaries of selected judgments): www.lawreports.co.uk/
The Times Law Reports: www.the-times.co.uk

Other Legal Materials

DIANA (database of links to human rights' topics): www.diana.law.yale.edu/
Human Rights on the Web (documents and links to resources): www.hrweb.org
Joseph Rowntree Foundation (JRF) (research reports, research materials): www.jrf.org.uk/
Legislation (full texts of Acts of Parliament published since January 1996, and explanatory notes of Acts from 1999, and summaries of earlier Acts): www.legislation.hmso.gov.uk

Official Documents (Command papers, including White Papers, Green Papers etc., plus links to other official document sites): www.official-documents.co.uk
UK Official Publications (UKOP) (indexes of all official publications, including HMSO and departmental or non-HMSO publications from 1980 onwards): www.ukop.co.uk
Web Journal of Current Legal Affairs: webjcli.ncl.ac.uk/

Other Websites

Butterworths (news service, on-line legal newspaper etc.): www.butterworths.co.uk/
Council of Europe (Human Rights' information, bulletins, case-law, text of European Convention on Human Rights etc.): www.dhdirhr.coe.fr/
Family Law (Jordans Publishing) (summaries of recent family law decisions, links to other websites): www.familylaw.co.uk/
Family Mediators' Association (responsible for providing mediation and for training and supporting mediators; explanations of what mediation is): www.familymediators.co.uk/
Family Policy Studies Centre (information and research on family policy): www.fpsc.org.uk/
Human Rights Act 1998 Information: www.homeoffice.gov.uk/hract/
The Law Society (includes general information on family matters): www.lawsoc.org.uk/
Legal Services Commission (LSC) (administers the scheme of publicly funded legal services; the 'Community Legal Service' replaces the old civil scheme of legal aid): www.legalservices.gov.uk/
Solicitors' Family Law Association (SFLA) (Code of Practice, mediation, details about choosing a solicitor, updates and press releases): www.sfla.co.uk/
SOSIG (Social Sciences Information Gateway) (useful for social science research on the family): www.sosig.ac.uk/
Sweet & Maxwell (includes case reports): www.smlawpub.co.uk/
UK College of Family Mediators (the professional standard-setting watchdog and public information providing body for family mediation in the UK, information on how mediation works etc.): www.ukcfm.co.uk/

Questions

1 Would you be in favour of allowing same-sex partners to enter into a marriage-type relationship by registering their partnership and thereby acquiring some (or all) of the legal effects of marriage?
2 Define what functions you consider family law to have, and under each of its functions make a list of those areas of family law which perform that function.

Part II

Marriage and Cohabitation

Part II looks at marriage and cohabitation and their legal consequences. Chapter 2 deals with marriage and Chapter 3 with the legal consequences of marriage and cohabitation. The property consequences of marriage and cohabitation are considered in Part III.

2 Marriage and the Law of Nullity

In this chapter we consider the institution of marriage today, how a valid marriage is created, and finally void and voidable marriages, in other words the law of nullity.

2.1 Marriage Today

Marriage today must be seen against a background of increasing cohabitation. Many couples choose to live together rather than marry. As a result of this trend, the number of marriages is declining. There are also other trends. Many marriages are second marriages. The age at which people are marrying is rising. And, many marriages end in divorce. Because of the declining popularity of marriage and increasing divorce, the institution of marriage is considered to be under threat. However, whether the law is responsible for the decline in marriage is difficult to establish. Some consider that more liberal grounds for divorce are responsible for marriage breakdown. However, although it has always been one of the main policy aims of divorce law to support the institution of marriage, it is questionable whether divorce law can actually do this. It is possible that marriages break down despite the law rather than because of it. A further problem is that there is always an inherent tension in divorce law between supporting marriage while simultaneously ensuring that marriages are brought to an end as smoothly as possible.

Fears about undermining the institution of marriage have been voiced not just in discussions about divorce reform but in discussions about reform of the law governing the property rights of cohabitants on relationship breakdown. There has been concern that reforms for cohabitants will lead to the erosion of the distinction between marriage and cohabitation, and further undermine the institution of marriage. Discussions about making pre-nuptial agreements enforceable in English law have also raised concerns about the institution of marriage. Some of the resistance to recognising pre-nuptial contracts in English law is because they might encourage people to believe that marriage is a short-term option.

The Government is keen to support the institution of marriage because of the supposed stability it creates in society and because it is considered to be the best environment in which to bring up children. In its Consultation Document (*Supporting Families*, 1998, The Home Office) the Government stated (at para. 8, p.4) that, although many lone parents and unmarried couples raised their children as successfully as married parents, marriage was still the 'surest foundation for raising children' and remained the choice of the majority of people in Britain. For these reasons the Government professed its wish to strengthen the institution of marriage to help more marriages to succeed.

With declining marriage and increasing cohabitation, perhaps parenthood, rather than marriage and cohabitation, should be recognised as the primary status relationship, and obligations towards children should be the prime consideration (see Drane and Phillimore, 1999). Indeed, this is the approach that the Government adopts in *Supporting Families*, where it stated that the first principle on which modern family policy must be based is that 'the interests of children must be paramount' (para. 6, p.4). This principle ranked ahead of the principle that the institution of marriage should be supported.

2.2   Who Can Marry?

To contract a valid marriage both parties must have the capacity to marry and must comply with certain legal formalities, otherwise the marriage may be void.

Section 11 of the Matrimonial Causes Act 1973 provides that a marriage is void if the parties lack the capacity to marry. The parties have capacity under s.11 if:

(a) they are not within the prohibited degrees of relationship;
(b) they are both over the age of 16;
(c) neither of them is already married; and
(d) one of them is male and the other female.

(a) Not Within the Prohibited Degrees of Relationship

A marriage is void if the parties are within what are called the prohibited degrees of relationship (s.11(a)(i)). In other words, marriages between certain relatives related by blood or by marriage are prohibited by the Marriage Acts 1949 to 1986. These prohibitions on marriage exist to prevent inbreeding and to discourage incest. However, they are not as strict as they once were. There are now fewer restrictions on relationships created by marriage, as a result of the Marriage (Prohibited Degrees of Relationship) Act 1986.

Under the rules of prohibited degrees of relationship, a man is prohibited from marrying his mother, grandmother, daughter, granddaughter, sister, aunt or niece, but he is not prohibited from marrying his step-daughter, step-mother, step-grandmother, step-daughter or mother-in-law. The same rules apply to a woman in respect of her male relations. There are further restrictions. Thus, a person can marry a step-child only if both parties are aged 21 or over, and the step-child has not at any time before the age of 18 been brought up by the other party as a step-child. A man can marry his daughter-in-law only if they are both aged 21 or over, and his wife and son are dead (the same is true for a woman and her son-in-law). Adopted children are generally in the same degrees of prohibited relationships in respect of their birth parents and other blood relatives, but fewer restrictions apply to relationships acquired by adoption. Thus, for example, a person can marry an adopted brother or sister.

(b) Over the Age of 16

A marriage is void if either party to the marriage is under the age of 16 (s.2 MA 1949; s.11(a)(ii) MCA 1973). However, where a party is aged 16 or 17, the following persons must give their consent (s.3 MA 1949): parents with parental responsibility; guardians; any person with whom the child lives under a residence order; the local authority if the child is in care; and where a residence order was in force immediately before the child was 16, the consent of the person(s) with whom the child lived under that order. The court's consent is required if the child is a ward of court (s.3(6) MA 1949). Consent can be dispensed with, however, where the person whose consent is needed is absent or inaccessible or suffers from some disability, or it can be dispensed with by the court (s.3(1)(a) MA 1949). If necessary, the court can give consent (s.3(1)(b) MA 1949). Where a marriage involving a party aged 16 or 17 has been solemnised without consent, the marriage will not, however, be void (s.24 MA 1949).

(c) Not Already Married

A party to a marriage must not be already married, otherwise the later marriage is void (s.11(b) MCA 1973). A spouse who remarries without his or her first marriage being terminated commits the crime of bigamy. Where a spouse has disappeared and/or is thought to be dead, the other spouse who wishes to marry can apply for a decree of presumption of death and dissolution of marriage (see 8.9), which, if granted, prevents the second marriage being bigamous even if the first spouse reappears.

(d) Respectively Male and Female

The parties to a marriage must be respectively male and female, otherwise the marriage is void (s.11(c) MCA 1973). Gay and lesbian marriages are not permitted. Although there have been developments in other countries (e.g. France and Denmark) to enable homosexual couples to marry, or more precisely to register their partnership and thereby acquire some of the legal effects of marriage, there are no proposals to do this in the UK.

The requirement that the parties be respectively male and female also extends to transsexuals (persons who have undergone a gender reassignment). It is not possible to contract a valid marriage with a person of the same biological sex. In the leading case of *Corbett* v. *Corbett (Otherwise Ashley)* [1971] P 83, [1970] 2 WLR 1306, Ormrod J held that a person's biological sex is fixed at birth and cannot be altered by a sex-change operation. In *Corbett*, the male partner petitioned for a decree of nullity against the respondent, a male-to-female transsexual. The marriage was held to be void as both parties were male. The court held that the respondent was male by chromosomal, gonadal and genital criteria, and it was irrelevant that the respondent considered herself philosophically, psychologically and socially to be a woman.

The decision in *Corbett* still represents the position taken by the English courts, despite medical research which has demonstrated that transsexualism may be a medically recognised condition. The test in *Corbett* therefore still governs the decision of the Registrar General to determine the sex of the child on a birth certificate (see *Re P and G (Transsexuals)* [1996] 2 FLR 90, where judicial review applications by two transsexuals against the Registrar General's refusal to allow their birth certificates to be changed were dismissed).

Some transsexuals feel that their psychological gender is more important than their biological sex and consider that the law discriminates against them, particularly in respect of formal documentation, such as birth certificates. They also consider that they have a fundamental human right to marry a person of the same biological sex. Because of these perceived injustices, transsexuals have brought applications under the European Convention for the Protection of Human Rights. In *Rees* v. *United Kingdom* (1986) 9 EHRR 56, [1987] 2 FLR 111, a female-to-male transsexual claimed that UK law violated art. 8 (right to a private and family life) by failing to provide measures that would legally constitute him as a male and allow him full integration into social life. He argued that the discrepancy between his apparent and legal sex as stated on his birth certificate caused him embarrassment and humiliation whenever the certificate was required to be produced. Rees also argued that the UK was in breach of art. 12 (right to marry and found a family) as he could not marry a woman. The European Court of Human Rights held by 12 to 3 votes that there had been no breach of art. 8 and unanimously held that there had been no breach of art. 12. Although conscious of the distress suffered by transsexuals, the European Court held that the UK should be left to decide whether it could meet the remaining demands of transsexuals. However, it did state that the need for appropriate legal measures should be kept under review having regard in particular to scientific and societal developments. *Rees* was endorsed by the Court of Human Rights in *Cossey* v. *United Kingdom* [1991] 2 FLR 492 but by less of a majority, which may indicate a slight change of attitude since *Rees*. In *B* v. *France* [1992] 2 FLR 249, on the other hand, where the facts were quite different from *Rees* and *Cossey*, a French transsexual's application to the European Court of Human Rights was allowed because French bureaucracy was such that it made the daily life of the applicant unbearable.

Although the European Court of Human Rights in *Rees* held that the law should be kept under review to allow for any scientific developments, in *Sheffield and Horsham* v. *UK* [1998] 2 FLR 928 the same approach was taken as in *Cossey* and *Rees*. In *Sheffield and Horsham*, two male-to-female transsexuals argued that the UK government was in breach of its obligations under arts. 8 and 12 because of difficulties and embarrassment they had encountered as a result of reassignment surgery, including that fact that their birth certificates and other records recorded their original gender. In Miss Horsham's case, she wished to marry a male partner in The Netherlands but had been informed that English law would not recognise her marriage. The European Court of Human Rights held by 11 to 9 votes that there had been no violation of art. 8 in either case. It held that their cases were essentially similar to *Rees* and *Cossey*, and that there had been no scientific or legal developments which persuaded the court to depart from those earlier decisions. The UK was still entitled to rely on a margin of appreciation to defend its refusal to recognise a post-operative transsexual's identity, and the detriment suffered by the applicants was not sufficiently serious to override that margin of appreciation. The Court also held by 18 to 2 votes that there had been no violation of art. 12. It reiterated the principles in *Rees*, and held that the right to marry guaranteed by art. 12 referred to the traditional marriage between persons of the opposite biological sex.

Another case involving a transsexual was *X, Y and Z* v. *UK* [1997] 2 FLR 892. Here a female-to-male transsexual (X) and his partner (Y) had a child (Z) as a result of artificial insemination by donor. X wished to be registered as the father of the child, but this was not permitted under English law as only a biological man could be regarded as the father for the purposes of birth registration. X brought an action against the UK government claiming violations of arts. 8 and 14. His application failed. The European Court of Human Rights, while recognising that 'family life' for the purposes of art. 8 was not confined solely to families based on marriage, held that there was a wide margin of appreciation and that where the community had interests in maintaining a coherent system of family law which prioritised the best interests of the child, it could be justifiably cautious about changing the law. The Court also stated that X was not prevented from acting as the child's father in a social sense and could apply for a joint residence order with Y in respect of the child, and thereby acquire parental responsibility.

Now that the Human Rights Act 1998 is in force, English courts are required to take account of the decisions of the European Court (see 1.5). However, although more challenges by transsexuals and homosexuals are likely to be brought before the English courts on the basis of breaches of their fundamental rights to marry and found a family under the Convention on Human Rights, it is unlikely that the English courts will take a different view from that taken by the European Court of Human Rights in the cases above – at least for the time being.

2.3   Formalities

As well as having the capacity to marry (see above), the parties must comply with certain preliminary formalities before the marriage ceremony can take place. The aim of these formalities is to establish that the required consents have been given and that there are no lawful impediments to the marriage taking place. In addition, the marriage must be registered, and the ceremony itself comply with certain formalities.

The rules are complex. Marriages can be celebrated in different ways with different preliminary formalities depending on whether the marriage is civil or religious. Special rules also apply in exceptional cases, e.g. where a party to a marriage is terminally ill or detained in prison.

(a)   *Preliminaries for All Marriages, Other than Church of England Marriages*

All marriages, whether civil or religious, except for those celebrated according to the rites of the Church of England, must be solemnised on the authority of: (i) a superintendent registrar's certificate without licence; (ii) a superintendent registrar's certificate with licence; or (iii) the Registrar General's licence.

(i) A Superintendent Registrar's Certificate Without Licence   Both parties must give written notice of the intended marriage to the local superintendent registrar in the area (or areas) in which each of them has resided for at least the previous seven days (s.27(1) MA 1949). A fee must be paid on giving notice and when the wedding takes place. The notice must be accompanied by a solemn declaration that there are no lawful impediments to the marriage, that the residence requirements have been satisfied and that the required consents have been given (see 2.2 above). Notice of the marriage is entered in the marriage book and publicly displayed in the register office for 21 successive days. After that period, provided there has been no objection to the marriage,

the registrar issues a certificate, after which the marriage must be solemnised within three months from the date of entry in the marriage notice book (s.31 MA 1949). The Marriage Act 1983 permits persons who are house-bound due to illness or disability (which is likely to last for at least three months), and persons detained in prison or detained due to mental ill-health, to marry on the authority of a superintendent registrar's certificate in the place where they are living or are detained.

(ii) A Superintendent Registrar's Certificate with Licence   This is similar to the superintendent registrar's certificate procedure above, except that only one party need give notice to the registrar in the district where either party has resided for the previous 15 days, provided the other party is resident in England and Wales. The notice is entered in the marriage notice book, but is not publicly displayed (s.32(1) MA 1949). A fee must be paid on giving notice and when the ceremony takes place. The marriage may take place at any time after the expiry of one whole day from the giving of notice (s.32(1) MA 1949), e.g. it may take place on Thursday if notice was given on Tuesday.

(iii) The Registrar General's Licence   This procedure is used only in exceptional circumstances, e.g. when a person is seriously ill and not expected to recover and cannot be moved to a place where the marriage can be solemnised. It authorises solemnisation of marriage in a place other than a register office, an Anglican church or a place registered for worship (Marriage (Registrar-General's Licence) Act 1970).

(b) Church of England Preliminaries

A Church of England marriage is solemnised according to the rites of the Church of England after: (i) the publication of banns; (ii) the grant of a common licence; (iii) the grant of a special licence (or after the grant of a superintendent registrar's certificate without licence, see above).

(i) Publication of Banns   The banns (notice of the marriage) are entered into an official register and publicly declared on three successive Sundays preceding the marriage (normally during morning service) by the clergyman in the church of the parish (or parishes) in which the parties reside, or in their respective parish churches. They may also be published in any parish church or authorised chapel which is the usual place of worship of one or both parties if the marriage is to take place there. Once the banns have been published and no one objects, the marriage takes place in one of the churches where the banns were published. There has been discussion by the General Synod of the Church of England about abolishing the requirement of banns.

(ii) Common Licence   A common licence is granted by the bishop of a diocese. It allows the parties to marry without the publication of banns. Before a common licence can be granted, one of the parties must make a sworn statement that there are no lawful impediments to the marriage, that the residence requirements are satisfied and that the required consents have been given or dispensed with. Once the licence is granted the marriage can take place at any time, but only in the parish where one of the parties has had his or her usual place of residence for 15 days immediately prior to the grant of the licence, or in the church that is the usual place of worship of either or both parties.

(iii) Special Licence   A special licence is granted (usually only in exceptional circumstances) by and at the discretion of the Archbishop of Canterbury. It allows a marriage to be solemnised according to the rites of the Church of England in any place and at any time. Special licences are often sought to authorise marriages in college chapels (e.g. at Oxford and Cambridge) and in churches with which neither party has the connection needed for banns or a common licence.

(c) Solemnisation of Marriage

(i) Civil Marriages   After the preliminary formalities above have been complied with, the marriage is solemnised in a register office or in 'approved premises' (or in the place where the person is house-bound or detained). As a result of recommendations made by the Government in its White Paper *Registration: Proposals for Change*, Cm 939, 1990, the Marriage Act 1994 was passed to enable marriages to take place in 'approved premises' (those approved by local authorities in accordance with regulations laid down by the Secretary of State). Many hotels, stately homes, castles and other places are registered, as well as some unusual places, such as Newcastle United Football Club and the First Class *Eurostar* waiting room at Ashford Station. A civil ceremony, whether held at the register office or in approved premises, is public and secular, but it may be followed by a religious ceremony in a church or chapel (s.46 MA 1949). However, it is the civil ceremony which is legally binding. A civil marriage must take place in the presence of the superintendent registrar and a registrar of marriages. The parties must declare that there are no lawful impediments to the marriage and exchange vows. The wedding must be witnessed by at least two witnesses. Some registrars remind the parties of the solemn nature of the vows they are making.

(ii) Church of England Marriages   After the preliminary formalities have been complied with, the marriage is solemnised by a clergyman according to the rites of the Church of England in the presence of at least two witnesses.

(iii) Other Religious Marriages   Religious marriages, other than Church of England, Quaker and Jewish marriages, can be solemnised by a religious ceremony after the parties have complied with one of the three civil preliminaries above. The certificate states where the marriage is to take place, but it usually takes place in a 'registered building' in the district where one of the parties lives, except where a person is house-bound or detained. A 'registered building' is one registered by the Registrar General as 'a place of meeting for religious worship' (s.41 MA 1949). Some Sikh and Hindu temples and Muslim mosques are registered. However, if a marriage takes place in a building which is not registered, it may be upheld as valid under the common law presumption of marriage from long cohabitation. In *Chief Adjudication Officer* v. *Bath* [2000] 1 FLR 8, the parties had married in a Sikh temple which had not been registered for the purpose of marriage. Despite this, the Court of Appeal held that they had validly married, despite the irregularity, because where a man and woman have cohabited for a long period of time, there is a strong presumption that they have agreed to do so in the proper form. Consequently, Mrs Bath was held to be entitled to a widow's pension. The Court of Appeal stated that where the law requires a marriage ceremony to take a certain form, the presumption operates to show that the proper form was observed, and the presumption can only be rebutted by positive, not merely clear evidence. Guilty knowledge by both parties was needed for a marriage to be void under s.49 MA 1949.

A non-Anglican religious marriage must be conducted by a registrar or an 'authorised person' (usually the religious person conducting the ceremony) and must take place in the presence of at least two witnesses and be open to the public. The ceremony can take any form, provided that during the ceremony the declarations required by the Marriage Act 1949 are made, namely that there are no lawful impediments to the marriage and that the parties take each other to be his or her lawful wedded wife or husband.

(iv) Quaker and Jewish Marriages   A Quaker or Jewish marriage can be solemnised after one of the civil preliminaries for marriage has been complied with (see above). Quakers must also make special declarations when giving notice (s.47 MA 1949) and both parties to a Jewish marriage must profess to belong to the Jewish faith (s.26(1)(d) MA 1949). Quaker and Jewish marriages are celebrated according to their own religious rites, but they need not take place in a registered building, in public or before an authorised person.

2.4   Void and Voidable Marriages – the Law of Nullity

The law of nullity is laid down in the Matrimonial Causes Act 1973. Like divorce, an annulment is granted in two stages: by decree nisi followed by decree absolute (s.1(5)) (see 8.1). Only after decree absolute is a marriage annulled. A decree of nullity can be sought at any time after marriage, unlike divorce, where one year must have passed before a petition can be sought. On or after the grant of a nullity decree, the court can make finance and property orders under Part II of the 1973 Act (see Chapter 9).

A decree of nullity can be sought on the basis that the marriage is void or voidable, the grounds for which are different.

(a) Grounds on which a Marriage is Void

A void marriage is one that is void *ab initio* (right from the beginning). In other words, there never was a valid marriage. For this reason a decree of annulment is not technically necessary to dissolve a void marriage, but it is useful because it gives the court power to make orders in respect of property and finance (see Chapter 9). A third party, not just a party to the 'marriage', may bring proceedings in respect of a void marriage.

Section 11 of the Matrimonial Causes Act 1973 provides that a marriage is void where:

'(a) ... it is not a valid marriage under the provisions of the Marriage Acts 1949 to 1986 (that is to say where—
   (i)   the parties are within the prohibited degrees of relationship;
   (ii) either party is under the age of sixteen; or
   (iii) the parties have intermarried in disregard of certain requirements as to the formation of marriage);
(b) that at the time of the marriage either party was already lawfully married;
(c) that the parties are not respectively male and female;
(d) in the case of a polygamous marriage entered into outside England and Wales, that either party was at the time of the marriage domiciled in England and Wales.'

These grounds, other than the polygamy ground, have been dealt with above (at 2.2). As far as polygamy is concerned, some British Moslems are expected to use the Human Rights Act 1998 to try and force the legalisation of polygamy in this country. However, they are unlikely to succeed.

For the purposes of s.11(a)(iii), not every breach of the formality requirements of the Marriage Acts necessarily invalidates a marriage. However, some breaches may attract criminal sanctions. For example, giving a false declaration is an act of perjury. However, an act of perjury is not necessarily a complete bar to a remedy in family law. Thus, in *J* v. *S-T (Formerly J) (Transsexual: Ancillary Relief)* [1997] 1 FLR 402, where a transsexual had committed an act of perjury by entering into a marriage after having concealed his true gender from the registrar, it was held that an act of perjury was not necessarily a complete bar to obtaining property and finance orders under Part II of the Matrimonial Causes Act 1973 on or after the grant of a decree of nullity (see Chapter 9).

There are no 'bars' (statutory defences) available for void marriages as there are for voidable marriages (see below). As far as children are concerned, a child born after a void marriage is treated in law as a legitimate child, if at the time of conception (or at the time of the marriage ceremony, if later) one or both parties reasonably believed that the marriage was valid (s.1 Legitimacy Act 1976, as amended by s.28 Family Law Reform Act 1987).

For the purpose of deciding whether a marriage is void under s.11, the court may have to decide whether the ceremony which took place can be regarded as a marriage ceremony, for if there was no marriage at all, a nullity decree is not needed and may be refused. In *Gereis* v. *Yagoub* [1997] 1 FLR 854, the marriage ceremony had taken place in a Coptic Orthodox Church, which was not licensed for marriages under the Marriage Act 1949, and had been conducted by a priest who was not licensed to conduct marriages under English law. In nullity proceedings, one of the parties submitted that a decree of nullity should not be declared as there never was a valid marriage. However, the court rejected this submission, as the church ceremony bore all the hallmarks of an ordinary Christian marriage and the marriage had been treated as a subsisting marriage by all those who had attended. The marriage was therefore capable of being declared void under s.11(a)(iii) and a decree of nullity was granted.

(b) Grounds on which a Marriage may be Voidable

A voidable marriage is a valid and subsisting marriage until annulled by a decree of nullity (s.16 MCA 1973).

Section 12 MCA 1973 provides that a marriage is voidable where:

(a) the marriage has not been consummated owing to the incapacity of either party to consummate it;

(b) the marriage has not been consummated owing to the wilful refusal of the respondent to consummate it;

(c) either party to the marriage did not validly consent to it, whether in consequence of duress, mistake, unsoundness of mind or otherwise;

(d) at the time of the marriage either party, though capable of giving a valid consent, was suffering (whether continuously or intermittently) from mental disorder within the meaning of the Mental Health Act 1983 of such a kind or to such an extent as to be unfitted for marriage;

(e) at the time of the marriage, the respondent was suffering from venereal disease in a communicable form;

(f) at the time of the marriage, the respondent was pregnant by some person other than the petitioner.

Most of the reported case-law has been concerned with non-consummation and lack of consent (particularly in consequence of duress). Some of these cases have occurred in the context of arranged marriages, where the civil ceremony has taken place, and has been followed later by a religious ceremony. Only after the religious ceremony are the parties deemed to be married in the eyes of their religion, and thereupon permitted to consummate their marriage. In some cases the religious ceremony has not taken place, and the marriage has not been consummated, as a result of which a party has been granted a nullity decree on the ground of non-consummation (see *Kaur* v. *Singh* [1972] 1 All ER 292 and *A* v. *J (Nullity)* [1989] 1 FLR 110). Sometimes a party to an arranged marriage has sought to have the marriage annulled because of duress caused by parental and family pressure to enter into the marriage (see *Hirani* v. *Hirani*, below).

As far as consummation is concerned, it must be 'ordinary and complete, and not partial and imperfect' (Dr Lushington in *D-E* v. *A-G* (1845) 1 Rob Eccl 279 at 298). It takes place whether or not a condom is used (*Baxter* v. *Baxter* [1948] AC 274), and whether or not a husband can ejaculate after penetration (*R* v. *R* [1952] 1 All ER 1194). With 'incapacity to consummate' (ground (a)) a party can petition on the basis of his own impotence or that of the respondent (*Harthan* v. *Harthan* [1948] 2 All ER 639). With 'wilful refusal' to consummate (ground (b)) there must be 'a settled and definite decision come to without just excuse' and the whole history of the marriage must be looked at (Lord Jowitt LC in *Horton* v. *Horton* [1947] 2 All ER 871 at 874).

When nullity proceedings are brought on the basis of duress, the test of duress is subjective (*Hirani* v. *Hirani* (1982) 4 FLR 232). The question to be asked by the court is whether the particular petitioner taking account of his or her personal qualities submits to the duress. In *Hirani*, a 19-year-old Hindu girl had entered into an arranged marriage after her parents had threatened to throw her out of the house if she did not go ahead with the ceremony. The court granted her a decree on the ground of duress as her will had been overborne. Her consent to the marriage had been vitiated.

Mistake vitiates consent only if the mistake is to the identity of the other party, and not as to his or her qualities, or there is a mistake as to the nature of the ceremony.

Bars to Nullity where the Marriage is Voidable

Section 13 of the Matrimonial Causes Act 1973 lays down bars (statutory defences) to nullity petitions in cases of voidable marriage. Thus, the court cannot grant a decree on any s.12 ground, if the respondent proves that the petitioner knew that he or she could have had the marriage voided, but whose conduct lead the respondent reasonably to believe that the petitioner would not do so, *and* it would be unjust to the respondent to grant the decree. Thus the defence allows a decree to be refused where there is approbation by the petitioner. Where a decree is sought on any ground other than non-consummation, a decree can be granted only where proceedings are brought within three years of marriage, although the court can grant permission to apply outside that period (s.13(2)) where the petitioner has suffered from a mental disorder under the Mental Health Act 1983 and it is just to grant such permission (s.13(4)). A decree can be granted on grounds (e) and (f) (venereal disease and pregnancy by some other person) only if the petitioner was ignorant of the disease or the pregnancy at the time of marriage (s.13(3)).

2.5   The Future of Nullity

Nullity petitions are extremely rare. In 1998, for example, only 505 nullity petitions were filed in the courts in England and Wales, and only 281 decrees nisi of nullity granted (*Judicial Statistics 1998*, Lord Chancellor's Department, www.open.gov/lcd). Because of the rarity of nullity, and because a divorce is now much easier to obtain, it must be questioned whether nullity should be retained. Obviously the concept of a void marriage must be retained because the grounds for void marriages are fundamental requirements of a valid marriage. However, the concept of the voidable marriage could be abolished and the law subsumed under the law of divorce. Indeed, the case for this is stronger now that the Church of England is willing to marry divorcees. When this was not possible, some persons would choose to petition for nullity, rather than divorce, so that they could contract a subsequent marriage in church at a later date. Nullity was also once more common than it is now, partly because of the social stigma attached to divorce. Another reason perhaps for getting rid of the grounds for voidable marriages is that they appear to be rather outdated. Venereal disease, for example, is a ground but AIDS is not. Furthermore, why should consummation be a ground? Although consummation is based on the religious view of marriage as a relationship based on procreation, increasing numbers of people are choosing not to have children and most of society has rejected religion and religious values. Several arguments can therefore be posited for abolishing the concept of voidable marriage, which is what has happened in Australia. However, perhaps the main reason for not subsuming voidable marriages into the law of divorce is that there is a fundamental difference between divorce and nullity in that the grounds for a voidable marriage relate to circumstances occurring at the time when the marriage was created. With divorce, on the other hand, the grounds relate to circumstances which occur after a valid marriage had been entered into – in some cases many years afterwards.

Had the reforms of divorce under Part II of the Family Law Act 1996 come into force (see Chapter 7), the grounds for void and voidable marriages would have remained unchanged. Had the new divorce law come into force, there might perhaps have been an increase in the number of nullity petitions because of the increased time scale for divorce.

2.6   Recognition of a Foreign Marriage

A foreign marriage is recognised as valid in England and Wales if: (i) each party has the capacity to marry according to his or her place of domicile; and (ii) the formalities required by the law of the place where the marriage was celebrated were complied with. A foreign marriage celebrated by local custom may be recognised, as it was in *McCabe* v. *McCabe* [1994] 1 FLR 410, where a marriage that had taken place in Ghana (involving a bottle of whisky and a sum of money) was upheld as valid with the result that the petitioner was entitled to divorce in the English courts. Special rules apply in certain cases, for instance where a party is serving in HM Forces (see Foreign Marriages Acts 1892–1947).

Summary

1 Marriage must be seen against a background of increasing cohabitation and a high incidence of divorce. The Government is keen to support the institution of marriage, and divorce law also attempts to do this.
2 To contract a valid marriage, the parties must have the capacity to marry and must comply with prescribed preliminary formalities and formalities in respect of the marriage ceremony. Failure to comply with these requirements may render the marriage void (s.11 Matrimonial Causes Act 1973).
3 Parties have the capacity to marry if they are: not within the prohibited degrees of relationship; are aged 16 or over; are not already married; and are respectively male and female.
4 Parties to a civil or religious marriage (other than a Church of England marriage) can marry on the authority of a superintendent registrar's certificate (with or without licence) or the Registrar General's licence, although special provision exists for house-bound and detained persons.
5 A Church of England marriage can take place after the publication of banns or after the grant of a common licence, special licence or a superintendent registrar's certificate without licence.
6 A nullity decree can be sought on the ground that a marriage is void or voidable. There is no prohibition on seeking a decree within the first year of marriage (s.3 MCA 1973).
7 A marriage is void (s.11 MCA 1973) if: there is no valid marriage under the Marriage Acts 1949 to 1986; the parties are within the prohibited degrees of relationship; either party is under the age of 16; either party is already married; the parties are not respectively male and female; or, in the case of a polygamous marriage, either party is domiciled in England and Wales.

8 A marriage is voidable (s.12 MCA 1973) on the following grounds: non-consummation (due to incapacity or wilful refusal); lack of consent (due to duress, mistake, unsoundness of mind, or otherwise); mental disorder; venereal disease; or the respondent was pregnant by some other person. Statutory bars (defences) exist (s.13 MCA 1973).

9 A decree of nullity allows the parties to apply for finance and property orders under Part II of the Matrimonial Causes Act 1973 (see Chapter 9).

10 Although decrees of nullity are rare, there are no proposals to change the law.

11 A foreign marriage is recognised as valid in England and Wales if each party has the capacity to marry according to the law of his or her domicile and the formalities of the place where the marriage was celebrated have been complied with.

Further Reading and References

Barton, 'The homosexual in the family' [1996] Fam Law 626.

Broberg, 'The registered partnership for same-sex couples in Denmark' [1996] CFLQ 149.

Drane and Phillimore, 'A change of status – Wave goodbye to marriage and say hello to parenthood' [1999] Fam Law 653.

Dupuis, 'The impact of culture, society and history on the legal process: An analysis of the legal status of same-sex relationships in the United States and Denmark' (1995) IJLF 86.

Katz, 'State regulation and personal autonomy in marriage: How can I marry and whom can I marry?', in Bainham (ed), *The International Survey of Family Law* (1998), pp.494–504.

Levy and Kashi, 'Getting married abroad' [2000] Fam Law 191.

Lewis, Marriage, *Cohabitation and the Law: Individualism and Obligation* (Lord Chancellor's Department, Research Series 1/99) (available from the LCD's website, www.open.gov.uk/lcd).

Lewis, *One-plus-One Marriage and Partnership Research. High Divorce Rates: The State of the Evidence on Reasons and Remedies* (Lord Chancellor's Department Research Series 2/99, available from the LCD's website, see above).

Nielsen, 'Family rights and the "registered partnership" in Denmark' (1990) Int J of Law and the Family 297.

Ogle, 'Marriage: Who needs it?' [1999] Fam Law 170.

Pickford, *Fathers, Marriage and the Law*, Family Policy Studies Centre for the Joseph Rowntree Foundation, 1999 (for website, see Chapter 1).

Probert, 'Displacing marriage – Diversification and harmonisation within Europe' [2000] CFLQ 153.

Questions

1 Is the institution of marriage really under threat? If so, why is it, and does it really matter if it is?

2 Would it be a good idea to introduce registered partnerships in this country for gay and lesbian couples? What would be the advantages and disadvantages of doing so?

3 The Legal Consequences of Marriage and Cohabitation

This chapter provides an overview of the legal consequences of marriage and cohabitation. Further reference should be made to other chapters where matters are dealt with in more detail.

3.1 The Legal Consequences of Marriage

Marriage creates a legal status from which various rights and duties flow.

(a) Separate Legal Personalities

Husbands and wives have separate legal personalities so that they can own property solely and can bring proceedings in tort and contract separately against each other or against third parties (Law Reform (Married Women and Tortfeasors) Act 1935; s.1 Law Reform (Husband and Wife) Act 1962). They can also enter into contracts with each other, although it may be difficult for family members to prove that there is an intention to create legal relations. Thus, in *Balfour* v. *Balfour* [1919] 2 KB 571, which is still the leading case, the Court of Appeal held that an agreement between a husband and wife in respect of maintenance was unenforceable because there was no intention to enter into legal relations. However, this is an old case, and times have changed since then. Today in family law there is a considerable emphasis on the importance of reaching agreement, and there has even been discussion about making pre-nuptial agreements enforceable. For these reasons, the presumption in *Balfour* against legal relations between family members is unlikely to apply, unless there is inequality of bargaining power or some other vitiating factor.

The fact that husbands and wives have separate personalities enables each spouse to make decisions about their own medical treatment. This even includes, rightly or wrongly, a wife being able to make a unilateral decision to abort the couple's unborn child. Thus, in *Paton* v. *British Pregnancy Advisory Service Trustees* [1979] QB 276, the husband failed to obtain an injunction prohibiting the defendants carrying out an abortion on his wife. Furthermore, as husbands and wives have separate personalities, a husband can be guilty of raping his wife. The House of Lords so held in *R* v. *R* [1992] 1 AC 599, where

Lord Keith said that marriage 'is in modern times regarded as a partnership of equals and no longer one in which the wife must be the subservient chattel of the husband.'

(b) Mutual Financial Obligations

Husbands and wives have a mutual duty to provide each other with financial support. Where one of them fails to provide such support, the other can apply for financial provision in the courts (see below). Applications during marriage, however, are rare in practice because a failure to provide financial support is likely to result in divorce, when any problem about financial provision and property matters can be settled by the divorce court (see Chapter 9). A spouse who does wish to seek financial provision during marriage can apply to a magistrates' family proceedings court, a county court or the High Court (see below). It is also possible for spouses to enter into maintenance agreements.

Financial Provision in the Magistrates' Court

Under the Domestic Proceedings and Magistrates' Courts Act 1978 the magistrates' family proceedings court can make periodical payments and lump sum orders, if an applicant spouse proves that the other spouse (s.1(1)): has failed to provide reasonable maintenance for the applicant; or has failed to provide, or to make proper contribution towards, reasonable maintenance for any child of the family; or has behaved in such a way that the applicant spouse cannot reasonably be expected to live with the respondent; or has deserted the applicant. Orders can be made in favour of the applicant or to or for the benefit of a child, but applications for child maintenance must usually be made to the Child Support Agency (see 14.2). When considering whether to make an order and, if so, in what manner, the magistrates must have regard to all the circumstances of the case (including certain specified matters), but with first consideration being given to the welfare of any child of the family (s.3). The court must not dismiss the application or make a final order, however, until it has considered whether it should exercise any of its powers under the Children Act 1989 with respect to any child of the family under the age of 18 (s.8, and see Chapter 12). As proceedings under the 1978 Act are family proceedings for the purposes of the Children Act, the magistrates can make any s.8 order (see 12.4) on an application, or of its own motion. The magistrates have the power to make consent orders (s.6), and can also make periodical payments orders where the parties have been living apart by agreement and one of the parties has been making periodical payments (s.7). Orders can be varied or revoked (s.20).

Financial Provision in the County Court or High Court

Under s.27 of the Matrimonial Causes Act 1973, county courts or the High Court can make orders for periodical payments and lump sums where the applicant proves that the other spouse has failed to provide reasonable maintenance for the applicant (s.27(1)(a)), or has failed to provide, or to make a proper contribution towards, reasonable maintenance for any child of the family (s.27(1)(b)). An order may be made in favour of the applicant and/or to or for the benefit of any child of the family, although applications for child support must usually be made to the Child Support Agency (see 14.2). The statutory criteria laid down in s.25 of the Matrimonial Causes Act 1973 (see 9.4) govern the exercise of the court's discretion.

Agreements about Maintenance

Married couples can enter into their own agreements about maintenance, but any provision in an agreement prohibiting any right to apply to the court for an order for financial provision is void, and the court can vary or revoke the terms of a maintenance agreement or insert new terms on an application by either spouse (see 9.8). Private maintenance agreements are not precluded by the Child Support Acts 1991 and 1995, but any provision in an agreement restricting the right of a person to apply for a maintenance assessment for a child is void (see 14.2).

(c) The Criminal Law

For the purposes of the criminal law, the spouse of the accused is a competent witness for the prosecution, the accused and any co-accused, except where the spouses are jointly charged, when neither is competent to give evidence for the prosecution if either of them is liable to be convicted (s.80 Police and Criminal Evidence Act 1984). A spouse can be compelled to give evidence against the other spouse, unless they are jointly charged, although even where jointly charged they can be compelled to give evidence where the offence involves certain offences against a child under 16 (s.80 Police and Criminal Evidence Act 1984). A husband can commit the crime of rape against his wife, as the common law rule that by marriage a wife impliedly consented to intercourse was overturned by the House of Lords in *R* v. *R* [1992] 1 AC 599.

(d) Property Rights

As married persons have separate personalities (see above), a husband and wife may own property solely or jointly. The rules governing ownership of property are generally the same for married couples as they are for other persons, except for some statutory provisions which apply only to spouses (see 4.2). The position is quite different, however, on divorce. Married persons, but not cohabitants, also enjoy statutory rights of occupation of the family home (see 4.2). Furthermore, a surviving spouse, unlike a surviving cohabitant, is treated favourably by the law when the other spouse dies intestate (see 5.2) and when he or she applies for financial provision under the Inheritance (Provision for Family and Dependants) Act 1975 (see 5.3).

(e) Parental Responsibility

Both married parents have parental responsibility for their children (see 11.6). This includes a duty to provide financial support for their children (see Chapter 14).

(f) Protection Against Violence

Spouses (and former spouses) may seek non-molestation and occupation orders under Part IV of the Family Law Act 1996 where the applicant or any child needs protection from violence (see Chapter 6).

(g) Rights on Marriage Breakdown

On marriage breakdown, a married person can petition for divorce, nullity or judicial separation under Part I of the Matrimonial Causes Act 1973 (see Chapter 8). Having obtained a decree, it is also possible to ask the court under Part II of the 1973 Act for property and financial orders, including orders in respect of the matrimonial home and orders in respect of pension entitlement (see Chapter 9).

(h) Rights in Respect of Adoption

Under the Adoption Act 1976, married couples can adopt a child jointly and both of them have the right to consent to (or refuse to consent to) the adoption of their own child (see Chapter 17).

(i) Citizenship and Immigration

In respect of British citizenship, married couples are treated more favourably by the law than other persons, including cohabitants. Under the British

Nationality Act 1981, a person who marries a British citizen can acquire British citizenship. A child born in the UK is a British citizen if either of his or her married parents (or unmarried mother) is a British citizen. Under the Immigration Act 1971, a British citizen has the right to live in and to enter and leave the UK. Whether or not a non-British spouse of a British citizen is able to live in and enter and leave the UK is governed by the immigration rules, but he or she is usually entitled to do so unless the immigration authorities consider that the marriage has been entered into purely to gain admission to the UK, in other words it is considered a 'sham'. However, because of the supremacy of European Community law, a non-British spouse who is an EC citizen or who is married to an EC citizen may be able to enter the UK under European Community law, despite UK rules to the contrary. Thus, in *R* v. *Immigration Appeal Tribunal, ex p Secretary of State for the Home Department* (C-370/90) [1992] 3 All ER 798, an Indian national, who had married a British national in the UK, was allowed to enter the UK from Germany under the European Community principle of free movement of workers which extends not only to workers but to their spouses and families.

3.2   The Legal Consequences of Cohabitation

Cohabitation, rather than marriage, is increasingly chosen by some couples. English family law, however, has generally only recognised cohabitation where it involves two people living together as husband and wife, although limited recognition has been given to homosexual cohabitants (see 1.2). Although many couples cohabit, they do not have the same legal rights and responsibilities as married couples. On relationship breakdown, in particular, cohabitants are in a vulnerable position compared with spouses, because the court has no discretionary jurisdiction as it has on divorce (see Chapter 9) to adjust their property and financial assets according to their needs and resources.

What is 'Cohabitation'?

Sometimes the court has had to consider what the term 'cohabitation' means. Thus in *G* v. *G (Non-molestation Order: Jurisdiction)* [2000] 2 FLR 533 the court had to consider whether the parties were cohabiting, for if they were the applicant would be able to apply for a non-molestation order under Part IV of the Family Law Act 1996. Wall J held that they were cohabiting as the 'signposts' set out in *Crake* v. *Supplementary Benefits Commission* [1982] 1 All ER 498 were present: there was a sexual relationship; some financial support; and the respondent's evidence demonstrated that from his perspective the parties were cohabiting. In *Kimber* v. *Kimber* [2000] 1 FLR 224, the court had to establish whether a divorced wife was cohabiting, because if she were her maintenance would have to be reduced under the terms of a consent order. Similar factors like those in *G* v. *G* were identified as being relevant to the question of whether there had been cohabitation: whether they lived together in the same household; whether they shared a daily life; whether their relationship was stable and permanent; how financial matters were arranged; whether there was a sexual relationship; how the children were treated; and what the intention and motivation of the parties were like in respect of their relationship.

Cohabitation Contracts

Cohabitants may, if they wish, enter into cohabitation contracts to regulate their affairs (e.g. to make arrangements about the allocation of property and other matters should their relationship break down). In practice, few couples do so. Today, courts are unlikely to hold such contracts void on grounds of public policy (i.e. because they undermine marriage), but a contract is likely to be carefully scrutinised by the courts if challenged. Cohabitants wishing to enter into a cohabitation contract should seek legal advice, otherwise they may find that the court sets it aside on the basis of some vitiating factor, such as duress, inequality of bargaining power, misrepresentation, or failure to make full and frank disclosure.

(a) Financial Obligations

Unlike married couples, cohabitants have no mutual duty during their relationship or on its breakdown to provide each other with financial support. Consequently they have no right to apply to the court for orders in respect of financial provision. However, both cohabitants, including the father whether or not he has parental responsibility, have a duty to maintain their children. Applications for child maintenance can be made to the Child Support Agency, except in a few special cases when they can be made to the court (see 14.2). Lump sum and property orders for children can be sought from the court (see Chapter 14).

(b) Property Rights

The property rights of cohabitants during their relationship and on relationship breakdown are governed by the general law of property (see Chapter 4). No special statutory provisions apply to them as apply to married couples either during their relationship or on relationship breakdown. Cohabitants must rely instead on equitable doctrines, such as trusts and proprietary estoppel, to establish interests. However, because of the unsatisfactory nature of equitable doctrines for determining property disputes between cohabitants, the Law Commission since 1995 has been considering reform in order to improve the legal position for cohabitants and other home-sharers. A report is still awaited. Cohabitants, unlike spouses, have no statutory rights of occupation of the family home and have no right to succeed to the deceased partner's estate on intestacy. However, a surviving cohabitant can apply under the Inheritance (Provision for Family and Dependants) Act 1975 (see 5.3) for financial provision out of the deceased cohabitant's estate, or claim a beneficial interest in the deceased cohabitant's property under a trust (see Chapter 4).

(c) Parental Responsibility

Cohabitants are not in the same position as married couples in respect of parental responsibility, as only the unmarried mother, not the unmarried father, has automatic parental responsibility for their children. However, unmarried fathers can acquire parental responsibility by agreement with the mother or by court order, and there are proposals to give some unmarried fathers automatic parental responsibility (see 11.7). Unmarried fathers (with or without responsibility) and unmarried mothers are parents for the purposes of the Children Act 1989 (see Chapter 12), but unmarried fathers without parental responsibility are not parents for the purposes of the Adoption Act 1976 (see Chapter 17) and cannot appoint a guardian for their children, except by making an application to the court (see 11.5).

(d) Protection against Violence

Like married couples, cohabitants (and former cohabitants) can seek non-molestation and occupation orders under Part IV of the Family Law Act 1996 to protect themselves and their children against a violent partner (see Chapter 6). Cohabitants, however, unlike spouses, do not have the advantage of having statutory rights of occupation of the family home.

(e) Rights on Relationship Breakdown

On relationship breakdown, cohabitants have a duty to give their children financial support by way of maintenance, but there is no such duty between the cohabiting partners themselves. Unlike married couples, the courts have no power to adjust the property entitlement of cohabiting partners according to their needs and resources. Instead, cohabitants must apply to the court using equitable doctrines such as trusts and proprietary estoppel. Doing this is time-consuming and costly. Because of the lack of jurisdiction in the court to adjust their property and financial matters, many cohabitants, particularly women, suffer on family breakdown, especially in respect of ownership and occupation of the family home and in respect of entitlement to the other partner's pension. There has, however, been considerable discussion about reforming the law applicable to cohabitants on family breakdown, although nothing, as yet, has been definitely proposed.

(f) Adoption Rights

Cohabiting couples are treated differently from married couples under the Adoption Act 1976. Thus, they cannot make a joint application to adopt a child. Instead, one of them will have to apply to adopt a child and then the other cohabitant (or both of them) will have to apply for a sole or joint residence order, which, if granted, will give one or both of them parental responsibility for the child (although the fact of adoption does itself confer parental responsibility on the adopter). As far as consent or refusal of consent to adoption is concerned, fathers without parental responsibility have no rights in this regard.

(g) British Citizenship and Immigration

Under the British Nationality Act 1981, it is more difficult for a non-British cohabitant partner of a British citizen to gain British citizenship by virtue of that partnership or to obtain permission to enter and remain in the UK. However, where a British citizen has a cohabitant partner who is not a British citizen, the latter may be entitled to enter the UK, despite UK immigration law to the contrary, under the European Community law principle of equal treatment, whereby an EC migrant worker and his family are entitled to enjoy the same 'social advantages' as nationals of the host Member State (see *Netherlands* v. *Reed* (Case 59/85) [1986] ECR 1283, where a cohabitant partner was allowed to enter The Netherlands). Another disadvantage of being a cohabitant is that a child born in the UK is a British citizen only if the child's mother is a British citizen or is settled in the UK, whether or not the father has parental responsibility for the child.

3.3 Are Cohabitants Discriminated Against?

Whether cohabitants should be given more rights similar to those possessed by married couples is a difficult question. Some couples have chosen cohabitation for the very reason that they do not wish the State to regulate the effects of their relationship. Nonetheless, it is generally felt that legislation is urgently needed to regulate the affairs of cohabitants on relationship breakdown, particularly as women sometimes fare less well than their male counterparts. Some cohabitants suffer a raw deal on relationship breakdown, particularly in respect of the home, and other substantial assets, such as pensions and investments, when they are owned by only one of them. Cohabitants who did not wish to be subject to new laws regulating the consequence of relationship breakdown could enter into cohabitation contracts in which they could expressly state that they wished to govern their own affairs, and not be subject to any discretionary adjustive jurisdiction in the courts.

Cohabitants also suffer tax disadvantages compared with husbands and wives. Thus, for example, if one spouse dies there is no inheritance tax on gifts or assets which pass to the other spouse, but if a cohabiting partner dies, the other partner is liable for inheritance tax on those assets if the estate is bigger than the current inheritance tax threshold. Another major disadvantage on death is that the surviving cohabitant does not automatically succeed to the other partner's estate on intestacy. Instead the estate passes to their children, or if there are no children, then to the deceased partner's family. Although amendments to the Inheritance (Provision for Family and Dependants) Act 1975 have improved the position for cohabitants, they are still not treated in the same way as married couples under the Act (see Chapter 5).

There are other ways in which cohabitants consider themselves discriminated against. One is in respect of parental responsibility. Unmarried fathers, unlike married fathers, do not have 'automatic' parental responsibility, but must acquire it. This may also discrimate against their children. However, this is one area where reform is imminent (see 11.7). Some consider that the law also discriminates against gay and lesbian partners because it does not allow them to marry and thereby acquire some of the legal effects of marriage. While in some countries, notably in the USA, The Netherlands and France, there have been developments to allow homosexual cohabitants to enter into marriage-type partnerships, the UK Government has no proposals to allow this in the UK. In fact, Jack Straw, the Home Secretary, announced on the implementation of the Human Rights Act 1998, that while he was a strong supporter of gay rights and treating people the same regardless of their sexual preference, marriage had a different purpose (see *The Times*, 2 October 2000). The Liberal Democrat Party, on the other hand, has proposed the introduction of a 'civil marriage' for both heterosexual and homosexual couples, whereby couples would be allowed to register their partnership and thereby acquire some, but not all, of the rights possessed by married couples. The Lib Dem proposals included property, inheritance and pension rights.

Now that the Human Rights Act 1998 is in force, human rights' challenges are likely to be made by both heterosexual and homosexual cohabiting couples in respect of their lack of family rights, in particular in respect of property and inheritance rights, and the lack of any right to enter into a registered partnership. How the courts will deal with such challenges remains to be seen.

Summary

1 Husbands and wives have separate legal personalities. They can therefore own property separately and can bring actions in tort and contact against each other, and separately or jointly against third parties. Husbands and wives have a mutual duty to provide each other with financial support, and either party may apply for financial provision from the magistrates' family proceedings court under the Domestic Proceedings and Magistrates' Courts Act 1978 or from the county court or High Court under s.27 of the Matrimonial Causes Act 1973. Married couples may make their own maintenance agreements. Both married parents have parental responsibility. Married couples have rights and remedies under the criminal and civil law to protect themselves and their children against domestic violence.

2 Cohabitation is common today, but cohabitants have fewer rights than spouses, particularly in respect of property, so that they are often in a vulnerable position on relationship breakdown or when their partner dies. Cohabitants have no obligation to maintain their partner but have an obligation to maintain their children. Only the unmarried mother has automatic parental responsibility for the children, but the unmarried father can acquire it. However, there are proposals to allow unmarried fathers registered on their child's birth certificate to have automatic parental responsibility. Cohabitants have rights and remedies under the criminal and civil law to protect themselves and their children against domestic violence. It is more difficult for a cohabiting partner to acquire British nationality than it is for a married partner. Cohabitants can make a cohabitation contract to govern their rights and obligations, but few do so.

3 A controversial issue is whether, and to what extent, the law should be changed to give cohabitants more rights, particularly in respect of property entitlement on relationship breakdown.

Further Reading and References

Bailey-Harris, 'Law and the unmarried couple – Oppression or liberation?' [1996] CFLQ 137.

Barlow, *Cohabitants and the Law* (2nd edn), Butterworths, 1997.

Barlow and Probert, 'Addressing the legal status of cohabitation in Britain and France: Plus ça change...?' [1999] 3 Web JCLI (webjcli.ncl.ac.uk/1999/issue3/barlow3.html).

Clive, 'Marriage: an unnecessary legal concept?', in Eekelaar and Katz (eds), *Marriage and Cohabitation in Contemporary Societies*, Butterworths, 1980.

Ermisch and Francesconi, *Cohabitation in Great Britain: Not for Long, but Here to Stay*, University of Essex, ESRC Research Centre on Micro-Social Change, 1998.

Lewis, *Marriage, Cohabitation and the Law: Individualism and Obligation*, Lord Chancellor's Department Research Series No 1/99 (available on the Lord Chancellor's Department's website, www.open.gov.uk/lcd/).

Lewis, 'Marriage and cohabitation and the nature of commitment' [1999] CFLQ 355.

Welstead, ' *M* v. *H*. Financial support for same-sex relationships – A Canadian constitutional solution' [2000] CFLQ 73.

Questions

1 What are the policy arguments for and against giving cohabiting partners the same rights as married couples?
2 Should reform of the law differ depending on whether cohabitants are heterosexual or homosexual partners?

Part III

Family Property

Part III deals with family property. Chapter 4 deals generally with family property, particularly ownership and occupation of the family home. It also considers local housing authorities' duties and powers under the homelessness legislation. Chapter 5 deals with family property on death and Chapter 6 with the occupation of the family home and protection against domestic violence. Property issues on divorce are dealt with in Part IV, Chapter 9.

4 Family Property

Although this chapter is entitled 'family property', it deals largely with ownership and occupation of the family home, because most property disputes which arise, and which get to court, are in respect of the home. This is because the family home is not only a valuable financial asset, but also provides a roof over the family's head. However, as we shall see when we come to consider divorce, occupational pensions are also a valuable family asset (see 9.7).

In this chapter, although the focus is on the property rights of married couples and cohabitants, the same rules (except for some statutory provisions which apply specifically to married couples) also apply to other family members. At the outset, however, it is important to understand that, although the rules in respect of property are largely the same for cohabitants and for spouses, the position is quite different for spouses on divorce, because the divorce court under its ancillary relief jurisdiction (see Chapter 9) can adjust the property rights of spouses according to their needs and resources and the needs of their children. Cohabitants, on the other hand, must rely instead on the general principles of contract and property law, particularly the law of equity. To this extent, spouses are in a considerably better position than cohabitants on relationship breakdown.

Before we look at the rules in detail, mention must be made of the fact that there are two sorts of ownership in English law: legal and equitable. Ownership in equity involves owning property as a beneficiary under a trust. A person can be an owner either in law or in equity, but it is possible for the same person to be simultaneously the owner of the same piece of property both in law and in equity. Thus, for example, one partner may be the owner in law of the family home but also hold it on trust for himself or herself and the other partner in equity. Many spouses and cohabitants, however, own property, particularly the family home, jointly as co-owners in law and in equity. Co-owners can own property either as joint tenants or as tenants in common. Joint tenants each own the whole interest in the property and as individuals own no separate share, so that on the death of one of them, the other is entitled to the whole property under the so-called 'right of survivorship'. Tenants in common, on the other hand, each own a separate share of the property. On death there is no automatic right of survivorship. The deceased's share passes in the will or according to the laws of intestacy (see Chapter 5). It is possible, however, to sever a joint tenancy and convert it into a tenancy in common by giving notice in writing, by mutual agreement, by alienation, or by conduct. A joint tenancy is also severed on bankruptcy. These rules about joint tenancies and tenancies in common are particularly important for cohabitants, as there is no adjustive jurisdiction available to them on relationship breakdown as there is for divorcing couples.

4.1   Property Rights of Engaged Couples

When an engagement breaks down, the Law Reform (Miscellaneous Provisions) Act 1970 gives engaged couples rights in respect of property similar to those of married couples (see below). Section 2(1) of the Act provides that when an engagement is terminated, any rule of law relating to the beneficial entitlement of spouses also applies to any property in which either or both parties had a beneficial interest during the engagement. Thus a person who is (or was) engaged can apply under s.37 of the Matrimonial Proceedings and Property Act 1970 and s.17 of the Married Women's Property Act 1882 (see below) for a property dispute to be settled. A s.17 application must be brought, however, within three years of the termination of the engagement (s.2(2)). It has been held that an application can be brought under s.17 even though an engagement is unenforceable, because one of the parties is already married (see *Shaw* v. *Fitzgerald* [1992] 1 FLR 357).

The 1970 Act also makes provision in respect of engagement gifts and engagement rings. Thus, the fact that one party was responsible for terminating the engagement does not affect any express or implied arrangement in respect of the return of engagement gifts as between the parties (s.3(1)). As far as engagement gifts from third parties (friends, relatives etc.) are concerned, whether they belong to one or both parties on termination of an engagement depends on the donor's intention. However, in the absence of intention, there may be an inference that any gift from a relative belongs to the engaged party to whom the relative is related (by analogy with *Samson* v. *Samson* [1982] 1 WLR 252, where this rule was applied to wedding gifts). An engagement ring, however, is presumed to be an absolute gift so that it can be kept, unless there is an express or implied condition that it is to be returned if the engagement comes to an end (s.3(2)). An engagement ring which is a family heirloom could be returned, for example.

Engaged couples are also entitled to apply for occupation orders and non-molestation orders under Part IV of the Family Law Act 1996 where there is domestic violence (see Chapter 6).

4.2   Property Rights of Married Couples

The principles which govern the ownership of property during marriage are generally the same as those which apply to cohabiting couples, but with some exceptions, notably in respect of occupation of the matrimonial home (see below). Property disputes, however, are rare during marriage. They are more likely to arise on marriage breakdown when they can be resolved by mediation or under Part II of the Matrimonial Causes Act 1973 by the divorce courts (see Chapter 9). Under Part II, divorce courts can make a range of different property orders taking into account the needs and resources of the parties and other factors, such as the parties' ages, contribution to the family, duration of the marriage and the needs of any children. When making orders, the court has a wide discretion and can override the property rights and entitlements of the parties, where appropriate.

(a) *Ownership of Property*

As husbands and wives have separate legal personalities and can therefore own property solely (see 3.1), any property owned before marriage continues to belong to the owner both on and during marriage, unless there is any express or implied intention to the contrary. There is therefore no concept of a presumption of joint ownership of property in English law, as there is in other European countries and in the USA. However, the possibility of introducing presumptive joint ownership of household goods (not land) was mooted by the Law Commission in 1988 (*Family Law: Matrimonial Property* (Law Com No 175)), but nothing was done about it, despite the fact that the Law Commission considered that the rules for determining ownership of property other than land were 'arbitrary, uncertain and unfair', as most couples intended property to be jointly owned even though according to the law it was not.

The following Acts of Parliament make provision in respect of property belonging to married couples, but they are rarely invoked today because most disputes arise as a result of divorce. When divorce was less common, however, these provisions had a greater role to play.

(i) Section 17 Married Women's Property Act 1882   Section 17 of the Married Women's Property Act 1882 gives county courts and the High Court power to make such orders as they think fit as to the ownership or possession of any property where a dispute arises between a married couple. However, s.17 only allows the court to *declare* existing rights of ownership. It does not allow the court to *create* rights (*Pettitt* v. *Pettitt* [1970] AC 777), as it can on divorce. In s.17 proceedings, the court also has power to order the sale of property, and make orders in respect of the proceeds of sale of any property representing the original property (ss.7(7) and 7(1) Matrimonial Causes (Property and Maintenance) Act 1958). An application can be made after divorce (or annulment), but it must be brought within three years (s.39 Matrimonial Proceedings and Property Act 1970). A s.17 application might be

useful, for example, when an application for a property adjustment order under the divorce legislation is prohibited because the applicant has remarried (s.28(3) MCA 1973). However, few applications are made.

(ii) Section 37 of the Matrimonial Proceedings and Property Act 1970   Under s.37, one spouse can apply against the other spouse for a share, or enlarged share, of the beneficial interest in any property, if the applicant spouse has made a substantial contribution in money or in money's worth to its improvement. The court may grant a share or, as the case may be, an enlarged share, provided there is no express or implied agreement to the contrary. Few applications are made under s.37 and reported cases on the section are virtually non-existent.

(iii) Section 1 of the Married Women's Property Act 1964   By virtue of this provision, any property bought by a wife with savings from housekeeping money given to her by her husband belongs to them both in equal shares. However, this provision is archaic and discriminatory. In 1988 the Law Commission recommended its repeal (see *Matrimonial Property*, Law Com 175), but this has not been done.

(b) Matrimonial Home Rights

Under Part IV of the Family Law Act 1996, a 'non-entitled' spouse (i.e. a non-owning spouse) has 'matrimonial home rights', which are conferred when (s.30(1)):

> '(a) one spouse is entitled to occupy a dwelling-house by virtue of –
> (i) a beneficial estate or interest or contract; or
> (ii) any enactment giving that spouse the right to remain in occupation; and
> (b) the other spouse is not so entitled.'

'Matrimonial home rights' consist of the following (s.30(2)):

> '(a) if in occupation, a right not to be evicted or excluded from the dwelling-house or any part of it by the other spouse except with the leave of the court given by an order under section 33;
> (b) if not in occupation, a right with the leave of the court so given to enter into and occupy the dwelling-house.'

These provisions apply only to a house which is, or was, intended by the spouses to be their matrimonial home (s.30(7)).

Where, during marriage, one spouse is entitled to occupy the matrimonial home by virtue of a beneficial estate or interest, then the other spouse's matrimonial home rights are a charge on that estate or interest (s.31). However, a charge will only bind a third party (such as a purchaser or a mortgagee), if it has been protected by registering a notice under the Land Registration Act 1925 (s.31(10) FLA 1996), or (if the title is not registered) by registering a Class F Land Charge under s.2(7) of the Land Charges Act 1972 (as amended by Sched. 8, para. 47 FLA 1996).

Part IV of the Family Law Act also makes provision in respect of mortgage payments (s.30(5)) and the rights of spouses to take part in possession proceedings where the house is subject to a mortgage (ss.54–56). Section 53 and Sched. 7 of the 1996 Act make provision in relation to the transfer of certain tenancies on marital and cohabitation breakdown (see 4.9).

4.3   Property Rights of Cohabiting Couples

(a) Ownership

During their relationship and on relationship breakdown, the property rights of cohabitants are governed by the general rules of property and contract law. There are no special statutory provisions for cohabitants as there are for married couples. Compared with married couples, cohabitants are therefore in a disadvantageous position on relationship breakdown, as the court has no discretionary jurisdiction equivalent to that of the divorce court to adjust their property rights according to their needs and resources and irrespective of their rights of ownership. (For a good comparison of property distribution on marriage and cohabitation, see Taylor, 1999.) A cohabitant who wishes to claim a share of the house will have to apply to the court for a declaration that he or she has an interest in the home in equity under a resulting or a constructive trust (see 4.5 below), or claim an interest under the equitable doctrine of proprietary estoppel (see 4.6 below). Where property is jointly owned, cohabitants can apply for sale and possession of property under the Trusts of Land and Appointment of Trustees Act 1996 (see below). Cohabitants and former cohabitants may also apply for occupation orders under Part IV of the Family Law Act 1996 (see 6.5).

The case of *Burns* v. *Burns* [1984] Ch 317 provides a good illustration of the disadvantages of being a cohabitant compared with a spouse on relationship breakdown. In *Burns*, the female cohabitant (she had taken her partner's name) had cohabitated with her partner for nearly 20 years, during which time she had brought up the children and looked after the home. On the breakdown of their relationship, she claimed a beneficial interest in the home which was solely owned by her partner. However, the Court of Appeal dismissed her claim and, while expressing sympathy for her, held that it was the responsibility of Parliament, not the judges, to change the law. In *Hammond* v. *Mitchell* [1991] 1 WLR 1127, *sub nom H* v. *M (Property: Beneficial Interest)* [1992] 1 FLR 229, on the other hand, the female cohabitant was successful in obtaining a beneficial interest in the home under a constructive trust on facts which were similar to those in *Burns*, but with the exception that Miss Mitchell and her cohabitant partner had exchanged a few words about the house at an earlier stage of their relationship. These few words were held to be sufficient evidence from which it could be inferred that she was to have an interest in the home under a constructive trust. The arbitrary and unsatisfactory nature of the law has led to increasing dissatisfaction and calls for reform (see 4.10).

(b) Occupation of the Family Home

Unlike married couples, cohabitants have no statutory right of occupation of the family home. Rights of occupation depend on whether a cohabitant possesses a right of ownership, or has a right to occupy the home under a tenancy, or a licence, or is in possession of an occupation order under Part IV of the Family Law Act 1996 (see 6.5).

4.4   Ownership of Family Property other than the Family Home

The rules for determining the ownership of property other than the home (and other land) are the same for married couples, cohabitants and other family members, with the exception of some statutory provisions which apply only to married couples (see above) and the exception of special provision on divorce. Entitlement to property other than land depends on whether there is a valid contract or an interest in equity under a trust. As a general rule, however, title passes to the person who purchases the property, subject to any evidence of a contrary intention. Thus, whichever family member buys the property (whether it be a car or a washing machine) owns it. As far as gifts are concerned, the general rule is that ownership passes to the recipient of the gift, provided the donor intended to transfer it and the gift was handed over.

However, it is possible to acquire a right of ownership by claiming an interest under a resulting or constructive trust (see further below). For example, a person who makes a payment of money into a bank account held in the sole name of another party can argue that he or she has an interest in equity under a resulting trust proportionate to that payment. It is also possible to argue that there is an express trust of property. In *Paul* v. *Constance* [1977] 1 WLR 527, for example, the female cohabitant was held to have an interest under an express trust in the bank account held in her cohabitant's sole name, as she had been authorised to draw on the account and he had told her on several occasions that the money in the account was as much hers as his. Similarly, in *Rowe* v. *Prance* [1999] 2 FLR 787 the applicant was held to be entitled to a half share in a valuable yacht owned by her married lover even though she had made no financial contribution to its purchase. The court accepted that the evidence was sufficient to constitute a trust in her favour. Her lover had spoken about 'our boat,' 'a share of the boat together' and had said 'your security is your interest in it.' They had had a close relationship for 14 years and she had given up her rented house and put furniture in storage in order to move into the boat which they intended to sail round the world together. The court held that the man had constituted himself an express trustee of the boat, and that no writing was required because the property in dispute was 'personal' property (property other than land).

Despite the successful outcome for the female cohabitants in *Paul* v. *Constance* and *Rowe* v. *Prance*, cohabiting couples should take heed of Waite J's words in *Hammond* v. *Mitchell* (above), where he said that cohabitants on family breakdown should be encouraged to do their best to settle disputes about chattels (household goods), on the understanding that in ordinary cases the court would divide them equally.

Bank Accounts

Disputes sometimes arise in respect of bank accounts, in respect of ownership of the funds and of property purchased with the funds. Where a bank account is held in one person's name, the money in the account belongs to that person, unless there is a contrary intention, or another person has made a contribution to the fund. Where a bank account is held in joint names, the money in the account belongs to both parties as beneficial joint tenants of the whole fund, unless there is a contrary intention, e.g. that the account was put into joint names only for the sake of convenience (*Marshall* v. *Crutwell* (1875) LR 20 Eq 328). However, even a joint account initially opened for convenience may be regarded as a true joint account after a period of time (*Re Figgis, dec'd* [1969] 1 Ch 123).

As a general rule, any property bought with funds from a bank account belongs to the purchaser. Thus, for example, if a husband draws money from a joint bank account to purchase shares in his name, then *prima facie* they belong to him. However, where the parties have pooled their resources, the court may adopt the approach laid down in *Jones* v. *Maynard* [1951] Ch 572, where Vaisey J treated the joint account as a 'common pool' and held that investments purchased by the husband with money from the account held jointly with his wife belonged to them both in equal shares, even though the husband had made larger contributions to the joint account than his wife.

4.5   Settling Disputes about the Family Home

Disputes about the family home can arise in many different situations. They can arise on relationship breakdown, in which case divorcing couples may have to resort to the divorce legislation and cohabitants to the law of equity. Another situation where a dispute might arise is in respect of a third party, such as a purchaser, a mortgagee or the trustee in bankruptcy. For example, one party might have mortgaged the home to a bank or building society either as security for a loan to pay for the house or to finance a business. If repayments to the mortgage are not made, the mortgagee may seek possession of the house and an order for sale. By way of defence, however, a home-sharer may claim that he or she has an overriding interest which defeats the claims of the third party. To establish an overriding interest, a person must be in actual occupation of the home and possess a beneficial interest in it (see s.70(1)(g) Land Registration Act 1925). To establish an overriding interest, a non-owner will therefore have to claim a beneficial interest (as Mrs Rosset tried to do in *Lloyds Bank plc* v. *Rosset* [1991] AC 107, see below). Another situation where a dispute about the home might arise is on death, where a cohabitant or other family member has received no share, or an insufficient share, of the interest in the home (see, for example, *Ivin* v. *Blake (Property: Beneficial Interest)* [1995] 1 FLR 70). Finally, a case about the home may come to court because there has been no mention of the parties' respective beneficial interests on the conveyance (see, for example, *Springette* v. *Defoe* [1992] 2 FLR 388).

The following procedures can be used to settle a dispute about property, although divorcing couples will seek remedies in the divorce court (see Chapter 9):

(i) A Declaration   County courts and the High Court can make declarations in respect of rights in property. For example, this is what each plaintiff sought in *Hammond* v. *Mitchell* (1991) and *Lloyds Bank plc* v. *Rosset* (1991).

(ii) An Order for Sale   Orders for sale and possession of land, including the family home, can be sought under the Trusts of Land and Appointment of Trustees Act 1996. Section 14 of the Act allows any trustee or beneficiary under a trust of land, or any secured creditor of a beneficiary, to apply to the court for an order for sale of the property. In exercising its discretion to decide whether or not to order sale, the court must take into account the following factors which are laid down in s.15:

- the intentions of the person(s) who created the trust;
- the purposes for which the trust is held;

- the welfare of any child who occupies, or who might reasonably be expected to occupy, any land subject to the trust as his or her home; and
- the interests of any secured creditor or beneficiary.

Applications for an order for sale are sometimes made on bankruptcy. In cases decided under the old law (s.30 Law of Property Act 1925), the wishes of the trustee in bankruptcy would usually prevail over the interests of the family in occupation of the home (*Re Citro (A Bankrupt)* [1991] Ch 142 and *Lloyds Bank plc* v. *Byrne and Byrne* [1993] 1 FLR 369). However, in *The Mortgage Corporation* v. *Shaire and Others* [2000] 1 FLR 973, Neuberger J was of the view that the law had been changed by s.15 of the Trusts of Land and Appointment of Trustees Act 1996, and that a different approach now applied in bankruptcy cases. His Lordship said that, as the new legislation intended to tip the balance more in favour of families and against banks and chargees, s.15 gave the court greater flexibility than it had under the old law. Neuberger J said that the old authorities decided under s.30 LPA 1925 should therefore be treated with caution, and would in many cases be unlikely to be of great assistance.

(iii) An Order under Part IV of the Family Law Act 1996 Orders in respect of the occupation of the home can be made under Part IV of the Family Law Act 1996 on the application of married couples and cohabitants – including former partners (see 6.5).

4.6 Acquiring a Right of Ownership in the Family Home under a Trust

A non-owner can claim a right of ownership in the home on the basis that he or she has a right of ownership in equity under a trust. Interests in land, trusts of land and contracts for the sale of land are required to be in writing, but provision is made for trusts to be claimed where there is no such writing. Thus, s.53(1)(a) of the Law of Property Act 1925 provides that interests in land can only be created or disposed of in writing, and s.53(1)(b) of the same Act provides that a declaration of trust in respect of land must be manifested and proved by writing. However, despite the absence of writing, an interest can be claimed by way of a resulting or constructive trust, as s.53(2) provides that the requirement of writing does not affect the creation or operation of resulting or constructive trusts. Written formalities are also required in respect of contracts for the sale of land (see s.2(1) of the Law of Property (Miscellaneous Provisions) Act 1989), but again the requirement of writing does not affect the creation or operation of resulting or constructive trusts (s.2(5)). It has also been held by the Court of Appeal that, as s.2(5) of the 1989

Act (like s.53(2) of the 1925 Act) was intended to save a range of equitable remedies, an interest can equally be claimed under proprietary estoppel (Beldam LJ in *Yaxley* v. *Gotts and Gotts* [1999] 2 FLR 941, and see 4.7 below).

A non-owner can therefore claim an interest in the home (or any other property) on the basis of a resulting or constructive trust. The principles which govern each of these two types of trust are quite different, although the principles have sometimes been merged, which has caused uncertainty and confusion (see Peter Gibson LJ in *Drake* v. *Whipp* [1996] 1 FLR 826 at 827). It is also possible to establish an interest in the home (and any other property) under the doctrine of proprietary estoppel (see below).

(a) Acquiring an Interest under a Resulting Trust

A resulting trust arises as a presumption of equity where someone makes a financial contribution to the purchase of property. In the absence of a contrary intention (e.g. that it was a gift or a loan, or that other shares were intended), a person who contributes money to the purchase of property acquires an interest under a resulting trust in equity proportionate to his or her contribution. In *Dyer* v. *Dyer* (1788) 2 Cox Eq Cas 92 at 93 and 94, Eyre CB stated:

> 'The clear result in all the cases, without a single exception, is that the trust of a legal estate ... whether taken in the names of the purchasers and others jointly, or in the names of others without that of the purchaser; whether in one name or several; whether jointly or successive – results to the man who advances the purchase-money.'

Thus, where a home is purchased in one person's sole name, a person who has contributed to the deposit or mortgage payments can claim an interest in the house under a resulting trust proportionate to that contribution.

A resulting trust was established in the case of *Sekhon* v. *Alissa* [1989] 2 FLR 94. Here the house had been bought in the name of the defendant daughter. She had contributed to the purchase price, but her mother had paid the balance. The mother claimed a share in the house under a resulting trust, arguing that, although it was bought in her daughter's name, it was purchased as a joint commercial venture and that they both intended to own it in proportion to their respective financial contributions. The daughter attempted to rebut the presumption of resulting trust by arguing that her mother's financial contribution was intended as a gift or a loan. The court therefore had to decide what was the actual or presumed intention of the parties at the time of the conveyance. Was the mother's financial contribution a gift or an unsecured loan, or was the mother intended to have a beneficial interest in the property? The Court of Appeal held that the law presumed a resulting trust in the mother's favour, and on the facts the presumption was not rebutted by the daughter's allegation that the money was a gift or a loan.

Another case where a claim was made under a resulting trust was *Springette* v. *Defoe* [1992] 2 FLR 388. In this case the parties, two elderly cohabitants, had bought their council house, but there was nothing in the registered transfer quantifying their respective beneficial interests in the property. Each party had paid half the mortgage instalments, but the plaintiff had paid most of the balance of the purchase price. When the relationship broke down, Miss Springette issued an originating summons claiming she was entitled to 75 per cent of the proceeds of sale, as this represented her contribution to the purchase. At first instance, the trial judge granted them an equal share of the beneficial interest, on the basis that it was their uncommunicated belief or intention that they were to share the property equally. However, the Court of Appeal allowed Miss Springette's appeal, holding that as there was no discussion between the parties at to their respective beneficial interests, there was no evidence to rebut the presumption that she was entitled to a 75 per cent of the beneficial interest under a resulting trust.

Another case which was argued on the basis of a resulting trust was *Tinsley* v. *Milligan* [1993] 2 FLR 963. Here the house in dispute had been acquired jointly by two women, but it had been registered in the sole name of one of them so that the other could make fraudulent social security claims. When the relationship broke down, the non-owner claimed an interest under a resulting trust, but the owner argued that her partner was not entitled to assert an interest because of the fraud. In other words, according to the maxim of equity, 'she had not come to equity with clean hands'. The House of Lords, by a majority, allowed the non-owner's claim and held that a completely executed transfer of property, or an interest in property made in pursuance of an unlawful agreement, was valid in law and in equity, and that the court would assist the transferee in the protection of that interest provided the claim itself was not based on the unlawful agreement. *Tinsley* v. *Milligan* was applied in *Lawson* v. *Coombes* [1999] 1 FLR 799, where a male cohabitant had perpetrated a fraud on his former wife by purchasing a house in his cohabitant's name so that his former wife should have no claim over the house on divorce. On relationship breakdown, the male cohabitant sought a declaration against his former cohabitant on the ground that the house was held by her on trust for them both in equal shares. He also sought an order for sale under the Trusts of Land and Appointment of Trustees Act 1996 (see above). At first instance, where illegality and *Tinsley* v. *Milligan* (above) were not argued, the trial judge held that, although it was the intention of the parties to purchase the house in equal shares, he was precluded from asserting his half interest in the house because of the fraud (applying *Tinker* v. *Tinker* [1970] P 136). However, the Court of Appeal allowed his appeal, holding that, as the case was one of illegality by reason of s.37 of the Matrimonial Causes Act 1973 (i.e. a transaction to defeat a claim to ancillary relief, see 9.10), it was governed by *Tinsley* v. *Milligan*. Thus, he could rely on the resulting trust which would give effect to the parties' beneficial interest in the home corresponding to their respective financial contributions to the purchase.

The Presumption of Advancement

Under the presumption of advancement, a transfer of property by a husband to his wife, or a father to his child, is presumed to belong to the transferee absolutely. This presumption can be used to rebut the presumption of resulting trust. Thus, for example, if a husband gives his wife money to purchase a house, she can argue that this rebuts a resulting trust in his favour because equity presumes that the money is an outright gift. However, as the presumption of advancement is archaic and discriminatory (because it only applies to gifts by husbands and fathers), it has little relevance today (see dicta in *Pettitt* v. *Pettitt* [1970] AC 777). Indeed, in *McGrath* v. *Wallis* [1995] 2 FLR 114, Nourse LJ said that in its application to a house acquired for joint occupation, it was a judicial instrument of last resort which could be easily rebutted.

(b) Acquiring an Interest under a Constructive Trust

An interest in the home (or any other property) can be claimed under a constructive trust, or what is more specifically sometimes called a 'common intention' constructive trust to distinguish it from other types of constructive trust which arise in other contexts. Unlike a resulting trust, financial contribution to the purchase of property is not needed. Instead, the emphasis is on finding an express or implied agreement that the non-owner is entitled to a beneficial interest. However, we shall discover below that, where there is no express agreement or arrangement to share property, then some financial contribution, however small, is likely to be needed.

Where a claim to property is sought on the basis of a constructive trust, the court conducts a two-stage process. First it looks at all the evidence to establish whether there is a constructive trust. If a trust is established, it then decides what size the beneficial interest should be. We have seen above that a successful claim by way of a resulting trust only gives the claimant a share of the equity proportionate to his or her financial contribution. With a constructive trust, on the other hand, the court determines the share by considering all the circumstances of the case. If a share larger than a proportionate share is required, then a claim will have to be brought on the basis of a constructive trust.

Judicial willingness to find interests under constructive trusts has fluctuated in the development of the law. During the late 1960s and early 1970s,

Lord Denning MR in the Court of Appeal was imposing constructive trusts on the basis of broad notions of justice or unconscionability, despite dicta to the contrary in two House of Lords' decisions (*Pettitt* v. *Pettitt* [1970] AC 777 and *Gissing* v. *Gissing* [1971] AC 886). After Lord Denning MR's retirement, however, the Court of Appeal in *Burns* v. *Burns* (1984) returned to the strict approach so that it became no longer possible to impose a trust merely to do justice in the particular case. If there was no intention or arrangement to share the house, then the court could not 'ascribe intentions which the parties in fact never had' (Lord Morris, in *Gissing*).

The leading case on constructive trusts of the home is *Lloyds Bank plc* v. *Rosset* [1991] 1 AC 107, [1990] 2 FLR 155, where Lord Bridge, who gave the leading opinion, laid down the approach to be adopted by the courts. In *Rosset*, the house had been purchased in the husband's sole name. Although his wife had helped to renovate the house, she had made no financial contribution to its purchase or renovation. Mr Rosset had charged the house to Lloyds Bank as security for a loan, but Mrs Rosset knew nothing of this. When Mr Rosset went into debt, the bank claimed possession of the house and an order for sale. Mrs Rosset, by way of defence to the bank's claim, argued that she had a beneficial interest in the house under a constructive trust and that this interest, coupled with her actual occupation, gave her an overriding interest under s.70(1)(g) Land Registration Act 1925 which would defeat the bank's claims. However, the House of Lords dismissed her appeal, holding that her activities in relation to the renovation of the house were insufficient to justify the inference of a common intention that she was entitled to a beneficial interest under a constructive trust. Lord Bridge, summarising and encapsulating the previous law as laid down in the two earlier House of Lords' decisions of *Pettitt* v. *Pettitt* (1970) and *Gissing* v. *Gissing* (1971), and referring also to the Court of Appeal decision in *Grant* v. *Edwards* [1986] Ch 638 (the leading case on detriment), said:

'The first and fundamental question which must always be resolved is whether, independently of any inference to be drawn from the conduct of the parties in the course of sharing the house as their home and managing their joint affairs, there has at any time prior to acquisition, or exceptionally at some later date, been any agreement, arrangement or understanding reached between them that the property is to be shared beneficially. The finding of an agreement or arrangement to share in this sense can only, I think, be based on evidence of express discussions between the partners, however imperfectly remembered and however imprecise their terms may have been. Once a finding to this effect is made it will only be necessary for the partner entitled to the legal estate to show that he or she has acted to his or her detriment or significantly altered his or her position in reliance on the agreement in order to give rise to a constructive trust or proprietary estoppel.

In sharp contrast to this situation is the very different one where there is no evidence to support a finding of an agreement or an arrangement to share, however reasonable it might have been for the parties to reach such an agreement if they had applied their minds to the question, and where the court must rely entirely on the conduct of the parties both as the basis from which to infer a common intention to share the property beneficially and as the conduct relied on to give rise to a constructive trust. In this situation direct contributions to the purchase price by the partner who is not the legal owner, whether initially or by payment of mortgage instalments, will readily justify the inference necessary to the creation of a constructive trust. But, as I read the authorities, it is at least extremely doubtful whether anything less will do.'

These words have formed the basis of the courts' approach to constructive trusts. According to Lord Bridge, there are two situations in which a constructive trust may arise: (i) where there is an express agreement, arrangement or understanding that the property is to be shared beneficially; and (ii) where there is no such express agreement, arrangement or understanding, but where an agreement can be inferred. In both situations, a claimant will also have to prove detrimental reliance. Detriment provides the consideration needed to satisfy the rule of equity that 'equity will not assist a volunteer' (a 'volunteer' is someone who has not provided consideration). Detrimental reliance is usually easily proved. Bringing up a family, running a home etc. can be used as evidence of detriment. The more difficult hurdle in a case will be proving the existence of an agreement, arrangement or understanding. A claimant may have to trawl back through the relationship to find evidence. Where a non-owner has not contributed to the purchase price in any way and there is no oral evidence from which an express agreement to share can be established, then a claim based on a constructive trust is unlikely to succeed.

Lord Bridge gave *Eves* v. *Eves* [1975] 1 WLR 1338 and *Grant* v. *Edwards* [1986] Ch 638 as examples of where there was an express agreement. In *Eves* v. *Eves*, the house had been purchased in the man's sole name but he told his partner he would have put it in her name had she been 21. He admitted later in evidence that this was just an excuse. She had done extensive and substantial decorative work on the house. The Court of Appeal held that she had a beneficial interest, as, despite the lack of writing, the parties had orally made their intentions plain. *Grant* v. *Edwards* was another 'excuse case'. Here the male cohabitant had told his partner that he had not put her name on the title as it might be detrimental to her pending divorce proceedings. This was also an excuse. He had paid the deposit and the mortgage and she had made a substantial contribution to the household expenses. The Court of Appeal, applying *Eves* v. *Eves*, held she was entitled to a beneficial interest in the house under a constructive trust. There was a common intention that she should have such an interest and evidence of conduct (substantial contribution to housekeeping and bringing up the children), which amounted to an acting on that intention (i.e. detrimental reliance), and on which it would not have been reasonable to have expected her to embark unless she was to have an interest.

As examples of the second situation in which a constructive trust can arise (i.e. where there is no express agreement, arrangement or understanding), Lord Bridge gave as examples *Pettitt* v. *Pettitt* and *Gissing* v. *Gissing* (see above), the two earlier House of Lords' cases on constructive trusts. Like *Rosset* itself, they were cases where there was no express evidence of an agreement or an arrangement to share. Neither was there any conduct, such as substantial work on the house, from which an intention could be inferred. The claims failed.

As a result of the decision in *Rosset*, if there is no express agreement to share and no direct financial contribution to the purchase which provides the evidence from which a common intention can be inferred, a claimant is unlikely to succeed. Furthermore, 'indirect contribution' to the purchase (e.g. contributing to the upkeep and care of children or running a household) is unlikely to be accepted as evidence from which the court can infer an intention. A constructive trust cannot be imposed merely to do justice. As Dillon LJ said in *Springette* v. *Defoe* [1992] 2 FLR 388 at 393, 'the court does not as yet sit, as under a palm tree, to exercise a general discretion as to what the man in the street, on the general view of the case, might regard as fair.' Even where there is financial contribution, this will not of itself suffice, as it is still necessary for an intention to be inferred from all the circumstances. The decision of the House of Lords in *Pettitt* v. *Pettitt* made this clear.

Lord Bridge's dicta in *Rosset* have been applied in many cases (see, for example, *H* v. *M (Property: Beneficial Interest)*, *sub nom Hammond* v. *Mitchell* (1991), and *Midland Bank plc* v. *Cooke* (1995), see below). In *Halifax Building Society* v. *Brown and Another*; *R Z Hemsley Ltd* v. *Brown and Another* [1996] 1 FLR 103, the plaintiffs, a building society and stockbrokers, sought possession of the matrimonial home registered in the husband's sole name, but the wife argued by way of defence that she had an overriding interest under s.70(1)(g) LRA 1925 by virtue of her beneficial interest in the property. The Court of Appeal, applying *Rosset*, said that whether the wife had a beneficial interest turned on whether there was any agreement between the parties or any contribution to the purchase price. It was held that, although there had been no agreement or discussion, a gift by the wife's mother-in-law in 1959 was capable of giving the wife a beneficial interest (see also *Drake* v. *Whipp* [1996] 1 FLR 826). Facts arising from the purchase of an earlier house can also give rise to a constructive trust in respect of a subsequent house which represents the proceeds of sale of an earlier house (*Halifax Building Society* v. *Brown* above and *McHardy and Sons (A Firm)* v. *Warren and Another* [1994] 2 FLR 338).

Quantification of the Beneficial Interest

Once the court is satisfied that the claimant is entitled to a beneficial interest under a constructive trust, it must then determine the size of that interest. To do this it considers what the parties intended, taking into account all the circumstances of the case, both of and financial and non-financial nature. It will often divide the property equally between the parties. The date for assessing what would be the equitable share of the beneficial interest is the date of sale and not the date of separation (*Turton* v. *Turton* [1988] Ch 542). The court has a wide discretion. In *Midland Bank* v. *Cooke and Another* [1995] 4 All ER 562, the husband purchased the matrimonial home for £8450, the purchase moneys consisting of £6450 by way of a mortgage, £1000 of his own savings and £1000 by way of a wedding gift from his parents to him and his wife. The wife had made no direct contribution to the purchase price, except for the £500 representing her half-share of the wedding gift, but she had made considerable financial contributions to the upkeep of the house and to the household. She claimed a beneficial interest in the home. At first instance, the county court judge held that her interest in the house amounted to a sum equivalent to 6.47 per cent of the value of the property, which represented her half-share of the wedding gift of £1000 advanced by her in-laws. She appealed. The Court of Appeal allowed her appeal, holding that, as she and her husband had agreed to share everything equally, including the house, she was entitled to half the beneficial interest. Waite LJ distinguished *Springette* v. *Defoe* (1992, above), preferring the approach in *McHardy and Sons (A Firm)* v. *Warren and Another* [1994] 2 FLR 338, where Dillon LJ said at 340:

'To my mind it is the irresistible conclusion that where a parent pays the deposit either directly to the solicitors or to the bride and groom, ... on the purchase of their first matrimonial home, it is the intentions of all three of them that the bride and groom should have equal interests in the matrimonial home, not interests measured by reference to the percentage the deposit [bears] to the full price.'

A similar approach was taken in *Drake* v. *Whipp* [1996] 1 FLR 826, where the Court of Appeal held that the case was one of constructive, not resulting trust, and that once a constructive trust was proved the court could adopt a broad-brush approach when determining the parties' respective shares.

4.7 Acquiring an Interest under the Doctrine of Proprietary Estoppel

An interest in the family home can be acquired under the equitable doctrine of proprietary estoppel, which can be invoked in respect of the home, or other land, even where the written formalities for land have not been complied with (see *Yaxley* v. *Gotts and Gotts* [1999] 2 FLR 941). The principle in its broadest form was described by Balcombe LJ in *Wayling* v. *Jones* [1995] 2 FLR 1029, at 1031:

'Where one person (A) has acted to his detriment on the faith of a belief, which was known to and encouraged by another person (B), that he either has or is going to be given a right in or over B's property, B cannot insist on his strict legal rights if to do so would be inconsistent with A's belief.'

Thus an interest under the doctrine of proprietary estoppel requires proof of an agreement or an expectation created or encouraged by one party, upon which the other party had acted to his or her detriment. There must also be a sufficient link between the promises relied upon and the conduct which constitutes the detriment (*Eves* v. *Eves* [1975] 1 WLR 1338 and *Grant* v. *Edwards* [1986] Ch 638). However, the promises relied upon do not have to be the sole inducement for the conduct; it is sufficient if they are an inducement (*Amalgamated Investment & Property Co (In Liquidation)* v. *Texas Commerce International Bank* [1982] QB 84 at pp. 104–5). Once it has been established that promises were made, and there has been conduct by the claimant of such a nature that inducement may be inferred, the burden of proof shifts to the defendant (the party creating the expectation of an interest in property) to show that his actions did not induce the other party to act in reliance of this expectation (*Greasley* v. *Cooke* [1980] 1 WLR 1306).

The Court of Appeal recently stressed in *Gillett* v. *Holt and Another* [2000] 2 FLR 266, however, that proprietary estoppel is a flexible doctrine, and, as the doctrine must reflect the fundamental principle that equity is concerned to prevent unconscionable conduct, the facts of a case must be looked at in the round. The Court of Appeal also said that detriment is not a narrow or technical concept, but one which must be approached as part of a broad inquiry in the case. It also stated that the issues of reliance and detriment were often intertwined – proprietary estoppel could not be treated as being divided into separate watertight compartments.

Once an estoppel is proved, the court must consider all the circumstances of the case and exercise its discretion to decide what remedy to give. However, the court adopts a cautious approach, in that the equitable relief granted need only be 'the minimum equity to do justice to the plaintiff' (Scarman LJ in *Crabb* v. *Arun District Council* [1976] Ch 179, at 198). For this reason, a claim based on estoppel may not be so advantageous to a claimant as one based on trusts, because the court may not grant a right of ownership. Instead, it may merely grant the claimant a licence to remain in the house (for life or for some other period), or order financial compensation to be paid. However, it is possible to obtain a right of ownership. For example, in *Gillett* v. *Holt* (above), the claimants, a husband and wife, were held to be entitled to the freehold interest in a farm, despite the deceased defendant's will to the contrary, on the basis that the defendant had promised it to them on his death. However, in *Matharu* v. *Matharu* [1994] 2 FLR 597, the successful party was granted only a licence to remain in the house in question. In *Matharu*, the plaintiff father had bought the house which had later become the matrimonial home of his son and daughter-in-law. The son had made extensive improvements to the house but had subsequently died. The father sought possession of the house against his daughter-in-law, but his action was dismissed on the ground that his daughter-in-law was entitled to an unquantifiable beneficial interest in the property by virtue of a proprietary estoppel in her favour. However, the Court of Appeal allowed the father's appeal in part, holding that, although an estoppel had been proved, the defendant daughter-in-law had not acquired a beneficial interest but merely a licence to remain in the property for life or for such shorter period as she might decide (see also, for example, *Wayling* v. *Jones* [1995] 2 FLR 1029 and *Baker* v. *Baker and Another* [1993] 2 FLR 247).

Estoppel has another disadvantage compared with trusts, which is that an estoppel arises only when the remedy is granted, whereas a beneficial interest under a trust arises when the claimant acted to his or her detriment on the basis of the common intention. This may be important when third-party interests are involved.

4.8   A Claim Based on Contract

An interest in property may be acquired under a contract, provided the legal requirements for creating a valid contract are satisfied, namely that there is offer and acceptance, an intention to create legal relations, consideration (unless the document is contained in a deed), and the contract is not void for some reason (e.g. on the ground of illegality or public policy). If a contract is in respect of the sale or disposition of land, it must be in writing (s.2 Law of Property (Miscellaneous Provisions) Act 1989), although this does not prevent the creation of a resulting or constructive trust, or the creation of an interest under the doctrine of proprietary estoppel (see *Yaxley* v. *Gotts and Gotts* (1999), above). In *Tanner* v. *Tanner* [1975] 1 WLR 1341, the plaintiff purchased a house for occupation by the defendant, his female partner, and their children. The defendant moved into the house, but when their relationship broke down the plaintiff sought possession on the basis that the defendant was only a bare licensee under a licence which he had revoked. However, the Court of Appeal held that there was an implied contractual licence, under the terms of which the defendant was entitled to occupy the house while the children were of school age, or until some other circumstance arose which would make it unreasonable for her to remain in possession. In *Layton* v. *Martin* [1986] 2 FLR 277, on the other hand, the Court of Appeal held that there was no intention to create a legally enforceable contract, with the result that the plaintiff mistress failed in her claim against the deceased's estate even though she had accepted his offer that, if she were to live with him, he would give her emotional security, and also financial security on his death. Despite living with him for five years after he had made the offer, and for 13 years in total, her claim failed.

4.9 Transfer of Tenancies

Under s.53 and Schedule 7 of Part IV of the Family Law Act 1996, county courts and the High Court have power to order the transfer of tenancies on divorce and on the breakdown of cohabitation. With married couples, the court can order a transfer of a tenancy if it has jurisdiction to make a property adjustment order under the Matrimonial Causes Act 1973 (see 9.1). With cohabitants, they must merely have ceased living together as husband and wife – there is no mention of them ceasing to live in the same 'household'.

A tenancy is transferred by the court making 'a Part II order', which it has power to make whether a spouse or cohabitant is solely or jointly entitled under a tenancy, *provided* the house was a matrimonial home in the case of a married couple, or, in the case of cohabitants, was a home in which the cohabiting couple lived together as husband and wife (para. 2 of Sched. 7 and s.62(1)). Para. 1 of Sched. 7 makes it clear that 'cohabitant' includes a 'former cohabitant'. There is no requirement that cohabitants must have lived together for a minimum period, although the court is required to take into account the length of the relationship when deciding whether or not to order a transfer. However, as cohabitants are defined as living together as husband and wife, the court cannot transfer tenancies between parties to gay or lesbian relationships. As far as 'entitlement' under a tenancy is concerned, it means present entitlement, in other words actual occupation at the time of the application or the making of the order (see *Gay* v. *Sheeran and Another* [1999] 2 FLR 519, where the Court of Appeal held that the tenancy in question could not be transferred, as the claimant was not 'entitled' to occupy the dwelling-house either in her own right or jointly with her former cohabitant who had left the house about 18 months earlier).

In determining whether to make a Part II order, and, if so, in what manner, the court must consider all the circumstances of the case including (see para. 5):

- the circumstances in which the tenancy was granted, or the circumstances in which either of the parties became tenant;
- the housing needs and housing resources of the parties and of any relevant child;

- the respective financial resources of the parties;
- the likely effect of any order (or no order) on the health, safety or well-being of the parties and of any relevant child;
- the conduct of the parties in relation to each other and otherwise; and
- the suitability of the parties as tenants.

Where the parties are cohabitants and only one of them is entitled to occupy the house under the tenancy, the court must also consider (see para. 5): the nature of their relationship; the length of time they have lived together as husband and wife; whether there are any children who are children of both parties or for whom both parties have or have had parental responsibility; and the length of time that has elapsed since the parties ceased to live together. Where the parties are council tenants, the housing policy of the local housing authority is a factor which the court can take into account (see *Jones* v. *Jones* [1997] Fam 39, [1997] 1 FLR 27).

Tenancies for the benefit of a child can be transferred under Schedule 1 to the Children Act 1989 (see 14.5).

4.10   Reform of the Law for Cohabitants

For many years there has been dissatisfaction with the law that applies to the adjustment of property rights on relationship breakdown, particularly for cohabitants, and particularly as cohabitation is increasing. Compared with divorcing couples, cohabitants are in a disadvantageous position on relationship breakdown, as the court has no power to adjust their property rights according to their respective needs and resources and the needs of their children. Cohabitants must turn to equitable remedies, notably trusts, in order to gain property interest. This is costly and time-consuming, and the law is insufficiently flexible to do justice between the parties. In particular, the principles that apply to constructive trusts are unsatisfactory, not only because they are based on the difficult and somewhat arbitrary task of establishing the intentions of the parties, but because the law encourages cohabitants to trawl back through their relationship to find evidence of intention, instead of encouraging them to look to the future, which is the approach adopted by the divorce courts. Future needs and resources are not considered by the court. The requirement that there be direct contribution to the purchase price (see *Lloyds Bank plc* v. *Rosset*, 1991) also means that some women will fail to acquire an interest in the home even though they have spent many years contributing to its upkeep and have looked after the family. The law is clearly unsatisfactory. Why should the female cohabitant in *Hammond* v. *Mitchell* (1991) be granted a half-share in the family home because of a short conversation with her former partner which took place many years earlier, while the plaintiff in *Burns* v. *Burns* 1984 gain nothing, despite her substantial contribution to the household and bringing up the family? The law on constructive trusts, as it now stands, may even encourage people to perjure themselves. For Lord Bridge, in *Rosset* (1991), said that express evidence of an intention to share the beneficial interest could be based on 'discussions between the partners, however imperfectly remembered and however imprecise their terms may have been.' Indeed Waite J in *Hammond* v. *Mitchell* hinted that the evidence of the parties in that case might not have been too sound, when he said that 'both parties were prone to exaggeration' and 'neither side had the monopoly of truth.' This is an unsatisfactory state for the law to be in. Furthermore, the terminology used by Lord Bridge in *Rosset* is somewhat unclear. For instance, his Lordship refers to 'any agreement, arrangement or understanding.' While it may be possible to prove the existence of an express common agreement or arrangement, it is dubious whether it is really possible to prove the existence of a common 'understanding'.

There is therefore considerable dissatisfaction with the law and, as a result of this dissatisfaction, the Law Commission has been considering the law with a view to making recommendations for reform for both cohabitants and other home-sharers. In May 1994 the Law Commission announced that the law relating to the ownership of property belonging to cohabitants and other home-sharers was arbitrary and unjust and needed reforming. However, despite the need for urgent reform, the Law Commission's recommendations are still awaited.

Possible options for reform include the introduction of registered partnerships, or encouraging cohabitants to enter into cohabitation contracts or to make declarations of beneficial interests, or introducing a discretionary adjustive system like that of the divorce courts. The Law Society (see [1999] Fam Law 747) has recommended changes to the remedies currently available, but has stated that any new remedies should not equate with those available for married couples, as this would undermine marriage. Its main recommendation is to allow cohabiting couples, depending on the nature of their relationship, to claim a capital sum, and to claim maintenance for up to four years after separation so as to enable the economically dependent partner to enjoy a period of skills training. Pension earmarking and enforceable cohabitation contracts have also been suggested. The Law Society considers that any reforms should apply equally to heterosexual and homosexual couples. The Solicitors' Family Law Association has also published proposals for reform (see [2000] Fam Law 210).

Any reform proposals, however, require important policy issues to be addressed. One is whether any reform of the law for cohabitants will undermine marriage. Another is how to give cohabitants who wish to do so the freedom to opt out of any new system for adjusting property rights. One way in which this could be done would be to give cohabitants the opportunity to make cohabitation contracts to that effect, provided they had received independent legal advice and there had been full and frank disclosure. Other important questions to be addressed are whether any reforms should also apply to homosexual couples, whether cohabitation relationships should be of a minimum duration and whether it should make any difference if there are children. Another question to be considered is whether any reforms should be integrated into any reform of ancillary relief on divorce, because there has also been some discussion about reforming this (see 9.14).

Thus, while reform is clearly needed, it will be difficult to find a perfect system for adjusting the parties' assets on relationship breakdown. As we shall see in Chapter 9, the current system for adjusting property on divorce is not perfect, because any system based on judicial discretion has its own set of drawbacks. Those responsible for reforming the law governing the property rights of cohabitants are therefore faced with the difficult task of having to balance competing social policies, in particular 'the competing demands of paternalism and self-determinism', and for this reason it may not be possible to achieve 'a perfection reconciliation' (see Bailey-Harris, 1998, Chapter 7, p.73).

4.11   Housing Homeless Families

Persons who are homeless can apply to their local housing authority for public sector housing. Housing authorities are responsible for managing, regulating and controlling housing vested in them, and have statutory duties and powers towards homeless persons under Part VII of the Housing Act 1996. When exercising their statutory duties and powers, housing authorities must comply with the *Homelessness Code of Guidance for Local Authorities* (ss.169(1) and 182(1)).

The duties and powers of housing authorities vary depending on whether a person is homeless or intentionally homeless and whether or not he or she has a priority need. A full housing duty is owed only to those persons who are not intentionally homeless and who also have a priority need. Special provision is made in the Housing Act 1996 for pregnant women, victims of domestic violence, persons with dependent children and those who are vulnerable as a result of old age, mental illness, or handicap or physical disability. Such persons have a 'priority need' under the legislation (see s.189(1)). Furthermore, in respect of domestic violence, the Housing Act provides that it is not reasonable for a person to continue to occupy accommodation if it is probable that this will lead to domestic violence against the applicant and any person who lives with (or might reasonably be expected to live with) the applicant (s.177(1)). Domestic violence includes actual and threatened violence between 'associated persons' (s.177(1)), which term is defined in the same way as 'associated persons' under Part IV of the Family Law Act 1996 (see 6.6).

Local housing authorities have various duties. Thus, for example, they have a duty to make inquiries where applicants are homeless or threatened with homelessness, in order to establish whether they are eligible for assistance and, if so, what duty is owed to them (s.184(1)). Local housing authorities also have a duty to provide appropriate advice and assistance to help applicants find accommodation where they are unintentionally homeless but have no priority need (s.192).

The full housing duty is owed only to applicants who are not intentionally homeless and who have a priority need, in which case the housing authority concerned must provide an applicant with accommodation (s.193(1)–(4)). The court has held that the duty to provide accommodation requires a housing authority to provide '*suitable*' accommodation (see *R* v. *Ealing London Borough Council ex parte Surdonja* [1999] 1 FLR 650, where the duty to provide accommodation was not discharged by providing accommodation for a family in separate dwellings, as families should be able to live together as a unit). Where a full housing duty is owed, but the applicant has a 'local connection' with another housing authority, the requesting authority may refer the applicant to the other authority, except where there is any risk that the applicant or any person living with the applicant will suffer domestic violence in the other district (s.198(1) and (2)). A 'local connection' is established if the applicant is (or was) normally resident in that district of his or her own choice, or is employed there, or has family associations there, or special circumstances exist (s.199(1)). Pending referral or a decision about a referral to another housing authority, the requesting authority has an interim duty to provide accommodation (s.200(1)).

Applications by Children

Children cannot apply for local authority housing under the Housing Act 1996 where their parents have been refused. In *R* v. *Oldham Metropolitan Borough Council ex parte G and Related Appeals* [1993] AC 509, after his application for housing had been rejected as he was intentionally homeless, a father made a fresh application in the name of his 4-year-old son. The House of Lords held that the application had been properly rejected, as to allow such an application would render the 'intentional homelessness' provisions redundant where there were dependent children. The court has also held that a family who has failed to obtain accommodation from a local housing authority cannot obtain housing by asking their local authority social services department for help on the basis that their children are children in need for the purposes of Part III of the Children Act 1989 (see 16.4).

Summary

1 There are two sorts of ownership in English law: ownership in law and ownership in equity under a trust.

2 Property can be owned jointly by the parties as joint tenants or tenants in common. Joint tenants each own the whole interest in the property, so that when one of them dies, unless there is anything to the contrary (e.g. in a will), the survivor is entitled to the whole interest. With a tenancy in common, the parties each own a separate share of the property. On death, the deceased's share passes to the deceased's estate according to the will or according to the rules of intestate succession (see 5.2).

3 Engaged couples have property rights similar to those possessed by married couples during marriage. An engagements ring is presumed to be an absolute gift.

4 Married couples have the same property rights during their marriage as other persons, so that who owns what depends on the general laws of contract and trusts. However, the following statutes make special provision for married couples: s.17 of the Married Women's Property Act 1882; s.37 of the Matrimonial Proceedings and Property Act 1970; and s.1 of the Married Women's Property Act 1964.

5 Married couples have 'matrimonial home' rights under s.30 of Part IV of the Family Law Act 1996 which gives non-owning spouses a right to remain in occupation of the home and to defeat the claims of third parties.

6 Spouses and cohabitants (and former spouses and former cohabitants) can apply for occupation orders and non-molestation orders under Part IV of the Family Law Act 1996 in cases of domestic violence (see Chapter 6).

7 There are no special statutory provisions for cohabitants in respect of property rights. Contract and trust law apply. The courts have no jurisdiction equivalent to the divorce court to adjust the property interests of cohabitants. Instead they must rely on equitable doctrines such as resulting and constructive trusts, and proprietary estoppel in order to establish an interest.

8 For married persons, cohabitants and other family members, ownership of personal property (property other than land) depends on the law of contract and trusts. As a general rule, property passes to the person who purchases it. Rights in personal property can be acquired expressly or impliedly (under a trust, estoppel or contract) and in many cases without written formalities.

9 Funds in a bank account presumptively belong to the party (or parties) in whose name(s) the account is held, but the presumption can be displaced by a contrary intention.

10 As far as the family home is concerned, trusts in respect of land and contracts for the sale of land must be in writing (s.53 of the Law of Property Act 1925 and s.2 of the Law of Property (Miscellaneous Provisions) Act 1989). However, despite the absence of writing, interests in land can be acquired under resulting or constructive trusts or under the doctrine of proprietary estoppel (s.53(2) LPA 1925 and s.2(5) LP(MP)A 1989).

11 An order for the sale and possession of land can be sought under s.14 of the Trusts of Land and Appointment of Trustees Act 1996.

12 A presumption of resulting trusts gives a claimant a share of the beneficial interest in property proportionate to his or her financial contribution.

13 A constructive trust arises where there is an express or implied agreement, arrangement or understanding that the claimant has an interest in property, and the claimant has acted to his or her detriment on the basis of that agreement, arrangement or understanding.

14 An interest in the family home can be acquired under proprietary estoppel where the claimant has acted to his or her detriment on the basis of a belief encouraged by the other party that he or she is to have an interest in the property in question and it would be inequitable to deny the claimant an interest. If successful, the claimant may be granted a licence to remain in the property, or financial compensation, or a right of ownership in the property.

15 Tenancies can be transferred between spouses and between cohabitants (and former spouses and cohabitants) under s.53 and Sched. 7 of Part IV of the Family Law Act 1996.

16 There has been increasing dissatisfaction with the law governing the property rights of cohabitants on relationship breakdown, and there is considerable pressure for reform.

17 Under Part VII of the Housing Act 1996, local authorities have powers and duties in respect of persons who are homeless.

Further Reading and References

Atkin, 'De factos down-under and their property' [1999] CFLQ 43.
Bailey-Harris (ed.), *Dividing the Assets on Family Breakdown*, Family Law, 1998.
Cooke, 'Reliance and estoppel' (1995) 111 LQR 389.
Gardner, 'Rethinking family property' (1993) 109 LQR 263.
Glover and Todd, 'The myth of common intention' (1996) 16 *Legal Studies* 325.
Lawson, 'The things we do for love: detrimental reliance in the family home' (1996) 16 *Legal Studies* 218.
O'Hagan, 'Quantifying interests under resulting trusts' (1997) 60 MLR 420.
Taylor, 'Section 25 – Quick, cheap and conciliatory' [1999] Fam Law 403.

Questions

1 What arguments are there for and against reforming the law of property for cohabitants on relationship breakdown?

2 What problems can you envisage reformers having to struggle with when considering making proposals for reform of the law applicable to the property rights of cohabitants on relationship breakdown?

5 Family Property on Death

This chapter looks at what happens to property on the death of a family member. It looks first at the legal rules which govern the devolution of property where the deceased leaves a will and then at the rules which apply on intestacy, in other words where there is no will, or no valid will. Finally, it considers the legal steps family members can take under the Inheritance (Provision for Family and Dependants) Act 1975 where a deceased person has failed to make adequate provision for certain persons on death. Reference should also be made to Chapter 4, as the equitable doctrines of trusts and estoppel can be used to claim a share of property from a deceased person's estate.

5.1 Devolution of Property by Will

There is complete freedom of testamentary disposition in England and Wales. Any adult person of sound mind can make a will disposing of his or her property to whomsoever he or she chooses. This rule applies to family members, whether they be husbands and wives, cohabitants or other persons, and for this purpose husbands and wives are separate persons. A will is valid if it is made in writing and is signed by the person making the will in the presence of at least two witnesses, each of whom must attest and sign the will, or acknowledge the signature of the person making it (ss.7 and 9 Wills Act 1837). A will is revoked by divorce or nullity. A will is also revoked by marriage (s.18 Wills Act 1837), unless made in contemplation of marriage (i.e. where the person making the will expects to marry a particular person and intends the will not to be revoked by the marriage). The same rule applies to dispositions in a will (s.18(3) and (4)). On divorce or nullity, the appointment of a former spouse as a child's guardian is also revoked (s.6(3A) Children Act 1989).

5.2 Devolution of Property Where There is no Will

Where a spouse dies intestate (without making a will), the law makes generous provision for the surviving spouse, then for the children (or the children of any deceased children) and finally for any other relatives. In many cases, unless the deceased spouse's estate is substantial, the surviving spouse inherits the whole estate. After the payment of debts and expenses, the personal representatives must distribute the estate according to the rules of intestate succession laid down in the Administration of Estates Act 1925. In outline the rules are as follows.

Where a deceased spouse leaves a surviving spouse and children (or grand-children) The surviving spouse takes the personal chattels absolutely, a statutory legacy of £125 000, plus a life interest in half the balance of the estate. The other half is held on the statutory trusts for the children (or grand-children), who during their minority can be paid maintenance out of income and lump sums out of capital. When they reach majority the children (or grandchildren) are entitled to the capital. The surviving spouse, if he or she so wishes, can insist on the personal representatives redeeming the life interest by paying the capital value (s.47A AEA 1925). The surviving spouse must elect to do so within 12 months after representation is taken out, but the court may extend this period (see s.47A(5)).

Where a deceased spouse leaves a spouse and no children (or grandchildren), but blood relatives (parent, brother, sister) or issue of such a brother or sister The surviving spouse takes the personal chattels absolutely, a statutory legacy of £200 000, plus an absolute interest in half the balance of the estate. The other half is held on trust for the deceased's parents in equal shares (or for one parent absolutely if only one parent is alive), otherwise the property is held on trust for the brothers and sisters, or the issue of any predeceased brother or sister.

Where a deceased spouse leaves a spouse but no children (or grandchildren) issue and no blood relatives The whole estate passes to the surviving spouse absolutely.

Where a deceased spouse leaves no surviving spouse but children (or grand-children), and blood relatives The estate is held on trust for any children (or grandchildren), otherwise the blood relatives take it in the following order of priority: parents; brothers and sisters; grandparents; uncles and aunts.

Where a deceased spouse leaves no surviving spouse, no children (or grand-children) and no blood relatives The estate passes to the Crown as *bona vacantia* (property having no owner), although the Crown can make discre-tionary provision for dependants and other persons for whom the deceased might reasonably have been expected to provide.

Rights in the Matrimonial Home

Where the matrimonial home was owned by the spouses as joint tenants, it devolves to the surviving spouse. Where the home was owned by them both as tenants in common, the deceased spouse's share forms part of his or her estate and passes according to the will or according to the laws of intestacy above.

On intestacy, however, the Intestates' Estates Act 1952 allows a surviving spouse in certain circumstances to retain the matrimonial home. Thus, a surviving spouse who was resident in the home at the time of the other spouse's death can require that the deceased's interest in the home be appropriated in or towards satisfaction of any absolute interest that he or she has in the estate, and if the value of the house exceeds the value of the surviving spouse's interest, then the survivor must pay the excess value to the representatives (sched. 2, paras. 1(1) and 5(2)). A surviving spouse who wishes to exercise this option must do so within 12 months of representation being taken out, but this period may be extended by the court (para. 3). As a result, the personal representatives must not sell the house within this 12-month period without the surviving spouse's written consent, unless sale is necessary for payment of expenses or debts (para. 4).

Cohabitants on Intestacy

Where a cohabitant dies without making a will, the surviving cohabitant has no automatic right to succeed to the deceased's estate. It passes to their children, otherwise to the parent(s) of the deceased. This is with the exception of any property which was jointly owned by the parties as joint tenants (e.g. the home or a bank account), when ownership passes to the survivor. As a surviving cohabitant is in a particularly vulnerable position on the intestacy of a partner, it is important for cohabitants to make a will. However, the disadvantageous position for surviving cohabitants has been improved to a certain extent by amendments to the Inheritance (Provision for Family and Dependants) Act 1975 (see below).

5.3   The Inheritance (Provision for Family and Dependants) Act 1975

Under the Inheritance (Provision for Family and Dependants) Act 1975, the court can make financial provision orders for certain family members and dependants out of a deceased person's estate where the deceased has failed under his or her will or under the law of intestacy (or both) to make reasonable financial provision for them. The Act only applies if the deceased was domiciled in England and Wales when he or she died (s.1(1)). Furthermore, any one who wishes to apply under the Act must do so within six months of the date on which probate or letters of administration were taken out, otherwise with permission of the court (s.4).

When considering any application under the Act, the court must ask two questions. First, it must ask whether reasonable financial provision was made for the applicant. This involves making an objective assessment of the facts.

Secondly, if the answer to the first question is 'no', it must then ask what financial provision ought to be made. When answering these questions, the court draws a distinction between spouses and other applicants. For applicants other than spouses, reasonable financial provision is such as would be reasonable for the applicant to receive by way of maintenance; whereas for spouses, maintenance is not the only consideration that can be taken into account by the court.

(a) Applicants

The following persons can apply for an order under the Act:

The Wife or Husband of the Deceased (s.1(1)(a)) This section also includes a spouse who contracted a void marriage in good faith (unless the marriage was dissolved or annulled, or the applicant contracted a later marriage during the deceased's lifetime (s.25(4)). It also includes a spouse who was granted a divorce (or annulment or judicial separation) in the year before the deceased's death, but where no order was made for ancillary relief (see Chapter 9). In such a case, the court, if just to do so, may treat the marriage as if it still existed (s.14(1)). A spouse who has been granted a decree of judicial separation can also apply under this section, provided the decree was in force and the parties were separated at the deceased's death (s.14(2)), and so too can a party to a polygamous marriage.

The Former Wife or Husband of the Deceased who has not Remarried (s.1(1)(b)) Remarriage is deemed to have taken place whether or not the previous or subsequent marriage is void or voidable (s.25(5)).

A Person who was Cohabiting with the Deceased When he or she Died (s.1(1)(ba)) This section was inserted into the 1975 Act by s.2 of the Law Reform (Succession) Act 1995 on the recommendation of the Law Commission (*Distribution on Intestacy* (1989), Law Com No 187, paras. 58–61). Prior to this new provision, surviving cohabitants could only apply under s.1(1)(e) (see below), and for this reason had to prove dependence on the deceased. Cohabitation is defined rather restrictively, for cohabitants are defined as persons living in the same household as husband or wife of the deceased, and the period of cohabitation must have been for a continuous period of at least two years before the deceased's death (s.1(1A)). Former cohabitants do not come within the definition. They will have to apply instead under s.1(1)(e) below. Although the Act has removed the need for a surviving cohabitant to prove dependency on the deceased, surviving cohabitants are not treated in the same way as surviving spouses, as they may receive only maintenance provision, not a capital share of the deceased's estate.

A Child of the Deceased (s.1(1)(c)) Any child of married or unmarried parents, and any adopted child, including any child born after the deceased's death, can apply (s.25(1)). Adult children of the deceased can apply but they may find it difficult to succeed, particularly where they are young and able-bodied, in employment and capable of maintaining themselves (see, for example, *Re Jennings deceased* [1994] Ch 286, *sub nom Re Jennings (Deceased), Harlow* v. *National Westminster Bank plc and Others* [1994] 1 FLR 536, where a claim failed). A claim by an adult son against his mother's estate was successful, however, in *Re Abram (Deceased)* [1996] 2 FLR 379, as he had worked for her in the family business for many years and for long hours and had received only a minimal wage. At one time it was thought that adult children would have to show special circumstances or that the deceased parent had a moral obligation to them. However, in *Re Hancock (Deceased)* [1998] 2 FLR 346 the Court of Appeal stated that, although the presence of special circumstances or a moral obligation may be relevant factors, particularly where the applicant is in employment or possessed of earning capacity, their absence does not necessarily preclude a successful claim (see also *Espinosa* v. *Bourke* [1999] 1 FLR 747, where the Court of Appeal allowed the 55-year-old daughter's appeal as the judge had erred in elevating moral obligation to a threshold requirement). The existence of a moral obligation may still be determinative, however, as it was in *Re Pearce (Deceased)* [1998] 2 FLR 705. Here the 29-year-old applicant was successful in his claim against his father's estate as his father was under a moral obligation, because the applicant son had done a substantial amount of work on his father's farm, and his father had made representations that his son would inherit it. The Court of Appeal awarded the son a lump sum, holding that, while awards are restricted to what is required for maintenance (except where the applicant is a surviving spouse), a lump sum could be justified where it would meet income needs of a recurrent nature.

Any Other Person (not Being a Child of the Deceased) who, in the Case of any Marriage to Which the Deceased was at any Time a Party, was Treated by the Deceased as a Child of the Family in Relation to that Marriage (s.1(1)d))   A step-child or foster-child treated by the deceased as a child of the family can apply under this section, whether or not he or she is a minor.

Any Other Person (not Being a Person Included in Paras (a) to (d) Above) who Immediately Before the Deceased's Death was Being Maintained, Wholly or Partly, by the Deceased (s.1(1)(e))   Applicants such as surviving relatives, friends, carers or cohabitants who do not come within s.1(1)(ba) above can apply under this section (see, for example, *Bouette* v. *Rose* [2000] 1 FLR 363, where a mother successfully applied against the estate of her deceased daughter). The Act provides that an applicant will be regarded as having been maintained by the deceased only if the deceased, otherwise than for full valuable consideration, was making a *substantial* contribution in money or in money's worth towards the reasonable needs of the applicant (s.1(3)). An application can therefore be struck out on the ground that there was no dependency. In order to decide whether there is dependency, the court balances what the deceased was contributing against what the applicant was contributing and, if the applicant made a greater or equal contribution, the application is struck out (see Stephenson LJ in *Jelley* v. *Iliffe* [1981] Fam 128). However, although dependency is a question of fact, not one of discretion, the court will look at the problem in the round and apply a common-sense sort of approach, avoiding fine balancing distinctions (see Butler-Sloss LJ in *Bishop* v. *Plumley* [1991] 1 All ER 236, where the Court of Appeal allowed the applicant's appeal despite the beneficiaries' argument that the applicant had given full valuable contribution by reason of her exceptional care of their father).

(b) 'Reasonable Financial Provision'

Any applicant must prove that the deceased's will or the law of intestacy (or both, if there is partial intestacy) failed to make 'reasonable financial provision' for the applicant (s.1(1)). The test is not whether reasonable provision has been made but the more rigorous test of whether the *failure* to make provision was unreasonable (Judge Roger Cooke in *Re Abram (Deceased)* [1996] 2 FLR 379). However, a surviving spouse is treated more generously than other applicants as 'reasonable financial provision' in the case of applicant spouses means 'such financial provision as it would be reasonable in all the circumstances of the case for a husband or wife to receive, *whether or not that provision is required for his or her maintenance*' (s.1(2)(a)). With all other applicants, 'reasonable financial provision' includes only *maintenance* (s.1(2)(b)). Surviving spouses are treated more favourably than other applicants, on the basis that they would normally expect to receive a share of the deceased spouse's estate or a share of a spouse's property had there been divorce not death. There is no definition of maintenance in the Act. What will be regarded as 'maintenance' will depend on the facts of each case, but it may be construed broadly, as it was in *Rees* v. *Newbery and the Institute of Cancer Research* [1998] 1 FLR 1041, where the provision of accommodation by the deceased for 10 years at less than market rent constituted 'maintenance' for the purposes of the Act.

(c) Orders That May be Made

The court may order out of the deceased's estate one or more of the following orders (s.2): periodical payments; a lump sum (which can be paid in instalments); a transfer of property; a settlement of property; acquisition of property and its transfer to the applicant or for the settlement of the applicant; and a variation of an ante-nuptial or post-nuptial settlement. The court can make an interim order if immediate financial assistance is needed (s.5). Periodical payments orders can be varied, discharged, suspended or revived (s.6). Any

periodical payments order made in favour of a former spouse or a spouse subject to a decree of judicial separation (where separation was continuing at
death) ceases to be effective on remarriage, except in respect of any arrears
due (s.19(1)).

(d) Factors to be Taken into Account

When deciding whether or not the deceased made reasonable financial provision for the applicant, and, what order, if any, to make, the court must consider
the following factors (s.3(1)):

'(a) the financial resources and financial needs which the applicant has or
      is likely to have in the foreseeable future;
(b) the financial resources and financial needs which any other appli-
      cant ... has or is likely to have in the foreseeable future;
(c) the financial resources and financial needs which any beneficiary of the
      estate of the deceased has or is likely to have in the foreseeable future;
(d) any obligations and responsibilities which the deceased had towards any
      applicant ... or towards any beneficiary of the estate of the deceased;
(e) the size and nature of the net estate of the deceased;
(f) any physical or mental disability of any applicant ... or any beneficiary
      of the estate of the deceased;
(g) any other matter, including the conduct of the applicant or any other
      person, which in the circumstances of the case the court may consider
      relevant.'

The weight given to each factor depends on the circumstances of each case.
For example, where an application is brought by an adult child against a
deceased parent, needs and resources under subs. (a) above and obligations
and responsibilities under subs. (d) are likely to be crucial (see, for example,
Espinosa v. *Bourke* [1999] 1 FLR 747).

Additional Factors to be Considered in Special Cases

Applications by Spouses and Former Spouses   Where the applicant is a spouse
or former spouse of the deceased, the court must also consider the applicant's
age, the duration of the marriage, and the applicant's contribution to the
welfare of the family (including any contribution made by looking after the
home or caring for the family) (s.3(2)). The court must also consider what provision the surviving spouse might reasonably have expected to receive if on the
date of death the marriage had been terminated by divorce rather than death
(s.3(2)). In *Moody* v. *Stevenson* [1992] Ch 486, for example, the court made a
similar order to that which the husband would have received in ancillary relief

proceedings on divorce. In *Davis* v. *Davis* [1993] 1 FLR 54, on the other hand, although it was clear that, if the marriage had ended in divorce, the divorce court would have ordered a clean break capital settlement, the Court of Appeal held that the wife's life interest in her deceased husband's estate was reasonable financial provision in the circumstances and her claim failed. The Court of Appeal has stressed, however, that the 'hypothetical divorce' approach in s.3(2) is only one of the factors for the court to consider, and is subject to the overriding consideration of what is reasonable in all the circumstances (see *Re Krubert (Deceased)* [1997]1 FLR 42).

Applications by Cohabitants Where the applicant is a cohabitant who is applying under s.1(1)(ba), the court must also have regard to the applicant's age, the duration of the cohabitation and the contribution which the applicant made to the welfare of the deceased's family, including any contribution made by looking after the home or caring for the family (s.3(2A)).

Applications by Children If the applicant is a child (under s.1(1)(c) or (d)), the court must also consider the manner in which the applicant was, or might be expected to be, educated or trained (s.3(3)). The court must also consider whether the deceased had assumed any responsibility for the applicant's maintenance (and, if so, its extent, basis and duration, and whether the deceased did so knowing that the applicant was not his child), as well as the liability of any other person to maintain the applicant (s.3(3)).

Applications by Dependants Where the applicant is a person who was being maintained by the deceased (under s.1(1)(e)), the court must also consider the extent, basis and duration of the deceased's responsibility for maintenance (s.3(4)).

(e) Restricting an Application under the 1975 Act after Divorce, Nullity or Judicial Separation

As part of the clean break policy on divorce (see 9.4), the divorce court on or after the grant of a decree nisi of divorce (or nullity or judicial separation) can, if just to do so, make an order under s.15 of the 1975 Act prohibiting the other spouse from making an application under the 1975 Act on the death of his or her spouse. A s.15 restriction is usually included in all clean break orders (see *Cameron* v. *Treasury Solicitor* [1996] 2 FLR 716).

(f) Other Powers under the 1975 Act

The court has other powers under the 1975 Act. It can vary or discharge a secured periodical payments order made on divorce, or revive the provisions of such an order which have been suspended in variation proceedings under s.31 MCA 1973 (s.16). A maintenance agreement between the applicant and the deceased which provides for maintenance on and after death can be varied or revoked (s.17). The court can also set aside a disposition made by the deceased within six months of death with the intention of defeating an application under the 1975 Act, provided the donee did not give full consideration and setting aside will facilitate making financial provision under the 1975 Act (s.10). Where a contract was made by the deceased without full valuable consideration with the intention of defeating an application for financial provision under the 1975 Act, the court can direct the personal representatives not to pass or transfer the whole or part of any money or property involved (s.11). To facilitate making payment to an applicant, the court can treat a deceased's interest in property under a joint tenancy or a joint interest existing immediately before death as a severable share of the net estate where just in all the circumstances to do so, provided the application is made within six months of the date on which a grant of representation to the deceased's estate was first taken out (s.9) (see, for example, *Jessop* v. *Jessop* [1992] 1 FLR 59).

Summary

1 Any adult person of sound mind can make a will leaving his or her property on death to whomsoever he or she chooses. A will is valid if it is made in writing and signed by the testator in the presence of two witnesses who must attest the will (ss.7 and 9 Wills Act 1837). A will made before marriage, unless made in contemplation of marriage, is revoked by marriage. A devise or bequest in a will is no longer effective after divorce or nullity, and neither is the appointment of the former spouse as trustee or executor.
2 Where a spouse has not made a will, his or her property passes under the rules of intestacy which are laid down in the Administration of Estates Act 1925.
3 Under the Inheritance (Provision for Family and Dependants) Act 1975, certain family members and other dependants, including spouses, former spouses and cohabitants, can apply for financial relief out of the deceased's estate where the deceased has failed to make reasonable financial provision either under the will or under the law of intestacy (or both).

Further Reading and References

Borkowski, '*Re Hancock (Deceased)* and *Espinosa* v. *Bourke* – Moral Obligations and Family Provision' [1999] CFLQ 305.
Bridge, 'For love or money? Dependent carers and family provision' [2000] CLJ 248.

Questions

1 Are cohabitants discriminated against in respect of property entitlement on death? Should the law make further changes? What would be the repercussions of any changes?

6 Domestic Violence and Occupation of the Family Home

6.1 The Problem of Domestic Violence

Domestic violence, in other words violence in the home, takes many forms. It includes not just physical assault, but psychological and emotional molestation or harassment, and also pestering, nagging, making nuisance telephone calls and intimidation. Sometimes the violence is extremely severe and results in a criminal conviction. Despite the difficulty of establishing what goes on behind locked doors, violence in the home is thought to be a widespread social problem existing at all levels of society, involving not just husbands and wives and cohabitants, but other family members. A study carried out by the Economic and Social Research Council has estimated that 570 000 domestic violence attacks occur each year, of which 81 per cent are attacks by men against women (see *Observer Newspaper*, 23 October 2000). Various factors have been posited as the causes of violence. Personality factors, such as psychopathic tendencies, aggression or jealousy may play a part, as may social factors, such as poverty, housing and unemployment. Most violence in the home (but not all) is by men against women.

Besides being extremely traumatic for the victim, and any children, violence can create housing problems. The victim may have to seek temporary accommodation in a women's refuge. Some victims may ask their local housing authority for accommodation and, provided they are not intentionally homeless, will qualify as persons with a priority need to whom a full housing duty is owed (see 4.11). Some victims, however, will end up divorcing and the divorce court may have to decide what is to happen in respect of ownership and occupation of the home (see 9.5). Sometimes it will be necessary to remove the perpetrator of violence from the home and allow the other party, and possibly any children, back in (see 6.5); but as we shall see below, moving a person from the home in which he or she has a proprietary interest is a remedy of last resort and usually only a short-term option. Where children suffer violence in the home, the criminal and civil law can provide some redress, but child protection measures may be needed (see Chapter 16). Violence in the home is very damaging for children who witness it (see Parkinson and Humphreys, 1998), and there is a link between violence in the home and child abuse (see Mullender and Morley, 1994). Violence in the home may also cause problems for children on contact visits (see 13.4).

Both the civil and the criminal law provide protection for those who suffer violence in the home.

6.2   The Criminal Law

The police may have to intervene in a domestic violence dispute, and will do so where necessary, as '[b]rutality in the home is just as much a crime as any other sort of violence' (Home Office Circular, No 60/1990). Police forces are in fact required to draw up clear policy statements about intervention in domestic violence cases, and also establish special domestic violence units.

Violence in the home is a criminal offence. The perpetrator of violence can be prosecuted for unlawful wounding, assault, grievous bodily harm, rape or even manslaughter or murder. Offences can also be committed under the Telecommunications Act 1984, which prohibits the sending of grossly offensive, indecent, obscene or menacing communications, and under the Malicious Communications Act 1988, which prohibits the sending of indecent or grossly offensive letters which are intended to create distress or anxiety. Under s.4A of the Public Order Act 1986 it is also an offence to cause intentional harassment, alarm or distress. Harassment is also a criminal offence under the Protection from Harassment Act 1997 (see 6.7 below). Victims of domestic violence may be entitled to compensation under the Criminal Injuries Compensation Scheme.

However, although police intervention may be required in some domestic violence disputes, recourse to the criminal law can be unsatisfactory, as it is a heavy-handed instrument in family disputes. Punishing a violent partner is likely to have disastrous emotional and financial consequences for the family and may lead to family breakdown. There may also be evidential difficulties proving violence. Victims may be unwilling to co-operate with the police and may withdraw their evidence, because of feelings of disloyalty, or because prosecution and possible conviction will ruin any chance of reconciliation, or because of fears of further violence. Protection for the family under the civil law is often the better solution.

6.3   Remedies under Part IV of the Family Law Act 1996

Part IV of the Family Law Act 1996 came into force on 1 October 1997, creating a unified body of law and procedure available in all family courts. Under the Act, magistrates' family proceedings courts, county courts and the High Court can grant 'non-molestation orders' and 'occupation orders' to protect victims of domestic violence. Part IV was enacted as a result of widespread criticism of the law. A major criticism of the law before Part IV came into force was that it was unnecessarily complex and confusing. Injunctions were available in different courts under different statutes according to different criteria. As Lord Scarman said in *Richards* v. *Richards* [1984] AC 174 (at 206–7), the law was 'a hotchpotch of enactments of limited scope passed into law to meet specific situations or to strengthen the powers of the specified courts.' Reform was therefore needed to create a coherent and comprehensive body of law. Another criticism of the old law was that injunctive protection under the family law statutes was available only to married persons and cohabitants. Former spouses and cohabitants were excluded, as were other family members, so that the only way they could obtain injunctive protection against violence in the home was to bring legal proceedings in respect of some substantive matter (e.g. in tort, or in respect of a property dispute, or in respect of their children), and then apply for an injunction ancillary to those proceedings. However, applying for an injunction in this way was unsatisfactory. Not only might an applicant have no legal or equitable right capable of being protected by injunctive relief, but the application was something of a fiction. What an applicant really wanted was an injunction to protect them from violence, not resolution of the substantive issue before the court. Where there were children at risk of violence, however, it was usually easier to obtain injunctive protection, because of the protective nature of the inherent jurisdiction where children were involved. But even here there were conflicting authorities in the Court of Appeal as to whether this jurisdiction was actually available.

In the late 1980s and early 1990s the Law Commission, as part of its comprehensive examination of family law, examined the law on domestic violence and occupation of the family home and made recommendations for reform. In its Report (*Family Law: Domestic Violence and Occupation of the Family Home*, Law Com No 207, 1992), the Law Commission stated that the civil remedies were 'complex, confusing and lacked integration', and recommended the introduction of a single but flexible range of remedies available in all courts having jurisdiction in family matters. It recommended the introduction of two new orders (a 'non-molestation order' and an 'occupation order') which would be available to a wider class of applicants. The Law Commission's proposals were adopted by the Government in its Family Homes and Domestic Violence Bill. However, the Bill was withdrawn because of concern expressed by some members of the House of Lords that to give occupation rights to cohabitants would erode the distinction between marriage and cohabitation, and to give persons associated only by a sexual relationship a right to apply to the courts would enable homosexual couples to do so. New proposals for reform in a much more diluted form and not as far-reaching as the Law Commission's original proposals were eventually introduced as Part IV of the Family Law Bill, which received the Royal Assent in July 1996, and eventually became Part IV of the Family Law Act 1996 (Parts I and II contained new proposals for divorce, see Chapter 8).

Part IV of the Family Law Act 1996 made significant improvements to the law. Not only did it streamline the old law to create two new orders available in all family courts, but it permitted a wider class of applicants to apply. Under the old law only spouses and cohabitants could apply for remedies in respect of violence and occupation of the home. Part IV of the Family Law Act, on the other hand, extended the availability of family remedies to spouses and cohabitants whose relationships had broken down, to engaged couples, to people living in the same household, and to relatives. It also extended protection to a wider range of children, and gave children the right to apply for orders in certain circumstances.

However, although the new law is a considerable improvement on the old, it has some drawbacks. First, it is complex, particularly in respect of the rules which apply to occupation orders, where the orders and the applicable criteria are all slightly different depending on the category into which the applicant falls. As far as non-molestation orders are concerned, the law is more straightforward, although what constitutes 'molestation' may cause difficulty. While the availability of orders to a wider range of parties is a great improvement on the old law, there is some criticism that the category of 'associated persons' is drawn too narrowly (see Hayes and Williams, 1999, at p.417). Another concern is that the different balance of harm tests for unentitled spouses and unentitled cohabitants is discriminatory. Where children are involved, there would seem to be no reason for having a different test depending on the status of the adult parties. There has also been some criticism of the differential treatment of cohabitants which requires the court when considering the nature of the relationship of cohabitants and former cohabitants 'to have regard to the fact that they have not given each other the commitment involved in marriage' (s.41). However, whether this requirement has much impact in practice is dubious. It was put into the Bill at the last minute to pacify those who thought that the Act would undermine marriage.

Despite these criticisms the Act is a considerable improvement on the old law, particularly as its remedies are open to a much wider range of family members. In fact, some of the cases brought under Part IV have quite a different 'flavour' from those brought under the old law. Thus, in *Chechi* v. *Bashier* [1999] 2 FLR 489, where there was a family feud about land, a brother sought a non-molestation order against his brother and nephews. Although the application was refused (because a power of arrest would give the applicant an unacceptable power over his family and because other civil proceedings were going to be brought), the Court of Appeal held that the trial judge had been wrong to refuse the order on the ground that the family relationship was incidental to the dispute, for the family relationship had clearly fuelled and magnified the original agreement.

Under Part IV of the 1996 Act, the courts have jurisdiction to make 'non-molestation orders' and 'occupation orders'.

6.4 Non-Molestation Orders under Part IV of the Family Law Act 1996

Section 42 of Part IV of the Family Law Act 1996 gives magistrates' family proceedings courts, county courts and the Family Division of the High Court power to make non-molestation orders. A non-molestation order is an order prohibiting the respondent from molesting the applicant and/or molesting a child (s.42(1)). An applicant cannot apply unless he or she is a person who is 'associated' with the respondent and any child must be a 'relevant' child (for definitions of 'associated persons' and 'relevant child', see 6.6 below). As well as making orders on application, the court in any family proceedings can make orders of its own motion (i.e. without an application having been made), s.42(2). (For the definition of 'family proceedings', see 6.6.) However, an order made in family proceedings ceases to be effective if the proceedings are withdrawn or dismissed (s.42(8)). Applications can be made by children, but those aged under 16 need the court's permission to do so, which it will grant if the child has sufficient understanding to make the application (s.43).

An order can refer to molestation in general and/or to particular acts of molestation (s.48(6)). It may be made for a specified period or until a further order is made (s.48(7)). Although the order is intended to give the parties a temporary breathing space, the Court of Appeal has held that an order can be made for an indefinite period in appropriate circumstances (see *Re B-J (Power of Arrest)* [2000] 2 FLR 443, which overruled *M* v. *W (Non-Molestation Order)* [2000] 1 FLR 107, where Cazalet J had held that an order must be made for a specified period, unless the circumstances are exceptional).

What is 'Molestation'?

'Molestation' is not defined in the Act but is interpreted widely to include not just violence, but pestering, harassment and threatening behaviour. 'Molestation' is a question of fact in each case. In *C* v. *C (Non-Molestation Order: Jurisdiction)* [1998] Fam 70, [1998] 1 FLR 554, Stephen Brown P said that there 'has to be some conduct which clearly harasses and affects the applicant to such a degree that the intervention of the court is called for.' In *C* v. *C*, the husband was granted a non-molestation order forbidding his wife procuring the publication of any account of personal or financial matters during their marriage, but the order was discharged on appeal as the material complained of was held to come nowhere near molestation as envisaged by s.42.

Criteria for Making Non-Molestation Orders

Section 42(5) provides that when deciding to make a non-molestation order and, if so, in what manner, the court must consider all the circumstances of the case, including the need to secure the health, safety and well-being of the applicant or the person for whose benefit the order would be made (if the court is considering whether to make it of its own motion), and of any relevant child (for definition of 'relevant child', see 6.6 below).

Ex parte *Orders (Orders Without Notice)*

As a speedy remedy is often required in domestic violence cases, the court, where just and convenient to do so, may make an *ex parte* non-molestation order, i.e. an order without the respondent being given such notice of the proceedings as would otherwise be required by the rules of court (s.45(1)). In deciding whether to make an *ex parte* order, the court must consider all the circumstances of the case, including (s.45(2)):

- the risk of significant harm to the applicant or any relevant child by the respondent if an order is not immediately made;
- the likelihood of the applicant being deterred or prevented from pursuing the application if an order is not immediately made; and
- whether there is reason to believe that the respondent is aware of the proceedings but deliberately avoiding service and that the applicant or relevant child will be seriously prejudiced by the delay in effecting service of proceedings or in effecting substituted service.

If the court makes an *ex parte* order it must afford the respondent an opportunity to make representations relating to the order as soon as just and convenient at a full hearing (s.45(3)). However, because of the natural justice implications of not allowing a person to argue their case, *ex parte* orders are not made routinely.

Undertakings

Instead of making a molestation order, the court may accept an undertaking (a promise to the court) from any party to the proceedings (s.46(1)). An undertaking is enforceable as if it were a court order (s.46(4)). As a power of arrest cannot be attached to an undertaking, the court will not accept an undertaking where a power of arrest is needed (s.46(2) and (3)). The advantage of an undertaking is that it carries less stigma for the respondent than a court order because the court does not make findings of fact about the respondent's behaviour.

Attaching a Power of Arrest

If it appears to the court that the respondent has used, or threatened to use, violence against the applicant or a relevant child, it is required to attach a power of arrest to any provision in a non-molestation order, unless it considers the applicant or child will be adequately protected without it (s.47(1) and (2)). In the case of *ex parte* orders, however, the position is different, for the court has a discretion whether to attach a power of arrest. Thus it *may* attach a power of arrest, but only if the respondent has used or threatened violence against the applicant or a relevant child, and there is a risk that the applicant or child will suffer significant harm as a result of the respondent's conduct if a power of arrest is not attached (s.47(3)). If a power of arrest is attached, a constable may arrest without a warrant a person whom he has reasonable cause to suspect is in breach of any provision in an order to which the power of arrest is attached (s.47(6)). The respondent must be brought before a judge or justice of the peace within 24 hours, and if the matter is not disposed of, the respondent may be remanded in custody or on bail (s.45(7)). The court can vary or discharge a power of arrest attached to any provision in an *ex parte* order whether or not an application for variation or discharge has been made (s.49(4)). The Court of Appeal has held that it is usually preferable for a power of arrest to have effect for the same period as the molestation (or occupation) order, but that the court can attach a power of arrest limited to a shorter period than the terms of the order, as this protects human rights by giving the court flexibility to limit the power of arrest to the period required to protect the victim (see *Re B-J (Power of Arrest)* [2000] 2 FLR 443, overruling *M* v. *W (Non-Molestation Order)* [2000], see above, where Cazalet J had held that a power of arrest which is of lesser duration than an order can only be made if the non-molestation order is made *ex parte*).

Enforcement of Orders

Non-molestation can be enforced by civil proceedings for contempt of court, and the contemnor can be punished by fine or, in the last resort, by imprisonment. Police intervention may be needed to enforce an order, and the courts' powers to attach a power of arrest (see above) make such intervention quicker and easier.

6.5   Occupation Orders under Part IV of the Family Law Act 1996

Sometimes a victim of violence may reach the point where she (or he) can no longer tolerate living under the same roof as the perpetrator of violence.

She may decide to leave home and find accommodation elsewhere, perhaps in a Women's Aid Refuge, or with relatives or friends. A victim of violence can protect herself by applying for an occupation order to remove the perpetrator from the house and to allow her back in. She (or he) may also wish to exclude the perpetrator from the area round the house. However, as an occupation order is a more severe order than a non-molestation order, occupation orders are not routinely made. They are considered to be Draconian orders of last resort. Furthermore, as the aim of an occupation order is to provide a temporary breathing-space, they are subject to strict time-limits.

Under Part IV of the Family Law Act 1996, magistrates' courts, county courts and the High Court have the power to make occupation orders (see ss.33, 35, 36 and 37). They can be made on application or by the court of its own motion in any family proceedings (i.e. without an application having been made) (s.39(1) and (2)). (For a definition of 'family proceedings', see 6.6. below.) Furthermore, as proceedings under Part IV of the 1996 Act are themselves family proceedings, the court may on an application or of its own motion make any s.8 order under the Children Act (see Chapter 12). The power to make occupation orders does not affect a person's claim to a legal or equitable interest in the home in any subsequent proceedings (including subsequent proceedings under Part IV) (s.39(4)). Provision is also made in Part IV for local authorities to apply to remove a child abuser from the home in cases of child abuse (see 16.8).

The court has wide powers. It can make *ex parte* occupation orders, accept undertakings, attach a power of arrest and enforce orders in the same way as it can non-molestation orders (see above). Children may apply for occupation orders, but children aged under 16 need the court's permission, which it will grant if the child has sufficient understanding to make the proposed application (s.43).

Applicants for occupation orders are either 'entitled' applicants or 'non-entitled' applicants. 'Entitled' applicants are persons with a right to occupy the home. 'Non-entitled' applicants have no such right of occupation. The courts' powers to make occupation orders is much wider in the case of 'entitled' applicants.

(a) 'Entitled' Applicants (s.33)

Section 33 deals with applications for occupation orders by 'entitled' persons. The right to apply under this section depends on:

- the applicant having a property entitlement (under a trust, contract, statute or by virtue of a 'matrimonial home right', see 4.2);
- the parties being 'associated persons' (see definition at 6.6. below); and
- the dwelling-house being their home.

The remedy under s.33 is open to a wide range of applicants, e.g. spouses, cohabitants, former spouses, former cohabitants, brothers and sisters, same-sex couples, relatives, etc. In fact, anyone living in the same household as an 'associated' person can apply (see 6.6 for definitions), provided the applicant satisfies the above requirements.

An occupation order under s.33 may declare that the applicant is an 'entitled' person for the purposes of s.33 (s.33(4)). Where the parties are married, and the applicant has 'matrimonial home rights', the court, where it is just and reasonable to do so (s.33(8)), may include a provision in the occupation order that those matrimonial home rights are not terminated by the other spouse's death or by divorce or nullity (s.33(5)). The order may be made for a specified period, until the occurrence of a specified event or until further order (s.33(10)). Thus, there is no fixed maximum time-limit in the case of orders for entitled persons as there is for orders in favour of unentitled persons (see below).

The court has wide powers. Under the terms of an occupation order made under s.33, it may (s.33(3)):

(a) enforce the applicant's entitlement to remain in occupation as against the respondent;
(b) require the respondent to permit the applicant to enter and remain in the home or part of it;
(c) regulate the occupation of the home by either or both parties;
(d) if the respondent is entitled to occupy the home, prohibit, suspend or restrict the exercise of that right;
(e) if the respondent has matrimonial home rights in relation to the home, and the applicant is the other spouse, restrict or terminate those rights;
(f) require the respondent to leave the home, or part of the home; or
(g) exclude the respondent from a defined area in which the home is included.

The Applicable Criteria

When deciding whether to exercise any of the above powers and, if so, in what manner, the court must have regard to all the circumstances of the case, including (s.33(6)):

'(a) the housing needs and housing resources of each of the parties and of any relevant child;
(b) the financial resources of the parties;
(c) the likely effect of any order, or of any decision by the court not to exercise any of the powers ... , on the health, safety or well-being of the parties and of any relevant child; and
(d) the conduct of the parties in relation to each other and otherwise.'

The 'Balance of Harm' Test

Before applying the above criteria, however, the court must apply the 'balance of harm' test laid down in s.33(7). This requires the court to consider first of all whether the evidence establishes that the applicant or any relevant child is likely to suffer significant harm attributable to the conduct of the respondent if any order is not made. If the court answers this question in the affirmative, then it must make an occupation order, unless balancing one harm against the other, the harm to the respondent or the child is likely to be as great or greater than to the applicant and any relevant child. If, however, the court answers the first question in the negative (i.e. the applicant or relevant child is not likely to suffer significant harm ...), then the court enters the discretionary regime provided by s.33(6) and must exercise a broad discretion having regard to all the circumstances of the case, including in particular those set out in the statutory checklist of (a)–(d) above. Thus, even where there is no likelihood of significant harm to the applicant or child, the court can nevertheless make an order by exercising its discretion in the light of the factors in s.33(6) (see above).

'Harm' in relation to children and adults covers physical or non-physical ill-treatment (including child sexual abuse) and impairment of physical or mental health, and in the case of a child includes impairment of development (s.63(1)). Where the question of whether harm suffered by a child is significant turns on the child's health or development, the court must compare the child's health or development with that which could reasonably be expected of a similar child (s.63(3)).

Judicial guidance on the application of the balance of harm test was given by the Court of Appeal in *Chalmers* v. *Johns* [1999] 1 FLR 39. Here the parties had cohabited for 25 years and had occupied the home as joint tenants for more than 20 years. They had an adult son and a 7-year-old daughter. Their relationship had always been tempestuous. There had been acts of violence by each party against the other, resulting in minor injuries. Alcohol abuse, particularly by the mother, had been responsible for much of this. The mother eventually left the house with their daughter and moved into temporary council accommodation. She applied *inter alia* for an occupation order. At first instance the judge made an interim occupation order requiring the father to vacate the family home seven days later. Although the judge recognised that this was not in ordinary terms a domestic violence case, she applied the balance of harm test and made the order on the basis that the mother and child were likely to suffer significant harm attributable to the father if the order were not made. However, the Court of Appeal allowed the father's appeal as the judge had incorrectly applied the statutory provisions, and because neither the mother nor child were likely to suffer significant harm attributable to the conduct of the father if the order were not made. As there was no real risk of violence or any other harm befalling the child, the matter was one in which the court would exercise its discretion by considering all the circumstances of the case and the prescribed factors in s.33(6). The Court of Appeal held that occupation orders which overrode proprietary rights (the father was a joint tenant) were justified only in exceptional circumstances. (This was the position taken by the courts in cases decided under the law before Part IV came into force.) The court held that the fact that the final hearing was to take place very shortly weighed against making such a Draconian order at an interlocutory (interim) hearing, particularly as there was no evidence that any further domestic disharmony could not be managed by the imposition of injunctive orders. Thorpe LJ explained the two-stage approach to applications for occupation orders (balance of harm test followed, where necessary, by the discretionary exercise, see above), and allowed the father's appeal because the trial judge had not clearly focused upon the alternative nature of the adjoining subsections of s.33(6) and s.33(7), but had treated them as though they were both simultaneously applicable to the facts of the case. Had she directed herself more closely to the statutory language, Thorpe LJ said that she would have seen that this was a case which came nowhere near s.33(7).

The balance of harm test was considered again in *B* v. *B (Occupation Order)* [1999] 1 FLR 715. Here the Court of Appeal had to weigh up the respective needs of two children living in different households. The wife had left the matrimonial home, where she and her husband lived as council tenants, taking with her their baby daughter, and leaving her husband in the matrimonial home with his 6-year-old son from a previous marriage. The Court of Appeal allowed the husband's appeal against an occupation order on the basis that the husband's child would suffer more harm if an occupation order were made than the wife and their baby daughter would suffer if it were not made. The Court of Appeal held that, while the husband's behaviour fully justified an occupation order, his position as a full-time carer had to be considered. If the occupation order were made, his 6-year-old son would be placed in unsuitable temporary council accommodation with the additional problem of having to change schools. In *G* v. *G (Occupation Order: Conduct)* [2000] 2 FLR 36, the trial judge had refused to make an occupation order on the ground that the husband's behaviour had not been intentional, so that the likelihood of any harm being suffered could not be attributed to him. The wife appealed. The Court of Appeal held that in considering for the purposes of the balancing test in s.33(7) whether any harm likely to be suffered by the applicant or child was attributable to the conduct of the respondent, the relevant factor was the effect of the conduct upon the applicant or child, not the intention of the respondent. It stated that, while intent might be a relevant consideration, it did not mean that significant harm could not be attributed to the respondent's conduct without lack of intention. However, the Court of Appeal dismissed the wife's appeal as the judge's conclusion was tenable on the facts, emphasising yet again the Draconian nature of an occupation order which excludes a person from his or her home.

(b) 'Non-entitled Applicants' (s.35)

The following 'non-entitled' applicants (persons who have no right to occupy the home) can apply for an occupation order:

(i) A Former Spouse Where the Other Former Spouse has a Right of Occupation (s.35)   On divorce or nullity, matrimonial home rights under s.30 terminate (see 4.2), which leaves former spouses in a vulnerable position if the other former spouse insists on his or her right to remain in the former matrimonial home. However, s.35 provides some protection as it allows former spouses without a right of occupation to apply for an occupation order against a former spouse who has a right to occupy the former matrimonial home (by virtue of a beneficial estate, contract etc.) (s.34(1), s.35(1)). If the applicant is in occupation, the order will give the applicant the right not to be evicted or excluded from the house or any part of it by the respondent for a specified period, and will prohibit the respondent from evicting or excluding the applicant during that period (s.35(3)). If the applicant is not in occupation, the order will give the applicant the right to enter into and occupy the house for a specified period, and require the respondent to permit the exercise of that right (s.35(4)). When exercising its powers to decide whether to make an order, and, if so, in what manner, the court must apply: the balance of harm test (see above); the same criteria which apply to an application by an entitled person (see above); and the following additional matters (s.35(6)):

- the length of time that has elapsed since the parties ceased living together;
- the length of time that has elapsed since the marriage was dissolved or annulled; and
- the existence of any pending proceedings between the parties for a property adjustment order under Part II of the Matrimonial Causes Act 1973, or an order settling or transferring property to or for the benefit of a child under sched. 1 Children Act 1989, or relating to the legal or beneficial ownership of the house.

An occupation order may incorporate terms (c), (d), (f) and (g) in s.33(3) (see p.95 above), which the court can make in the case of entitled applicants (s.35(5)). An order can be made to last for up to six months, but may be extended on one or more occasions for a further period of up to six months (s.35(10)). While the order is in force, the applicant is treated as if he or she possesses 'matrimonial home rights' under s.30 of the Act and the respondent were the other spouse (s.35(13)).

(ii) A Cohabitant or Former Cohabitant Where the Other Cohabitant or Former Cohabitant has a Right of Occupation (s.36) A cohabitant or former cohabitant with no right to occupy the home (or who has an equitable interest in the home or its proceeds of sale but in whom the legal estate is not vested, s.36(1)) may apply for an occupation order under s.36 where the respondent cohabitant or former cohabitant has a right of occupation, provided the dwelling-house is the home in which they live (or have lived or intended to live) together as husband and wife (s.36(1) and (2)). If the applicant is not in occupation, the occupation order will contain a provision giving the applicant the right to enter into and occupy the home for a specified period and requiring the respondent to allow the exercise of that right (s.36(4)). The order may also (s.36(5)): regulate the occupation of the home by either or both parties; prohibit, suspend or restrict the exercise of the respondent's right of occupation; require the respondent to leave the home or part of it; or exclude the respondent from a defined area in which the home is situated. The same criteria apply as those which apply to the making of an order in favour of a non-entitled former spouse (see above), but omitting any references to marriage or divorce (see ss.36(3)–(7). The balance of harm test must be applied, but the test is more restricted. Section 36(7) provides that when considering whether to include any provision in an order (see s.36(5)), and (if so) in what manner, the court must have regard to whether (s.36(8)): the applicant or any relevant child is likely to suffer significant harm attributable to the conduct of the respondent if the subsection (5) provision is not included in the order; and whether the harm likely to be suffered by the respondent or child if the provision is included is as great as or greater than the harm attributable to the conduct of the respondent which is likely to be suffered by the applicant or child if the provision is not included. Thus the balance of harm test does not create a duty in respect of the order itself, but only in respect of any provision in an order. When considering the nature of the parties' relationship, the court must also take into account the fact that the parties have not given each other the commitment involved in marriage (s.41). The duration of any order is limited in the same way as an order for former spouses (see above), and for the duration of the order a former spouse is treated as if he or she has 'matrimonial home rights' under s.30 of the Act (s.36(13)).

(iii) Spouse or Former Spouse Where Neither Party has a Right of Occupation (s.37) Where both spouses (or former spouses) occupy a dwelling-house which is or was the matrimonial home, but neither is entitled to remain in occupation, either one of them may apply against the other for an occupation order (s.37(1) and (2)). The order may: require the respondent to permit the

applicant to enter and remain in or in part of the house; regulate the occupation of the house by either or both parties; require the respondent to leave the house or part of it; or exclude the respondent from a defined area in which the house is included (s.37(4)). The criteria which the court must apply when deciding whether to make an order, and (if so) in what manner, are the same as those which apply under s.33(6) when the court is considering whether to make an order in favour of an 'entitled person' (see above), and the balance of harm test must also be applied (see above) (s.37(4)). The order is limited to six months, but can be extended on one or more occasions by a further period of up to six months (s.37(5)).

(iv) A Cohabitant or Former Cohabitant Where Neither Party has a Right of Occupation (s.38) Where both cohabitants or former cohabitants occupy a dwelling-house which is the home in which they live, or have lived, together as husband and wife, but neither is entitled to remain in occupation, either of them may apply against the other for an occupation order (s.38(1) and (2)). The order may make the same provisions as a s.37 order above (s.38(3)). The same criteria apply as apply to a s.37 order (s.38(4)) (see above), and the court must apply the balance of harm test (s.38(5)). The order is limited to six months, but can be extended on one or more occasions by a further period of up to six months (s.38(6)).

(c) Ancillary Powers

On or after making an occupation order under ss.33, 35 or 36 (not ss.37 and 38) the court has a range of ancillary powers (s.40(1)). Thus it can impose a repair and maintenance obligation, require a party to pay the rent, mortage or other outgoings, and lay down certain obligations in respect of the furniture or other contents of the house (e.g. grant the use or possession of furniture or other content, and order a party to take reasonable care of them). It can also require a party to keep the house, furniture and any other contents secure. When deciding whether and, if so, how to exercise these ancillary powers, the court must consider all the circumstances of the case, including the parties' financial needs and resources, and their present and future financial obligations, including their financial obligations to each other and any relevant child (s.40(2)). Ancillary orders are only effective for the duration of an occupation order (s.40(3)). In *Nwogbe* v. *Nwogbe* [2000] 2 FLR 744 the Court of Appeal, however, drew attention to the fact that there is no power to permit enforcement of these ancillary powers and said that this was a serious omission in the statutory provisions and required urgent Parliamentary attention. In *Nwogbe*, an occupation order had been made on terms that the husband was to pay the monthly rent, water rates, council tax and other expenses relating to the property under s.40.

He defaulted on the payments, but the Court of Appeal held there was no power to commit him to prison and no power to enforce the orders, so that such orders were of no value to spouses and cohabitants.

(d) Restrictions on the Powers of Magistrates

The magistrates' court cannot hear an application or make an occupation order where the proceedings involve a disputed question about a party's right to occupy the home, unless it is not necessary to determine that question in order to deal with the application or to make the order (s.59(1)). The magistrates' court can also decline jurisdiction if it considers that the case can be dealt with more conveniently by another court (s.59(2)).

(e) Undertakings, Ex parte Orders, Powers of Arrest and Enforcement of Occupation Orders

The rules are the same as they are for non-molestation orders (see 6.4 above).

6.6 Definitions for the Purposes of Part IV of the Family Law Act 1996

The following are definitions for the purposes of Part IV of the Family Law Act 1996:

'Cohabitants' and 'Former Cohabitants'

Cohabitants and former cohabitants are defined as a man and a woman who, although not married to each other, are living (or have lived) together as husband and wife, but this does not include former cohabitants who have subsequently married each other (s.62(1)).

'Relevant Child'

A 'relevant child' is defined as (s.62(2)):

● any child who is living with, or might reasonably be expected to live with, either party to the proceedings;

- any child in relation to whom an order under the Adoption Act 1976 or the Children Act 1989 is in question in the proceedings; and
- any other child whose interests the court considers relevant.

This broad definition highlights the importance of protecting *any* child from domestic violence. The child need not be related to the applicant, nor be a child of the family.

'Associated' Persons

The following persons are defined as 'associated' persons (s.62(3)):

- spouses, or former spouses;
- cohabitants, or former cohabitants;
- persons who live, or have lived, in the same household, otherwise than merely by reason of one of them being the other's employee, tenant, lodger or boarder;
- relatives;
- engaged, and formerly engaged, couples;
- in relation to any child, they are parents, or have (or have had) parental responsibility for the child (see s.62(4));
- parties to the same family proceedings, other than Part IV FLA 1996 proceedings.

The term 'associated persons' is likely to be broadly construed in order to bring persons needing protection within the scope of the Act. In *G* v. *G (Non-molestation Order: Jurisdiction)* [2000] 2 FLR 533, for instance, the magistrates held that the applicant was not entitled to a non-molestation order as the parties were neither cohabitants nor 'associated persons' because they did not live in the same household. However, Wall J held on appeal that they did come within the Act, for although they lived in separate households, they could be described as being cohabitants within the meaning of s.62(3)(b). There was a sexual relationship, some form of financial support and the respondent's evidence demonstrated that from his perspective they were cohabiting. Wall J said that it would have been better if the justices had decided the cohabitation point first, after which it would have been open to them to have considered whether or not they qualified as living in the same household. Wall J ordered a rehearing, and stated that it would be most unfortunate if the term 'associated persons' were construed too narrowly to exclude borderline cases from the scope of the Act. His Lordship was of the view that the provisions of the Act dealing with non-molestation should be purposively construed and that the courts should not decline jurisdiction unless the facts of the case were plainly incapable of being brought within the statute.

A 'Relative'

A 'relative' in relation to a person is defined as (s.63(1)):

'(a) the father, mother, stepfather, stepmother, son, daughter, stepson, step-daughter, grandmother, grandfather, grandson or granddaughter of that person or of that person's spouse or former spouse; or

(b) the brother, sister, uncle, aunt, niece, or nephew (whether of the full blood or of the half blood or by affinity) of that person or of that person's spouse or former spouse,

and includes, in relation to a person who is living or has lived with another person as husband or wife, any person who would fall [within (a) or (b)] if the parties were married to each other.'

Engagements

Where an engagement is terminated, an application for an occupation order or a non-molestation order must be made within three years of its termination (ss.33(2) and 42(4)). The court will require written evidence of an engagement, unless it is satisfied that the engagement is evidenced by an engagement ring or an engagement ceremony (s.44).

Adopted Children

If a child has been adopted or freed for adoption, two persons are associated with each other if: one of them is the natural parent of the child or a parent of such a natural parent; and the other is the child or any person who has become a parent of a child under an adoption order or has applied for an adoption order, or a person with whom the child has at any time been placed for adoption (s.62(5)).

'Family Proceedings'

Family proceedings are defined as (s.63(1) and (2)):

● any proceedings under the inherent jurisdiction of the High Court in relation to children (s.63(1)); or

● proceedings under: Parts II and IV FLA 1996; the Matrimonial Causes Act 1973; the Adoption Act 1976; the Domestic Proceedings and Magistrates'

Courts Act 1978; Part III Matrimonial and Family Proceedings Act 1984; Parts I, II and IV Children Act 1989 (but also in the case of a non-molestation order, proceedings in which an emergency protection order has been made under s.44 CA 1989 which includes an exclusion requirement, s.42(3)); and s.30 Human Fertilisation and Embryology Act 1990.

6.7   Remedies for Persons not Protected under Part IV of the Family Law Act 1996

Some persons are afforded no protection under Part IV of the Family Law Act 1996. Imagine the following scenario:

> Sue and Dave met when she was 19 and he was 21. They became friends. Eventually Sue told Dave that she wanted no more to do with him. However, Dave was unable to accept that their relationship was over, and over a period of time he assaulted her, threatened her with violence, behaved aggressively to her and followed her around shouting abuse. He pestered her with telephone calls at the homes of her parents and grandmother. Dave was eventually arrested, but when released from custody he continued to threaten Sue, and even threatened to kill her. Sue and Dave were not engaged, not married and had never cohabited.

These facts actually occurred in the case of *Khorasandjian* v. *Bush* [1993] QB 727, [1993] 2 FLR 66 (although the names have been changed), where the victim sought injunctive protection in tort proceedings on the basis of the tort of nuisance. She had to do this, as she did not come within the family legislation in force at the time when the case was decided as it only provided protection against violence for spouses and cohabitants. Furthermore, at the time of the case the Protection from Harassment Act 1997 (see below) had not been enacted. She was granted an injunction at first instance prohibiting the defendant from using violence, harassing, pestering or communicating with her. The decision was upheld by a majority of the Court of Appeal, despite the fact that she had no property right capable of being protected by an injunction, and even though it is a fundamental principle of English law that where there is no right, there is no remedy. In *Burris* v. *Azadani* [1995] 4 All ER 802, the Court of Appeal affirmed *Khorasandjian* and held that there was a tort of harassment in English law. However, both cases were short-lived, for the House of Lords in *Hunter* v. *Canary Wharf Ltd* [1997] AC 655, [1997] 2 FLR 342 subsequently overruled them, holding that only a person with a proprietary right (not a licensee or occupier) can bring an action in nuisance.

Despite the implementation of Part IV of the Family Law Act 1996 (see above), a person in the same position as Sue in the scenario above has no remedy under Part IV, as she and David are not 'associated persons' (see 6.6). Persons who' are boarding in a household are also outside its scope, so that lodgers and possibly au pairs are excluded. Persons with no remedy under Part IV have two options: (a) they can apply for an injunction ancillary to civil proceedings; or (b) seek a remedy under the Protection from Harassment Act 1997.

(a) Injunctions Ancillary to Legal Proceedings

A victim of violence who is not afforded protection under Part IV of the Family Law Act can seek an injunction in the county court or High Court ancillary to civil proceedings, e.g. ancillary to an action in tort or a property dispute or to proceedings involving children. These courts have jurisdiction under s.38 of the County Courts Act 1984 and s.37 of the Supreme Court Act 1981 respectively to grant an interlocutory or final injunction 'in all cases in which it appears to the court to be just and convenient to do so.' However, the court can only grant an injunction if the applicant has a legal or equitable right which is capable of being protected, e.g. a cause of action in tort, or a proprietary interest, or a right to exercise parental responsibility for a child. The applicant must himself or herself possess the right; it is not sufficient if another member of the family has the right (see *Hunter* v. *Canary Wharf Ltd* above). Another option is for a person to seek civil or criminal redress under the Protection from Harassment Act 1997.

(b) The Protection from Harassment Act 1997

The Protection from Harassment Act 1997, which came into force on 16 June 1997, was enacted as a result of considerable public concern about 'stalking' (the obsessive harassment of one person by another), one of Britain's fastest growing crimes. The 1997 Act is unusual, indeed novel, in providing both (i) criminal and (ii) civil remedies for harassment.

Criminal Remedies

Two criminal offences of harassment exist under the 1997 Act. One is the summary offence of harassment, which must involve a 'course of conduct', i.e. there must be harassment on at least two occasions (ss.1, 2(1) and 7(3)). The other is the aggravated indictable offence of harassment, that of conducting a course of conduct which causes another person to fear, on at least two occasions, that violence will be used against him or her. Criminal courts also have the power to make injunctive-style restraining orders against persons convicted of either of the two criminal offences, which prohibit offenders from further conduct which causes, or will cause, victims fear of violence (s.5). Breach of a restraining order is a criminal offence (s.5(6)). Both offences of harassment are subject to statutory defences (ss.1(3) and 7(3)), for instance that the course of conduct was pursued for the purpose of preventing or detecting crime, or that the pursuit of the course of conduct was reasonable.

Civil Remedies

In addition to the two criminal offences, the Act creates civil remedies. In respect of the s.1 offence of harassment, s.3 creates a statutory tort of harassment by providing that an actual or apprehended breach of s.1 may be the subject of a claim in civil proceedings by the person who is, or may be, the victim of the course of conduct in question. On such a claim, damages may be awarded for 'any anxiety caused by the harassment and any financial loss resulting from the harassment' (s.3(2)). The Act makes no mention of any right to sue for an injunction to protect a victim from harassment, but as the county court and High Court have the power to grant injunctions where it appears 'just and convenient to do so' (see above), then injunctions can be granted ancillary to proceedings brought under the 1997 Act. There are various procedures for enforcing civil injunctions. Thus, where a court grants an injunction in the county court or High Court to restrain a defendant from pursuing any course of conduct which amounts to harassment, and the plaintiff considers that the defendant has done anything which he is prohibited from doing by injunction, the plaintiff may apply for the issue of a warrant for the arrest of the defendant (s.3(3)). Breach of an injunction restraining the defendant from pursuing any conduct which amounts to harassment is a criminal offence (s.3(6)). It is not punishable as a contempt of court (s.3(7)).

Compared with the detailed provisions of Part IV of the Family Law Act 1996 above, the 1997 Act is loosely drafted. How it will work in the family context for persons who have no remedy under the 1996 Act remains to be seen.

Summary

1 Domestic violence is a widespread phenomenon existing at all levels of society.
2 The criminal law provides protection, but it has drawbacks for families. Protection under the civil law is usually the better solution.
3 Under Part IV of the Family Law Act 1996, magistrates' courts, county courts and the High Court have jurisdiction to make occupation orders and non-molestation orders for a wide class of applicants, including spouses and cohabitants, former spouses and cohabitants, and other persons who come within the definition of 'associated persons'.

4 The court can accept undertakings from respondents instead of making orders and can make *ex parte* orders and attach a power of arrest to an order. The jurisdiction to remove a respondent from his or her home, particularly where he or she has a proprietary interest, is used with extreme caution because of the severity of ordering someone from their home.

5 County courts (under s.38 of the County Courts Act 1984) and the High Court (under s.37 of the Supreme Court Act 1981) have jurisdiction to grant injunctions ancillary to other proceedings where it is just and convenient to do so, provided the applicant has a legal or equitable right which needs injunctive protection. These powers may be useful for persons who do not come within the scope of Part IV of the Family Law Act 1996.

6 The Protection from Harassment Act 1997 makes harassment a criminal offence and also provides civil remedies for harassment.

Further Reading and References

Addison and Lawson-Cruttenden, *Harassment Law and Practice*, Blackstone Press, 1999.

Bird, *Domestic Violence and Protection from Harassment* (3rd edn), Family Law, 2001.

Gardner, 'Stalking' (1998) LQR 33.

Hayes and Williams, *Family Law: Principles, Policy and Practice* (2nd edn), Butterworths, 1999.

Kaganas, '*B* v. *B (Occupation Order)* and *Chalmers* v. *Johns* – Occupation orders under the Family Law Act 1996' [1999] CFLQ 193.

Law Commission, *Domestic Violence and Occupation of the Family Home*, LC No 207, 1992.

Lawson-Cruttenden and Addison, *Blackstone's Guide to the Protection from Harassment Act 1997*, Blackstone Press, 1997.

Lockton and Ward, *Domestic Violence*, Cavendish Publishing, 1997.

Mullender and Morley, *Children Living with Domestic Violence*, Whiting and Birch, 1994.

Parkinson and Humphreys, 'Children who witness domestic violence – The implications for child protection' [1998] CFLQ 147.

Von Heussen, 'The law and 'social problems': The case of Britain's Protection from Harassment Act 1997' [2000] Web JCLI (webjcli.ncl.ac.uk/2000/issue1/vonheussen1.html).

Websites

Domestic Violence Data Source (DVDS) (provides up-to-date facts and figures about domestic violence, as well as details of research projects being conducted): www.domesticviolencedata.org/

Home Office Domestic Violence Website: www.homeoffice.gov.uk/domestic-violence/index.htm

Women's Aid Federation (A national charity for women and children experiencing physical, sexual or emotional abuse in their home – information, and facts and figures): www.womensaid.org.uk/

Questions

1 What are the good and bad things about Part IV of the Family Law Act 1996?

2 What problems might domestic violence cause for those who are participating in mediation on divorce?

Part IV

Divorce and its Consequences

Part IV considers the law of divorce and its consequences. Chapter 7 deals with the development of divorce law, including consideration of the new law which was due to come into force in the year 2000 but which was eventually scrapped in December 2000 because of concerns that it would not achieve its policy aims in practice. Chapter 8 deals with obtaining a divorce. Chapter 9 deals with financial and property matters on divorce. Arrangements for children on divorce are dealt with in Chapter 13.

7 The Development of Divorce Law

7.1 Divorce Today

Although divorce is a world-wide phenomenon, Britain has one of the highest divorce rates. In fact it heads the European 'league table' for divorce. There are more than 140 000 divorces each year in England and Wales. In fact there has been a slight decline in the last few years (from 146 700 in 1997 to 145 200 in 1998, and about 141 000 in 1999, see *Population Trends*). The average length of marriages which end in divorce is 9–10 years. As about 40 per cent of marriages end in divorce, many spouses and children experience divorce. Sometimes this can be very traumatic for the parties and their children. It can have a considerable emotional, and financial, impact on families.

The reasons for the high divorce rate are complex. Greater social mobility, the liberation of women, the social acceptability of divorce, the desire to form companionate marriages, the rise of the permissive society and changing attitudes to marriage and cohabitation have no doubt been influential factors. The decline of religion and the erosion of the ecclesiastical concept of the sanctity of marriage have also had an impact. Divorce law itself may have had an effect on the divorce rate, for with each change in the law and the introduction of more liberal divorce laws the number of divorces has risen. Whether the new divorce law (see 7.5), had it been implemented, would have had an impact on the divorce rate is unclear. However, as divorces under the reformed law would have taken longer to obtain than under the present law, there might have been a decline in the divorce rate. On the other hand, it may be the case that divorce law itself has little effect on the number of divorces. Perhaps people divorce not because of the law but because of the strains and stresses of the human condition.

7.2 The Development of Divorce Law

Until the mid-nineteenth century both the ordinary courts and the ecclesiastical courts had no jurisdiction to grant decrees of divorce, although the latter could annul marriages and could grant a limited sort of divorce called a divorce *a mensa et thoro*, which, like the decree of judicial separation today, relieved the parties of the legal obligation to live together, but did not leave them free to remarry. The Christian idea of marriage as an indissoluble life-long union prevailed. Anyone wishing to divorce could do so only by private Act of Parliament, a complex, lengthy and expensive procedure only available to a small minority of people.

In order to remedy the inadequacies of the Act of Parliament procedure, the Matrimonial Causes Act 1857 was passed permitting judicial rather than legislative divorce by establishing the Court for Divorce and Matrimonial Causes with jurisdiction to grant decrees of divorce, nullity and judicial separation. However, divorce continued to be difficult to obtain as there was only one ground for divorce, namely that the respondent had committed adultery. This was an acceptable ground to the Church as there was biblical precedent for it. In addition to adultery, a party also had to prove the absence of any collusion, condonation or connivance between the parties. Divorce was thus only available to an innocent petitioner where the respondent had committed the matrimonial offence of adultery. The terminology was that of the criminal law. However, divorce under the 1857 Act was more difficult for wives than husbands, as they had to prove aggravated adultery (adultery plus some additional factor, such as incest, cruelty, bigamy, sodomy or desertion). Eventually, however, after considerable pressure for reform by the female emancipation movement, aggravated adultery was abolished by the Matrimonial Causes Act 1923.

After considerable criticism of the fact that the sole ground for divorce was adultery, the Matrimonial Causes Act 1937 was enacted introducing additional grounds for divorce, namely cruelty, desertion for a continuous period of at least three years and incurable insanity. Divorce continued to require proof of a matrimonial offence (except in cases of incurable insanity). In addition to new grounds, the 1937 Act also introduced an absolute bar on divorce in the first three years of marriage, unless the petitioner had suffered exceptional hardship, or the respondent had shown exceptional depravity. This bar was introduced in response to concern that the new, more liberal grounds for divorce would undermine the institution of marriage. The aim of the three-year bar was to deter trial marriages and hasty divorces. Condonation, connivance and collusion also remained as bars.

After the 1937 Act, and particularly after the Second World War, there was a sharp rise in the number of people wishing to divorce, and a growing dissatisfaction with the law. It seemed wrong to have to prove a matrimonial offence, thereby apportioning blame, when both spouses were often responsible for marriage breakdown. It seemed wrong for a restrictive divorce law to perpetuate a dead marriage which had completely broken down. It was also easy to abuse the system, for example by fabricating adultery. In response to this general dissatisfaction, a Royal Commission, the Morton Commission, was established, which in its Report in 1956 (Cmd 9678) recommended the retention of the matrimonial offence doctrine as the basis for a good divorce law. This was a considerable set-back for the proponents of reform, and it was not until the mid-1960s that the publication of two reports (one by the Church of England and the other by the Law Commission) led to changes in the law. In 1963 the Archbishop of Canterbury appointed a Committee to study divorce, which in its report (*Putting Asunder*, 1966) recommended that the doctrine of the matrimonial offence should be abolished and be replaced by a principle of irretrievable breakdown of marriage, which would be proved by holding an inquest into the causes of breakdown. Shortly after the publication of *Putting Asunder*, the Law Commission published a Report (*Reform of the Grounds of Divorce: The Field of Choice*, Cmnd 3123, 1966) stating that the objectives of a good divorce law should be:

'(i) To buttress, rather than to undermine the stability of marriage; and

(ii) When, regrettably a marriage has irretrievably broken down, to enable the empty legal shell to be destroyed with the maximum fairness, and the minimum bitterness, distress and humiliation.'

The Law Commission concluded that a divorce law based on a matrimonial offence failed to satisfy both these objectives, and, while agreeing with the Archbishop's Committee that irretrievable breakdown should be the sole ground for divorce, rejected its proposal that breakdown should be established by holding an inquest into the causes of breakdown. The Law Commission considered that such an inquest would be distressing for the parties, expensive, time-consuming and essentially untriable. It proposed instead that breakdown should be established on proof of one or more of five facts, three of which would be based on the old matrimonial offences, and the other two on periods of separation. The five facts proposed were: adultery plus intolerability; unreasonable behaviour; desertion for a period of at least two years; two years' separation with consent to the divorce; and five years' separation. The Law Commission also recommended that the new divorce law should incorporate certain policy objectives. It should encourage reconciliation, prevent injustice to economically vulnerable spouses, and should protect children. It also recommended that the bar on divorce within the first three years of marriage should be replaced with a one-year bar, as the three-year bar prolonged poor marriages or encouraged allegations of exceptional hardship or depravity which were difficult to adjudicate, and also caused hostility and bitterness between the parties. It also caused duplicity of proceedings, as an unhappily married spouse would petition for a decree of judicial separation which would be followed not long afterwards by a petition for divorce. The Law Commission recommended a one-year bar, as it felt that to have no bar at all would undermine the sanctity of marriage.

The Law Commission's recommendations were eventually enacted in the Divorce Reform Act 1969, which came into force on 1 January 1971 (the 1969 Act was later re-enacted as Part I of the Matrimonial Causes Act 1973). Except for certain amendments (notably the 'clean break' provisions introduced by the

Matrimonial and Family Proceedings Act 1984) the reforms introduced by the 1969 Act remain the law today. We therefore have a hybrid law of divorce with fault and no-fault grounds, so that the matrimonial offence doctrine remains, and is particularly prevalent, as most divorces are sought on the basis of adultery or unreasonable behaviour as these grounds enable a party to obtain a 'quick' divorce. The Law Commission's belief that most couples would use the new separation grounds was never realised in practice. However, since the introduction of these grounds in 1971 there has been considerable dissatisfaction with the law, both the grounds and procedure for divorce, and this dissatisfaction eventually led to the passing of a fundamentally different divorce law laid down in Part II of the Family Law Act 1996 (see 7.5 below). These reforms were due to come into force in 2000 but in December 2000 the Lord Chancellor, Lord Irvine, announced that the law would be scrapped, despite the general consensus that there is an urgent need for reform.

7.3   The Development of Divorce Procedure

In addition to changes to the grounds for divorce, there have been changes over the years in respect of divorce procedure. Initially, because divorce was considered such a serious matter, proceedings were heard only in London and only by senior judges. Later on, however, undefended divorces were heard by specially designated divorce county courts (or the Divorce Registry in London). Defended divorces, however, continued to be heard in the High Court. All divorces were heard in open court with the petitioner giving oral evidence to prove the fact(s) alleged. Eventually, it became increasingly recognised that hearing divorces in court was distressing for the parties, who would have intimate marital details exposed in open court, and also that the divorce process was unnecessarily expensive and time-consuming for both the parties themselves and for the court. Divorce was failing to achieve one of its main policy aims: the burial of a dead marriage with the minimum of distress and humiliation.

With the sharp increase in the divorce rate, particularly in the early 1970s after the introduction of the more liberal grounds for divorce under the Divorce Reform Act 1969, the courts became overloaded, even though most undefended divorces were taking as little as ten minutes to be heard. Eventually, a new divorce procedure, the 'special procedure', was introduced to remedy the defects in procedure and with the aim of achieving simplicity, speed and economy. In 1973 it was introduced for childless couples divorcing with consent, but in 1975 was extended to all childless couples, except those petitioning on the basis of unreasonable behaviour. In 1977 it was extended to all undefended divorces.

All undefended divorces today are therefore dealt with in what is essentially an administrative procedure with minimal judicial involvement. The district judge examines the papers and a sworn written statement made by the petitioner in order to establish whether the fact alleged is proved, whether the marriage has irretrievably broken down, and whether there is any reason for not granting a divorce. A list of petitioners who have satisfied the district judge is drawn up and later read out in open court by the judge's clerk after which the judge pronounces decrees nisi of divorce on block. This judicial pronouncement is the last vestige of the public hearing of divorce. If a divorce is undefended neither party need attend court. Defended divorces, on the other hand, which are virtually non-existent, are still required to be heard in open court with the parties giving oral evidence.

7.4   A New Divorce Law: The Background

After the introduction in 1971 of the Divorce Reform Act 1969 (later re-enacted as Part I of the Matrimonial Causes Act 1973) there was increasing dissatisfaction with the grounds for divorce, in particular adultery and unreasonable behaviour, because allegations of adultery and behaviour caused hostility and bitterness between the parties, when one of the main policy objectives of the 1969 reforms had been to minimise such hostility and bitterness. Adultery and behaviour were also fault grounds, when it had been a major aim of the 1969 reforms to move away from fault. These two grounds were also felt to be leading to too many 'quickie' divorces. It was also felt that the law 'steamrollered' too many couples towards divorce once they had started the process in motion. Couples needed time to reflect and consider whether divorce was the right step to take. There was also criticism that the process of obtaining the decree of divorce was quite separate from ancillary matters. It was felt that ancillary matters should be more closely integrated into the divorce process, particularly as there was evidence that some couples would never have divorced had they realised the problems they would encounter in sorting out the consequences.

There was also concern about divorce procedure. As a result, the Booth Committee on Procedure in Matrimonial Causes (chaired by Hon Mrs Justice Booth) was set up by the Government to look at divorce procedure, its remit being to make recommendations to mitigate the intensity of disputes, encourage settlements, and to provide further for the welfare of the children of the family. The Committee, which reported its findings in 1985, found among other things that under the special procedure the registrar (now the district judge) could do no more than merely 'rubber stamp' applications, as he or she was not in a position in most cases to make findings of fact, e.g. to establish the effect of the respondent's behaviour on the petitioner. The Committee felt that the law was little respected and little understood and that the special procedure increased bitterness. With these criticisms in mind it recommended several reforms, including allowing joint applications for divorce and a system of initial hearings in which the parties would be able to reach a settlement or identify areas in dispute. The Committee also recommended changes of terminology to make the law more understandable. Some of these recommendations are in fact reflected in recent changes to the law, in particular the introduction of a First Directions Appointment and the Financial Dispute Resolution (FRD) scheme for ancillary relief cases (see 9.2).

It was concern, however, about the ground for divorce, not procedure, that led the Law Commission in 1988 to publish a discussion paper, *Facing the Future: A Discussion Paper on the Ground for Divorce* (Law Com No 170), which discussed whether the law had succeeded in satisfying the objectives of a good divorce law which it had laid down in its 1966 Report, *Reform of the Grounds of Divorce: The Field of Choice* (Cmnd 3123): to buttress, rather than to undermine the stability of marriage and when a marriage had irretrievably broken down, to enable the empty legal shell to be destroyed with the maximum fairness, and the minimum bitterness, distress and humiliation. It also considered whether the law avoided injustice to economically weak spouses, whether it protected the interests of children, and whether it was understandable and respected.

Although the Law Commission considered the law to be a considerable improvement on the earlier law, it felt that the major aim of the 1969 reform to move away from fault had not been achieved in practice, as most divorces were sought on the basis of adultery and unreasonable behaviour. Divorce was a hybrid system of fault and no-fault grounds. As a result, many parties continued to apportion blame, with one party being unfairly stigmatised when often both parties were to blame. Allegations of fault also encouraged the parties to adopt entrenched and hostile positions, thereby making settlement about ancillary matters more difficult. The Law Commission therefore concluded that the law had not achieved its objectives. It was neither easily understandable nor respected. Proving a fact had become a meaningless formality, with petitioners exaggerating a fact in order to obtain a divorce. The law was also illogical because in some cases, although a marriage had irretrievably broken down, it was not possible to grant a decree, as a fact could not be proved. The Commission also considered divorce law had a juggernaut effect, because once the parties had started out on the divorce process there was little scope for reconciliation, conciliation and negotiation. Most of all, the Law Commission felt that the law failed to recognise that divorce is not a final product but part of a massive transition for the parties and their children. It therefore made proposals for reform which would introduce a truly, and not artificially, no-fault divorce which would encourage the parties to reach agreement and to consider and face up to the consequences of marriage breakdown.

The Law Commission discussed various options for reform, but concluded that a no-fault model was best. After discussing the advantages and disadvantages of different no-fault models (marriage breakdown, separation, mutual consent and unilateral demand), it recommended retaining irretrievable breakdown as the ground for divorce, but with divorce available at the end of a period of time. The Commission felt that divorce over a period of time had many advantages. It would encourage the parties to co-operate and to consider the practical consequences of divorce and would reinforce the idea that divorce is a process and not an event. Furthermore, it considered that conciliation and mediation would fit in well with the proposed model, as would the procedural reforms recommended by the Booth Committee (see above).

The Law Commission's Discussion Paper was followed in 1990 by its Report, *Family Law: The Ground for Divorce* (Law Com No 192) in which it outlined in more detail its recommendation for a divorce over a period of time. The Report also included a draft Bill. The proposals included changes in terminology to make divorce law more understandable. 'Petitioner' and 'respondent' would become 'applicant' and 'respondent'. A 'petition' would become an 'application', and a 'decree' an 'order'. The period over time would be set in motion by a joint or sole initial statement in prescribed form that the marriage had broken down, which would be lodged at the court with other documents. After that there would be a 12-month period for consideration and reflection, during which proof of breakdown would be established, practical difficulties resolved, and the consequences of divorce considered. Optional conciliation, mediation and counselling would be available during that period. No later than 12 weeks from making the initial statement, the court would hold an initial hearing to make a preliminary assessment to monitor the progress of the arrangements being made, to identify issues in dispute and to dispose of any matters which could be disposed of. Financial provision and property adjustment orders could be made at this hearing, and the court could also consider arrangements for the children. During this period the parties would be free to apply for s.8 orders under the Children Act 1989 and orders for ancillary relief under Part II of the Matrimonial Causes Act 1973. The court would have the power to make orders in respect of financial provision and property adjustment at any time during the period of reflection and consideration, rather than leaving them until decree nisi as at present. The court, of its own motion or on application, would also have power to postpone divorce: where it would be likely to exercise its powers under the Children Act 1989; where financial provision for a spouse or child had not been made; and where, in exceptional circumstances, a respondent would suffer hardship. At the end of the 12-month period an application for divorce could be made by one or both of the spouses together with a declaration that their marriage had irretrievably broken down and a request for a divorce order, which the court would automatically issue, provided the application had been made in the required form, the period of time for reflection and consideration had passed and the statement of marital breakdown had not been withdrawn. Spouses would be able to make a statement of marital breakdown within the first year of marriage but an application for a divorce would not be possible unless at the time of the application the parties had been married for one year and eleven months.

The Government subsequently adopted most of the Law Commission's proposals, some of the Booth Committee's proposals, as well as proposals for an increased role for mediation. In 1993 these proposals were published in a Consultation Paper, *Looking to the Future: Mediation and the Ground for Divorce* (Cm 2424), in which the Government said the law was not working well as:

- it allowed divorce to be obtained quickly and easily without the parties being required to have regard to the consequences;
- it did nothing to save the marriage;
- it could make things worse for the children;
- it was unjust and exacerbated bitterness and hostility;
- it was confusing, misleading and open to abuse;
- it was discriminatory; and
- it distorted the parties' bargaining positions.

In 1995, after responses to the Consultation Paper had been processed, the Government published a White Paper, *Looking to the Future: Mediation and the Ground for Divorce. The Government's Proposals* (Cm 2799), in which its stated objectives for a better divorce process were:

- to support the institution of marriage;
- to include practicable steps to prevent the irretrievable breakdown of marriage;
- to ensure that the parties understand the practical consequences of divorce before taking any irreversible decision;
- where divorce is unavoidable, to minimise the bitterness and hostility between the parties and reduce the trauma for the children; and
- to keep to the minimum the cost to the parties and the tax-payer.

The White Paper was followed in November 1995 by the publication of the Family Law Bill. Parts I and II of the Bill contained the reforms of divorce law and Part III made proposals for mediation in family matters. The Bill had a stormy ride through Parliament with many last-minute amendments made, but on 4 July 1996 the Bill received the Royal Assent.

The new law of divorce laid down in Part II of the Family Law Act 1996 was expected to come into force on 1 January 1999, but was postponed until the year 2000 as the Government decided to conduct a pilot scheme to see how the information meetings in the Act would work in practice. Thus between June 1997 and June 1999 fourteen information meeting pilots were launched in England and Wales, covering eleven different areas and using six different models. However, in June 1999 the Lord Chancellor, Lord Irvine, unexpectedly announced that implementation of the new law would be indefinitely suspended, as the pilot project to test the provision of information meetings had been disappointing, in view of the Government's objectives of saving saveable marriages and encouraging the mediated settlement of disputes. According to a press release issued by the Lord Chancellor's Department, only 7 per cent of those attending the pilots had been diverted into mediation and only 39 per cent of those attending had reported that they were more likely than before to go to a solicitor. The research also showed that the vast majority of people attended without their spouse, when many of the options described to them under the new law required the commitment of both spouses. The Lord Chancellor stated that, before the new law could be implemented, the Government must be satisfied that the new arrangements for divorce would work in practice.

Postponement of the proposed reforms was greeted with considerable relief by those who thought it would never work in practice (for a critique, see 7.6). Eventually, in December 2000, the Lord Chancellor announced that the proposed reforms would not come into force at all. Consequently we are left with an unsatisfactory divorce law which is still in urgent need of reform.

7.5   An Outline of the Proposed Reforms

The current law of divorce is described in Chapter 8, but an outline of the Government's proposals for a reformed new law which was due to come into force under Part II of the Family Law Act 1996 is given here because a knowledge of the proposals throws light on the limitations and inadequacies of the current law, and because it is possible that divorce law will be reformed in the future.

Had the new divorce law ('divorce over a process of time') been implemented, it would have radically changed the law, for with the exception of the retention of irretrievable breakdown as the sole ground for divorce, virtually everything else would have changed. Part II would have emphasised that divorce is a process, not an event, and would have introduced a truly no-fault divorce. Arrangements for the future would have had to be made before rather than after a divorce was granted. The parties would have been given more information about divorce, and there would have been a greater emphasis on mediation.

Under the new law, a divorce would have been available only after compulsory attendance at an information meeting, followed at least three months later by the filing of a statement of marital breakdown, followed in turn by a nine or fifteen months' period for reflection and consideration, during which time the divorcing couples would be required to spend time reflecting on whether their marriage could be saved, and, if not, then facing up to the consequences of divorce by making arrangements for the future. Had the new law come into force, amendments would have been made to the law on ancillary relief (see Chapter 9) and to the provisions governing arrangements for children (see Chapter 13).

(a) The Part I General Principles Governing the Grant of a Divorce

Part I of the Family Law Act 1996 laid down the following set of principles which judges and persons involved in the divorce process must consider when exercising any of their powers and functions in respect of divorce:

> '(a) that the institution of marriage is to be supported;
> (b) that the parties to a marriage which may have broken down are to be encouraged to take all practicable steps, whether by marriage counselling or otherwise, to save the marriage;
> (c) that a marriage which has irretrievably broken down and is being brought to an end should be brought to an end—
>> (i) with minimum distress to the parties and to the children affected;
>> (ii) with questions dealt with in a manner designed to promote as good a continuing relationship between the parties and any children affected as is possible in the circumstances; and
>> (iii) without costs being unreasonably incurred in connection with the procedures to be followed in bringing the marriage to an end; and
> (d) that any risk to one of the parties to a marriage, and to any children, of violence from the other party should, so far as reasonably practicable, be removed or diminished.'

These principles are in fact already in force, having been brought into effect without the implementation of the new law. The first two principles emphasise the importance of supporting marriage, while the second two focus on bringing marriage to an end smoothly. This juxtaposition reflects an inherent tension in divorce law. However, while the aim of smoothing the divorce process is laudable, it is questionable whether divorce law can, and indeed should, support the institution of marriage. It is difficult to disagree with Walker (2000) whose evaluation of information meetings suggested that 'saving marriages is an objective distinct from securing civilised divorce.'

(b) Establishing Irretrievable Breakdown of Marriage

There were no facts for establishing irretrievable breakdown under the proposed reforms. Instead marriage breakdown would have been inferred if (see s.5(1)): one party (or both) had made a statement of marriage breakdown; the required period for reflection and consideration had ended; and one party (or both) had made a declaration stating that, having reflected on the breakdown, and having considered the requirements as to the parties' arrangements for the future, he or she believed that the marriage could not be saved.

(c) The Divorce Process

To obtain a divorce, an applicant would have had to have taken the following steps in the following order:

- attend an **information meeting**;
- make a **statement of marital breakdown** at least three months after attendance at an information meeting;
- pass a specified **'period for reflection and consideration'** (nine months in some cases and 15 months in others) after the making of the statement of marital breakdown during which the applicant(s) must spend time reflecting on whether the marriage can be saved and, if not, then making financial arrangements and arrangements for the children;
- make an **application for a divorce order** which must (except in specified circumstances) be accompanied by prescribed evidence about arrangements for the children and financial matters and a declaration by the applicant for divorce that he or she believes the marriage cannot be saved.

In some circumstances, the court would have been able to make an 'order preventing divorce' under s.10 (see below), even though the marriage had irretrievably broken down and all the above steps have been satisfactorily completed.

The Information Meeting

The aim of the information meeting (see s.8) was to provide relevant information about matters which might arise in connection with divorce, and to provide and encourage marriage counselling. Legal advice would not have been available at the meeting. One spouse or both spouses would have attended, but respondents would have been compelled to attend if they had contested ancillary matters or arrangements for their children.

The Statement of Marital Breakdown

The statement of marital breakdown (see s.6) would have been made by one or both spouses three months or more after the information meeting. The statement would merely have stated that the marriage had broken down, but it would also have included a statement by each party stating that he or she was aware of the purpose of the period for reflection and consideration and wished to make arrangements for the future. A statement made during the first year of marriage or without attendance at an information meeting would have been ineffective. Receipt of the statement by the court would have marked the start of legal proceedings, and 14 days later the period for reflection and consideration would have started to run. Once the statement had been received the court would have been able to make directions requiring the parties to attend a meeting at which mediation was explained, and the court would also have been able to make interim orders for ancillary relief and orders under the Children Act 1989. A statement of marital breakdown could have been withdrawn on a joint application by both parties, and would have lapsed one year after the period for reflection and consideration had passed (although interruptions during that year for attempted reconciliations of up to 18 months would have been permitted).

The Period for Reflection and Consideration

Fourteen days after receipt of the statement of marital breakdown, the period for reflection and consideration would have started to run, at the end of which a divorce order could be applied for by one or both parties. During the period for reflection and consideration the parties would have been expected to spend time reflecting on whether their marriage could be saved, considering whether to effect a reconciliation, or otherwise considering and making arrangements for the future. The length of the period for reflection and consideration was 9 months, or 15 months if there were children aged under 16, or a party had asked for further time for reflection. However the period would not have lasted for 15 months where an occupation order or non-molestation order (see 6.5 and 6.6) was in force or where delay would have been significantly detrimental to the welfare of any children. The court would have been able to extend the 9-month period where an applicant had delayed in serving a copy of the statement of marital breakdown on the other party. Periods of attempted reconciliation would not have been taken into account when calculating the appropriate period of reflection.

The Application for a Divorce Order

At the end of the period for reflection and consideration one party (or both) would have been able to apply for a divorce order. The application would have been accompanied by (i) a declaration that, having reflected on the breakdown and having considered their arrangement for the future, the applicant(s) believed that the marriage could not be saved, and (ii) evidence about finance and property matters and arrangements for children. Evidence would have taken the form of a court order (made by consent or otherwise), a negotiated agreement, or a declaration. However, the court would have been able to waive the requirement for evidence about finance and property matters where there was delay or obstruction by the other party, ill-health, disability or injury, or where a party could not be contacted or where there was domestic violence.

The court would have been able to make a divorce order, provided it was satisfied that (s.3(1)): the marriage had irretrievably broken down; the information meeting requirements had been satisfied; the parties had made the required arrangements for the future; the application for divorce had not been withdrawn; one (or both) parties had satisfied the domicile requirements; no order preventing divorce was in force; and the requirements in respect of the welfare of the children had been satisfied.

An 'Order Preventing Divorce'

Under s.10 of the Act, the court would have been able to make an 'order preventing divorce' in cases where it considered that dissolution of the marriage would result in substantial financial or other hardship to the other party, or to a child of the family, and it would be wrong in all the circumstances for the marriage to be dissolved. This hardship bar would have been similar to the hardship bar in the current law of divorce under s.5 of the Matrimonial Causes Act 1973 (see 8.3), except that the hardship bar would have applied to all divorces and used the term 'substantial' rather than 'grave' hardship, and would have applied not only to respondents but to children. Had the new law been introduced, it is likely that the 'order preventing divorce' would have remained a 'sticking point' for many divorces, and might have had a subversive effect on the aims of the new law to move away from fault. However, the requirement that the court must be satisfied that it would be wrong in all the circumstances to dissolve the marriage, would have meant that, despite proof of substantial hardship, it could nevertheless have been able to grant a divorce. The rationale for the 'order preventing divorce' was to enable the wishes of those who were unwilling to divorce to be taken into account. To what extent the courts would have used the order to prevent a divorce is hard to predict, but it is likely that, although many parties would have applied for the order, the court would have refused to grant it, in much the same way as it refuses to grant an order under s.5 of the 1973 Act except in truly exceptional cases.

Mediation

To facilitate the resolution of disputes (about finance, property, or children), the court, after receiving a statement of marital breakdown, would have been able to give a direction requiring each party to attend a meeting at which mediation could be explained and at which the parties could take advantage of mediation (s.13). Furthermore, legal aid would not have been available in most cases unless the parties had investigated the possibility of mediation.

Separation Orders

The court would have had jurisdiction to make separation orders (see s.2(1)) where: the applicant(s) could show that the marriage had irretrievably broken down; they had attended an information meeting; a statement of marital breakdown had been made; the period for reflection and consideration had been satisfied; and arrangements in respect of finance, property and children had been made. Unlike divorce, a statement of marital breakdown would have been capable of being made in the first year of marriage. A separation order could have been converted into a divorce order. There would have been no power to grant an order preventing a separation.

Finance and Property

Had the new divorce law been implemented, Sched. 2 to the Family Law Act 1996 would have amended the current law on ancillary relief laid down in Part II of the Matrimonial Causes Act 1973 to give the court power to make orders for financial provision before a divorce or separation order was granted. The court would have continued to make the same range of finance and property orders, but changes would have been made in respect of when they could be applied for and when they would take effect. Periodical payments and lump sum orders would have been available for spouses and children on an interim or final basis, but maintenance pending suit would have disappeared. Amendments to the variation provisions would also have been made. Under the new law, the s.25 guidelines and the clean break provisions would have continued to govern the exercise of the court's discretion.

7.6   The Proposed New Law: a Critique

The proposed new law aimed to revolutionise divorce law and had ambitious policy objectives. These were to strengthen the institution of marriage; and to minimise hostility and bitterness between the parties by removing allegations of fault and by encouraging the parties to reach agreement. Reducing hostility and bitterness was intended to benefit not just the parties but their children. Another aim of the new law was to place a greater emphasis on mediation. Except for the increased emphasis on mediation, the policy aims of the new law were in fact the same as those adopted by the Law Commission in 1966 as the basis for a good divorce law, but which according to the Law Commission in its 1988 Discussion Paper and 1990 Report (see above) had not been achieved in practice. However, it is possible that the new law might also have failed to have achieved its professed objectives.

Would the New Law Have Strengthened Marriages?

The need to buttress the institution of marriage was a major policy objective of the new law, as it has always been with divorce law. The new law aimed to fulfil this objective in various ways. First, parties would have been given the opportunity to effect a reconciliation and to reflect on whether their marriage could be saved. Secondly, parties would have been encouraged to seek marriage counselling. Thirdly, the period for reflection and consideration might have prevented some couples being 'steam-rollered' into divorce. Fourthly, attendance at an information meeting might have provided the parties with information which would have made them decide not to go ahead with divorce. However, although all these devices were put in place to attempt to strengthen the institution of marriage, it is difficult to assess whether many marriages would have been saved in practice. It is also questionable whether it should be the role of divorce law to attempt to save marriages, if indeed it ever can. Divorce, like marriage, is perhaps a social than a legal institution. The ability of the law to modify and shape human behaviour is arguably limited, and in the case of divorce, it would seem that relationships break down despite the law, rather than because of it.

The new law placed considerable emphasis on mediation. However, while mediation would have reduced hostility and bitterness in some cases, it is never a universal panacea. In fact, mediation and pressure to reach agreement may create their own set of problems. Parties may enter into an unsatisfactory agreement just to obtain a divorce (see *Edgar* v. *Edgar* [1980] 1 WLR 1410, and also 10.7), or they may be pressurised by the other party into making an agreement. A wife, for example, might agree to an unsatisfactory arrangement for fear of losing the children or in fear of violence. Mediation must therefore develop the same sorts of safeguards that exist for the adjudication of marital disputes, particularly in respect of non-disclosure.

A rather ironical twist of the new law is that it might well have undermined the institution of marriage. Some commentators (notably Ruth Deech, see *The Independent*, 2 November 1990) were strongly opposed to the new law as they believed it was likely to lead to a rise in divorce, because every previous reform of divorce law had done so. However, the reverse might have occurred had the new law been introduced. Previous reforms of divorce had introduced more liberal grounds for divorce with the result that divorce became easier and easier to obtain. With the new law, on the other hand, it is difficult to decide whether it would have introduced a more liberal or a more restrictive divorce law. It is true that it would have removed the need to prove fault, but the requirement that the parties undergo a period of reflection and consideration during which time they would have been required to make arrangements for the future might have made divorce more difficult. Divorcing couples would have to have gone through a protracted and complicated process. No longer would it have been possible to divorce easily and quickly. The reforms, had they been implemented, might have led to more couples choosing to cohabit rather than marry because of the difficulty of obtaining a divorce should their marriage break down. The end result of the new law might somewhat ironically have been to undermine rather than to buttress the institution of marriage.

Would the New Law have Minimised Hostility and Bitterness?

Although it is felt by some that the removal of fault might have undermined the moral basis of marriage and divorce, the removal of fault is nevertheless considered to be a major priority of any reform as it is believed to reduce hostility and bitterness between the parties and facilitate agreement about the consequences of divorce. However, it is possible that the new law might have encouraged hostility and bitterness, particularly because of the protracted nature of divorce. Tactical manoeuvres by the parties might have encouraged hostility, such as one party applying for a 'no divorce order' or a request that the period of reflection and consideration be shortened or waived. Some parties might have adopted delaying and obstructive tactics in respect of financial arrangements in order to drag out the divorce. While it does seem more rational to integrate the financial and property consequences of divorce with the actual process of dissolving the marriage, the inevitable drawback of such a development is that many divorcing couples would have found themselves involved in a lengthy, drawn-out experience causing uncertainty, frustration, and, in some cases, hostility and bitterness.

Another criticism of the new law was that it would arguably have expected too much of human nature. Many couples in the throes of marriage breakdown with the emotional turmoil which that involves might well have found it difficult, if not impossible, to sit down and discuss arrangements for the future. Cretney (1995 at 304) was of the opinion that the Government's white paper on divorce seemed 'curiously naive' about what was likely to happen during the period of reflection. He said that some couples would not spend time considering whether their marriage could be saved or making arrangements for the future but would be spending time conceiving children, or exploiting their emotional or financial advantage or brooding on their grievances. According to

Freeman (1997) the 'subtext' of the new law was about marriage, and he criticised the length of the divorce process because he considered it would create 'more conflict, more tension, more domestic violence, unnecessary abortions and more children who [would] experience their parents' divorce while still of pre-school years' (p.414). Furthermore, Freeman found it hard to believe that the one-year bar on divorce was never questioned throughout discussions leading up to the reforms. He also said that while the new law could mandate the passage of time – it could not mandate reflection and consideration (p.416).

In brief, the new law can be criticised for being unnecessarily complicated and possibly unworkable in practice. Administrative processes (i.e. information meetings, mediation and marriage-saving) would have all become part of the ground for divorce, thereby creating an unnecessarily complex and multi-purpose law. The policy objectives of the new law were also open to question. Should it be the function of divorce law to save marriages? In most cases it will be too late to save a party's marriage. Marriages need earlier intervention if they are to be saved. Another concern was in respect of the information meetings. Eekelaar (1999) criticised the need for information meetings before divorce, on the ground that they represented a form of 'social engineering'. While divorcing couples and their children need access to information about divorce, compulsory attendance at an information meeting might not have been the best way of conveying information, except possibly where divorcing couples had children (see Richards and Stark, 2000). However, what is clear is that creating a coherent, workable and understandable divorce law is a difficult, and perhaps virtually impossible, task. Finding the best model for a good divorce law is a difficult matter. However, although looking for a perfect divorce law is like searching for the Holy Grail, law reformers must be sure that any new law is significantly better than the old before they decide to change it.

7.7   Divorce Law: The Future

As we have seen, the Government has scrapped the introduction of the new law and given no indication of when, if at all, reform will take place. The future of divorce law therefore hangs in the balance. However, despite the fact that the new law has been criticised as being unnecessarily complicated and unworkable in practice, the general consensus is that divorce reform is urgently needed. Indeed the Rt. Hon Dame Elizabeth Butler-Sloss at her inaugural press conference on becoming President of the Family Division described the current common practice of obtaining a divorce on the ground of unreasonable behaviour as a 'hypocritical charade' and she stressed the need to introduce a truly no-fault divorce.

The courts are currently administering an outmoded, illogical, misleading and confusing divorce law which came into force more than 30 years ago.

Not only is the mixture of fault and no-fault grounds confusing, but some feel that divorce law fails to protect children. Smart (1999) has said that, although the new divorce law might not have been perfect, its demise has resulted in important opportunities and initiatives to improve matters for children being lost. The information meetings, she says, would have provided an opportunity to raise with parents the question of how children might feel about, or react to, their parents' divorce, and also an opportunity to present children with information designed to meet their specific needs and interests.

Although the introduction of the proposed new law will not now take place, it is likely that reform in some form or other will eventually take place. Reform is particularly pressing because of recent changes to ancillary relief procedure (see 9.2), which require both parties to attend court and place an increased emphasis on mediation. As the law now stands, however, the grounds for divorce encourage hostility while the law on ancillary relief encourages agreement and amicable settlement. What may eventually happen, however, is that the Government will introduce a new divorce built around the existing law but incorporating some of the good features of the proposed, but now rejected, reforms.

Summary

1 Divorce is common world-wide, but is particularly common in the UK.
2 Legislative divorce was introduced into England and Wales by the Matrimonial Causes Act 1857 (before that it was only possible to divorce by private Act of Parliament), but the sole ground was adultery. Wives, not husbands, had to prove 'aggravated adultery' (adultery plus some other factor such as incest, bigamy, sodomy or desertion). Aggravated adultery was abolished by the Matrimonial Causes Act 1923.
3 The grounds for divorce were extended by the Matrimonial Causes Act 1937 to include not just adultery but cruelty, three years' desertion and incurable insanity. The Act also imposed an absolute bar on divorce within the first three years of marriage unless the petitioner had suffered exceptional hardship, or the respondent had shown exceptional depravity.
4 The Divorce Reform Act 1969 introduced the present grounds for divorce – irretrievable breakdown of marriage plus proof of one or more of the following: adultery (plus intolerability); unreasonable behaviour; two years' desertion; two years' separation with consent to the divorce; and five years' separation. The Divorce Reform Act was re-enacted in Part I of the Matrimonial Causes Act 1973 and these grounds remain the law today.
5 All divorces originally took place in open court, but in the 1970s the special procedure (an administrative form of divorce) was introduced for all undefended divorces.
6 There has been considerable dissatisfaction with the law, in particular that it is fault-based, and that settling the consequences of divorce (property, finance and children) is remote from the process of obtaining the divorce itself.
7 As a result of this dissatisfaction, Parts I and II of the Family Law Act 1996 were enacted to introduce a new form of divorce, which would have been granted after

a period for reflection and consideration during which time the parties would in most cases have been required to have sorted out their ancillary matters (finance, property and children). At the end of the period for reflection, the divorce order would have been granted. The new law would also have placed a greater emphasis on mediation. However, in June 1999, just before the new law was about to be introduced, the Lord Chancellor, Lord Irvine, announced that implementation was postponed indefinitely because the pilot schemes which had been introduced to look at how information meetings worked had shown it to be unsatisfactory. The Government considered it unwise to change the law unless it could be sure that the policy objectives of the new law could be achieved in practice. In December 2000 the Government announced that the reforms would not come into force.

8 Thus, we have a situation where there is a consensus that the law needs changing, but uncertainty as to what form a new law of divorce should take.

Further Reading and References

Bridge, 'Diversity, divorce and information meetings – ensuring access to justice' [2000] Fam Law 645.
Collier, 'The dashing of a "liberal dream"? – The information meeting, the "new family" and the limits of law' [1999] CFLQ 257.
Cretney, 'The Divorce White Paper – Some Reflections' [1995] Fam Law 302.
Day-Slater and Piper (eds), *Undercurrents of Divorce*, Dartmouth, 1999.
Eekelaar, 'Family law – Keeping us "on message"' [1999] CFLQ 387.
Freeman (ed.), *Divorce – Where Next?* Dartmouth, 1996.
Freeman, 'Divorce gospel style' [1997] Fam Law 413.
Lewis, 'Relationship breakdown, obligations and contracts' [1999] Fam Law 149.
McCarthy, Walker and Hooper, 'Saving marriage – a role for divorce law?' [2000] Fam Law 412.
Richards and Stark, 'Children, parenting and information meetings' [2000] Fam Law 484.
Smart, 'Shelving Part II of the Family Law Act – Shelving children?' [1999] Fam Law 801.
Thorpe, Rt Hon Lord Justice, and Clarke (eds), *No Fault or Flaw: The Future of the Family Law Act 1996*, Family Law, 2000.
Walker, 'Information meetings revisited' [2000] Fam Law 330.

Questions

1 Why is it generally agreed that divorce law needs reforming?
2 What were the strengths and weaknesses of the proposed new law?
3 What would be the arguments for and against introducing divorce by unilateral demand, or divorce by mutual consent?

8 Obtaining a Divorce

8.1 Introduction

The law governing divorce is laid down in the Matrimonial Causes Act 1973 and procedural rules are laid down in the Family Proceedings Rules 1991. Part I of the Matrimonial Causes Act 1973 contains the law on the ground for divorce. Part II contains the law on property and finance on divorce (see Chapter 9). The rules governing jurisdiction to grant a divorce are laid down in the Domicile and Matrimonial Proceedings Act 1973, which provides that the divorce courts in England and Wales have jurisdiction to hear a petition for divorce (and for nullity and judicial separation) if either party to the marriage is domiciled in England or Wales when divorce proceedings are commenced; or either party was habitually resident in England and Wales for one year before commencement of divorce proceedings. Jurisdiction is not lost by a change of domicile or residence after commencement of proceedings. Under the Domicile and Matrimonial Proceedings Act 1973 the divorce court in England and Wales may stay (stop) the proceedings if divorce proceedings are pending in another country. Thus, for example, in *S* v. *S (Divorce: Staying Proceedings)* [1997] 2 FLR 100, Wall J in the High Court granted the husband's application for a stay of the English proceedings as the New York court was the appropriate forum for the divorce.

An undefended divorce in this country is obtained under the so-called 'special procedure', which is essentially an administrative form of divorce. The divorce can be granted in a matter of weeks without the need for either party to the marriage to attend court, in most cases. A defended divorce, on the other hand, takes longer to obtain, as proceedings must be heard in open court. In practice, defended divorces are virtually non-existent. While an undefended divorce can be obtained in as little as six weeks, ancillary matters (property, finance and arrangements for children) often take many months, even years, to conclude, depending on the complexity of the case and the willingness of the parties to reach agreement. Divorce is a two-stage procedure. A decree nisi of divorce is obtained first, and this is followed by a decree absolute. Only on the grant of decree absolute is a marriage terminated.

Divorce is very common in this country. In fact the UK has the highest divorce rate in Europe, with approximately 145 000 divorces granted annually. The latest figures available show that 141 543 decrees nisi of divorce were granted in 1998 (*Judicial Statistics 1998*, Lord Chancellor's Department). As we saw in the previous chapter, the law of divorce, both substance and procedure, has been strongly criticised and new provisions introducing a fundamentally reformed divorce law were due to come into force in the year 2000 under Part II of the Family Law Act 1996. However, in June 1999 the Lord Chancellor announced that implementation of these radical reforms was postponed because of the failure of the pilot schemes for information meetings to live up to expectations. This has created considerable uncertainty, for while the current law of divorce law is generally considered to be wholly unsatisfactory, the proposed new law had not escaped criticism. In fact the Lord Chancellor's announcement that implementation would be delayed was heartily welcomed in some quarters. Eventually, in December 2000 the Lord Chancellor announced that the implementation of 'divorce over a period of time' would be scrapped. Thus we are left with an unsatisfactory divorce law which needs reforming (see Chapter 7). When this will be, and what form it will take, remain to be seen.

8.2   The Ground for Divorce and the Five Facts

Irretrievable breakdown of marriage is the sole ground for divorce (s.1(1)), but it is established by proving one or more of the following five 'facts' (s.1(2)):

'(a) that the respondent has committed adultery and the petitioner finds it intolerable to live with the respondent;

(b) that the respondent has behaved in such a way that the petitioner cannot reasonably be expected to live with the respondent;

(c) that the respondent has deserted the petitioner for a continuous period of at least two years immediately preceding the presentation of the petition;

(d) that the parties of the marriage have lived apart for a continuous period of at least two years immediately preceding the presentation of the petition ... and the respondent consents to a decree being granted;

(e) that the parties to the marriage have lived apart for a continuous period of at least five years immediately preceding the presentation of the petition.'

Once a fact has been proved the court must grant a decree nisi of divorce, unless it is satisfied on all of the evidence that the marriage has not irretrievably broken down (s.1(4)). The requirement that the petitioner must prove both irretrievable breakdown and a fact has led to some rather unsatisfactory and illogical decisions. For example, in *Richards* v. *Richards* [1972] 1 WLR 1073 the petitioner had satisfied the court that her marriage had irretrievably broken down, but failed to satisfy the court that her husband, who was mentally ill, had behaved in such a way that she could not reasonably be expected to live with him. Similarly in *Buffery* v. *Buffery* [1988] 2 FLR 365 the Court of Appeal was satisfied that the marriage had irretrievably broken down, but was not satisfied that unreasonable behaviour had been proved.

The Five Facts

(a) Adultery (s.1(2)(a))

Adultery involves an act of voluntary heterosexual intercourse between two people who are not married to each other, and at least one of whom is married to a third party. Adultery does not include involuntary intercourse (e.g. as a result of rape, duress, intoxication, or mental disorder) and homosexual intercourse. Adultery is proved by the respondent simply answering 'yes' to the question 'Do you admit the adultery alleged in the petition?' and signing the form (Appendix 1, FPR 1991). Where there is no such admission, then proof of adultery is needed, and for this purpose the degree of proof is thought to be slightly higher than on the balance of probabilities (*Serio* v. *Serio* (1983) 4 FLR 756).

In addition to proving adultery, the petitioner must prove that he or she finds it intolerable to live with the respondent (s.1(2)(a)). This intolerability requirement was added to buttress the stability of marriage (a policy aim of the 1969 divorce reforms), so that a single act of adultery on its own would be insufficient to end a marriage. Adultery and intolerability are two separate and unrelated facts (*Cleary* v. *Cleary* [1974] 1 WLR 73). In practice, the petitioner must simply answer the question 'Do you find it intolerable to live with the respondent?' (Appendix 1, FPR 1991).

A petition based on adultery cannot be heard if the parties have lived together for more than six months (in one period or several periods aggregated) after the petitioner discovered the adultery (s.2(1)), but the period of living together is disregarded by the court when it is determining the question of whether the petitioner finds it intolerable to live with the respondent (s.2(2)).

(b) Behaviour (s.1(2)(b))

Under s.1(2)(b) the petitioner must prove that the respondent has behaved in such a way that the petitioner cannot reasonably be expected to live with the respondent. Although this fact is always referred to as 'unreasonable behaviour', this is a misnomer, because it is the effect of the respondent's behaviour on the petitioner which is relevant, not whether the respondent's behaviour is unreasonable.

The test for establishing unreasonable behaviour is both objective and subjective. It is objective as the court must establish whether the petitioner can reasonably be expected to live with the respondent, but it is also subjective, as the court must consider the effect of the respondent's behaviour on the particular petitioner. In *Ash* v. *Ash* [1972] Fam 135, Bagnall J said that the question to be asked was 'can this petitioner, with his or her character and personality, with his or her faults and other attributes, good and bad, having regard to his or her behaviour during the marriage, reasonably be expected to live with this respondent?' His Lordship said by way of example that a violent or alcoholic petitioner could reasonably be expected to live with a respondent with similar attributes. In *Livingstone-Stallard* v. *Livingstone-Stallard* [1974] Fam 47, Dunn J adopted the following test:

'Would any right-thinking person come to the conclusion that this husband has behaved in such a way that this wife cannot reasonably be expected to live with him, taking into account the whole of the circumstances and the characters and personalities of the parties?'

This test was approved by the Court of Appeal in *O'Neill* v. *O'Neill* [1975] 1 WLR 1118, and endorsed by the Court of Appeal in *Buffery* v. *Buffery* [1988] 2 FLR 365. In *Birch* v. *Birch* [1992] 1 FLR 564, the wife petitioned for divorce on the basis of her husband's unreasonable behaviour. She claimed that his attitude to her was dogmatic, nationalistic and dictatorial. She said that she was sensitive and had taken a passive role during their 20-year marriage, putting aside her own interests until the children had grown up. The county court judge dismissed her petition, but the Court of Appeal allowed her appeal and granted a decree because the judge had used an objective test when the correct test was subjective.

Divorces are granted for a wide range of different sorts of behaviour, including both acts and omissions. In *O'Neill* v. *O'Neill* (above), for example, the petitioner stated that her husband had a withdrawn personality, had doubted the paternity of their children, and had spent two years 'improving' the flat, which included mixing cement on the living-room floor and leaving the lavatory door off for about eight months. Financial irresponsibility has been held to constitute unreasonable behaviour (see, for example, *Carter-Fea* v. *Carter-Fea* [1987] Fam Law 131). So too has evidence of violence or drunken behaviour (see, for example, *Ash* v. *Ash* above). Some behaviour, however, may be too trivial and a decree will be refused, as it was in *Buffery* v. *Buffery* above, where the wife alleged that her husband was insensitive, never took her out, and after their children had left home they had nothing to talk about and nothing in common. Her petition was dismissed, as her husband's behaviour was insufficient to satisfy the behaviour ground. An accumulation of trivial incidents may, however, be sufficient to constitute unreasonable behaviour as they were in *Livingstone-Stallard* v. *Livingstone-Stallard* (above), where, according to Dunn J, the wife 'was subjected to a constant atmosphere of criticism, disapproval and boorish behaviour on the part of her husband.' However, as each case depends on its own facts, an accumulation of various minor matters will not necessarily result in a decree being granted. Thus, in

Butterworth v. *Butterworth* [1997] 2 FLR 336, for example, the decree of divorce was set aside by the Court of Appeal as the petition was severely defective. The husband had denied the wife's allegations that he was a violent, possessive, sexually demanding, jealous alcoholic who stopped her going to church. The Court of Appeal stressed that English divorce law still gave the respondent the right to oppose a divorce, and to have the allegations in the petition properly proved. The Court of Appeal held that the court had not applied the correct test for unreasonable behaviour, or anything like it.

In some cases the court will have to decide whether to grant a divorce where the behaviour is not the respondent's fault, e.g. where the respondent is mentally or physically ill. Whether a divorce will be granted will depend on the facts of the case, and, although the court will be cognisant of the fact that marriage entails a commitment, which includes caring for a sick spouse, it is likely to be sympathetic to the plight of the petitioner and the fact that illness can place severe strains on a marriage. A divorce may therefore be granted even though a respondent is not responsible for his or her own 'behaviour'. Thus, in *Katz* v. *Katz* [1972] 1 WLR 955, the wife succeeded in obtaining a decree where her husband had suffered from manic depression. In *Thurlow* v. *Thurlow* [1976] Fam 32, the wife was an epileptic who suffered from a severe neurological disorder. She was bed-ridden and bad-tempered, threw objects at her husband and wandered the streets causing him distress. He worked full-time and found it difficult to care for her, and the stress affected his health. Rees J granted a decree, and stated that:

> 'If the behaviour stems from misfortune such as the onset of mental illness or from disease of the body or from accidental physical injury the court would take full account of all the obligations of the married state. These would include the normal duty to accept and to share the burdens imposed upon the family as a result of the mental or physical ill-health of one member. It would also consider the capacity of the petitioner to withstand the stresses imposed by the behaviour, the steps taken to cope with it, the length of time during which the petitioner had been called upon to bear it, and the actual or potential effect upon his or her health.'

In order to encourage reconciliation, spouses are permitted to live together for up to six months (in one period or several aggregated) after the last instance of behaviour alleged, without losing the right to petition for divorce, and the court must ignore this period when determining whether the petitioner can reasonably be expected to live with the respondent (s.2(3)). If the spouses live together for more than six months after the last proven instance of behaviour, the court can, however, take that into account when determining what is reasonable.

(c) Desertion (s.1(2)(c))

A divorce can be granted where the respondent has deserted the petitioner for a continuous period of at least two years immediately preceding the presentation of the petition. Divorces based on desertion are rare, however, as petitioners tend to rely instead on other facts. Desertion requires proof of: factual separation; an intention by the respondent to desert; no consent by the petitioner to the desertion; and no just cause to desert. Constructive desertion is also possible, whereby one spouse's behaviour is so bad that the other spouse is forced to leave the home. Desertion is also possible where the parties are living under the same roof. To encourage reconciliation, a period of up to six months' resumed cohabitation does not prevent the desertion being continuous (s.2(5)).

(d) Two Years' Separation with Consent to the Divorce (s.1(2)(d))

To succeed on this fact the petitioner must prove that the parties have lived apart for a continuous period of at least two years immediately preceding the presentation of the petition, and that the respondent consents to a decree being granted. The respondent must have the capacity to consent and must be given such information as will enable him or her to understand the effect of a decree being granted (s.2(7)). The respondent notifies the court of his or her consent by filing a notice to that effect signed by the respondent personally, but a statement in the Acknowledgement of Service signed by the respondent (and solicitor, if any) is also treated as notice of consent (r.2.10). Consent may be withdrawn at any time before decree nisi, whereupon the proceedings must be stayed (r.2.10). At any time before decree absolute, the respondent may apply to have the decree nisi rescinded if the petitioner intentionally or unintentionally misled the respondent about any matter which the respondent took into account in deciding whether to consent to divorce (s.10(1)).

As far as separation is concerned, a husband and wife are treated as living apart unless they are living with each other in the same household (s.2(6)). However, it is possible for there to be factual separation where the parties are living under the same roof. What matters is that they are not living in the same household. Thus, for example, in *Fuller* v. *Fuller* [1973] 1 WLR 730 a decree was granted where the husband lived as a lodger with his wife and her new male friend. In *Mouncer* v. *Mouncer* [1972] 1 WLR 321, on the other hand, a decree was refused because, although they slept in separate bedrooms, the spouses were not living in separate households. They ate their meals with the children and they shared household chores. Facts similar to those in *Mouncer* may nevertheless justify the grant of a divorce, particularly as it would seem perfectly reasonable for a parent, like the father in *Mouncer*, to stay in the house for the sake of the children, despite the marriage having broken down.

Where a divorce is sought on the basis of two years' separation, the respondent may be able to postpone decree absolute under s.10 (see 8.3 below). In order to facilitate reconciliation, calculation of the separation period takes no account of periods of up to six months (in one period or several aggregated) during which the parties resumed living together, but there must still be an aggregated period of actual separation for at least two years (s.2(5)). If the period of resumed cohabitation is more than six months, the two-year period of separation starts to run again.

(e) Five Years' Separation (s.1(2)(e))

To succeed on this fact, the parties must have lived apart for a continuous period of at least five years immediately preceding the presentation of the petition. Consent to the divorce is not needed. The petitioner must establish factual separation, but separation is possible even though the spouses live under the same roof. In five-year separation cases a decree absolute can be delayed or a decree nisi refused (see 8.3 below). A reconciliation period of up to six months can be ignored provided the parties have separated for an aggregated period of at least five years, but if the reconciliation is for more than six months, then the five-year period begins to run again (s.2(5)). In practice, few spouses petition for divorce on this fact because of the need to wait five years.

8.3   Protection for Respondents

Sections 10 and 5 of the Matrimonial Causes Act 1973 provide protection for 'innocent' respondents, in other words respondents who are being divorced on the basis of two or five years' separation, and who have therefore committed no matrimonial offence. A similar restriction on divorce was included in the reforms of divorce under Part II of the Family Law Act 1996, where the court was given the power to grant a 'no divorce order' under s.10 of the Act in the case of any divorce.

(a) Section 10 MCA 1973

Under section 10(2) a respondent to a divorce based on two or five years' separation can ask the court by notice in Form B to consider whether his or her financial situation after divorce will be satisfactory. If such an application is made, the court may refuse to grant a decree absolute unless it is satisfied: that the petitioner should not be required to make financial provision for the respondent; or that the provision made by the petitioner for the respondent is reasonable and fair, or the best that can be made in the circumstances (s.10(3)). The court may, however, grant a decree absolute in any event if it is desirable to do so without delay and it has obtained a satisfactory undertaking from the petitioner that he or she will make such financial provision as the court may approve (s.10(4)).

Although few applications are made under s.10, an application may be useful as a tactical manoeuvre to put pressure on a petitioner to sort out the parties' financial position, particularly where there may be a problem in enforcing an ancillary relief order. Thus, in *Garcia* v. *Garcia* [1992] 1 FLR 256, for example, an application to delay decree absolute was used to enforce maintenance payments for a child where the petitioner had failed to keep up with those payments under a separation agreement made in Spain. The Court of Appeal held that the protection afforded to respondents under s.10 was not just confined to future financial provision, but could be used to remedy past financial injustice and unfulfilled past obligations, as the duty of the court in a s.10 application was to consider all the circumstances of the case (s.10(3)).

Applications under s.10 have been used to provide protection for respondents (particularly wives) who are going to lose pension entitlement as a result of divorce (see, for example, *Griffiths* v. *Dawson & Co.* [1993] 2 FLR 315, and *Jackson* v. *Jackson* [1993] 2 FLR 848), but, as the position in respect of pensions on divorce has now been improved (see 9.7), s.10 applications are now less likely to be made.

(b) *Section 5 MCA 1973*

Section 5 of the Matrimonial Causes Act 1973 gives respondents to a divorce based on five years' separation a complete defence to divorce. The aim of s.5 is to safeguard the position of 'innocent' spouses who do not wish to be divorced. In practice it is rarely invoked, and even if it is, rarely succeeds. To succeed in having a decree nisi refused, a respondent must prove two things: first that he or she will suffer grave financial or other hardship if the divorce is granted; and secondly, if such hardship is proved, that it would be wrong in all the circumstances to grant the divorce. The alleged hardship must arise as a result of the dissolution of the marriage, not from the fact of marriage breakdown or separation. Furthermore, the Act provides that hardship can include the loss of the chance of acquiring a benefit which the respondent might acquire if the marriage were not dissolved (s.5(3)). Such a loss might include, for example, loss of a right to succeed under the other spouse's will, or intestacy, or loss of pension rights. Most cases brought under s.5 have been in relation to pension rights (see, for example, *Le Marchant* v. *Le Marchant* [1977]

1 WLR 559, *Mathias* v. *Mathias* [1972] Fam 287 and *Archer* v. *Archer* [1999] 1 FLR 327). Although s.5 refers to 'other hardship', not just financial hardship, 'other hardship' defences are rare. Those that have been brought have been based on religious or social hardship. For example, respondents have argued that they will suffer ostracism in the community because of social or religious attitudes to divorce (see, for example, *Banik* v. *Banik* [1973] 1 WLR 860 and *Rukat* v. *Rukat* [1975] Fam 63).

Defences under s.5 are extremely rare, and will be even more rare now that pensions can be taken into account on divorce (see 9.7). Even where they have been pleaded they have rarely been successful as financial loss to the respondent can usually be compensated for in other ways (e.g. by state benefits or a proposal put forward by the petitioner). In *K* v. *K (Financial Relief: Widow's Pension)* [1997] 1 FLR 35, for example, the High Court adjourned proceedings on an application under s.5 by the wife who would lose her widow's pension on divorce, in order to allow her husband to make a reasonable financial proposal. He eventually did so. In most cases the court will therefore consider it best to end a marriage, despite the possibility of a respondent suffering grave financial or other hardship.

8.4   Protection for Children

Where there are children of the family aged under 16, or whom the court expressly directs should be included (e.g. because of disability), the court must consider the parents' proposed future arrangements for their children and decide whether it should exercise any of its powers under the Children Act 1989 (see Chapter 13).

8.5   Protection for Parties with Religious Beliefs

Jewish couples who undergo an English divorce may not be regarded as having been divorced according to Jewish religious law, unless and until the marriage is terminated by a 'get' (a Jewish religious divorce), which requires the husband to consent to the divorce. Sometimes a husband may refuse to consent, perhaps because of jealousy or spite, or because he wishes to blackmail his wife into a less favourable settlement in respect of financial and property matters on divorce. If a husband refuses to give his consent to the divorce, his wife remains chained to him as an 'agunah', and under Jewish religious law she is unable to remarry and any children born from a new marriage will be disadvantaged. To remedy this problem the Divorce (Religious Marriages) Bill has been introduced to give divorce courts power, on the application of either party to a Jewish marriage, to refuse a decree absolute (if just and reasonable to do so), until both parties have made a declaration that they have taken the steps required to dissolve the marriage in accordance with Jewish religious principles. The Bill re-enacts the principle already approved by Parliament in s.9(3) of Part II of the Family Law Act 1996. The Bill is still to be finally debated in Parliament, and there has been discussion about whether it should be extended to include other religious divorces.

8.6 Divorce Procedure

Divorce procedure differs according to whether a divorce is undefended or defended, but in practice virtually all divorces are undefended, because of the expense and futility of defending a divorce. Disputed issues often arise, however, in respect of finance and property on divorce (ancillary relief) (see Chapter 9), living and contact arrangements for children (see Chapter 13) and also financial provision for children (see Chapter 14).

(a) Undefended Divorce

An undefended divorce is obtained under the 'special procedure', which is essentially a paper exercise. There is usually no need for the parties or their legal representatives (if any) to attend court.

In order to commence divorce proceedings, the petitioner must present a divorce petition to a divorce county court or, in London, to the Divorce Registry alleging that the marriage has irretrievably broken down (s.1(1)) and alleging one or more of the five facts in s.1(2) (see 8.2 above). A petition cannot be presented to the court before one year has expired from the date of the marriage (s.3(1)). This is a strict rule (see *Butler* v. *Butler* [1990] FLR 114), although anything that happened during that year (e.g. evidence of unreasonable behaviour or adultery) can be used as evidence in divorce proceedings (s.3(2)).

The petition must contain the information specified in r.2.2 of the Family Proceedings Rules 1991, for example names and addresses of the parties and their children under 16 or in full-time education, occupations of the parties and details of the marriage. The petition must also contain: a statement that the marriage has irretrievably broken down; the fact or facts relied on; brief particulars of such individual fact or facts; and a prayer setting out any ancillary relief claimed.

The petition is sent to the court and must be accompanied by the following: the marriage certificate; the statement of arrangements for the children on Form M4 (if there are children under 16 or in full-time education); a reconciliation certificate on Form M3; and a written sworn statement verifying the contents of these documents. The reconciliation certificate is a document signed by the petitioner's solicitor (if any), certifying whether he or she has discussed with the petitioner the possibility of a reconciliation and has given details of persons qualified to help to effect a reconciliation (s.6(1)). A fee must be paid on presentation of the petition.

After the papers are filed at the court, a copy of the petition is sealed by the court and served on the respondent. This is accompanied by forms known respectively as Notice of Proceedings (explaining the effect of the petition and informing the respondent of the procedure involved) and Acknowledgement of Service, which latter document the respondent must complete, sign and return to the court within eight days, failing which a further copy of the petition may be served upon him personally and a sworn written statement filed to prove such service. In the Acknowledgement of Service the respondent must state whether the petition has been received, whether he or she intends to defend the divorce, whether consent to the divorce is given (if sought on the basis of two years' separation with consent), and also whether he or she intends to apply for ancillary relief or for orders in respect of the children. The Acknowledgement of Service may be signed by either the respondent or his solicitor, save that, where the fact relied upon is two years' separation with consent of the respondent and the respondent does in fact consent, then the respondent must sign in person.

Once the Acknowledgement of Service has been returned to the court and the respondent does not wish to defend, the petitioner (or the petitioner's solicitor) must file a written request for 'directions for trial' together with a written statement and questionnaire in specified form, sworn by the petitioner and providing evidence of the fact(s) relied on. The district judge gives 'directions for trial' by entering the cause in the special procedure list and thereafter considers the evidence filed by the petitioner both for procedural regularity and to establish that there is sufficient evidence to prove the fact alleged. The district judge may request further information or evidence if needed. If he is satisfied that the fact is proved and that the marriage has irretrievably broken down, he files a certificate to that effect and a date, time and place are fixed for the judge to pronounce decree nisi. Both parties receive a certificate and notice of the date and place for the pronouncement of decree nisi by the judge in open court, which neither the parties nor their legal representatives need attend. The process of pronouncement is a mere formality. The decrees are listed together in batches and collectively mentioned before the judge who gives his consent either orally or by nodding. If the district judge is not satisfied that the case for divorce is made out, he will move the case from the special procedure list and require that it be heard before the judge.

The marriage is not terminated by decree nisi but by decree absolute, which is automatically granted on the application of the petitioner or otherwise the application of the respondent. The petitioner can apply for decree absolute six weeks or more after decree nisi by lodging a notice on Form M8 (r.2.49(1) FPR 1991). If the petitioner fails to apply for a decree absolute, the respondent may apply at any time after three months have elapsed from the earliest date on which the petitioner may apply for decree absolute (s.9(2)). However, the court cannot grant the respondent a decree absolute without a hearing and adjudication by a judge or district judge, after giving at least four days' notice of the hearing to the petitioner (r.2.50 FPR 1991). A fee must be paid for the application of decree absolute. These rules are strict. Thus, if a decree absolute is obtained in breach of the rules, the divorce is void (see *Dennis* v. *Dennis* [2000] 2 FLR 231).

The purpose of the gap between decree nisi and decree absolute is to enable a respondent to appeal and the Queen's Proctor and other persons to intervene to show just cause why a decree should not be made absolute. Such intervention was formerly a real possibility (e.g. if the parties were found to have colluded, the decree absolute would be refused), but is now rare (but see *Moynihan* v. *Moynihan (Nos. 1 and 2)* [1997] 1 FLR 59). Where there are children, the divorce cannot be made absolute until the district judge has considered whether the court should exercise any of its powers under the Children Act 1989 (s.41) (see 13.2). Where a divorce is sought on the basis of two or five years' separation, a decree absolute may be refused where a respondent has not been satisfactorily financially provided for by the petitioner (see 8.3 above).

(b) Defended Divorce

Defended divorce proceedings begin in the same way as an undefended divorce, but the respondent in the Acknowledgement of Service indicates an intention to defend. Such an indication does not of itself cause the proceedings to become defended, but must be followed by the filing of an answer within 29 days of receipt of the notice of proceedings. There is then exchange of pleadings by counsel and the hearing takes place in open court with oral evidence being given and cross-examination of both parties.

8.7 Effects of Divorce

Once a decree absolute has been granted the marriage is dissolved and each party is free to remarry. A decree absolute also has other legal consequences. Financial provision and property adjustment orders made under Part II of the Matrimonial Causes Act 1973 (see Chapter 9) in favour of the parties to the marriage can take effect and orders for settlement or variation of a settlement can take effect in respect of any child of the family. All other orders for children take effect as soon as they are made. Divorce also has an effect on a will made by either party to the marriage (see 5.1). Social Security and pension rights and taxation are also affected, and both parties lose rights under certain matrimonial legislation, notably 'matrimonial home rights' (see 4.2). However, as far as children are concerned, divorced parents both retain parental responsibility for their children (see 11.6) and are obliged to provide them with financial support (see Chapter 14).

8.8   Recognition of a Foreign Divorce

Part II of the Family Law Act 1986 lays down rules for the recognition in the UK of divorces (and annulments and separations) obtained overseas. The Act makes a distinction between divorces obtained in judicial or other proceedings and those otherwise obtained. Recognition is much broader for divorces obtained in proceedings. A foreign divorce granted in proceedings is recognised in the UK if it is effective under the law of the country where it was obtained and at the commencement of those proceedings either party was habitually resident or domiciled in that country or was a national of that country (s.46(1)). A foreign divorce obtained otherwise than in proceedings is recognised in the UK, if it is effective in the country where it was obtained and at the date it was obtained one or both parties were domiciled there, or one party was domiciled there and the other party was domiciled in a country which recognised the divorce, and in any case neither party was habitually resident in the UK for one year immediately preceding the divorce (s.46(2)) (see, for example, *Wicken* v. *Wicken* [1999] Fam 224, [1999] 1 FLR 293, where Holman J held that a 'divorce letter' was effective under Gambian law to dissolve the marriage and could be recognised as a divorce in the UK).

The English courts have a discretion to refuse recognition of a foreign divorce, whether or not it was obtained in proceedings. Thus, for example, the court may refuse to recognise a foreign divorce granted in proceedings where a party was not given notice of the proceedings, or not given an opportunity to take part in them, or recognition would be manifestly contrary to public policy (s.52). In *Eroglu* v. *Eroglu* [1994] 2 FLR 287, a wife who wished to divorce in England argued that her Turkish divorce should not be recognised in England and Wales on the ground of public policy since it had been obtained by fraud (they had divorced in Turkey so that her husband could avoid Turkish national service). However, the English court held that the Turkish divorce was valid and dismissed the English petition (see also *D* v. *D (Recognition of Foreign Divorce)* [1994] 1 FLR 38). In *Eroglu*, Thorpe LJ said that it is difficult to argue that a divorce should not be recognised on public policy grounds. A foreign divorce obtained other than in proceedings may be refused recognition, for example, where no document of divorce exists, or where it would be manifestly contrary to public policy. Recognition may also be refused where a foreign divorce is irreconcilable with a previous decision about the subsistence or validity of the marriage or there was no subsisting marriage under UK law.

Some divorces are 'transnational' – they take place in two different countries. The Jewish get and the Muslim talaq are examples. The English courts have refused to recognise transnational divorces even though this creates a 'limping marriage' (a marriage which is recognised as valid in one country but not in another). Thus, in *R* v. *Secretary of State for the Home Department ex parte Ghulum Fatima* [1986] AC 527 the House of Lords refused to recognise a Muslim talaq (a unilateral foreign divorce pronounced by a husband which does not require the wife's consent). However, the courts' power to recognise or fail to recognise a foreign divorce, even a talaq, is discretionary, and in *El Fadl* v. *El Fadl* [2000] 1 FLR 175 a talaq divorce registered with the Sharia court in Lebanon was recognised by the English High Court, and the wife's petition for an English divorce dismissed. Recognition of the talaq was not held to be contrary to public policy, even though such a divorce might offend English sensibilities. In *Berkovits* v. *Grinberg (Attorney-General Intervening)* [1995] Fam 142, the court, applying *Fatima* above, refused to recognise a Jewish get written by the husband in London but delivered to his wife in Israel.

8.9   Other Decrees

Under Part I of the Matrimonial Causes Act 1973 the divorce court also has jurisdiction to grant decrees of nullity (see Chapter 2), decrees of judicial separation and decrees of presumption of death.

(a)   Decree of Judicial Separation

Under s.17 of the Matrimonial Causes Act 1973, divorce county courts and the High Court can grant a decree of judicial separation provided a petitioner can prove one of the five facts in s.1(2) (adultery, unreasonable behaviour etc., see 8.2 above). There is no need to prove irretrievable breakdown of marriage. Most decrees are undefended and heard under the special procedure (see para. 8.5 above), but contested cases may be heard in open court. There is no two-stage procedure (decree nisi followed by decree absolute) as there is for divorce. The effect of a decree is to relieve the petitioner of the obligation to continue living with the respondent (s.18(1)), but the spouses are not obliged to separate. Where a decree of judicial separation is in force and separation is continuing, the surviving spouse is not entitled to succeed to the deceased's spouse's property on his or her intestacy, but judicial separation does not affect a will (s.18(2)). On the grant of a decree, the court has jurisdiction to make orders for ancillary relief under Part II of the Matrimonial Causes Act 1973 (see Chapter 9). Divorce is not precluded by a previous judicial separation and the divorce court can treat the decree of judicial separation as proof of one or more of the five facts alleged for divorce (s.4). Decrees are rarely sought, but a decree may be useful for a spouse who does not wish to divorce (e.g. for religious reasons) or who cannot divorce because one year of marriage has not elapsed. In 1998, 519 decrees nisi of judicial separation were granted (see *Judicial Statistics 1998*).

(b) Decree of Presumption of Death

Where a spouse is missing and thought to be dead, the other spouse can petition for a decree of presumption of death and dissolution of marriage under s.19 of the Matrimonial Causes Act 1973. If a decree is granted, the petitioner can contract a valid new marriage, which remains valid, even if the spouse who is presumed dead subsequently reappears. The court will grant a decree if it is satisfied that reasonable grounds exist for supposing the petitioner's spouse is dead. A spouse is presumed dead if he or she has not been seen for a continuous period of at least seven years. The petitioner must, however, have made reasonable enquiries to establish whether or not the other spouse is alive.

Summary

1 Nearly all divorces today are undefended and dealt with under the special procedure. The law is laid down in Part I of the Matrimonial Causes Act 1973. Procedural rules are laid down in the Family Proceedings Rules 1991.
2 A divorce is commenced by the petitioner presenting a divorce petition to a divorce county court (or the Divorce Registry in London). The other party is called the respondent. Divorce involves a two-stage procedure, i.e. decree nisi and then decree absolute. Only after decree absolute is the marriage terminated.
3 Divorce is not possible within the first year of marriage (s.3(1)).
4 There is one ground for divorce, namely irretrievable breakdown of marriage (s.1(1)). Breakdown is established on proof of one or more of five facts (s.1(2)): (a) adultery; (b) unreasonable behaviour; (c) desertion for a period of at least two years; (d) two years' separation with consent to the divorce; and (e) five years' separation. There must be proof of irretrievable breakdown and proof of at least one fact.
5 The adultery fact requires proof of adultery and proof that the petitioner finds it intolerable to live with the respondent, although the intolerability need not relate to the adultery.
6 The test for 'unreasonable behaviour' is not whether the behaviour is unreasonable, but whether the petitioner can reasonably be expected to live with the respondent.

7 Desertion must be for a continuous period of at least two years and requires: factual separation; an intention to desert; no consent by the petitioner to the desertion; and the respondent must have no just cause to desert. Constructive desertion is possible.

8 For the separation grounds (two years and five years) there can be separation under the same roof, provided the parties are living in separate households (a question of fact in each case).

9 Under s.10 a respondent can ask the court to delay decree absolute until it is satisfied about financial arrangements made by the petitioner for the respondent.

10 Section 5 provides a complete defence to divorce for a respondent to a petition brought on the basis of five years' separation, if the respondent can prove that the dissolution of the marriage will cause him or her grave financial or other hardship, and it would be wrong in all the circumstances to grant the divorce.

11 There are proposals to remove some of the difficulties caused for those who suffer as the result of religious divorce, in particular the Jewish 'get'.

12 The court has jurisdiction to grant a decree of judicial separation if one of the five facts in s.1(2) is proved (see s.17). It also has jurisdiction to grant a decree of presumption of death (see s.19).

Further Reading

See Further Reading and References at the end of Chapter 7.

Questions

1 What criticisms can be made of the law of divorce laid down in Part I of the Matrimonial Causes Act 1973?

2 How could the law be improved?

9 Ancillary Relief on Divorce

9.1 Ancillary Relief

This chapter deals with ancillary relief, in other words finance and property matters, on divorce. It is called 'ancillary relief', as the relief is ancillary to the divorce petition. The law is laid down in Part II of the Matrimonial Causes Act 1973. Procedural rules are contained in the Family Proceedings Rules 1991. The same rules apply to annulments and judicial separations.

Had the new divorce law come into force under Part II of the Family Law Act 1996 (see 7.5), the law on ancillary relief would have been amended, as in most cases the parties would have had to sort out their financial and property matters before obtaining a divorce. Under the present law, however, the situation is different, as obtaining a divorce and sorting out finance and property matters are quite separate. In practice a divorce can be obtained in a matter of weeks, but it can take many months to sort out the financial and property consequences of marriage breakdown.

Although some cases are dealt with in court proceedings, in practice few get to court, as most couples reach agreement about property and finance with or without negotiation and mediation (see 1.3). Many solicitors are members of the Solicitors' Family Law Association whose Code of Practice encourages conciliatory approaches to the resolution of divorce disputes. Settlement and agreement are good both for the parties and for the children. They reduce cost and remove the unpredictability of going to court. If, however, court proceedings are necessary, the court has wide discretionary powers to distribute and reallocate resources according to statutory criteria, such as the needs and resources of the parties. Any arguments based on property law principles such as trusts (see 4.5) do not require investigation, except where there is a genuine third-party interest in any property (Thorpe LJ in *Tee* v. *Tee and Hillman* [1999] 2 FLR 613). While discretion has the advantage of being flexible, it can create uncertainty and unpredictability, and it also involves the court in a time-consuming and expensive exercise.

Despite the emphasis on settlement, some couples still manage to spend vast sums of money on legal costs, particularly where they have substantial assets to fight over. For example, in *F* v. *F (Ancillary Relief: Substantial Assets)* [1995] 2 FLR 45, the wife's costs were £733 521 and the husband's £777 182. Even where the parties assets are not substantial the legal costs may still be high, as they were in *Piglowska* v. *Piglowski* [1999] 2 FLR 763, where they were estimated to exceed £120 000. In *Evans* v. *Evans (Practice Note)*

[1990] 1 WLR 575, where the parties had run up costs of £60000, Booth J, with the approval of the President of the Family Division, issued guidelines to be followed by practitioners in the preparation of cases in order to reduce costs. These included keeping clients informed of the costs at all stages of proceedings and requiring parties to obtain joint valuations of matrimonial property. However, under the recently reformed ancillary relief rules (see below), judges now have greater powers to control proceedings with the aim of reducing costs in property and finance cases.

The courts exercise their discretionary powers across a wide spectrum of human life. In *Dart* v. *Dart* [1996] 2 FLR 286, Butler-Sloss LJ stated at 303:

'The Matrimonial Causes Act 1973, as amended in 1984, provides the jurisdiction for all applications for ancillary relief from the poverty-stricken to
the multimillionaire. It is obvious that a court, in the exercise of the discretion provided by ss.25 and 25A, will apply the relevant criteria according to
the widely differing facts of each case before it .... '

Where the parties are wealthy, orders for vast sums of money may be made, but at the other end of the spectrum the court may have to consider finance and property issues in the context of state benefits and local authority housing. In low-income cases, 'the assessment of the needs of the parties will lean heavily in favour of the children and the parent with whom they live' (Butler-Sloss LJ in *Dart* above, at p.303).

Until the decision of the House of Lords in *White* v. *White* [2000] 2 FLR 981, in 'big money' cases the courts had adopted a 'reasonable requirements' approach rather than dividing the property equally. In *Dart* above, Thorpe LJ said (at p.296) that the essential function of the judge is 'to declare the bound-ary between the applicant's reasonable and unreasonable requirements, apply-ing all the statutory criteria to the myriad relevant facts of the case.' In *Dart*, the wife was awarded £9 million, despite her husband's wealth which was in excess of £400 million. Had a presumption of a 50/50 split existed in English law, as exists in some other jurisdictions, then Mrs Dart would have obtained much more (see also *Conran* v. *Conran* [1997] 2 FLR 615).

However, in *White* v. *White* (above), where the House of Lords for the first time had to consider broad questions about how the courts should exercise their powers under s.25(2) of the Matrimonial Causes Act (see below) in 'big money' cases, Lord Nicholls said that the aim in ancillary relief cases is for the court to make fair financial arrangements on divorce, and that as a general guide equal division of matrimonial assets on divorce should be departed from only if there is good reason for doing so. Only in this way could discrimina-tion be avoided. Thus in *White*, where the husband and wife had been in busi-ness together, the House of Lords rejected the husband's argument that the wife's reasonable requirements were to be regarded as determinative (see further at 9.4 and 9.7 below).

As far as trends are concerned, Barton and Bissett-Johnson (2000) have analysed applications for ancillary relief by looking at *Judicial Statistics* from 1985 to 1998. They have noted a 'modest rise' in lump sum and property orders and a 'severe drop' in periodical payment orders for spouses and for children. They say that the reason for this trend has been the introduction of the 'clean break' provisions (see 9.4) and the introduction of child support (see 14.2). Although there has been a sharp increase in the number of consent orders granted in the last 15 years (39 per cent of orders made in 1985 compared with 75 per cent in 1998), overall the number of claims for ancillary relief has declined. Barton and Bissett-Johnson identify two major factors responsible for this decline: the increase in the number of short marriages, and child-free divorces involving parties who have not built up much equity in their family home; and the introduction of child support maintenance. They suggest, however, that 'the essential point' of the *Judicial Statistics* is the fact that the emphasis is now on settlement, and a non-adversarial culture.

9.2   Procedure in Ancillary Relief Applications

In June 2000 important changes were made to the ancillary relief rules, after a successful pilot scheme involving a new procedure formulated in 1992 by the Lord Chancellor's Advisory Group on Ancillary Relief Procedure had been conducted in selected county courts throughout the country and in the Principal Registry of the Family Division (see *Practice Direction: Ancillary Relief Procedure: Pilot Scheme* [1996] 2 FLR 368). The new scheme was implemented nationwide in all courts on 5 June 2000. The new rules are laid down in the Family Proceedings (Amendment No 2) Rules 1999, which has amended the Family Proceedings Rules 1991. They were introduced because, despite the guidelines in *Evans* (see above), ancillary relief cases were taking too long, costing too much and too few parties were reaching settlement. The new rules apply to all applications commenced after 5 June 2000. Cases commenced before that date are governed by the old rules, although the court can direct that the new rules shall apply.

A hearing for ancillary relief takes place before the district judge in the divorce county court (or the Principal Registry in London) seized of the divorce petition, but the case can be referred to the judge (r.2.65), and a complex or serious case can be transferred to the High Court (s.39 Matrimonial and Family Proceedings Act 1984). Except for maintenance pending suit and orders to or for the benefit of any child of the family, an order cannot be made unless a decree nisi has been granted and, if made, cannot take effect until decree absolute. The court can stay ancillary relief proceedings on an application where they will be more appropriately decided in a foreign juris-diction (*W* v. *W (Financial Relief: Appropriate Forum)* [1997] 1 FLR 257).

Under the new rules the parties must attend a First Appointment before the district judge where the issues are defined and directions made, where neces-sary. At the next stage, the parties attend a Financial Dispute Resolution (FDR) appointment where the district judge helps the parties reach agreement. If this fails, the dispute must be decided in court proceedings. Thus, litigation only takes place if all else fails. Written estimates of costs must be provided at each hearing (on Form H), so that parties are fully aware of the costs being incurred (r.2.61F(1)).

The aim of the new rules is to reduce delay, facilitate settlement, and limit costs by giving the court greater control over the conduct of proceedings. It is the court, rather than the parties (or their lawyers) that manages the way in which proceedings progress. The new scheme also aims to encourage unifor-mity of practice and procedure between courts. Under the rules, the court must actively manage cases to ensure that all couples co-operate in the conduct of proceedings. The district judge must encourage the parties to settle differences through mediation, fix timetables, restrict expert evidence and make use of information technology. The parties are required to further the overriding objective of dealing with cases justly (see below). Previous case-law still continues to apply.

The Overriding Objective

The 'overriding objective' in ancillary relief cases is that they must be dealt with 'justly' (r.2.51B(1)). Dealing with a case justly requires the district judge, so far as is practicable, to deal with the case with a view to (r.2.51B(2)): ensuring parties are on an equal footing; saving expense; dealing with cases in ways which are proportionate to the amount of money involved, the impor-tance of the case, the complexity of the issues, and to the financial position of each party; ensuring that the case is dealt with expeditiously and fairly; and allotting to cases an appropriate share of the court's resources, while taking into account the need to allot resources to other cases. The court must give effect to the overriding objective when exercising any power or interpreting any rule (r.2.51B(3)), and the parties themselves are required to help the court to further the overriding objective (r.2.51B(4)).

Active Case Management

To further the overriding objective of dealing with cases justly, the district judge must engage in active case management (r.2.51B(5)), which includes (r.2.51B(6)): enouraging parties to co-operate with each other in the conduct of proceedings; encouraging the parties to settle by mediation, if appropriate; identifying issues; regulating the disclosure of documents and expert evidence so that they are proportionate to the issues in question; helping parties to settle the whole or part of a case; fixing timetables or otherwise controlling the progress of the case; making use of technology; and giving directions to ensure that the trial of a case proceeds quickly and efficiently.

Making an Application for Ancillary Relief

To commence proceedings, an application for ancillary relief is made by notice in Form A (Notice of Intention to Proceed with an Application for Ancillary Relief) (r.2.61A(1)), which is filed by the applicant in the court seized of the divorce petition (r.2.61A(2)). Where the applicant requests an order to be made under s.25B or s.25C in respect of a pension, the terms of the order requested must be specified in the notice in Form A (r.2.61A(3)). Once Form A is filed, the court fixes a time for the First Appointment (which will be between 12 and 16 weeks of filing Form A), gives notice of that date, and serves a copy of Form A on the respondent within 4 days of it being filed (r.2.61A(4)). The date for the First Appointment can only be cancelled with the permission of the court, but if it is cancelled, the court must immediately fix a new date (r.2.61A(5)).

The First Appointment

The aim of the First Appointment is to define the issues and make directions, so that the parties can reach agreement, if possible. This early Appointment is similar to the system of 'initial hearings' recommended by the Booth Committee in 1985 (see 7.2 and 7.3). Both parties must attend (unless the court orders otherwise) (r.2.61D(5)). The Appointment is fixed by the court and the district judge's duty is to conduct the Appointment with the objective of defining the issues and saving costs (r.2.61D(1)).

Before the First Appointment, both parties must, at the same time, exchange with each other, and each file with the court, a statement in Form E which must be signed by the party who made the statement, be sworn to be true, and contain the required information and have attached to it the required documents (r.2.61B(1)). Form E is an important form, as it seeks to limit the evidence to current circumstances and to avoid provocative allegations in relation to the history of the marriage which might encourage hostility and reduce the chances of a settlement. It replaces the old affidavit (sworn statement).

Form E must be exchanged and filed not less than 35 days before the date of the First Appointment (r.2.6B(2)). It must have attached to it the required documents (and no others), and any documents needed to explain or clarify any of the information contained in Form E (r.2.61B(3) and (4)). At least 14 days before the First Appointment, each party must file with the court and serve on the other party: a concise statement of the issues between the parties; a chronology; a questionnaire setting out by reference to the concise statement of issues any further information and documents requested from the other party, or a statement that no information and documents are required; and a notice on Form G (Notice of Response to First Appointment) stating whether that party will be in a position to proceed on that occasion to a Financial Dispute Resolution (FDR) appointment (r.2.61B(7)).

At the First Appointment the district judge has various powers (r.2.61D(2)), such as directing that further documents be produced, giving directions about the valuation of assets, directing that the case be referred to a Financial Dispute Resolution (FDR) Appointment, or directing a further Directions Appointment. The district judge can also direct that an appointment be fixed for making an interim order, or that the case be fixed for a final hearing, or that the case be adjourned for out-of court mediation or private negotiation. The district judge may also (r.2.61D(2)) make an interim order, or treat the appointment (or part of it) as a FDR Appointment.

The Financial Dispute Resolution (FDR) Appointment

Both parties must personally attend the Financial Dispute Resolution (FDR) Appointment, unless the court orders otherwise (r.2.61E(9)). Not later than seven days before the FDR Appointment, the applicant must file with the court details of all offers and proposals, and responses to them (r.2.61E(3)). The aim of the FDR Appointment is for an attempt to be made to reach a negotiated settlement through the intervention of a third party (usually the district judge) but without the third party having the power to impose a solution. The emphasis at the FDR Appointment is on encouraging the parties to settle their dispute. They must use their 'best endeavours to reach agreement on the matters in issue between them' (r.2.61E(6)). The FDR Appointment may take place at the First Appointment (see above), or subsequently. At the FDR Appointment, proposals for resolving the application are discussed in circumstances of privilege. For this reason the district judge (or judge) must have no further involvement with the application, other than to conduct any further FDR Appointment, or to make a consent order or a further directions hearing order (r.2.61E(2)). The Appointment may be adjourned from time to time (r.2.61E(7)). At the conclusion of the Appointment the court may make the appropriate consent order, but otherwise must give directions for the future course of proceedings, including, where appropriate, the filing of evidence and fixing a final hearing date (r.2.61E(9)).

A Practice Direction (*Practice Direction (Ancillary Relief Procedure) (25 May 2000)* [2000] 1 FLR 997) clarifies the new rules. It emphasises the importance of the FDR Appointment in the settlement process and states that the parties should approach it openly and without reserve. It also emphasises the privileged nature of the Appointment and the rule in *In Re D (Minors) (Conciliation: Disclosure of Information)* [1993] Fam 231 that any statements made at the Appointment cannot be used as evidence in subsequent court proceedings, other than in exceptional circumstances. Annexed to the *Practice Direction* is a 'Pre-Application Protocol' which outlines the steps parties must take to seek and provide information. It also lays down a set of rules governing ancillary relief applications, for example the importance of resolving disputes justly and speedily, safeguarding the interests of children, ensuring that costs are not out of proportion to the assets available, clarifying aims and identifying issues. The court expects the parties to comply with the terms of the Protocol.

If agreement cannot be reached at the FDR Appointment, the case proceeds to a full court hearing.

Appeals in Contested Cases

As the court in ancillary relief cases has wide discretionary powers, an appeal against a decision will only be successful if there has been an error of law or the decision was outside a band of reasonable discretion. In *G* v. *G (Minors: Custody Appeal)* [1985] 1 WLR 647, Lord Fraser at 651–652 laid down the following principle:

> 'It is, of course, not enough for the wife to establish that this court might, or would, have made a different order. We are here concerned with a judicial discretion, and it is of the essence of such a discretion that on the same evidence two different minds might reach widely different decisions without either being appealable. It is only where the decision exceeds the generous ambit within which reasonable disagreement is possible, and is, in fact, plainly wrong, that an appellate body is entitled to interfere.'

In *Piglowska* v. *Piglowski* [1999] 2 FLR 763 Lord Fraser's words were approved by the House of Lords and Lord Hoffmann, who gave the leading opinion, explained some of its implications. His Lordship said that an appeal court must bear in mind the advantage which the trial judge has had in seeing the parties and the other witnesses, and that this did not just apply to questions of credibility and findings of fact, but also to the judge's evaluation of facts. Lord Hoffmann also warned that an appeal court should not override a trial judge's discretion by a narrow textual analysis of the judgment in order to claim that the judge had misdirected himself. As the s.25 factors and any guidelines laid down by the court involve value judgments on which reasonable people, including judges, may differ, the appeal court must permit a degree of pluralism in these matters. Lord Hoffmann also referred to the principle of proportionality between the amount of property assets at stake and the legal resources of the parties and the community. For this reason, Lord Hoffmann said it was important for appeals to be made only where cases raised an important point of principle or practice, or where there was some compelling reason for an appeal. Parties should therefore be aware of the difficulty of bringing an appeal, and if so, of being successful.

A Duty of Full and Frank Disclosure

Both parties have a duty to make full and frank disclosure of all matrimonial assets and other relevant up-to-date information, for without this the court will be unable properly to exercise its discretion. This strict rule applies both to mediation sessions and court proceedings. Without full disclosure the court will be unable to satisfy the overriding objective which is to deal with cases 'justly' (see above). Failure to make full and frank disclosure is a serious matter and may result in an order being set aside (*Jenkins* v. *Livesey (formerly Jenkins)* [1985] AC 424, *sub nom Livesey (Formerly Jenkins)* v. *Jenkins* [1985] FLR 813, see 9.10 below). The court is also entitled to draw appropriate adverse inferences from any failure to make full and frank disclosure (see *Baker* v. *Baker* [1995] 2 FLR 829). Although the court may impose the penalty of costs on a dishonest party, it cannot reduce a party's share of the assets as a penalty (*P* v. *P (Financial Relief: Non-Disclosure)* [1994] 2 FLR 381).

9.3   Orders that can be Granted

Under Part II of the Matrimonial Causes Act 1973 the court can make the following orders:

(a) Maintenance Pending Suit (s.22)

Maintenance pending suit takes effect on commencement of proceedings but terminates when the divorce suit is determined, unless the court makes the order for a shorter period. The court is required to make such order as it thinks 'reasonable'. The s.25 guidelines (see below) do not apply, but the court performs a similar exercise. The court has a wide discretion and in a suitable case may order substantial maintenance (see, for example, *F* v. *F (Ancillary Relief: Substantial Assets)* [1995] 2 FLR 45, where the husband was ordered to pay maintenance pending suit of £360 000 p.a.).

(b) Financial Provision Orders (s.23)

The following orders for financial provision can be made in favour of a spouse and to or for the benefit of any child of the family aged under 18 or who is being educated or trained (or where special circumstances exist) (ss.23(1), 29(1) and (3)).

(i) Periodical Payments Orders

Periodical payments can be made in favour of a spouse and to or for the benefit of children, although child maintenance in most cases must be sought from the Child Support Agency, not the court (see 14.2). Periodical payments can be secured or unsecured. If unsecured, payment is made from unsecured income. If secured, capital assets or other property are charged as security for payment, with the exception of the matrimonial home, which the court does not usually charge. Periodical payments in favour of a spouse automatically terminate on the payee spouse's remarriage (s.28(1)).

(ii) Lump Sum Orders

Lump sum orders can be made in favour of a spouse and to or for the benefit of any children (s.23(1)). A lump sum order may be ordered to enable liabilities and expenses reasonably incurred by a spouse or a child prior to the application to be met (s.23(3)(a) and (b)). A lump sum can be ordered to be paid in instalments (s.23(3)(c)), and may incur interest if the order is deferred or payable by instalments (s.23(6)).

A lump sum is usually ordered in preference to periodical payments because it effects a clean break between the parties. A lump sum can be made to represent 'capitalised maintenance', whereby the sum is invested to provide the recipient with an income. Substantial sums are sometimes ordered (see for example, *Gojkovic* v. *Gojkovic* [1992] Fam 40, where the wife received a lump sum of £1.3 million). To help calculate a lump sum representing 'capitalised maintenance', a computer program called the *'Duxbury* calculation' is sometimes used in cases involving substantial assets. The program, named after *Duxbury* v. *Duxbury* [1987] 1 FLR 7, where it was first mentioned, takes into account variables (e.g. inflation, life expectancy, income tax, capital growth of and income from investments) to calculate a lump sum which, when invested, will produce sufficient income for the payee for life. Although the *Duxbury* program is a useful tool, the court will not allow it to derogate in any way from its wide discretionary powers (see, for example, *Vicary* v. *Vicary* [1992] 2 FLR 271, *B* v. *B (Financial Provision)* [1990] 1 FLR 20 and *White* v. *White* [2000] 2 FLR 981). Thus the court can order a lump sum which is larger or smaller than the sum calculated under a *Duxbury* calculation, and in an appropriate case can ignore it altogether. In *A* v. *A (Elderly Applicant: Lump Sum)* [1999] 2 FLR 969, for example, Singer J reduced the lump sum payable, as the *Duxbury* technique, however flexibly applied, would not meet the justice of the case. Here, the elderly husband's significant contribution to the lengthy marriage needed recognition in monetary terms. The *Duxbury* formula was also held to be inappropriate in *Fournier* v. *Fournier* [1999] 2 FLR 990, where the wife had a life expectancy exceeding 40 years. The *Duxbury* calculation is therefore only 'a starting-point or guide' (Holman J in *F* v. *F (Duxbury Calculations: Rate of Return)* [1996] 1 FLR 833). In *White* v. *White* (2000, see above) the Court of Appeal held that the *Duxbury* guidelines would be irrelevant and misleading where both parties worked together in a business partnership, and stressed that the *Duxbury* method ought to be applied flexibly.

A lump sum made in favour of a spouse is a final order which cannot be varied under s.31, and only one lump sum order can be made (the plural reference to 'lump sums' in s.23(1)(c) is to allow payment by instalment). However, to avoid the potential injustice caused by the finality of lump sum orders, proceedings may be adjourned. In *MT* v. *MT (Financial Provision: Lump Sum)* [1992] 1 FLR 363, the spouses had no assets from which a lump sum could be ordered other than a substantial sum which the husband was certain to inherit under German law from the estate of his father aged 83. Bracewell J held that to do justice in a case where there was a long marriage, the court has a discretion to adjourn proceedings where there is a real possibility of capital from a specific source becoming available in the near future (see also *Michael* v. *Michael* [1986] 2 FLR 389 and *Milne* v. *Milne* (1981) FLR 286). The court might, for example, be prepared to adjourn proceedings where a pension is about to be paid.

Lump sum orders in favour of a child are not final orders, as the power to make orders for children is 'exercisable from time to time' (s.23(4)). However, in practice, lump sums are rarely made for children, unless substantial assets are available. The court may be unwilling to order a lump sum to be paid to a spouse for the benefit of a child as the spouse may dissipate the fund and use it for the wrong purpose (*Griffiths* v. *Griffiths* [1974] 1 WLR 1350). A lump sum order made in favour of a child must take effect during the child's minority (*Kiely* v. *Kiely* [1988] 1 FLR 248).

(c) Property Adjustment Orders

(i) A Transfer of Property Order (s.24(1)(a))

A transfer of property order directs one spouse to transfer specified property to the other spouse and/or to or for the benefit of a child of the family. Any property can be transferred, but the order is commonly used to transfer the matrimonial home – usually to the party with whom the children will live. The transferee may be given a charge over the house for a fixed amount or a percentage of the value, which is realisable at a later date, for example when the house is sold. The transferee may be ordered to pay the transferor a lump sum representing the latter's share in the former matrimonial home. A transfer of property is a useful way of effecting a 'clean break' (see below), e.g. a husband could be ordered to transfer investments to his wife so that she can live on the income; or he could be ordered to transfer the matrimonial home to his wife, with her agreeing to forego any claim for spousal maintenance.

(ii) A Settlement of Property Order (s.24(1)(b))

This order directs a spouse to settle property for the benefit of the other spouse and/or any child of the family. Under a settlement, property is held on trust for certain beneficiaries who have an interest in the property.

(iii) A Variation of Settlement (Ante-nuptial or Post-nuptial) Order (s.24(1)(c) and (d))

This order can be made for the benefit of the parties and/or any child of the family. As settlements are rare, so are variations of settlements (but see *E* v. *E (Financial Provision)* [1990] 2 FLR 233, where £1.25 million was ordered to be transferred to the wife and children from a settlement held on discretionary trusts, and *Brooks* v. *Brooks* [1996] 1 AC 375, where a pension arrangement was construed as a post-nuptial settlement and thereby capable of variation).

(d) Order for the Sale of Property (s.24A)

The court can make an order for the sale of property (or proceeds of sale of property) in which one or both spouses has a beneficial interest, but it can only do so if it makes, or has made, a secured periodical payments, lump sum or property adjustment order. The power to order sale gives the court a useful enforcement mechanism where there is, or is likely to be, non-compliance with an order. For example, where a spouse has failed to pay a lump sum, the court can order that property belonging to that spouse be sold and direct that the proceeds of sale be paid to the party who should have received the lump sum (s.24A(2)(a)). The court can defer sale until a specified event has occurred or a specified period of time has expired (s.24A(4)). It can also order that property be offered for sale to a specified person or persons (s.24A(2)(b)). A third party with an interest in the property in dispute (e.g. a mortgagee) must be allowed to make representations to the court, and the third-party's interest must be included as one of the circumstances of the case when the court performs its discretionary exercise (s.24A(6)).

9.4   How the Court Exercises its Powers

The court has considerable discretion when exercising its powers under Part II of the Matrimonial Causes Act 1973. In *Thomas* v. *Thomas* [1995] 2 FLR 668, Waite LJ said at p.670:

'The discretionary powers conferred on the court by the amended ss.23–25A of the Matrimonial Causes Act 1973 to redistribute the assets of spouses are almost limitless. That represents an acknowledgement by Parliament that if justice is to be achieved between spouses at divorce the court must be equipped, in a society where the forms of wealth-holding are diverse and often sophisticated, to penetrate the outer forms and get to the heart of ownership … .'

However, judicial discretion is not completely unchecked as the court must apply the s.25 guidelines, and consider whether to effect a clean break between the parties. Because the court reaches a decision based on the facts of each case, earlier cases do not create precedents in the strict sense. In *White* v. *White* [2000] 2 FLR 981, the Court of Appeal emphasised the width of discretion in ancillary relief proceedings, and warned against too rigid an application of reported decisions. Thorpe LJ (at p.318) stressed that each case depended on its own unique facts, and that those facts determined which of the eight factors in s.25(2) should be given particular prominence. Butler-Sloss LJ (at p.22) warned family law practitioners of the danger of attempting to apply earlier decisions too rigidly without sufficiently recognising that each case involving a family has to be decided upon broad principles adapted to the facts of the individual case. In *Piglowska* v. *Piglowski* (1999), Lord Hoffmann also warned against a rigid application of guidelines laid down in earlier cases.

At one time the courts used the so-called 'one-third' rule as a starting point for assessing the parties' income and capital needs (see *Wachtel* v. *Wachtel*

[1973] Fam 72). Applied to income it would order the husband to pay periodical payments to his wife to bring her income (if any) up to one-third of their joint income. The one-third approach, however, was discredited in later decisions and is rarely used (but see *Bullock* v. *Bullock* [1986] 1 FLR 372 and *Dew* v. *Dew* [1986] 2 FLR 341 where it was used as a starting point to calculate capital distribution). Today, when it is lump sums, rather than periodical payments, which are ordered, the 'one-third' rule has little application.

In recent cases, particularly 'big money' cases, it has been argued (usually by wives) that a 50/50 division of matrimonial assets should be the starting point for the court. For example, in *Dart* v. *Dart* [1996] 2 FLR 286 the wife argued in favour of a 50/50 starting point and sought a lump sum of £122 million and the matrimonial home in the USA. However, the Court of Appeal held that it was not the practice of the English courts to be bound by any fixed percentage. The s.25 criteria must be applied. There was no justification for applying a mathematical solution in such a case. The correct test for assessing the quantum was the applicant's reasonable requirements, while having regard to the other criteria in s.25. There was no justification for going beyond the spouse's needs, based on homes, children and life-style. However, Butler-Sloss LJ did express some reservation as to whether 'the courts may not have imposed too restrictive an interpretation upon the words of s.25 and given too great weight to reasonable requirements over other criteria set out in the section.' *Dart* can be contrasted, however, with *Burgess* v. *Burgess* [1996] 2 FLR 34, where the Court of Appeal held that equal division or some other proportion could be a starting point, provided that such a starting point was never allowed the status of a rule or principle governing, as opposed to initiating, the exercise of judicial discretion.

In *White* v. *White* [2000] 2 FLR 981, the House of Lords (see further at 9.6) made some important statements of principle about how the court should perform its discretionary exercise under s.25 of the Matrimonial Causes Act. Lord Nicholls, who gave the leading opinion, stressed the importance of achieving a fair result in ancillary relief cases:

> 'Self-evidently, fairness requires the court to take into account all the circumstances of the case ... But there is one principle of universal application which can be stated with confidence. In seeking to achieve a fair outcome, there is no place for discrimination between husband and wife and their respective roles.... There should be no bias in favour of the money-earner and against the home-maker and the child-carer.'

Lord Nicholls then went on to say, however, that although there was no presumption of equal division of matrimonial assets on divorce, as a general guide equal division of assets should be departed from only if there is good reason for doing so. His Lordship said that the 'need to consider and articulate reasons for departing from equality would help the parties and the court to focus on the need to ensure the absence of discrimination.' His Lordship said:

'This is not to introduce a presumption of equal division under another guise. Generally accepted standards of fairness in a field such as this change and develop, sometimes quite radically, over comparatively short periods of time. The discretionary powers, conferred by Parliament 30 years ago, enable the courts to recognise and respond to developments of this sort. These wide powers enable the courts to make financial provision orders in tune with current perceptions of fairness. Today there is greater awareness of the value of non-financial contributions to the welfare of the family. There is greater awareness of the extent to which one spouse's business success, achieved by much sustained hard work over many years, may have been made possible or enhanced by the family contribution of the other spouse .... There is increased recognition that, by being at home and having and looking after young children, a wife may lose for ever the opportunity to acquire and develop her own money-earning qualifications and skills ....

Despite these changes, a presumption of equal division would go beyond the permissible bounds of interpretation of section 25 .... A presumption of equal division would be an impermissible judicial gloss on the statutory provision .... Whether there should be such a presumption in England and Wales, and in respect of what assets, is a matter for Parliament.'

White v. *White* therefore provides highest judicial authority for a greater emphasis on equal division than has hitherto been the case, and the decision is likely to have a considerable influence on the way in which the courts will exercise their discretionary powers under s.25 to adjust matrimonial assets on divorce. (For more discussion on the introduction of a 50/50 split of assets on divorce, see 9.14.)

(a) The 's.25 Guidelines'

When exercising its powers to make orders (except maintenance pending suit) the court must consider all the circumstances of the case, but give first consideration to the welfare of any child of the family aged under 18 (s.25(1)). When exercising its powers in favour of a party to a marriage, it must also consider the factors laid down in s.25(2). Which of the factors in s.25(2) will carry most weight depends on the facts of each case; s.25(2) does not create a hierarchy of factors (Lord Hoffmann in *Piglowska* v. *Piglowski* (2000), see above).

S.25(2)(a) The income, earning capacity, property and other financial resources which each of the parties to the marriage has or is likely to have in the foreseeable future, including in the case of earning capacity any increase in that capacity which it would in the opinion of the court be reasonable to expect a party to the marriage to take steps to acquire The court is 'not obliged to limit its orders exclusively to resources of capital or income which are shown actually to exist' (Waite LJ in *Thomas* v. *Thomas* [1995] 2 FLR 668 at 670). It may in an appropriate case impute a notional earning capacity, or infer that unidentified resources are available from a spouse's expenditure or style of living. Future earning potential is a particularly important consideration when the court is deciding whether to terminate the financial obligations of the parties to effect a clean break.

In *Schuller* v. *Schuller* [1990] 2 FLR 193 the Court of Appeal stated that the word 'resources' is entirely unqualified; there are no words of limitation on it. Thus the court can take into account resources such as business profits, interest on investments, insurance policies, pension rights and welfare benefits. As future financial resources must be considered, the court may postpone making an order if financial resources are likely to be available, or likely to increase, in the relatively near future. Future financial resources might include gratuities receivable upon retirement or upon termination of employment, or inheritances (*Michael* v. *Michael* [1986] 2 FLR 389, *H* v. *H (Financial Provision: Capital Allowance)* [1993] 2 FLR 335), or interests under a trust, or assets tied up in a business which are realisable at a later date. Damages for personal injury have been taken into account (*Daubney* v. *Daubney* [1976] Fam 267, *Wagstaff* v. *Wagstaff* [1992] 1 WLR 320, *C* v. *C (Financial Provision: Personal Damages* [1995] 2 FLR 171) and a beneficial interest under a discretionary trust outside the jurisdiction (*Browne* v. *Browne* [1989] 1 FLR 291). The income of a new spouse or cohabitant may be taken into account (*Macey* v. *Macey* (1982) FLR 7). The court is also required to take into account any pension scheme which a party to a marriage has or is likely to have, and in relation to the benefits in a pension scheme, s.25(2)(a) must be read as if the words 'in the foreseeable future' were omitted (s.25B(1)).

S.25(2)(b) The financial needs, obligations and responsibilities which each of the parties to the marriage has or is likely to have in the foreseeable future Financial needs include, for example, the provision of accommodation and general living expenses. If there are children, the financial needs of the parent with whom the children are to live are likely to be greater than those of the other parent, particularly if the residential parent is not working. The court will take these factors into account. The court used to consider only reasonable needs. In *Leadbetter* v. *Leadbetter* [1985] FLR 789, for example, it was held that the wife could not justify the purchase of a three-bedroomed house even though her husband's assets totalled about £1.5 million. By contrast, in *Delaney* v. *Delaney* [1990] 2 FLR 457 it was reasonable for the husband to take out a mortgage to buy a house for his new partner which would provide a place where the children of his former marriage could stay. However, in *White* v. *White* (above) Lord Nicholls disapproved of the principle of reasonable needs or requirements laid down in earlier cases, and held that the 'financial needs' of the parties should not be allowed to prevail over the general principle that the division of matrimonial assets should be fair in all the circumstances. Lord Nicholls said:

'On the facts of a particular case there may be good reason why the wife should be confined to her needs and the husband left with the much larger balance. But the mere absence of financial need cannot, by itself, be a sufficient reason. If it were, discrimination would be creeping in by the back door.'

S.25(2)(c)   The standard of living enjoyed by the family before the breakdown of marriage   However, it is often impossible, unless there are substantial assets available, for the parties to enjoy the same standard of living as they did before divorce.

S.25(2)(d)   The age of each party to the marriage and the duration of the marriage   The ages of the parties and the duration of the marriage are relevant to the parties' financial needs and obligations. The needs and resources of a young couple whose marriage has been short are likely to be quite different from those of an older couple after a long marriage. As far as cohabitation before marriage is concerned, the general rule is that it will not be counted, as marital obligations and needs begin on, and not before, marriage (*Foley* v. *Foley* [1981] 2 All ER 857). However, pre-marital cohabitation may be taken into account in exceptional cases, as it was in *Kokosinski* v. *Kokosinski* [1980] Fam 72, where the parties were unable to marry for many years because of political reasons. In exceptional cases, periods of cohabitation after divorce may be considered (*Chatterjee* v. *Chatterjee* [1976] Fam 199). Each case, however, depends on its facts, and as cohabitation is now more common and socially acceptable, the courts may be more willing to take it into account.

S.25(2)(e)   Any physical or mental disability of either of the parties to the marriage

S.25(2)(f)   The contribution which each of the parties has made or is likely in the foreseeable future to make to the welfare of the family, including any contribution by looking after the home or caring for the family   Contribution to the welfare of the family, including looking after the home, is also considered. Failure to make a contribution may also be taken into account, as it was in *West* v. *West* [1978] Fam 1, where the wife refused to set up home with her husband but looked after the children at her parents' house. In *Vicary* v. *Vicary* [1992] 2 FLR 271, the wife's contributions to the family were taken into account, even though she had made no financial contribution to the family assets. Purchas LJ held that no distinction should be made between a wife who had contributed directly to a business and one who had supplied the infrastructure and support for the family, while the husband was able to prosper and accumulate wealth. The wife's contributions to the family were also considered to be important in *Piglowska* v. *Piglowski* (1999), see above.

S.25(2)(g)   The conduct of each of the parties, if that conduct is such that it would in the opinion of the court be inequitable to disregard it   Only conduct of an extreme kind is taken into account, otherwise it would contradict the policy of divorce law, which is not to apportion blame. In *Wachtel* v. *Wachtel* [1973] Fam 72, Lord Denning MR said that conduct must be 'obvious and gross' before it can be taken into account. In *Duxbury* v. *Duxbury* [1987] 1 FLR 7, the husband's argument that his wife's adultery should be taken into account was rejected by the Court of Appeal, with Ackner LJ stating that the s.25 exercise was essentially a financial and not a moral exercise. The following conduct, for example, has been taken into account: causing serious injury to a spouse (*Jones (M)* v. *Jones (W)* [1976] Fam 8); malicious persecution by a schizophrenic spouse (*J (HD)* v. *J (AM) (Financial Provision: Variation)* [1980] 1 WLR 124); dissipating family assets (*Martin* v. *Martin* [1976] 2 WLR 901); committing adultery with a father-in-law (*Bailey* v. *Tolliday* [1983] 4 FLR 542); alcoholism causing disagreeable behaviour and neglect of the home (*K* v. *K (Conduct)* [1990] 2 FLR 225); inciting the murder of a spouse (*Evans* v. *Evans* [1989] 1 FLR 351); and assisting a spouse's suicide (*K* v. *K (Financial Provision: Conduct)* [1988] 1 FLR 469). However, even where there is serious misconduct, the court retains a discretion to discount it. Thus, in *A* v. *A (Financial Provision: Conduct)* [1995] 1 FLR 345, a depressed and suicidal husband had assaulted his wife with a knife, but Thorpe J allowed his appeal, holding that although an assault constituted conduct which it would be inequitable to disregard, other s.25 factors had to be taken into account. A recent case where a wife's conduct was taken into account was *Clark* v. *Clark* [1999] 2 FLR 498. Here the marriage had not been consummated, and the wife had induced her husband, who was 36 years her senior, to buy property most of which was transferred into her name. She relegated him to a caravan in their garden, and later on made him a virtual prisoner in his own home.

If the court considers that the conduct is sufficiently serious to be taken into account, it has a discretion to decide what order, if any, to make, taking into account all the other matters in s.25. In *H* v. *H (Financial Provision: Conduct)* [1998] 1 FLR 971, where the husband's conduct was held to be too inequitable to ignore (he had transferred money for three years into a Swiss bank account), Singer J said that the approach to be taken was not to fix a sum as a 'penalty', but to carry out an evaluation based on all the relevant factors taken in the round. Where there is misconduct in respect of the process of the case (e.g. failure to give full and frank disclosure) this generally only affects costs (see *Tavoulareas* v. *Tavoulareas* [1998] 2 FLR 418 and *Young* v. *Young* [1998] 2 FLR 1131), but in an exceptional case (as in *Clark* above), it can be taken into account when assessing the substantive order. In some cases the court may dismiss the application without making an order at all. Thus, in *Whiston* v. *Whiston* [1995] 2 FLR 268, a person who had committed bigamy was barred from seeking ancillary relief, and in *S-T (formerly J)* v. *J* [1998] Fam 103 *sub nom J* v. *S-T (Formerly J)(Transsexual: Ancillary Relief)* [1997] 1 FLR 402 a transsexual's deception as to his sexual identity led to his application for ancillary relief in nullity proceedings being dismissed on the grounds of public policy.

S.25(2)(h)   In the case of proceedings for divorce or nullity of marriage, the value to each of the parties to the marriage of any benefit which by reason of the dissolution or annulment of the marriage, that party will lose the chance of acquiring   On divorce a spouse may lose certain property rights and interests, for example the benefit of a pension, the surrender value of an insurance policy, future business profits, or being able to succeed to the other spouse's estate. The court can take these and other lost future benefits into account. It might, for example, decide to increase an order for financial provision to compensate for the loss of future benefits or make a deferred lump sum order or adjourn proceedings. However, the position in respect of pensions has been improved (see 9.7 below).

(b) The 'Clean Break' Provisions

Under s.25A, when exercising its powers to make ancillary relief orders in favour of a spouse (not a child), the court must consider whether to effect a 'clean break' between the parties either to take effect immediately or at some time in the future. The clean break provisions were inserted into Part II of the Matrimonial Causes Act 1973 by Part II of the Matrimonial and Family Proceedings Act 1984 after the Law Commission (*The Financial Consequences of Divorce*, Law Com No 112) had recommended that greater weight should be given to a divorced wife's earning capacity and to the desirability of spouses becoming financially self-sufficient on divorce, where possible. Before the 1984 Act a clean break could be imposed only if a spouse agreed to it (see *Dipper* v. *Dipper* [1981] Fam 31, [1980] 1 FLR 286). The clean break was introduced to encourage the parties to put the past behind them and to begin a new life which was not overshadowed by the relationship which had broken down (see Lord Scarman, *Minton* v. *Minton* [1979] AC 593).

The court must therefore consider whether it is appropriate to exercise its powers to make orders in favour of spouses so that 'the financial obligations of each party towards the other will be terminated as soon after the grant of the decree as the court considers just and reasonable' (s.25A(1)). The court can effect a clean break between the parties in an application for periodical payments by:

- dismissing the application;
- making a limited-term periodical payments order (s.25A(2));
- dismissing the application with a direction that the applicant shall not make further application (s.25A(3));
- making a limited-term periodical payments order (s.25A(2)) with a direction that no application for variation of that term should be sought in variation proceedings under s.31 (s.28(1A)); or
- ordering a lump sum representing capitalised periodical payments.

There are other clean break provisions. Thus when making a periodical payments order for a fixed term, the court can make a direction that no application can be made in variation proceedings for an extension of that term (s.28(1A)). A clean break can also be imposed in s.31 variation proceedings, when the court can make a limited term order 'to enable the party in whose favour the order was made to adjust without undue hardship to the termination of those payments' (s.31(7)). A clean break provision also exists in the Inheritance (Provision for Families and Dependants) Act 1975 (see 5.3).

Although the court is under a duty to consider whether or not to effect a clean break, there is no presumption that a clean break must be ordered (Butler-Sloss LJ in *Barrett* v. *Barrett* [1988] 2 FLR 516 and Hale J in *SRJ* v. *DWJ (Financial Provision)* [1999] 2 FLR 176 at 181). Indeed, the Court of Appeal has warned against treating the clean break as a principle (*Clutton* v. *Clutton* [1991] 1 FLR 242). The court is unlikely, however, to order a clean break where to do so would make unrealistic expectations of a spouse's capacity for economic independence. In *M* v. *M (Financial Provision)* [1987] 2 FLR 1, for example, the husband contended that periodical payments to his wife should be terminated under s.25A(2) after five years, but Heilbron J held that it would be inappropriate, unjust and unrealistic in view of the wife's age (she was 47) and her inability to find employment, despite her genuine attempt to do so. She had also lost the chance of a secure future which her husband's pension would have provided, and, in any event, the husband could apply in the future in s.31 variation proceedings should his financial position deteriorate. However, in *C* v. *C (Financial Provision)* [1989] 1 FLR 1, on the other hand, a clean break was considered appropriate as the wife had considerable earning capacity. As a result, the court made a deferred order whereby the lump sum and maintenance for the wife would terminate in three years. In *Waterman* v. *Waterman* [1989] 1 FLR 380, where the marriage had been very short and the wife had earning capacity, the court ordered that periodical payments to the wife should terminate in five years (see also *Mawson* v. *Mawson*

[1994] 2 FLR 985). In cases where there is ill-health, the court may be unwilling to order a clean break. In *M* v. *M (Property Adjustment: Impaired Life Expectancy)* [1993] 2 FLR 723 it was held that a clean break could not be achieved, because of the wife's reduced life expectancy due to ill-health. In *Purba* v. *Purba* [2000] 1 FLR 444, the Court of Appeal also refused to order a clean break because of the wife's ill-health.

Although the first consideration of the court when exercising its powers is the welfare of any child of the family (s.25(1)), a clean break can be imposed upon the parties where the parties have children (*Suter* v. *Suter and Jones* [1987] Fam 111). In some cases, however, the court may decide to make a deferred order or a nominal order (e.g. for £10 p.a.). A nominal order provides a 'backstop', in other words an order which can be varied in the future should circumstances change. Thus, in *Whiting* v. *Whiting* [1988] 1 WLR 565 a nominal order was upheld by a majority of the Court of Appeal even though the wife had qualified as a teacher and had a steady job. Balcombe LJ, however, dissented, saying that to make a nominal order just in case something should happen in the future was to negate entirely the aim of the clean break. A nominal order was also made in *SRJ* v. *DWJ (Financial Provision)* [1999] 2 FLR 176, as the Court of Appeal considered that a clean break order was inappropriate on the facts.

9.5 The Family Home on Divorce

The future of the family home is often an important matter on divorce. Not only is the home a valuable capital asset, but it also provides accommodation for the family. Indeed, the provision of accommodation will be a primary consideration for the court. In *M* v. *B* [1998] 1 FLR 53, Thorpe LJ said at p.60:

'In all these cases, it is one of the paramount considerations, in applying the section 25 criteria, to endeavour to stretch what is available to cover the need of each for a home, particularly where there are young children involved. Obviously the primary carer needs whatever is available to make the main home for the children, but it is of importance, albeit it is of lesser importance, that the other parent should have a home of his own where the children can enjoy their contact time with him. Of course there are cases where there is not enough to provide a home for either. Of course there are cases where there is only enough to provide one. But in any case where there is, by stretch and a degree of risk-taking, the possibility of a division to enable both to rehouse themselves, that is an exceptionally important consideration and one which will almost invariably have a decisive impact on outcome.'

In *M* v. *B* the principal issue in dispute was the wife's housing needs. The Court of Appeal allowed the husband's appeal as the judge had failed to take into account the importance of the parent who was not the primary carer having a home of his own where the children could enjoy contact. It was therefore held that the wife should have a cheaper house so that her husband would have enough money to buy a property of his own, where the children could visit him. *M* v. *B* was discussed by Lord Hoffmann in *Piglowska* v. *Piglowski* (1999), where the question for the House of Lords was whether the wife should have a cheaper house so that her husband could buy himself a house in England, even though he had accommodation in Poland. Lord Hoffman said, however, that to treat *M* v. *B* as a case laying down the rule that both spouses invariably have a right to purchase accommodation was a misuse of authority, and his Lordship distinguished *M* v. *B* on the basis that the children in *Piglowska* were adults, so that there was no question of the husband needing a home to receive them. Lord Hoffmann also stated that he saw no reason why the courts should not take into account the rationality of a party's intentions which gave rise to their needs (in *Piglowska*, whether it was reasonable for the husband to wish to return to live in England when he already had accommodation in Poland). His Lordship said that judges are free to make value judgments about the facts of cases. The House of Lords warned against treating earlier cases as binding precedents and restored the order of the trial judge, which had given particular weight to the wife's need to stay in the matrimonial home (s.22(2)(b)) and the fact that she had not only looked after the home and cared for the family, but had made a substantially greater financial contribution to the matrimonial assets (s.25(2)(f)).

When deciding what should happen to the home, the court has various options available, depending on the facts. It might, for example, order one party to transfer the house or his or her share of the house to the other party with or without the transferee making any compensating payment. It might order a transfer but subject to a charge in favour of the transferor, representing the value of the transferor's interest in the home which will be realised on sale at a later date (see, for example, *Knibb* v. *Knibb* [1987] 2 FLR 396 and *Popat* v. *Popat* [1991] 2 FLR 163). The house might be transferred to effect a clean break. It might, for instance, be transferred to the wife, with her forbearing to claim periodical payments.

Sometimes the courts have made a '*Mesher* order' (named after *Mesher* v. *Mesher* [1980] 1 All ER 126) under s.24(1)(b), whereby the home is settled on both parties on trust in certain shares but with the sale postponed until an event in the future, e.g. until the children have reached a particular age or have finished full-time education, or until death, remarriage, or cohabitation of the other party. *Mesher* orders were once popular with the courts, but they became increasingly unpopular because of their drawbacks. In many cases, wives found they had insufficient funds from the eventual proceeds of the sale to rehouse themselves, and the children continued to need accommodation even after the event-triggering sale had occurred. *Mesher* orders were also contrary to the clean break, as, until sale, the parties were tied together as joint owners, thereby restricting their chances of financial self-sufficiency.

Mesher orders also had drawbacks because, like other property adjustment orders, they were final orders which could not be varied (see, for example, *Omielan* v. *Omielan* [1996] 2 FLR 306 and *Carson* v. *Carson* [1983] 1 WLR 285). Another problem with a *Mesher* order occurred in *Thompson* v. *Thompson* [1986] Fam 38, [1985] FLR 863, where the husband refused to agree to his wife selling the house before the triggering event (when the youngest child reached 17 or finished full-time education). However, the Court of Appeal allowed her appeal and granted her an order enforcing sale, holding that it had jurisdiction to hear an application provided the object of the application was to give effect to the spirit and purpose of the original order.

Despite the drawbacks of *Mesher* orders, the Court of Appeal in *Clutton* v. *Clutton* [1991] 1 FLR 242 said that an order might be appropriate where family assets were sufficient to provide both parties with a roof over their heads if the matrimonial home were sold at a later date, but the interest of the parties required the children to stay in the matrimonial home. However, Lloyd LJ stressed that where there were any doubts about a wife's eventual ability to rehouse herself, then a *Mesher* order should not be made. The Court of Appeal held that a *Martin* order did not suffer from the same disadvantages. A *Martin* order (named after *Martin* v. *Martin* [1978] Fam 12) is an order giving one party a right to occupy the house until his or her death, remarriage or cohabitation, after which the proceeds of sale are divided in certain shares (see, for example, *Harvey* v. *Harvey* [1982] Fam 83). A *Martin* order effectively gives the party in occupation a life interest in the house, unless a specified event occurs.

The court can order that the home be sold under s.24A, but this can only be done ancillary to the court's power to make an order for financial provision or property adjustment. Thus, for example, the court could order sale of the home so that one of the parties receives a lump sum from the proceeds of sale. If there is any danger that the spouse who owns the home will sell it to a third party before the court has exercised its powers under ss.24 and 24A, the non-owning spouse should register his or her matrimonial home rights under Part IV of the Family Law Act 1996 (see 4.2), or obtain an order under s.37 of the Matrimonial Causes Act or under the inherent jurisdiction of the court to prevent or set aside an actual or threatened sale of the property (see 9.10 below).

As far as tenancies of the home are concerned, s.53 and sched. 7 Family Law Act 1996 make provision for the transfer of tenancies on divorce (see 4.7). A tenancy can also be transferred under s.24 of the Matrimonial Causes Act (see 9.3 above). Where the tenancy is a joint council tenancy, the court is entitled to take into account the effect on either party of the local authority's housing policy (*Jones* v. *Jones* [1997] Fam 59, [1997] 1 FLR 27).

9.6   A Family Business

Before the case of *White* v. *White* [2000] 2 FLR 981, in 'big money' cases where one party ran a business, the court would usually not divide the wealth between the parties equally, but would exercise its discretion by considering the reasonable needs of the spouse who was not the business earner (see *Dart* v. *Dart* [1996] 2 FLR 286 and *Conran* v. *Conran* [1997] 2 FLR 615). However, whether or not the spouses are in business together, the court may now decide to divide the parties' matrimonial assets equally, as the Court of Appeal did in *White* v. *White* (above). Here the husband and wife had entered into an equal farming partnership on marriage. After 33 years of marriage, the wife obtained a divorce and sought enough capital to set herself up independently in farming, arguing that her equal contribution to their farming business throughout their long marriage justified her claim to an equal share of the assets. Her husband argued, however, that she should only be given enough to satisfy her reasonable needs. At first instance, the judge, adopting a reasonable needs approach, on the basis that it was impractical for her to continuing farming, awarded her one-fifth of their joint assets, and ordered that the farming business remain with her husband. However, the Court of Appeal allowed the wife's appeal. Butler-Sloss LJ said that partnership cases where a wife was an equal business partner were in a wholly different category from 'big money' cases such as *Dart* v. *Dart* [1996] 2 FLR 286 and *Conran* v. *Conran* [1997] 2 FLR 615 where 'the origin of the wealth was clearly on one side and the emphasis was rightly on contribution not entitlement.' The Court of Appeal held that the starting-point for the exercise of the court's discretion under s.25 ought to be their respective financial position at the end of the business relationship. Only after that should the court go on to consider whether to exercise its powers to make finance and property orders, having regard to all the circumstances in s.25, so as to increase or decrease each party's share of the assets. Furthermore, the Court of Appeal said it was not the function of the judge to criticise the wife's plans to carry on farming. The Court of Appeal awarded her a lump sum of £1.5 million. The husband's appeal was dismissed by the House of Lords which applied a yardstick of equality. Lord Nicholls upheld the decision of the Court of Appeal, and said that the case was a good illustration of the unsatisfactory results which could flow from the 'reasonable requirements' approach taken by Holman J at first instance. Lord Nicholls said:

> ' ... I can see nothing, either in the statutory provisions or in the underlying objective of securing fair financial arrangements, to lead me to suppose that

the available assets of the respondent become immaterial once the claimant wife's financial needs are satisfied.... If a husband and wife by their joint efforts over many years, his directly in his business and hers directly at home, have built up a valuable business from scratch, why should the claimant wife be confined to the court's assessment of her reasonable requirements, and the husband left with a much larger share?'

However, although the wife in *White* was given a larger share than her reasonable requirements demanded, it must be remembered that each case turns on its own facts. Earlier cases do not necessarily create precedents. In *White*, both parties traded as *equal* partners. Where a spouse is involved in a business partnership or enterprise with the other spouse, but to a lesser degree, the court may take a different view and prioritise the s.25 criteria in a different way. However, what *White* has done is make it more likely that wives, in particular, whether or not they are engaged in a business partnership, will obtain larger shares of matrimonial assets than hitherto.

9.7 Pensions on Divorce

Loss of a pension on divorce can be a substantial loss, particularly for wives, many of whom will have made no, or inadequate, pension arrangements. Although pension entitlement has always been a relevant consideration for the court on divorce under the s.25(2) guidelines, changes have been made in recent years to improve the position in respect of pensions on divorce. Loss of pension rights on divorce (and on judicial separation and annulment) can therefore be compensated for in the following ways by the court:

(i) making compensatory adjustments of matrimonial assets generally by taking account of a pension under the s.25 discretionary exercise;
(ii) varying a pension, if it can be construed as a settlement;
(iii) 'earmarking the pension'; or
(iv) making a 'pension sharing order'.

(i) Compensatory Adjustments   To allow for loss of pension rights, the court in the exercise of its discretionary powers under s.25 can make compensatory adjustments in respect of matrimonial assets other than the pension itself. It could, for example, order that the matrimonial home be transferred to the person without the pension provision, or order payment of a larger lump sum. Section 25(2)(h) expressly requires the court to take into account 'any benefit' that a party will lose the chance of acquiring (which can include a pension), and a pension can also be taken into account under s.25(2)(a) as a 'financial resource' which a party has or is likely to have in the future. The court may, if retirement is reasonably imminent, adjourn the proceedings, or make a deferred order to take effect on retirement (see, for example, *Milne* v. *Milne* (1981) FLR 286).

(ii) Variation of a Settlement   A pension arrangement has been construed as an ante-nuptial or post-nuptial settlement under s.24(1)(c), which is thereby capable of being varied under s.31. It was not until the decision of the House of Lords in *Brooks* v. *Brooks* [1996] 1 AC 375, [1995] 2 FLR 13 that the possibility of this construction was highlighted (see also *W* v. *W (Periodical Payments: Pensions)* [1996] 2 FLR 480). However, although *Brooks* was considered a 'landmark' decision, its impact was limited, as the House of Lords was keen to stress that not every pension scheme constituted a marriage settlement for the purposes of s.24(1)(c) and even if a scheme did, it would not be right for the court to vary one scheme member's rights to the prejudice of other members. The decision in *Brooks* was therefore limited to its own facts. The pension scheme in question had only one beneficiary, the husband, and the wife had earnings of her own from the same employer which would sustain provision of an immediate pension for her. The new pension provisions now expressly exclude the possibility of a pension being construed as a settlement (see below).

(iii) Earmarking   Although the court has always had to take pensions into account under s.25 (see above), in practice little emphasis had been given to pensions. As a result of pressure for reform, the position was eventually improved by ss.25B–25D, which were inserted into the Matrimonial Causes Act 1973 by s.166 Pensions Act 1995. These provisions gave the divorce court power to 'earmark' pension payments, so that pension-splitting can take place at retirement. Thus when the pensioner begins to draw pension benefits, a proportion of those benefits becomes payable to the former spouse. The Pensions Act 1995 also made changes to the s.25 guidelines to give greater emphasis to pensions. Thus, s.25(2)(a) is to be read as though the words 'in the foreseeable future' had been removed, as far as they apply to consideration of a pension as a future resource.

Under the earmarking provisions, the court performs a two-stage exercise. First, it asks whether a financial provision order should be made to take account of any benefits, or lost benefits, under a pension scheme (s.25B(2)). If the answer to this question is 'yes', it must then decide whether to make an order requiring the trustees or managers of the pension fund to make payments out of the pension to the other spouse (s.25B(4)). However, any payment ordered must not exceed the amount of payment due to the pension holder (s.25B(5)). Where the benefits under a pension scheme include a lump sum payable in respect of the pension holder's death, the court can, for example, require the pension trustees or managers to pay the sum in whole or in part, or require the pension holder to nominate that the other spouse be entitled to payment in whole or in part (s.25C(1) and(2)). Earmarking orders must be expressed in percentage terms (s.25B(5)). The court cannot make an earmarking order in relation to a pension arrangement which is the subject of a pension sharing order (s.25B(7B) and s.25C(4)). The s.25 guidelines (see 9.4 above) must be applied by the court when it is exercising its earmarking powers.

Although the court has a duty to consider pension entitlement on divorce, it has a discretion whether to make an order. There is no automatic entitlement to an earmarking order. The earmarking powers are merely one part of the court's discretionary powers to adjust assets on divorce. In *T* v. *T (Financial Relief: Pensions)* [1998] 1 FLR 1072, the wife asked the judge to earmark part of her husband's pension to compensate for her lost pension rights. She argued that the Matrimonial Causes Act obliged the court to compensate her for her lost pension rights. However, Singer J rejected her argument, holding that the Act required the court to consider: first, whether a periodical payments order or a lump sum was appropriate; and secondly, how pension considerations should affect the terms of any such order. His Lordship said that the answer to the second question might be 'not at all'. Singer J also stated that an earmarking order is subject to the same restrictions as a conventional order. It is a financial provision order under s.23, not a new or distinct species of order. Thus, it can be varied during the payer's lifetime but terminates on the payee's death or remarriage. According to District Judge Roger Bird (at [2000] Fam Law 455), the courts have adopted a cautious approach to earmarking. He says that the number of earmarking orders has been small, and that most of them are contained in consent orders (see also *Burrow* v. *Burrow* [1999] 1 FLR 508).

(iv) A Pension Sharing Order The earmarking provisions above have improved the pension position on divorce, but they are not completely satisfactory. They can create uncertainty and insecurity as to when the payments will take effect and how long they will last. They are also contrary to the policy of the 'clean break' (see above), as the parties continue to be financially tied to each other.

As a result of continuing concerns about pensions on divorce, steps were taken to enable pension splitting to take place at the time of divorce. The Conservative Government made proposals to introduce pension splitting at the time of divorce, but failed to do so before the Labour Government came to power (see the Consultation Paper, *The Treatment of Pension Rights on Divorce* (Cm 3345, July 1996) and the White Paper, *Pension Rights on Divorce* (Cm 3564, February 1997)). In June 1998, the Labour Government published a Consultation Paper, *Pension Sharing on Divorce: Reforming Pensions for a Fairer Future*, and after consultation and consideration, new provision for pension sharing on divorce (annulment and judicial separation) was made.

These new provisions permitting pension sharing at the time of divorce are laid down in the Welfare Reform and Pensions Act 1999 (WRPA 1999), which makes amendments to Part II of the Matrimonial Causes Act 1973, and to Part III of the Matrimonial and Family Proceedings Act 1984 (financial relief after a foreign divorce). Under the new scheme (which came into force on 1 December 2000) the divorce court can make 'a pension sharing order' which takes effect at the time of divorce, so that one spouse becomes a member of the other spouse's pension scheme, or takes a transfer of a designated amount into his or her own pension arrangement (s.21(2A)(2)). A 'pension sharing order' is an order directing the trustees or managers of a pension scheme to allocate all or part of the pension rights to be awarded to the pensioner's other spouse at divorce. The order transfers rights to the other party, and specifies the percentage value to be transferred (s.21A(1)). There is no presumption of an equal distribution; the order may be made in any percentage. More than one pension sharing order can be made, provided each one is made in respect of a different pension arrangement (ss.24B(1), (3) and (4)). The order does not take effect until decree absolute (s.24B(2)). An order cannot be made where an earmarking order in relation to a particular pension arrangement is in force (s.24B (5)). The s.25 guidelines apply (see 9.4 above).

The new provisions are not retrospective. They apply only to divorces and annulments commenced after 1 December 2000. They do not apply to the basic state retirement pension. A pension sharing order can be made in respect of a pension already being paid. Divorcing couples are not obliged to seek a pension sharing order, and earmarking (above) remains available as an alternative option, as do the courts' powers to offset pension rights against other assets under its general discretionary powers on divorce. However, it is no longer possible to obtain a variation of settlement order in respect of a pension as in *Brooks* v. *Brooks* (see above). The courts therefore possess a range of available powers in respect of pensions. At the time of writing, it is impossible to predict how pension sharing will work, or to what extent it will be used. It has been predicted by Salter (2000), however, that pension sharing orders will be made in about one in three divorces.

9.8   Reaching Agreement

Many couples, instead of litigating, reach agreement about property and financial matters with or without the assistance of lawyers, mediators and the district judge. Some may make separation or maintenance agreements. Others may make agreements which are incorporated into a court order known as a consent order. However, despite the emphasis on agreement, the courts retain a supervisory role. The parties are not completely free to make their own agreements.

(a) Separation and Maintenance Agreements

Married couples can make their own separation or maintenance agreements but the divorce court has the power to alter such agreements (ss.34 and 35), and any provision in a maintenance agreement restricting any right to apply to the court for financial provision is void (s.34(1)). The court can also alter the terms of an agreement where circumstances change and where there is no provision in the agreement for financial provision for a child of the family (s.35(2)(a) and (b)). The court may insert new terms, or may vary or revoke the order.

While private maintenance or separation agreements have the advantage of encouraging amicable settlement, they can have disadvantages as the case of *Edgar* v. *Edgar* [1980] 1 WLR 1410 shows. In *Edgar*, the parties entered into a separation agreement in which the husband, a multi-millionaire, agreed to pay his wife a lump sum of £100 000 and in which she agreed to seek no further provision. The wife entered into the agreement even though her solicitor had advised her that she would obtain a better settlement in divorce proceedings. She was subsequently granted a lump sum of £760 000 in ancillary relief proceedings, but the Court of Appeal set aside the order on the basis that she was bound by the terms of the original agreement. There was no evidence that she had been exploited. She had received legal advice and there had been no adverse conduct by her husband during negotiations leading up to the agreement. The Court of Appeal held that a large disparity between the sum agreed and the sum that she might have been awarded in divorce proceedings was insufficient on its own for the court to ignore the agreement. In *Camm* v. *Camm* (1983) 4 FLR 577, on the other hand, *Edgar* v. *Edgar* was distinguished on its facts and the wife was awarded substantial periodical payments, as she had entered into a disadvantageous agreement under extreme pressure and with poor legal advice.

The principle in *Edgar* also applies to an agreement about periodical payment incorporated in a consent order. It cannot be varied in s.31 proceedings (see *B* v. *B (Consent Order: Variation)* [1995] 1 FLR 9). In *Richardson* v. *Richardson (No 2)* [1996] 2 FLR 617, the wife applied for variation of a consent order in which she had agreed to receive periodical payments of £8000 p.a. for three years. She applied for variation of the order, but the Court of Appeal, following *Edgar*, held that, although the weight attached to a consent order must depend on the facts of the case, formal agreements, properly and fairly arrived at with competent legal advice, should not be displaced unless there were good and substantial reasons for concluding that an injustice would be done by holding the parties to their terms. However, in *Pounds* v. *Pounds* [1994] 1 FLR 775, Hoffmann LJ expressed concern about the unsatisfactory state of the law created by the decision in *Edgar* and its progeny because of the lack of certainty it had created as to whether or not an agreement is legally binding (see also *Smith* v. *McInerney* [1994] 2 FLR 1077).

(b) Consent Orders

Agreements made by the parties about finance and property on divorce can be incorporated into an order known as a consent order, which the court has jurisdiction to make under s.33A of the 1973 Act. Consent orders must contain only those orders which the court has power to make under the 1973 Act (see 9.3 above). Consent orders encourage settlement and reduce the cost of litigation. However, to ensure they are made with full disclosure, certain safeguards exist. Thus, the parties must provide the court with prescribed information (see s.33A and r.2.61), e.g. the duration of the marriage, the age of the parties and children, an estimate of the approximate value of their capital resources, accommodation arrangements for them and the children, and whether either party has remarried or intends to marry or cohabit. Failure to provide the required information can result in a consent order being set aside (see 9.11 below), although the court will not do so lightly, because consent orders are intended to encourage settlement and finality. Furthermore, although consent orders are based on an agreement, they are not treated as ordinary contracts (see *Potter* v. *Potter* [1990] 2 FLR 27). Thus, general contract principles do not determine the outcome of a case. It is the consent order itself which determines the rights and duties of the parties, not the agreement, which in most cases will have been made before the order (see *De Lasala* v. *De Lasala* [1980] AC 546 and *Xydhias* v. *Xydhias* [1999] 1 FLR 683).

When considering whether to make a consent order, the court does not just 'rubber-stamp' the proposed agreement. It considers all the circumstances and applies the s.25 guidelines and the clean break provisions. However, the court will usually approve the agreement, as the fact that it has been drawn up and agreed to by the parties, often with legal advice, is *prima facie* proof of its reasonableness. The terms of a consent order can be varied but only those which refer to periodical payments (see 9.11 below).

9.9   Enforcing Orders for Ancillary Relief

(a) Periodical Payments

Periodical payments can be enforced in the same way as lump sums (see below) and also by:

(i)   *an attachment of earnings order*, whereby the payer's employer is ordered to deduct payment from earnings;

(ii) *registration in the magistrates' court* (which can be done at the time the order is made if non-payment is likely), whereby payment is made to the clerk of the justices and a record of payment is kept (no record exists in county courts or the High Court), and where the magistrates have a power of committal to prison for those who default.

With secured periodical payments there is no problem with enforcement because property belonging to the payer is charged with payment. Under the

Maintenance Enforcement Act 1991, magistrates' courts, county courts and the High Court, when making or varying orders for child or spousal maintenance, can order that payment be made by standing order and can order a payer to open a bank account for that purpose. The court can also make an attachment of earnings order at the time of making the order.

(b) Lump Sums

A lump sum can be enforced by:

(i) *an order for sale of property under s.24A* made in the original order or at a later date (the district judge can execute the transfer or conveyance if necessary);

(ii) *a writ of execution*, whereby the bailiff in the county court (sheriff in the High Court) seizes goods belonging to the payer representing the value of the lump sum;

(iii) *garnishee proceedings*, whereby payment is ordered to be made by a third party (e.g. bank or building society);

(iv) *a charging order* charging some capital asset (e.g. land) with the lump sum owed; or

(v) *a judgment summons*, whereby an order is made for payment by a certain date and by instalments where appropriate, and which can be reinforced by a suspended committal order (an order that the payer be committed to prison if the lump sum is not paid). An order for payment of school fees can be enforced in this way (*L* v. *L (School Fees: Maintenance: Enforcement)* [1997] 2 FLR 252).

9.10 Protecting Matrimonial Assets Pending Ancillary Relief Proceedings

Sometimes a party may dispose of, or attempt to dispose of, matrimonial assets in order to defeat the other party's claim to finance and property on divorce, for example by selling them, giving them away or sending them out of the jurisdiction. To prevent this happening, the court can make a 'freezing order' under s.37 of the Matrimonial Causes Act 1973 (see, for example, *Roche* v. *Roche* [1981] Fam Law 243 and *Sherry* v. *Sherry* [1991] 1 FLR 307) or under the High Court's inherent jurisdiction (see s.37(1) of the Supreme Court Act 1981). A freezing order under the inherent jurisdiction (formerly called a '*Mareva* injunction') may be useful where the necessary intention required for s.37 of the 1973 Act is absent (see *Shipman* v. *Shipman* [1991] 1 FLR 250). Overseas assets can be frozen, except where there are problems enforcing an order in a foreign court (*Hamlin* v. *Hamlin* [1986] 1 FLR 61). A freezing order will not usually freeze all the defendant's assets; it will usually be restricted to the maximum amount of property likely to be awarded in the divorce proceedings (*Ghoth* v. *Ghoth* [1992] 2 All ER 920).

Another order which is available to protect matrimonial assets pending ancillary relief proceedings is an *Anton Piller* order, which can be granted by the High Court under its inherent jurisdiction. The aim of this order is to ensure that the respondent does not dispose of evidence which may be useful at the ancillary relief hearing, and is sometimes used in cases of suspected non-disclosure (see, for example, *Emmanuel* v. *Emmanuel* [1982] 1 WLR 669). The order allows a named person to enter premises to search for and seize documents which might be useful as evidence in court proceedings. However, as Waite LJ stressed in *Burgess* v. *Burgess* [1996] 2 FLR 34, the use of *Anton Piller* relief in family proceedings 'remains a rare weapon for use only in extreme or exceptional cases.' Strict rules apply to the grant of an order and to the way in which the entry and search powers can be exercised.

In an emergency the orders above can be granted without the applicant giving notice to the other party, but a hearing with both parties present must take place as soon as possible afterwards. The applicant has a duty of full and frank disclosure and can be asked to give an undertaking in damages lest the injunction is wrongly granted. Breach of an injunction is contempt of court, which can result in committal to prison. It must be stressed, however, that freezing orders and *Anton Piller* orders are both considered to be Draconian orders, which are to be granted only in exceptional cases. Thus in *Araghchinchi* v. *Araghchinchi* [1997] 2 FLR 142, applications by a wife for an *Anton Piller* order and a freezing order were refused even though her husband had been devious and dishonest.

Where there is a danger that a party may leave the jurisdiction before a claim for ancillary relief has been settled, a writ *ne exeat regno* can be sought, but this order is rarely made because of the civil liberties implications of restricting a person's liberty. The order directs the tipstaff, an officer of the court, to arrest the respondent and bring him or her before a judge. The respondent's passport may be seized.

9.11   Challenging an Order for Ancillary Relief

An order for finance or property on divorce can be challenged in various ways:

(i) by asking for a rehearing;
(ii) by applying to have the original order varied under s.31 MCA 1973;

(iii) by appealing against the order (which may require an application for permission to appeal out of time if the time for lodging an appeal has passed);

(iv) by applying to have the original order set aside on the basis of something being wrong at the time the order was made, or because of some subsequent change of circumstances.

(i) A Rehearing

Where a party considers that there was something fundamentally wrong with the way in which the case was heard (e.g. there was non-disclosure or perjury), an application can be made for a rehearing. Sometimes an appeal court will order a rehearing because the order is fundamentally flawed (see further below).

(ii) Variation under s.31 MCA 1973

Under s.31 the court has wide powers to vary or discharge certain orders (whether or not made by consent), or to temporarily suspend and revive any provision contained therein (s.31(1)). The following orders can be varied (s.32(2)): maintenance pending suit; periodical payments; the instalments by which a lump sum is payable; and an order for the sale of property. Lump sum orders and property adjustment orders cannot be varied. They are 'once and for all' orders, which are intended to create finality in litigation so that the parties can plan for the future without worrying about whether an order will be overturned. A person who wishes to challenge a lump sum or property adjustment order will have to do so by other means.

When exercising its powers in variation proceedings, the court must consider all the circumstances of the case, but with first consideration being given to the welfare of any child of the family aged under 18, and the changes of circumstance include any change in any of the matters to which the court was required to have regard when making the original order (s.31(7)). The court must also consider whether to effect a clean break. Thus, it must consider whether it is appropriate to vary a periodical payments order so that payments will be made for a limited term sufficient to enable the payee to adjust without undue hardship to the termination of those payments (s.31(7)(a)). The court has other powers. It can remit payment of all or part of any arrears due under any periodical payments order, including maintenance pending suit and interim maintenance (s.31(2A)). Where a periodical payments order was for a limited term, it can extend that term, unless the original order prohibited it (s.28(1A)).

The court has a wide discretion in variation proceedings (see, for example, *Cornick* v. *Cornick (No 2)* [1995] 2 FLR 490). It can take into account increases in both the capital and income resources of the payer (*Boylan* v. *Boylan* [1988] 1 FLR 282 and *Primavera* v. *Primavera* [1992] 1 FLR 16). In *Flavell* v. *Flavell* [1997] 1 FLR 353, the Court of Appeal held that when seeking variation of periodical payments, there is no need to show a change of circumstances, or an exceptional or material change of circumstances. As the court has an absolute discretion, it can look at the case afresh, and need not regard the original order as the starting point. However, the court will be vigilant to ensure that the variation application is not a disguised form of appeal. In *Flavell* (above) the Court of Appeal held, however, that it is usually inappropriate to dismiss all claims for periodical payments for dependent or partially dependent wives in their mid-fifties.

An application for variation of periodical payments should be made well in advance of the cut-off date for a variation or extension of a periodical payments order (see *G* v. *G (Periodical Payments: Jurisdiction)* [1998] Fam 1, [1997] 1 FLR 368, where the Court of Appeal held that a wife was not able to apply after the child's eighteenth birthday for variation of a periodical payments order which had terminated on the child reaching 18).

There has been some uncertainty in the law as to whether an extension of time to pay a lump sum or to transfer property is a variation prohibited by s.31, because lump sum and property orders cannot be varied. However, in *Potter* v. *Potter* [1994] 2 FLR 27 the Court of Appeal held that a time limit in a lump sum or property order could be varied to give effect to the spirit and purpose of a consent order. In *Potter*, the purpose of the time limit had been to allow the wife to buy out her husband's interest in the home, and was only inserted to clarify the time in which the wife had to raise the money. On this construction, the Court of Appeal held that it was unnecessary to decide as a matter of law whether there was jurisdiction to vary a lump sum by varying the time limit (see also *Masefield* v. *Alexander (Lump Sum: Extension of Time)* [1995] 1 FLR 100). Although a property adjustment order is a final order, a charge in respect of a former matrimonial home can be redeemed at an earlier date than that specified in the order (unless the terms of the order prohibit redemption), because an order authorising redemption of a charge is not a variation under s.31 (*Popat* v. *Popat* [1991] 2 FLR 163).

Until 1998 the divorce court had no power to discharge a periodical payments order and substitute it with a lump sum or property order (see *S* v. *S* [1987] 1 FLR 71). To remedy this, s.31(7B) was brought into force on 1 November 1998 (by Sched. 8, para. 16(7) of the Family Law Act 1996) to give the court power in variation proceedings to order a lump sum or a property adjustment order in favour of a spouse as a means of effecting a variation (e.g. to compensate for loss of, or failure to pay, periodical payments). The amendment to s.31 allows a clean break to be achieved in variation proceedings where it was not possible at the time when the original order was made. In *Scheeres* v. *Scheeres* [1999] 1 FLR 241, the wife's application for a lump sum was dismissed, but Thorpe LJ stated that if the husband's financial position improved the parties could negotiate a commutation of the periodical payments to a single capital payment under the new provision in s.31(7B).

(iii) Appeals and Permission to Appeal out of Time

A person can appeal against an original order, which may, if the date for lodging an appeal has passed, require the court's permission (leave) to bring the appeal. (In most cases an appeal must be lodged within 14 days.) Sometimes an appeal is combined with an application to set aside the original order (see below). With an application for permission to appeal out of time, the applicant is not saying that the original order was wrong or that facts were not disclosed to the court, but that changes have occurred since the original order was made and after the time for an appeal has expired.

However, because of the need to create certainty and finality in litigation and to stop the courts being flooded with appeals, the courts are unwilling to set orders aside easily. In *Barder* v. *Barder (Caluori Intervening)* [1988] AC 20, [1987] 2 FLR 480, Lord Brandon held that leave to appeal out of time would not be granted for every unforeseen change of circumstances. It would only be granted where:

- the new events relied on had invalidated the fundamental basis or assumption on which the original order had been made, so that, if leave to appeal were granted, the appeal would be certain or very likely to succeed;
- the new events had occurred within a relatively short time of the original order being made – probably less than a year;
- the application for leave to appeal had been made promptly; and
- the grant of leave would not prejudice third parties who had acquired in good faith and for valuable consideration an interest in the property subject to the order.

In *Barder*, a consent order in full and final settlement was made, in which the husband agreed to transfer his half-share in the matrimonial home to his wife. However, four weeks after the order was made, but outside the time limit for lodging an appeal, the wife killed the children and committed suicide. Her will provided that her mother should inherit her estate. The husband sought leave to appeal out of time against the order (it could not be varied under s.31 as it was a property order), arguing that the basis on which the order had been made had been fundamentally altered by the unforeseen change of circumstances – the death of his wife and children. The House of Lords gave leave to appeal out of time, and, having heard the appeal, held that the order should be set aside.

Lord Brandon's principles (the '*Barder* principles') apply to orders made in contested proceedings and by consent. The operative date for determining whether permission to appeal has been sought promptly is not when the order was implemented but when it was made (Ward J in *B* v. *B (Financial Provision: Leave to Appeal* [1994] 1 FLR 219). However, not every application will result in permission to appeal being granted and an order being set aside. Indeed in *Thompson* v. *Thompson* [1991] 2 FLR 530 Mustill LJ stated that lawyers advising parties who might be considering appealing out of time, should be aware of the severity of the *Barder* principles to make sure the courts are not swamped by meritless applications. In *McGladdery* v. *McGladdery* [1999] 2 FLR 1102, the Court of Appeal held that the *Barder* principles could not be used to allow the court to rewrite an order merely because a person had failed to comply with it. Here, the husband had argued that his wife's dishonourable conduct in failing to comply with an order constituted a change of circumstances under the *Barder* principles. His argument was not accepted, and Thorpe LJ emphasised the importance of final orders being treated as final.

How the court should exercise its jurisdiction once permission to appeal has been granted was considered in *Smith* v. *Smith (Smith and Others Intervening)* [1992] Fam 62, [1991] 2 FLR 432. Here a lump sum order had been made in favour of a wife, which represented half the family assets, but six months later she committed suicide leaving her whole estate, including the lump sum, to her daughter. In the Court of Appeal, Butler-Sloss LJ stated that the correct approach was to start the s.25 exercise from the beginning and consider what order should be made on the basis of the new facts (here that the wife was known only to have a few months to live). Applying the s.25 guidelines to the facts, Butler-Sloss LJ reduced the lump sum (see also *Barber* v. *Barber* [1993] 1 FLR 476).

Appeals and appeals out of time have been brought in a wide range of different situations, for example: in respect of fluctuations in property valuations where a party has delayed in effecting sale (see, for example, *Heard* v. *Heard* [1995] 1 FLR 970; *Penrose* v. *Penrose* [1994] 2 FLR 621; *Worlock* v. *Worlock* [1994] 2 FLR 689); unforeseen death or serious illness (see, for example, *Amey* v. *Amey* [1992] 2 FLR 89); unexpected remarriage or cohabitation (see, for example, *Wells* v. *Wells* [1992] 2 FLR 66; *Chaudhuri* v. *Chaudhuri* [1992] 2 FLR 73); and misrepresentation (see, for example, *Ritchie* v. *Ritchie* [1996] 1 FLR 898).

(iv) Setting the Original Order Aside

An application can be made to set aside an order which has been made on an improper basis, for example where there has been non-disclosure, fraud, duress or misrepresentation, or where changes of circumstances have occurred which were unforeseen when the original order was made. An application to set an order aside will often be made in conjunction with an appeal out of time (see above).

Applications have been made where there has been a failure to disclose information prescribed by the rules of court. In *Jenkins* v. *Livesey (Formerly Jenkins)* [1985] AC 424, *sub nom Livesey (Formerly Jenkins)* v. *Jenkins* [1985] FLR 813, the leading case on setting aside orders for non-disclosure, a clean break consent order had been made in which the parties had agreed that the husband would transfer to his wife his half-share in the home on her foregoing all claims to ancillary relief. Three weeks after the house had been transferred, however, the wife remarried and two months later she put the home up for sale. The husband appealed out of time, asking for the consent order to be set aside on the grounds of misrepresentation and non-disclosure on the part of his wife. The House of Lords allowed his appeal, and held that parties who wished the court to exercise its discretionary powers under ss.23–25 of the 1973 Act were under a duty in contested or consent proceedings to make full and frank disclosure of all material matters, so that the court could exercise its discretion properly. However, because of the importance of encouraging a clean break, the House of Lords held that orders should not be lightly set aside. They would be set aside only if the absence of full and frank disclosure had led the court to make an order which was substantially different from that which would have been made had there been full and frank disclosure. On the facts, the wife's engagement was held to be a material circumstance directly relevant to the parties' agreement about ancillary relief, so that she was under a duty to disclose it before the agreement was put into effect by means of the consent order. Her failure to disclose the engagement invalidated the order, which was set aside and the case remitted for a rehearing.

Non-disclosure on its own is not a sufficient ground for an order to be set aside. With applications for permission to appeal out of time and applications to set aside orders, the change of circumstances must be such that a fundamentally different order would have been made had the circumstances been known. The policy of the law is to encourage finality in litigation, particularly where an order has been made to effect a clean break between the parties, and where it has been made by consent. However, as it would be unjust for an order to be upheld if relevant circumstances had not been put before the court, either because they were not disclosed or because they were not known or foreseen at the time the order was made, the court will sometimes set aside an order, as it did in *T* v. *T (Consent Order: Procedure to Set Aside)* [1996] 2 FLR 640. Here a consent order was set aside because of fraudulent non-disclosure by a husband. He had sold his company for £1.6 million two months after a consent order had been made.

In *Harris* v. *Manahan* [1997] 1 FLR 205, the Court of Appeal had to consider whether a consent order could be set aside because a party had received bad legal advice. Approaching the question in the light of *Edgar* v. *Edgar* and *Camm* v. *Camm* (see 9.8 above), the Court of Appeal held that the requirement of public policy that there be finality in litigation also required, save in the most exceptional cases of the cruelest injustice, that bad legal advice should not be a ground for interfering with a consent order. The rationale for such an approach is that, once an agreement has been embodied in a consent order, the source of the obligation becomes the court's order rather than the agreement made by the parties (*De Lasala* v. *De Lasala* [1980] AC 546). However, where any agreement about property and finance has not been embodied in a consent order, then the court may take into account the quality of any legal advice.

Where an order is set aside, the Court of Appeal has held that it is preferable for the circuit judge or High Court judge to look at the matter again, but that in exceptional cases, where the appellate court has all the information that the judge was likely to have, then the appellate court itself can make the order (see *Middleton* v. *Middleton* [1998] 2 FLR 821, where the Court of Appeal set aside a consent order, and made new orders on the basis of the evidence before it).

9.12   The Impact of a New Partner

When exercising its powers to make finance and property orders on divorce, the court can take account of the fact that a party is living with a new partner, as this is likely to affect the parties' financial resources and financial needs under s.25(2)(a) and (b). A divorcing spouse must also disclose whether or not he or she has remarried or is cohabiting, or intends to do so, as this is relevant to the proper exercise of the court's discretion. Where a party fails to disclose a new relationship, an order may be set aside (see *Jenkins* v. *Livesey* above), and some orders (e.g. *Mesher* orders, *Martin* orders and consent orders) are made subject to a party's marriage, or settled cohabitation.

Whether and to what extent the court will take into account a new partner depends on the facts of each case. In *MH* v. *MH* [1982] 3 FLR 429, for instance, the maintenance payable by the husband was reduced because his former wife was receiving financial support from her cohabitant, and in *Suter* v. *Suter and Jones* [1987] Fam 111 it was held that the divorced wife's cohabitant should be expected to make a contribution to their living expenses in order to reduce the obligations of her former husband. In *Atkinson* v. *Atkinson (No. 2)* [1996] 1 FLR 51, the wife's periodical payments of £30 000 p.a. were reduced to £10 000 when she began to cohabit with a new partner after the original order had been made. However, each case depends on its own facts. Thus, in *S* v. *S* [1987] 1 FLR 71 a lump sum of £400 000 was ordered to be paid to a wife even though she was living with a wealthy boyfriend, and in

Duxbury v. *Duxbury* [1987] 1 FLR 7 the wife's cohabitation was ignored in calculating capitalised maintenance, payable by her husband, a millionaire. Periodical payments automatically terminate on a payee's remarriage, but not on a payee's cohabitation. This distinction is perhaps open to criticism because it encourages cohabitation after divorce. Furthermore, the court has refused to equate long-term or settled cohabitation after divorce with remarriage, because of the impossible task it would be faced with if it had to make qualitative judgments about different sorts of cohabitation. In *Atkinson* v. *Atkinson* [1988] Ch 93, the husband applied in variation proceedings for periodical payments to his wife to be discharged or reduced to a nominal amount, as his wife was cohabiting with someone. He argued that her long-term and fixed cohabitation should be equated with remarriage so that his periodical payments to her should terminate, as they would have done under s.28(1) had she been married. The Court of Appeal rejected his argument, holding there was no statutory requirement or binding or persuasive authority that the courts should give decisive weight to an ex-wife's cohabitation or that a settled state of cohabitation should be equated with remarriage. However, the Court of Appeal held that her cohabitation and her reasons for not marrying constituted a change of circumstances within s.31(7) which it would be inequitable to disregard as conduct under s.25(2)(g). However, as the evidence showed that she would be unable to adjust without undue hardship to the termination of maintenance, the husband's appeal was dismissed (see also *Hepburn* v. *Hepburn* [1989] 1 FLR 373, where the Court of Appeal refused to overturn a nominal periodical payments order to a wife, even though she was cohabiting with a wealthy man, as long-term cohabitation could not be equated with remarriage).

9.13 Applications for Ancillary Relief after a Foreign Divorce

Under Part III of the Matrimonial and Family Proceedings Act 1984, a person who has divorced outside England and Wales can with the court's permission apply for ancillary relief in the English courts. The court can only grant permission if there is a substantial ground for making the application (s.13). When deciding whether to grant permission, it must consider whether England and Wales is the appropriate venue for the application (s.16(1)) and must have regard to a number of specific matters (s.16(2)), e.g. the connection the parties have with England and Wales, the country where they were divorced and with any other country, and any financial benefit the applicant or child of the family has received or is likely to receive by agreement or operation of law in another country. Once permission has been granted, ss.17 and 18 provide that the court can exercise its ancillary relief powers under Part II of the Matrimonial Causes

Act 1973 (see *Hewitson* v. *Hewitson* [1995] 1 FLR 241 and *Z* v. *Z (Financial Provision: Overseas Divorce)* [1992] 2 FLR 291).

However, because of the need for finality in litigation and the principle of comity between nations, permission to apply for ancillary relief in this country is unlikely to be granted unless the facts are exceptional (see Russell LJ in *Holmes* v. *Holmes* [1989] Fam 47 at p.59). As the purpose of the 1984 Act is 'to remit hardships which have been experienced in the past in the presence of a failure in a foreign jurisdiction to afford appropriate financial relief' (Purchas LJ in *Holmes* v. *Holmes*), the courts' power to grant permission has been used sparingly. Thus, in *Hewitson* v. *Hewitson* (1995), for example, the Court of Appeal refused to grant permission to the wife, as a court of competent jurisdiction in California had made the consent order, which had been negotiated by lawyers, and which was designed to be comprehensive and final. In *M* v. *M (Financial Provision after Foreign Divorce)* [1994] 1 FLR 399, an application by a wife for ancillary relief in England after a French divorce was refused. But, in *Lamagni* v. *Lamagni* [1995] 2 FLR 452, on the other hand, a wife, who had been divorced in Belgium 12 years earlier, was granted permission to apply for financial relief in the English courts because of her fruitless attempts to enforce Belgian court orders for financial relief. Applications for permission to apply for ancillary relief in England and Wales are unlikely to succeed where they are made for the sole purpose of enforcing a foreign order, unless foreign enforcement procedures and reciprocal enforcement procedures have been exhausted or are manifestly inadequate (see *Jordan* v. *Jordan* [1999] 2 FLR 1069, where the wife's application to seek ancillary relief in the English courts after her Californian divorce was refused as it was in essence an application to enforce a Californian court order).

9.14   Ancillary Relief: The Future

During the past few years the discretionary system for allocating property and finance on divorce has been criticised and proposals for reform have been discussed. While the discretionary approach has the advantage of flexibility, it creates unpredictability and uncertainty. The possibility of introducing clearer rules has been mooted, but there is not complete agreement on whether reform is necessary. While Dnes (1998), for example, believes that clear rules may reduce a litigious approach, encourage agreement and reduce the cost of disputes, there is no evidence available to show that firmer rules necessarily make agreement any easier. It has also been said that the unpredictability of the present system may actually encourage agreement and settlement (see Davis, Cretney and Collins, 1994).

As far back as 1991, the Family Law Committee of the Law Society discussed the possibility of reforming the law on ancillary relief (*Memorandum: Capital*

Provision on Divorce, see www.lawsoc.org.uk/). It looked at three possible options for reform: the introduction of a system of community of property; a greater emphasis on marriage agreements, particularly pre-nuptial agreements; and the introduction of a set of principles like those in Scotland. However, no reforms took place as a result of these discussions, as it was felt that more research was needed.

At the end of the 1990s there was renewed discussion of reform. In 1998 the Government proposed changes to ancillary relief (see its Green Paper, *Supporting Families*, published by the Home Office), which included the possible introduction of a 50/50 split of matrimonial assets and the introduction of binding pre-nuptial contacts subject to certain safeguards. However, the proposal for a 50/50 split was eventually rejected by the Government after the Lord Chancellors's Ancillary Relief Advisory Group (chaired by the Rt Hon Lord Justice Thorpe) had looked at possible reforms of ancillary relief, in particular a 50/50 split, pre-nuptial contracts and a set of general principles, but had concluded that there was still need for research and wide consultation, which should encompass both social and public policy issues. The Group was unanimous in its opposition to the introduction of a presumptive 50/50 division of property and also considered that the Scottish system would be inappropriate for England and Wales. There was, however, unanimous agreement that there was a strong case in principle for the codification of the principles that are currently applied by the courts. Some of the Group, however, urged the retention of the status quo.

The two options for reform which have been most discussed are a recognition of pre-nuptial or post-nuptial agreements and a presumptive 50/50 split of matrimonial assets. The two options for reform would work together. Thus, a couple would be able to contract out of the presumption of a 50/50 split by making a pre-or post-nuptial agreement to the contrary. Such agreements and presumptive equal divisions of property are common in European jurisdictions and in some states of the USA.

As far as pre- or post-nuptial agreements are concerned, they are not recognised in English law on grounds of public policy. It is considered that to make them enforceable would undermine the concept of marriage as a life-long union. For this reason, Wall J in *N* v. *N (Jurisdiction: Pre-nuptial Agreement)* [1999] 2 FLR 745 refused to recognise and enforce a pre-nuptial agreement made by a Jewish couple, which dealt primarily with property matters, and in which they agreed to submit to the authority of the Jewish religious court in London. However, despite their unenforceability in English law, pre- and post-nuptial agreements can be taken into account by the court when it conducts its discretionary exercise under s.25 of the Matrimonial Causes Act (see 9.4). The existence of a pre- or post-nuptial agreement made abroad may also be highly relevant when the court is considering whether to stay (stop) divorce proceedings taking place in England and Wales.

Although pre-nuptial and post-nuptial agreements might create greater certainty for the parties, as the parties themselves, not the State, are responsible for regulating financial and property matters, they are not an ideal solution. First of all, there is the problem of drafting them. Couples should seek legal advice, but many might be unwilling and unable to pay for this. Such agreements are more likely to be used by wealthy persons wishing to safeguard their assets. There may also be problems with non-disclosure, duress, mistake and inequality of bargaining power. Another problem is the difficulty of predicting what may happen in the future, for instance whether the couple will have children, whether one of them will suffer ill-health, or lose a job, or receive a windfall, such as an inheritance or even a lottery win. The birth of children is likely to cause problems, because although it may be appropriate for a party to the agreement to contract out of any financial obligation, the parental obligation to support children cannot be terminated by agreement. Thus, any reform would have to make provision for pre- and post-nuptial agreements to terminate on the birth of a child and possibly other triggering events. This would lead to complexity in the law. Marital agreements are therefore not a universal panacea for solving the problems inherent in a discretionary system. Indeed, according to Milligan (1999), US family law practitioners do not like them because they create problems not just for the parties but for the lawyers who have to draft them. Not only do lawyers risk having negligence claims brought against them, but attacking pre-nuptial agreements (e.g. on the grounds of duress, non-disclosure, incapacity and hardship) has become a new field of law for US practitioners. Milligan states that while pre-nuptial agreements would take away from the court some of the ancillary relief work, their introduction would open up new cases for the court and new types of work for lawyers. Because of the problems which marital agreements create, there is considerable opposition to them, including strong opposition to them from the Solicitors' Family Law Association (see Hodson, 1999).

The other major proposal is the introduction of a presumptive 50/50 division of assets on divorce which would be rebuttable if there was a pre-nuptial agreement to the contrary. However, a 50/50 split has drawbacks. Thus, while such a split might create a fairer and more equitable result for middle- and upper-income families (see Cleverely, 1999), it would be likely to create hardship for poorer families, because a 50/50 split would give many parties insufficient funds to rehouse themselves. This would cause hardship for children and injustice for the parties. It is for this reason that the Government has decided not to introduce a 50/50 presumptive share of matrimonial property on divorce, at least for the time being.

Eekelaar (1998) has acknowledged that s.25 of the Matrimonial Causes Act can be criticised, but he says that it is hard to find evidence of any strong dissatisfaction with the way it is working. He suggests that reform should only proceed after careful consideration of existing practice, and only on the basis of clear principle and policy. He recommended the introduction of a first principle which would put the provision of accommodation both for children and the parties first, where possible. After that he says that all property should be subject to a presumption of equal sharing but only if the parties have lived together for a specified period of time, and (unless the circumstances are exceptional) only if the parties have brought up at least one child together during at least part of that period. If the parties have lived together for less than the set period (he suggests 15 years), then the allocation of property should, he suggests, be made in proportions other than 50/50. He suggests 10/90 after 3 years, 20/80 after 6, 30/70 after 9, and 40/60 after 12. What is particularly interesting about his proposed approach is that it could be used for both married and cohabiting couples whose relationships have broken down, at least for cohabitants who have children. He says (at p.473):

' ... [T]he proposed approach holds out the possibility of unifying the law as between married and unmarried parents. The self-proclaimed upholders of 'family values' may like to maintain distinctions between married and unmarried partners. It will be harder to argue for their retention as between married and unmarried parents, especially those who have lived together for many years while performing the socially useful task of bringing up their children. After all, is that not what family values, in common parlance, are largely about?'

As reform of the law relating to the property ownership of cohabitants is urgently needed (see 4.10), perhaps reform for cohabitants and reform for ancillary relief on divorce should be looked at together. However, important policy issues would need to be addressed first, in particular whether the law should undermine the autonomy of those who choose to cohabit rather than marry, and whether any integrated reform would undermine the institution of marriage. What is clear, however, is that it will always be extremely difficult to devise a fair, just and effective system for adjusting finance and property matters on relationship breakdown which is both predictable but at the same time flexible enough to deal with the infinite variety of family life. Reforms of child support have been riddled with the same problems.

Summary

1 The emphasis today is on mediation, negotiation and settlement, with court proceedings to settle property and financial issues on divorce being sought only as the last resort.
2 If the parties cannot reach agreement, then financial provision and property adjustment orders can be sought on divorce (or on nullity or judicial separation) in ancillary relief proceedings under Part II of the Matrimonial Causes Act 1973.

Orders can be made for a spouse and/or to or for the benefit of a child of the family, although child maintenance must be sought in most cases from the Child Support Agency (see 14.2).

3 The procedure for ancillary relief applications is laid down in the Family Proceedings Rules 1991, as amended. Important procedural changes came into force on 5 June 2000. Under the new procedure, the emphasis is on reaching agreement, saving cost and reducing delay. The district judge must 'actively manage' the case to achieve these aims. Both parties must personally attend a first appointment (unless the court orders otherwise). At this hearing the district judge will define the issues, recommend the parties to mediation, set an appointment for the next hearing etc. The parties will then be encouraged to settle their dispute at a Financial Dispute Resolution (FDR) appointment where the district judge will effectively act as a mediator. If the parties are still unable to settle their differences, then the case will proceed to a contested hearing. Appeals against court decisions are rarely successful, unless the judge has erred in law or has exercised his discretion outside a reasonable band of discretion and is plainly wrong.

4 There is a duty of full and frank disclosure in ancillary matters.

5 The court in ancillary relief proceedings can make the following orders: maintenance pending suit (s.22); periodical payments order (s.23); lump sum order (s.23); property adjustment order (s.24); and order for the sale of property (s.24A).

6 The court must apply the s.25 guidelines when considering whether to make an order, and, if so, in what manner.

7 The court must apply the clean break provisions when making orders in favour of spouses in original proceedings (s.25A) and in variation proceedings (s.31(7)).

8 Various orders may be made in respect of the matrimonial home. Tenancies can be transferred under s.24 MCA 1973 or under s.53 and Sched. 7 Family Law Act 1996.

9 A family business can be taken into account and if both parties have contributed equally then the assets available to the parties on divorce may be divided equally. However, each case depends on its own facts.

10 Pensions can be taken into account by the court: making compensatory adjustment of matrimonial assets; or by 'earmarking' a pension so that it can be divided between the spouses on retirement. New provisions came into force on 1 December 2000, allowing the court to divide pensions at the time of divorce by making a 'pension sharing order'.

11 Private agreements may be made on divorce. The court has jurisdiction to make a consent order (a court order incorporating an agreement in respect of periodical payments, lump sum and property adjustment), but only if prescribed information has been provided by the parties. Consent orders can be set aside for non-disclosure and on other grounds.

12 Orders can be enforced in various ways.

13 An order under s.37 Matrimonial Causes Act 1973 or a 'freezing order' can be granted to protect matrimonial assets pending the outcome of ancillary relief proceedings. An *Anton Piller* order can be used to gain entry to premises to take out and copy evidence relevant to ancillary relief proceedings. These orders are only granted in exceptional circumstances because of their Draconian nature.

14 An order for ancillary relief can be challenged in the following ways: by asking for a rehearing; by applying to have the order varied under s.31; by appealing against the order, which may require an application for permission to appeal out of time; and by applying to have the order set aside.

15 Applications for appeals out of time and applications to set orders aside are only granted in exceptional circumstances. The court will not grant permission to appeal out of time, unless the *Barder* principles are satisfied. An application to

set aside an order will only be granted if the order is fundamentally unsound (e.g. for non-disclosure, fraud, mistake etc.).

16 The existence of a new partner after divorce may be taken into account by the court when making orders for ancillary relief. Periodical payments automatically terminate on remarriage but not on cohabitation. Settled cohabitation is not treated as being equivalent to remarriage, although cohabitation may be considered under the s.25 guidelines.

17 An application for permission to seek ancillary relief in the English courts after a foreign divorce can be sought under Part III of the Matrimonial and Family Proceedings Act 1984.

18 The law on ancillary relief has been criticised because the discretionary jurisdiction creates uncertainty and predictability. Reforms have been recommended (in particular, a presumption in favour of a 50/50 split of matrimonial property and encouraging pre-nuptial agreements), but nothing has been done to implement these because it is felt that more research and consultation are needed, and because they have their own disadvantages.

Further Reading and References

Bailey-Harris (ed.), *Dividing the Assets on Family Breakdown*, Family Law, 1998.

Bailey-Harris and Coleridge, 'Family assets, costs and avenues of appeal' [1999] 115 LQR 551.

Barton and Bissett-Johnson, 'The declining number of ancillary relief orders' [2000] Fam Law 94.

Bird, *Pension Sharing: The New Law*, Family Law, 1999.

Bird, *Ancillary Relief Handbook*, Family Law, 2000.

Burrows, *Ancillary Relief: The New Rules*, Family Law, 2000.

Cleverely, 'Statutory reform of Matrimonial Causes Act 1973, s.25 – an opportunity missed?' [1999] Fam Law 326.

Cretney 'Contract not apt in divorce deal (*Xydhias* v. *Xydias*)' [1999] 115 LQR 361.

Cretney, 'Trusting the judges – Money after divorce' (2000) *Current Legal Problems* 286.

Davis, Cretney and Collins, *Simple Quarrels*, Clarendon Press, 1994.

Davis, Pearce, Bird, Woodward and Wallace, 'Ancillary relief outcomes' [2000] CFLQ 43.

Dnes, *An Economic Analysis of a Proposal to Reform the Discretionary Approach to the Division of Marital Assets in England and Wales* (1998), Lord Chancellor's Department (can be accessed at www.open.gov.uk/lcd).

Dnes, 'Pension splitting in England and Wales' (1999) JSWFL 41.

Eekelaar, 'Should s.25 be reformed?' [1998] Fam Law 469.

Eekelaar, 'Back to basics and forward into the unknown' [2001] Fam Law 30.

Hodson, 'Government proposed reforms of ancillary relief' [1999] Fam Law 265.

Hodson, '*White*: Equality on divorce?' [2000] Fam Law 870.

Jackson, Wasoff, Maclean and Emerson, 'Financial support on divorce: The right mixture of rules and discretion' (1993) IJLF 230.

KPMG Study of the Ancillary Relief Pilot Scheme, Lord Chancellor's Department Research Series 1998 (can be accessed at www.open.gov.uk/lcd).

Memorandum: Maintenance and Capital Provision on Divorce – Recommendations for Reform of the Law and Procedure made by the Family Law Committee, The Law Society, 1991 (can be accessed at www.lawsoc.org.uk/).

Milligan, 'Pre-nuptials beware' [1999] Fam Law 483.

Oliver and Clements, *Enforcing Family Finance Orders*, Family Law, 1999.

Salter, *Pensions and Insurance on Family Breakdown* (2nd edn), Family Law, 1999.
Salter, 'A practitioner's guide to pension sharing, Parts I and II' [2000] Fam Law 489
    and 543.

Questions

1 Would it be a good idea to create a statutory presumption of a 50/50 split of matri-
    monial assets on divorce?
2 What do you think of Eekelaar's proposals above for the reform of ancillary relief?
3 To what extent should any reforms of the law relating to property distribution on
    cohabitation breakdown be assimilated into any reforms of ancillary relief on
    divorce?
4 According to research by the Institute of Social and Economic Research, divorce
    makes men richer and wives poorer. The research showed that men's disposable
    income increased by an average of 15 per cent after divorce, while women's fell by
    around 28 per cent (mirroring the average gain they experienced on marrying).
    Does this surprise you, and what do you think the explanation for this is?
5 Has *White* v. *White* added certainty and coherence into the law of ancillary relief,
    or has it done the opposite?

Part V

Children

Part V considers the law relating to children. Chapter 10 deals with the emergence of children's rights and looks in particular at the *Gillick* case and its impact on the law relating to children. Chapter 11 deals with parents and their rights and responsibilities to children, as well as the law on establishing parentage. Chapter 12 deals with the Children Act 1989. The remaining chapters deal with more specific aspects of child law, namely children on family breakdown (Chapter 13), financial support for children (Chapter 14), child abduction (Chapter 15), child protection (Chapter 16) and finally adoption (Chapter 17).

Part 5

Children

10 Children's Rights

10.1 Children's Rights

Over the centuries, but particularly during the twentieth century, children have acquired more rights and more freedom to make their own decisions, particularly when they are mature and intelligent enough to do so. This has not always been the case, for at one time a child's wishes were largely ignored, as parents, particularly fathers, had more or less absolute rights over their children. In *Re Agar-Ellis* [1883] 24 Ch D 317, for example, the father had taken his children away from their mother after a dispute about whether they should be brought up as Roman Catholics or Anglicans. One of the children, a girl aged 16, wished to spend her holidays with her mother and an application was made to the court. Cotton LJ dismissed the application, holding that, in the absence of any fault on the father's part, the court had no jurisdiction to interfere with a father's legal right to control the custody and education of his child, which at common law were vested entirely in a father. The extent to which the position of children has changed can be seen if we compare *Re Agar-Ellis* with *Gillick* v. *West Norfolk and Wisbech Area Health Authority* [1986] AC 112 (see below), where the House of Lords held that a child of sufficient age and understanding could consent to contraceptive treatment without parental consent. Today, the father in *Re Agar-Ellis* might have been guilty of the criminal offence of abduction (see 15.5).

Since the end of the Second World War the children's rights movement has grown. In 1959 the United Nations passed a Declaration of the Rights of the Child. In 1979 during the International Year of the Child, the Children's Legal Centre was established, and in 1989 the United Nations' Convention on the Rights of the Child was adopted (see below).

Various theories of children's rights have been posited and discussed, usually by philosophers rather than family lawyers (see Fortin, Chapter 1, 1998, for a useful overview, and Alston *et al.*, 1992). The impetus for children's rights was the 'children's liberationists' movement in the 1970s, which was responsible for generating debate about the extent to which children should have rights. The children's liberationists took the view that children had the right to enjoy adult freedoms, in particular the right to have freedom of choice to make decisions about themselves (see Archard, 1993, Part II). Other theorists have taken a different view. They have argued that children have a right not to be forced into adulthood, and have rights to be protected and cared for.

It has been argued that to give children autonomous rights undermines and inhibits parental authority and has repercussions for children.

While some theorists have argued that children have rights, others have preferred not to use 'rights talk', because they consider there are theoretical difficulties in doing so. One difficulty is that children are often too powerless and dependent to enforce any rights they may have. They need adults to champion their rights. This is why there have been arguments in favour of appointing a Children's Ombudsman or Children's Rights Commissioner. Instead of rights, some theorists have preferred to talk about children's 'interests' (see Eekelaar, 1986), or to view children's rights in terms of the obligations adults owe them (see O'Neill in Alston *et al.*, 1992).

If it is conceded that children do have rights, then the next question to ask is what sorts of rights children should have. One way to think about this is to adopt some sort of classification of rights. Various attempts have been made to do this. Freeman (1983), for instance, has proposed four categories of rights: welfare rights; protective rights; rights grounded in social justice; and rights based on autonomy. Bevan (1989), on the other hand, has divided children's rights into the two broad categories of 'protective' and 'self-assertive' rights. Fortin (1998, at p.18) prefers Bevan's categorisation because it 'reflects the fundamental conflict currently underlying the whole of child law as it is developing in practice – that is the conflict between the need to fulfil children's rights to protection and to promote their capacity for self-determination.'

One of the central dilemmas for those involved with children, whether they be law reformers, lawyers, social workers or doctors, or parents, is the extent to which paternalistic approaches should be adopted, or whether, and if so, to what extent, children should have rights of self-determination or autonomy. We shall see in the chapters that follow that in the development of children's rights there has been a move away from authoritarian and paternalistic approaches towards more permissive and liberal ones. However, while some advocates of children's rights have argued in favour of greater autonomy for children, the law must inevitably attempt to strike a balance between recognising that children have greater rights of self-determination as they near majority, while at the same time recognising that they need the protection of the law.

Another issue which has concerned some theorists is the extent to which the State should intervene in children's lives. Some theorists, in particular Goldstein, Freud and Solnit (1973 and 1980), have argued in favour of family privacy and minimum state interference in family life, on the basis that families are most successful if they are allowed to establish their own sets of rules and values. They argue that the state has insufficient resources and sensitivity to take on a parental role. We shall see that the Children Act 1989 (see Chapter 12) adopts a non-interventionist approach. Furthermore, the European Convention for the Protection of Human Rights upholds such an approach in art. 8 which guarantees a right to a private and family life (see 1.5).

10.2   The UN Convention on the Rights of the Child 1989

The UN Convention on the Rights of the Child 1989 was created with the aim of encouraging governments world-wide to recognise the importance of children in society and to recognise that children have rights. The Convention applies to all children and has the following four general aims: prevention; protection; provision; and participation. These are known as the '4 Ps'. However, the UN Convention on the Rights of the Child does not have the same force in English law as the European Convention for the Protection of Human Rights, which has now been woven into the fabric of English law by the Human Rights Act 1998 (see 1.5). Although the UK has ratified the UN Convention, it has not been incorporated into English law and no court exists under the Convention to enforce its provisions. However, despite these drawbacks, the Convention is referred to by English judges in their judgments and is of persuasive value in legal argument. Furthermore, the UN Committee on the Rights of the Child monitors the implementation of the Convention in Member States and by means of its reports brings pressure to bear on Member States to change the law where it fails to promote the rights and best interests of children.

It is not possible to mention all 54 articles which make up the Convention, but of particular importance is art. 3 which provides that in 'all actions concerning children, whether undertaken by public or private social welfare institutions, courts of law, administrative authorities or legislative bodies, the best interests of the child shall be a primary consideration.'

Under the Convention, children have rights, for example: to life (art. 6); to freedom of expression (art. 13); to freedom of association and freedom of peaceful assembly (art. 15); to a private and family life (art. 16); to freedom of thought, conscience and religion (art. 14); to education (art. 28); to enjoy minority rights (art. 30); to rest and leisure (art. 31); to a standard of living adequate for the child's physical, mental, spiritual, moral and social development (art. 27); to protection against economic exploitation and from performing work which will interfere with the child's education or health or development (art. 32); and to social security benefits (art. 26).

Children also have a right to have contact with both parents on a regular basis, except when a court decides that such contact is contrary to the child's best interests (art. 9). States Parties must also protect children from all forms of abuse, neglect, maltreatment, exploitation and sexual abuse while in the care of their parents or other persons (art. 19). Children must be protected against drugs (art. 33), sexual exploitation (art. 34), other forms of exploitation (art. 36), abduction (art. 35), and cruel, inhuman or degrading treatment or punishment (art. 37). The Convention also makes provision for refugee children (art. 22), disabled children (art. 23) and for health care and medical provision for children (art. 24).

The Convention recognises the importance of parents in the upbringing of children. It provides that respect must be afforded to the parental responsibilities, rights and duties of parents, members of the extended family or community and others who are legally responsible for children (art. 5). It also recognises the importance of both parents having common responsibilities for the upbringing and development of children, and having the primary responsibility for bringing up their children (art. 18). Parents and others responsible for children must ensure that the child's living conditions are the best that can be secured in the circumstances (art. 27(2)) and States Parties must take all appropriate measures to recover maintenance for children from parents having financial responsibility (art. 27(4)).

10.3   The *Gillick* Case

Gillick v. *West Norfolk and Wisbech Health Authority* [1986] AC 112 was a landmark case in the development of the law. First, it gave greater recognition to the right of children to make decisions for themselves without parental interference. Secondly, it emphasised that parents do not have rights in respect of their children but responsibilities and duties, and it is this concept of parental responsibility which is enshrined in the Children Act (see 11.6).

In the development of children's rights, *Gillick* was hailed as a landmark decision, because it brought about a recognition that children, particularly those of sufficient age and understanding, should have a greater say in decisions concerning them. This recognition was also reflected in the drafting of the Children Act 1989, as in contested s.8 order proceedings (see 12.4) and in care and supervision proceedings (see 16.5) the court must have regard to the ascertainable wishes and feelings of the child concerned (considered in the light of his or her age and understanding) (s.1(3)(a)). A child can also apply for s.8 orders, with the permission of the court (s.10(8)). Under the Children Act, a child also has a right to refuse to consent to medical or psychiatric examinations or other assessments, provided he or she has sufficient understanding to make an informed decision.

However, although *Gillick* had an impact on the content of the Children Act 1989 and children of sufficient understanding are given greater recognition, a child does not necessarily have the final say. It is always open to the court to overrule the child's wishes (and sometimes those of parents) on the basis that the child's welfare requires it to do so. It is the child's welfare, not the child's wishes, that is paramount, and, although there are many references to the child's welfare in the Children Act and in other child legislation, nowhere is there any express reference to children's 'rights'. Furthermore, the child is not necessarily a party to all proceedings and the child's consent is not needed for removal from the jurisdiction and for a change of surname (see 13.5 and 13.6).

In *Gillick*, a Department of Health and Social Security (DHSS) circular was sent to doctors advising them that they would not be acting unlawfully if in exceptional circumstances they prescribed contraceptives to girls under the age of 16 without first obtaining parental consent, provided they did so in good faith. Mrs Gillick, an ardent Roman Catholic with teenage daughters, brought an action against the DHSS and her local hospital authority, seeking a declaration that the circular was illegal on two grounds. First, it enabled doctors to break the criminal law by causing or encouraging unlawful sexual intercourse under the Sexual Offences Act 1956; and secondly, the circular was inconsistent with her parental rights. The case went to the House of Lords, which held that there was no rule of absolute parental authority over a child until a fixed age, but that parental authority dwindled as the child grew older and became more independent. The law recognised parental rights only in so far as they were needed for the child's protection, so that it was more appropriate to talk of duties and responsibilities than rights. Parental rights, if any, yielded to the right of the child to make his or her own decisions if of sufficient understanding and intelligence. Consequently a girl under 16 did not merely by reason of her age lack legal capacity to consent to contraceptive treatment. Neither had any offence under the Sexual Offences Act 1956 been committed as the *bona fide* exercise of a doctor's clinical judgement negated the necessary *mens rea*. Lord Scarman, drawing on Blackstone's *Commentaries on the Laws of England*, stated ([1986] AC 112 at 186):

'The underlying principle of the law was exposed by Blackstone and can be seen to have been acknowledged in the case-law. It is that parental right yields to the child's right to make his own decisions when he reaches a sufficient understanding and intelligence to be capable of making up his own mind on the matter requiring decision.'

However, *Gillick* did not give children absolute rights. In fact, the House of Lords itself stressed that, as far as contraception was concerned, only in exceptional cases would there be no parental involvement.

Gillick – *its Progeny*

Despite being hailed as a 'landmark' decision for children's rights, the impact of *Gillick* has not been as great as was anticipated at the time it was decided. Subsequent case-law has shown that the scope of children's rights depends on all the circumstances of the case and that the wishes of a '*Gillick* competent' child (a child who is mature and intelligent enough to make an informed decision) can be overridden. '*Gillick* competence' is only one of the circumstances of the case. The outcome of a case depends not just on the maturity of the child in question, but also on the seriousness of the decision to be taken. Thus, in a series of cases where children have refused to consent to medical treatment (*Gillick* was about consent, not refusal) the courts have overridden the wishes of children and authorised medical treatment, even where the child concerned has been mature enough to make an informed decision.

In *Re R (A Minor)(Wardship: Medical Treatment)* [1992] Fam 11, the Court of Appeal held that a *Gillick*-competent child could consent to medical treatment, but where such a child refused to give consent, then consent could be given by someone else with parental responsibility, including the court. In *Re R* the child, a girl aged 15 who had a serious mental illness, had been placed in an adolescent psychiatric unit. The local authority applied in wardship for her to be given psychiatric treatment without her consent. The Court of Appeal allowed the application, holding that she was not *Gillick*-competent as her mental state fluctuated from day to day, but, even if she had been, the court would still have had the power to override her refusal. Lord Donaldson MR was also of the opinion that a *Gillick*-competent child's refusal to have treatment could be overridden if a person with parental responsibility gave consent. *Re R* was applied in *Re K, W and H (Minors)(Medical Treatment)* [1993] 1 FLR 854, where it was held that three teenage children in secure accommodation were not *Gillick*-competent and that, even if they had been, their refusal to consent to medical treatment would not have exposed the doctors to civil or criminal proceedings, as parental consent had been given.

In *Re W (A Minor)(Medical Treatment: Court's Jurisdiction)* [1993] Fam 64, a local authority was granted permission by the court under its inherent jurisdiction (see 12.8) to authorise medical treatment in respect of a 16-year-old girl, who was suffering from anorexia nervosa. Her condition was rapidly deteriorating, but she had refused treatment. The Court of Appeal held that it had jurisdiction to override a *Gillick*-competent child's refusal to consent to medical treatment, despite the provision of s.8 of the Family Law Reform Act 1969 (which allows 16- and 17-year-olds to give valid consent to surgical, medical and dental treatment), as the court under its inherent *parens patriae* jurisdiction had theoretically limitless powers extending beyond the powers of natural parents. In *Re M (Medical Treatment: Consent)* [1999] 2 FLR 1097, Johnson J, following *Re W*, authorised that a 15-year-old girl undergo an urgent heart transplant operation as she had refused to give her consent. In several cases the courts have overridden the refusal of children who are Jehovah's Witnesses to submit to medical treatment on religious grounds (see *Re E (A Minor)(Wardship: Medical Treatment)* [1993] 1 FLR 386, *Re S (A Minor)(Consent to Medical Treatment)* [1994] 2 FLR 1065 and *Re L (Medical Treatment: Gillick Competency)* [1998] 2 FLR 810). However, recent changes to allow Jehovah's Witnesses to undergo medical treatment in life-threatening situations will mean that fewer cases like this will come to court.

The power of the court to override the wishes of a mature minor also prevails despite statutory provisions to the contrary. In *South Glamorgan County Council* v. *W and B* [1993] 1 FLR 574, the court had made an interim care order in respect of a severely disturbed 15-year-old girl with directions under s.38(6) of the Children Act 1989 that she receive a psychiatric examination and assessment. When she refused to consent to the examination and assessment, the court under its inherent jurisdiction overrode her wishes and gave the local authority permission to take the necessary steps for her to be treated and assessed. The court so decided, despite the fact that s.38(6) expressly states that a child of sufficient understanding to make an informed decision may refuse to submit to the examination or other assessment, and notwithstanding that she was *Gillick*-competent.

These cases clearly show that the *Gillick* principle is limited. A child has no absolute power of veto over medical treatment. The court can always intervene to override the child's wishes. Thus, while children may have greater rights of self-determination then they used to have, they do not have absolute autonomy.

10.4   The Corporal Punishment of Children

The development of society's attitude to the corporal punishment of children illustrates how differently children are treated today. At one time it was acceptable for parents to beat their children. Today, however, while parents are not prohibited from using physical punishment, it must be reasonable, otherwise they may commit a criminal offence or the child may be taken into care. In some countries (e.g. Sweden and Norway) physical punishment of children is prohibited, and there have been calls to outlaw it in this country, particularly by a pressure group called EPOCH (End Physical Punishment of Children). However, because of the decision of the European Court of Human Rights in *A* v. *United Kingdom (Human Rights: Punishment of Child)* [1998] 2 FLR 959, the UK Government has now been forced to change the law.

In *A* v. *United Kingdom (Human Rights: Punishment of Child)*, a boy aged 9 had been beaten by his step-father with a garden cane which he had used with considerable force. The step-father was charged with assault but was acquitted because of the defence of 'reasonable chastisement' (a defence which has its origins in Victorian times). The case was subsequently heard by the European Court of Human Rights, which unanimously held that the UK was in breach of art. 3 of the European Convention for the Protection of Human Rights (right not to be subject to inhuman and degrading treatment). The European Court held, however, that the ill-treatment must attain a minimum level of severity in order to fall within art. 3. On the facts, the step-father's ill-treatment of the child had reached the level required by art. 3, taking into account the age of the child and the severity of the treatment.

However, although the UK Government is obliged to change the law as a result of the decision in *A* v. *UK*, it is not obliged to outlaw physical punishment by parents completely, because the decision of the European Court was based on the *degree of severity* of the step-father's ill-treatment, and not on the fact that he had used physical punishment. The Government has taken the same approach and not prohibited physical punishment completely. In its Consultation Document, *Protecting Children, Supporting Parents: A Consultation Document on the Physical Punishment of Children* (Department of Health, 2000, available at www.open.gov.doh), the Government stated at para. 1(5) that, while harmful and degrading treatment of children could never be justified, it did not consider that the right way forward was to make unlawful all smacking and other forms of physical rebuke. It said that there was 'a common sense distinction to be made between the sort of mild physical rebuke which occurs in families and which most loving parents consider acceptable, and the beating of a child.' Some commentators (such as Barton, 1999) have been strongly critical of this approach, however, and have argued in favour of an absolute ban on the physical punishment of children by their parents.

As far as physical punishment in schools is concerned, it has been outlawed in state schools by the Education Act (No 2) 1986, and under the Children Act 1989 it is banned in all children's homes. Corporal punishment is not, however, banned in public schools, and in *Costello-Roberts* v. *UK* (1994) 19 EHRR 112 the European Court of Human Rights rejected the claim that the UK had breached the human rights of a 7-year-old pupil at a private school who had been beaten by his headmaster. The punishment was not severe enough to constitute degrading treatment under art. 3 of the Convention. The UN Committee on the Rights of the Child, which was set up under the UN Convention to monitor abuses of children's rights in Member States which have implemented the Convention, has criticised the UK for permitting corporal punishment by parents and in public schools. The Committee may well decide that the proposed reforms of physical punishment of children by parents have not gone far enough.

10.5   Children of Unmarried Parents

Many children today are born outside marriage. At one time such children were stigmatised and treated much less favourably by the law than those born to married parents. They could not be buried in consecrated ground and were not entitled to succeed to property on intestacy or to receive maintenance. Over the years, however, the law has attempted to remove the stigma against the children of unmarried parents. In fact it is now considered inappropriate to refer to such children as 'illegitimate' children. The preferred term is 'non-marital' or 'extra-marital' children.

The Family Law Reform Act 1987 was responsible for removing some of the legal discrimination against non-marital children after recommendations were made by the Law Commission (*Illegitimacy*, Law Com No 118, 1982). Section 1(1) of the Act lays down a general principle that with respect to any laws passed or instruments made after the commencement of the Act (4 April 1988), any 'references (however expressed) to any relationship between two persons shall, unless the contrary intention appears, be construed without regard to whether or not the father and mother of either of them, or the father and mother of any person through whom the relationship is deduced, have or had been married to each other at any time.' On intestacy, children of unmarried parents are now entitled to succeed to property under the Administration of Estates Act 1925 in the same way as the children of married parents (ss.18–21 FLRA 1987). Under the Legitimacy Act 1976, non-marital children can be legitimised in various ways. Under s.1, a child born of a void marriage can be treated as legitimate if at the time of insemination, conception or celebration of marriage one or both parents reasonably believed the marriage was valid (reasonable belief is now presumed, see s.28 FLRA 1987). A non-marital child can also be legitimised by his or her parents' marriage (ss.2 and 3 LA 1976). Financial provision orders for children born to unmarried parents and for other children can be sought under s.15 and Sched. 1 to the Children Act 1989, and maintenance can be sought from the Child Support Agency (see 14.2).

However, some discrimination against children born outside marriage still remains. For instance, as s.1 of the Family Law Reform Act 1987 does not apply retrospectively, it does not apply to the British Nationality Act 1981. For this reason, children of unmarried parents can acquire British citizenship only if their *mother* is a British citizen, whereas children of married parents can acquire it if either parent is British. It is also more difficult under the immigration rules for children born overseas of unmarried parents to enter and reside with a parent in the UK than it is for children of married parents. Children of unmarried parents are discriminated against in other respects. They are arguably discrimated against because unmarried fathers do not have automatic parental responsibility, although legislative reform is expected to change this for some fathers in the near future. They are also discriminated against on the breakdown of their parents' relationships, because the lack of power in the court to adjust their parents' property rights may result in non-marital children suffering greater hardship than children on divorce.

10.6   Children as Parties in Legal Proceedings

The rules for representation of children in legal proceedings differ depending on whether the case is brought in private law or public law.

(a) Private Law Cases

As a general rule, a child cannot bring or defend legal proceedings otherwise than through a next friend (e.g. parent, relative or friend) or a guardian *ad litem* (RSC Ord. 80 r.2(1)), whose task it is to instruct a solicitor, serve and accept service of documents etc. However, a child with 'sufficient understanding', with permission of the court, can apply for a s.8 order under the Children Act (see s.10(8) CA 1989), or bring proceedings under the inherent jurisdiction of the court (see 12.8) without a next friend or guardian *ad litem*, or can apply during such proceedings to discharge the next friend or guardian (r.9.2A FPR 1991). The test of whether a child has sufficient understanding is one of *Gillick* competence (see 10.3 above), but only older teenagers are likely to be held to have sufficient understanding (see *Re T (A Minor)(Child Representation)* [1994] Fam 49 and *Re C (Residence: Child's Application for Leave)* [1995] 1 FLR 927). An application for permission to apply must be made to the High Court (*Practice Direction: Children Act 1989 – Applications by Children* [1993] 1 FLR 668). The court can hear the views of other parties who may be involved in the application (r.4.3 FPR 1991). The court also has the power to order that a child be separately represented in any family proceedings, but this power is rarely used (r.9(5) FPR 1991, and see *L v. L (Minors)(Separate Representation)* [1994] 1 FLR 156).

An issue which is sometimes raised is whether the involvement of children in private law proceedings, and in mediation sessions, should be increased. Some feel that children are not involved enough in family proceedings, and that they should be given a greater voice, otherwise, as Piper (1999) has said, there is 'a real danger that children's interests cannot be promoted if we artificially limit our gaze by our presumptions about them' (p.375). As a result of pressure from children's rights organisations, provision was made in the Family Law Act 1996 to give the Lord Chancellor power to make regulations to provide for separate representation of children in specified private law proceedings, including divorce proceedings, but this has not been implemented.

(b) Public Law Cases

In public law proceedings (see Chapter 16) it is mandatory for a guardian *ad litem* to be appointed unless the court is satisfied that such an appointment is unnecessary (see s.41 CA 1989 and rr.4.10–12 of Part IV of the FPR 1991). The guardian has a duty to safeguard the child's interests (s.41(2)(b)) and must, unless he or she is the Official Solicitor, appoint a solicitor to represent and advise the child (r.11(2), (2A)). The guardian must inform the court if it appears to him or her that the child is instructing a solicitor direct, or is intending to do so, or is capable of conducting the proceedings on his or her own behalf (r.4.11(3)). Thereafter, the guardian must perform such duties and take such part in the proceedings as the court directs, and may, with the permission of the court, have legal representation (r.4.11(3)). The guardian, unless excused, must attend court (r.4.11(4)) and advise the court of various matters, including: whether the child has sufficient understanding for any purpose; what the child's wishes are; and what options are available to the court (r.4.11(4)). Where there is no guardian and the child wishes and has sufficient understanding to instruct a solicitor, the court may appoint a solicitor to act for the child (ss.41(3) and (4)). The solicitor (whether appointed by the guardian or by the court) must act in accordance with the instructions given by a child of sufficient understanding if these instructions conflict with those of the guardian (r.4.12(1)). Where no instructions are given by the guardian or child, the solicitor must act in furtherance of the child's best interests (r.4.12(1)(c)). A child (r.4.12(3)) and a guardian (r.4.12(4)) can each apply to the court for the appointment of a solicitor to be terminated.

Summary

1 It is now recognised that children have rights and that parents have responsibilities. Children also have greater rights of self-determination than they once had, particularly after the decision of the House of Lords in *Gillick*, but the court can override the wishes of a '*Gillick* competent' child where the child's welfare requires it. Proponents of children's rights feel that the law has not gone far enough, and that, in particular, children are given an insufficient voice in legal proceedings.

2 The law is currently in the process of being reformed to give children better protection from corporal punishment by their parents, after the European Court of Human Rights ruled in *A* v. *UK* (1998) that the UK was in breach of art. 3 of the European Convention on Human Rights (right not to be subject to human and degrading treatment), because the criminal law made it easy for parents to escape conviction. However, some proponents of children's rights believe that there should be an absolute ban on corporal punishment as there is in some countries.

3 Various theories of children's rights have been put forward, but some have argued that 'rights talk' is not appropriate in the context of children.

4 The UN Convention on the Rights of the Child 1989 has been ratified by the UK but it is not part of English law and neither does it have its own court. Enforcing the provisions of the Convention is therefore difficult. However, arguments based on the Convention can be used persuasively in court and judges sometimes refer to the Convention in their decisions.

5 The *Gillick* case (1986) was important in the development of children's rights. In *Gillick*, the House of Lords said that, where necessary, doctors could prescribe contraceptives to children under the age of 16 without parental consent. Section 8 of the Family Law Reform Act 1969 allows children aged 16 and 17 to give valid consent to medical and dental treatment. Cases since *Gillick* have shown that children's rights are not absolute, and that they cannot have the final say about medical treatment (and other matters), particularly if a course of action, or inaction, is contrary to their welfare. *Gillick* was also important for emphasising that parents have responsibilities, not rights.

6 A child cannot bring private law proceedings other than through a next friend (e.g. parent, guardian, relative or friend) or a guardian *ad litem*, although a child can apply for s.8 orders in his or her own right under the Children Act 1989 (see 12.4) with the permission of the court, which it can grant if the child has sufficient understanding to make the application (s.10(8) CA 1989). In public law proceedings, a guardian *ad litem* must be appointed, unless the court considers the appointment is unnecessary (see also 16.5).

Further Reading and References

Alston, Parker and Seymour (eds), *Children, Rights and the Law*, Clarendon Press, 1992.

Archard, *Children: Rights and Childhood*, Routledge, 1993.

Barton, '*A* v. *UK* – The thirty thousand pound caning – An "English vice" in Europe' [1999] CFLQ 63.

Barton, 'Physical punishment of children – The Consultation Document' [2000] Fam Law 257.

Bevan, *Child Law*, Butterworths, 1989.

Brazier and Bridge, 'Coercion or caring – Analysing adolescent autonomy' (1996) *Legal Studies* 84.

Bridge, 'Religion, culture and conviction – The medical treatment of young children' [1999] CFLQ 1.

Douglas and Sebba (eds), *Children's Rights and Traditional Values*, Dartmouth, 1998.

Eekelaar, 'The emergence of children's rights' (1986) 6 OJLS 161.

Eekelaar, 'The importance of thinking that children have rights' in Alston, Parker and Seymour (see above), at p.221.

Eekelaar, 'The interests of the child and the child's wishes: the role of dynamic self-determinism' (1994) 8 IJLF 42.

Fortin, *Children's Rights and the Developing Law*, Butterworths, 1998.

Fortin, 'Rights brought home for children' (1999) 62 MLR 350.

Fortin, 'The HRA's impact on litigation involving children and their families' [1999] CFLQ 237.

Freeman, *The Rights and Wrongs of Children*, Frances Pinter, 1983.

Goldstein, Freud and Solnit, *Beyond the Best Interests of the Child*, New York Free Press, 1973.

Goldstein, Freud and Solnit, *Before the Best Interests of the Child*, Burnett Books Limited, 1980.

Herring, 'The Human Rights Act and the welfare principle in family law – Conflicting or complementary?' [1999] CFLQ 223.

Huxtable, '*Re M (Medical Treatment: Consent)* – Time to remove the "flak jacket"' [2000] CFLQ 83.

Kilkelly, 'The UN Committee on the Rights of the Child – An evaluation in the light of recent UK experience' [1996] CFLQ 105.

Landsdown, 'Implementing the UN Convention on the Rights of the Child in the UK' [1995] CFLQ 122.

McCafferty, 'Won't consent? Can't consent! Refusal of Medical Treatment' [1999] Fam Law 335.

Piper, 'Barriers to seeing and hearing children in private law proceedings' [1999] Fam Law 394.

Sawyer, 'Conflicting rights for children: implementing welfare, autonomy and justice in family proceedings' (1999) JSWFL 99.

Sawyer, 'One step forward, two steps back – The European Convention on the Exercise of Children's Rights' [1999] CFLQ 151.
Sawyer, 'Hitting people is wrong' [2000] Fam Law 655.
Timms, 'The tension between justice and welfare' [1997] Fam Law 38.

Websites

Centre for Europe's Children (the documentation and information centre for the Programme for Children within the Council of Europe, which in co-operation with UNICEF promotes the United Nations Convention on the Right of the Child): eurochild.gla.ac.uk/
Children's Legal Centre (publications, press releases, *Childright* journal, research): www2.essex.ac.uk/clc/
CRIN (Children's Rights Information Network) (includes the text of the UN Convention on the Rights of the Child, and weblink to EPOCH – End Punishment of Children): www.crin.org/
National Children's Bureau (organisation devoted to promoting the well-being and interests of children; undertakes research projects, which can be accessed): www.ncb.org.uk/
Save the Children Fund: www.savethechildren.org.uk/

Questions

1 What are the arguments for and against the complete abolition of physical punishment of children by their parents?
2 Do children have duties? If so, what are they? Should the law give them greater emphasis?

11 Parents

11.1 Parents and Parenthood

The Government recognises the importance of parents and is keen to support them, for by doing so it says that it demonstrates its commitment to supporting families. In its Consultation Document (*Supporting Families*, 1998, Home Office), the Government stated that 'Good parenting benefits us all' and that 'All parents need support with their children's health, education and welfare and many also want advice and guidance on how to bring up their children' (paras. 1.1 and 1.2, p.6). However, as the Government felt that there was insufficient support for parents (para. 1.3) it introduced new initiatives to support them. Thus, in December 1999 the National Family and Parenting Institute (NPI) was launched under the chairmanship of Dame Margaret Booth DBE to provide helpful guidance and to develop more and better parenting support. A national parenting telephone helpline has also been set up. The Government also intends to introduce education for parenthood in the school curriculum.

The judges also recognise the importance of parents. They do so by upholding the principle that, other things being equal, it is in a child's best interests to be brought up where possible by his or her natural parents. In *Re KD (A Minor)(Ward: Termination of Access)* [1988] AC 806 at 812 Lord Templeman said:

> '[T]he best person to bring up a child is the natural parent. It matters not whether the parent is wise or foolish, rich or poor, educated or illiterate, provided the child's moral and physical health are not endangered.'

As a result of this parental presumption, in *Re D (Residence: Natural Parent)* [1999] 2 FLR 1023, for example, a residence order made in favour of the child's aunt was overturned by Johnson J as the justices had misdirected themselves in law. For while the child's welfare was the court's paramount consideration, there was a strong supposition that a child should remain with his or her natural parents. The presumption in favour of parents is also enshrined in the Children Act 1989, because taking a child away from his or her parents and intervention into family life are seen as remedies of last resort. The Act is based on a policy of minimum state intervention. In this way it upholds the right to a private and family life guaranteed by art. 8 of the European Convention for the Protection of Human Rights.

11.2 Becoming a Parent

The word 'parent' covers many different types of persons. Married parents, unmarried parents, parents-in-law, adoptive parents, step-parents and foster-parents are all 'parents'. The court in respect of wards of court and local authorities in respect of children in care are also 'parents' in the sense that they stand *in loco parentis* to the child. With some parent–child relationships there is a biological relationship between the parent and child which gives rise to a legal relationship, but with others the relationship is created or imposed by the law.

Some couples who are unable to have a child resort to medically assisted techniques. The law makes provision in respect of children born by such techniques, and also for children born as a result of a surrogacy arrangement. Thus, s.27 of the Family Law Reform Act 1987 provides that, where a child's mother is married and her husband has consented to her being artificially inseminated, the child is treated in law as the child of the parties to that marriage and not a child of any other person. Modern technological advances in the field of assisted reproduction have raised difficult ethical issues. Because of these developments, the Warnock Committee into Human Assisted Reproduction and Embryology was established to look into the subject of assisted reproduction and in 1984 published a Report, the '*Warnock Report*' (Cmnd 9314). Its findings resulted in the Human Fertilisation and Embryology Act 1990 being passed. The Human Fertilisation and Embryology Authority is responsible under the Act for regulating treatment and research in the field of fertility treatment. It maintains a Code of Practice and issues licences to clinics to enable them to carry out fertility treatment. As a public authority, the authority is also open to challenges under the Human Rights Act 1998 (see 1.5). The 1990 Act also makes provision for parental orders to be made for parents who have children as a result of assisted reproduction (see below).

Some couples may decide to resort to surrogacy to have a child. Under a surrogacy arrangement a surrogate mother acts as the birth mother for the commissioning parents and agrees to hand the child over to them soon after birth (see, for example, *Re C (A Minor)(Wardship: Surrogacy)* [1985] FLR 846, and *Re P (Minors)(Wardship: Surrogacy)* [1987] 2 FLR 421). Although surrogacy arrangements between private individuals are permitted, it is a criminal offence under the Surrogacy Arrangements Act 1985 to set up a surrogacy agency commercially, to advertise surrogacy services and to negotiate a surrogacy arrangement for money. Before the Human Fertilisation and Embryology Act 1990 came into force, the commissioning parents, including the genetic father, had to adopt the child in order to become the child's legal parents. However, the position has changed, for under s.30 of the 1990 Act the court has the power to make a 'parental order' (see below).

11.3   Obtaining a Parental Order

Under s.30 of the Human Fertilisation and Embryology Act 1990, married commissioning parents of a surrogacy arrangement or married parents of a child conceived by assisted reproduction can apply to the court for a 'parental order', which is an order for a child to be treated in law as a child of the parents' marriage. The procedure is laid down in *Circular – The Principal Registry of the Family Division: The Human Fertilisation and Embryology Act 1990)* [1994] 2 FLR 1098.

The court can make a parental order under s.30 in respect of a child of a married couple where one parent is the genetic parent, provided (s.30(2)–(7)):

- the application is made within six months following the child's birth;
- at the time of the application and order the child's home is with the husband and wife;
- the husband and wife (or one of them) is domiciled in the UK, Channel Islands or Isle of Man;
- the husband and wife are aged over 18;
- no money or other benefit (other than reasonable expenses) has been given or received by the husband or wife for the arrangement, unless authorised by the court; and
- the child's father (whether or not he is the husband) and the woman who carries the child have freely, and with full understanding of what is involved, agreed unconditionally to the order being made.

As a general rule, the child's legal father is the man whose sperm led to the child's creation, except where the sperm is used after a man's death or where the man is a donor for the purpose of licensed treatment under Sched. 3 (s.28(6)). However, where the child was conceived by an embryo or sperm and eggs being placed in a wife, or she was inseminated with sperm that was not her husband's, he is treated as the child's father, unless he did not give consent to the embryo or sperm and eggs being placed in her or did not consent to her insemination (s.28(2)). Where, however, the fertility treatment is carried out under a licensed arrangement, and the embryo or the sperm and eggs were placed in a woman, or she was artificially inseminated, the man is treated as the father of the child (s.28(3)). In *Re CH (Contact: Parentage)* [1996] 1 FLR 569, the child had been conceived by artificial insemination by donor (AID), as the husband had had a vasectomy during a previous marriage. He was present at the birth and regarded himself as the child's father. The marriage broke down and the wife remarried. She sought to deny her former husband contact with the child *inter alia* on the ground that he was not the child's biological father. Callman J held, however, that he was the child's biological parent under s.28 of the 1990 Act.

In *Re Q (Parental Order)* [1996] 1 FLR 369, an unmarried woman acted as a surrogate mother for a married couple and carried and gave birth to a child created from an egg of the wife fertilised by sperm donated at a clinic under a licensed arrangement. The question arose as to who was to be treated as the father for the purpose of giving consent to a s.30 parental order. Johnson J, construing s.28, held that on a proper application of the 1990 Act there was no man who could be treated as the father and whose consent was necessary to the making of a parental order.

A mother who gives birth to a child is treated in law as the child's mother whether or not the child is genetically related to her (ss.27(1) and 29(1)). As proceedings for a s.30 parental order are family proceedings for the purposes of the Children Act 1989 (s.30(8)(a)), the court may make any s.8 order under the Children Act (see 12.4) in s.30 proceedings, either on an application or of its own motion.

11.4   Establishing Paternity

Under the presumption of legitimacy, a child born of married parents is presumed to be the child of the husband, unless and until proved otherwise (i.e. by blood testing and DNA profiling). The presumption of parentage arises from the relationship. The presumption applies to any child conceived or born during marriage, or born within the normal gestation period after the marriage has been terminated by death or divorce. The burden of proof lies on the mother to rebut the presumption. The presumption of parentage does not apply to unmarried parents except where the unmarried father's name appears on the child's birth certificate (s.34(4) Births and Deaths Registration Act 1953).

Blood Tests

In some circumstances it may be necessary to establish the child's paternity, for example for the purposes of contact and maintenance (although special provisions exist under the child support legislation, see 14.2). Under s.20(1) of the Family Law Reform Act 1969, the court in any civil proceedings in which the question of the child's paternity is in issue may on application by a party to those proceedings, or of its own motion, make a direction that a blood test be taken to establish the child's paternity.

A direction will usually be made as the court generally takes the view that a child has a right to know the truth about his parents. In *Re H (Paternity: Blood Tests)* [1997] Fam 89, [1996] 2 FLR 65, Ward LJ referred to art. 7 of the UN Convention on the Rights of the Child 1989 which provides 'that a child has, as far as possible, the right to know and be cared for by his or her parents' (see also *Re G (Parentage: Blood Sample)* [1997] 1 FLR 360). Although the court can direct a blood test be made to establish paternity even where it might not benefit a child (see *S v. S; W v. Official Solicitor* [1970] 3 All ER 107), it may decide not to do so where it will disturb the stability of the child's family unit. In *Re F (A Minor)(Blood Tests: Parental Rights)* [1993] 3 All ER 596, [1993] 1 FLR 598 the Court of Appeal refused to order a blood test, as it would destabilise the child. Balcombe LJ laid down the following principles: that public policy no longer required any special protection to be given to the status of legitimacy; that the interests of justice and the child's welfare normally required the truth to be ascertained; and that it did not protect a child to ban a blood test on a vague and shadowy conjecture that the test might turn out to be to the child's disadvantage. In *Re K (Specific Issue Order)* [1999] 2 FLR 280, where the mother had an obsessional hatred of the father, it was held not to be in the child's bests interests to be told the identity of the father as it would cause the child emotional disruption.

Consents Required

Consent of the person submitting to the blood test is needed if that person is aged over 16 (s.21(1) and (2) FLRA 1969). However, if a person refuses to consent, the court can draw such inferences from a refusal as it thinks fit. Indeed in *Re A (A Minor)(Paternity: Refusal of Blood Test)* [1994] 2 FLR 463 the Court of Appeal held that if a claim were made against someone who could possibly be the father and that person chose not to be tested, the inference that he was the father would be virtually inescapable unless he could give very clear and cogent medical reasons for his refusal. However, a refusal is not always determinative (see *Re H (Paternity: Blood Tests)* [1997] above).

Where the person submitting to the blood test is a child under 16, the blood sample can only be taken with the consent of the person who has care and control of the child (s.21(3)). Where a person with care and control refuses consent to the blood test, it was held by Wall J in *Re O and J (Paternity: Blood Tests)* [2000] 1 FLR 418 that neither the 1969 Act nor the inherent jurisdiction (see 12.9) could provide redress. His Lordship overrode the decision of Hale J in *Re R (Blood Test: Constraint)* [1998] Fam 66, [1998] 1 FLR 743, where she had made a direction under s.20 but had ordered that the child be delivered into the care and control of the Official Solicitor for the purpose of consent to the blood test. Wall J in *Re O and J* called upon Parliament to implement reform as the law did not protect the best interests of children and might not comply with the Human Rights Act 1998. Not only does the question of consent need to be looked at, but it has also been argued (for example, by Sharp, 2000) that UK law governing scientific testing for paternity needs reforming so that saliva, skin or hair roots can be used, instead of blood sampling alone.

11.5 'Alternative' Parents

Most children are brought up by parents with whom they have a biological link, but some children are cared for and brought up by step-parents, foster-parents or a guardian. Some children are brought up by adoptive parents (see Chapter 17).

(a) Step-Parents

With the high rate of divorce, many children are brought up by step-parents. A step-parent is not a biological parent but a parent created by marriage. Step-parents have legal obligations towards their step-children, in particular to provide financial support for the child (see Chapter 14). Step-parents also have certain rights in respect of a step-child. Thus they can apply for adoption (see Chapter 17) and can apply for s.8 orders for a step-child (see 12.4).

(b) Foster-Parents

A foster-parent is a person who acts *in loco parentis* for a child on a fairly settled basis. There are two types of foster-parent: those who care for children under a private fostering arrangement; and those who look after children in local authority care. Although both types of foster-parent have no parental responsibility for the child in law, they may acquire it under a residence order (see 12.4), or by being appointed a guardian (see below). Even where they have no such responsibility, they have an obligation to care for the child. Both types of foster-parent are subject to the control and supervision of local authorities, but different rules and regulations apply to each group.

(c) Guardians

Sections 5 and 6 of the Children Act 1989 make provision in respect of the appointment of guardians. A guardian can be appointed privately or by the court.

(i) Private Appointment A parent (or both parents) with parental responsibility, or a guardian, can appoint a guardian (s.5(3), (4) and (10)). An appointment can be made in a will or otherwise, but it must be in writing, and be dated and signed by the appointor, or signed at the direction of the testator in accordance with s.9 of the Wills Act 1837 (if made in a will), or signed at the

direction of the appointor in his or her presence and in the presence of two witnesses who must each attest the signature (s.5(5)).

(ii) Appointment by the Court   The court on the application of any person (but not a local authority), or of its own motion in any family proceedings (see 12.4), may appoint a guardian if the child has no parent with parental responsibility, or a parent or guardian who had a residence order in his or her favour has died while the order was in force (s.5(1) and (2)). The court can appoint more than one guardian and can make an appointment even though a guardian has been privately appointed. When deciding whether or not to make an appointment, the child's welfare is the court's paramount consideration and the 'no delay' principle and the 'no order presumption' apply (see 12.3). As the appointment of a guardian is itself family proceedings (s.8(4)), the court instead of, or in addition to, appointing a guardian can on an application, or of its motion, make any s.8 order under the Children Act 1989 (see 12.4).

(iii) Revocation and Disclaimer of Appointment   A later private appointment revokes an earlier private appointment made by the same person in respect of the same child, unless the clear purpose of the later appointment is to appoint an additional guardian (s.6(1)). A person who has appointed a guardian can revoke that appointment by a written and dated instrument signed by him, or signed at his direction in his presence and in the presence of two witnesses each of whom must attest the signature (s.6(2)). Where a guardian has been appointed, other than by will or codicil, the appointor can revoke that appointment by destroying the instrument or getting someone else to destroy it in his presence (s.6(3)). Revocation of a will or codicil in which a guardian has been appointed revokes that appointment (s.6(4)). A person appointed a guardian by private appointment can disclaim appointment by an instrument in writing signed by him within a reasonable time of his first knowing the appointment has taken effect (s.6(5)). Any appointment of a guardian can also be terminated by court order on the application of any person with parental responsibility for the child (including a local authority), or on the application of a child, provided the child has permission of the court (s.6(7)). The court in any family proceedings (see 12.5) may of its own motion also terminate an appointment (s.6(7)).

(iv) Effects of Guardianship   Guardianship takes effect: on the death of the appointor, if the child has no parent with parental responsibility (s.5(7)(a)), or on the death of the appointor if the appointor had a residence order in his or her favour in respect of the child, except where the residence order was also made in favour of a surviving parent (ss.5(7)(b) and (9)). Guardians have parental responsibility for the child (s.5(6)) and, like parents, have certain duties (e.g. to care for the child and see that the child is educated) and rights in respect of the child (e.g. to apply for orders under the Children Act 1989 and to consent to the child's adoption). However, unlike parents, a guardian has no

legal duty to make financial contribution towards a child (as this might deter people becoming guardians). Consequently, child support and orders for financial relief (see Chapter 14) cannot be made against a guardian. Furthermore, a guardian has no right to succeed to the child's property on the child's intestacy, and a child cannot become a British citizen under the British Nationality Act 1981 by virtue of his guardian being resident or settled in the UK.

11.6 Parental Responsibility

The term 'parental responsibility', not 'parental rights', is the term used to describe parental interests in children. 'Parental responsibility' was adopted by the Children Act 1989 in order to reflect the idea that children are persons to whom duties are owed, rather than persons over whom power is wielded. The emphasis on parental responsibility arose partly as a result of the influence of the *Gillick* case on discussions leading up to the Children Act (see 10.3). In *Gillick*, Lord Scarman had stated that parental rights are derived from parental duty.

Who has Parental Responsibility?

At the time of writing, married parents (s.2(1)) and the unmarried mother (s.2(2)) have 'automatic' parental responsiblity for their child. Unmarried fathers do not have automatic parental responsibility but can acquire it if they wish (see below). However, because it has been increasingly felt that unmarried fathers are discriminated against, the Government is proposing to introduce legislation giving automatic parental responsibility to unmarried fathers who are registered as the father on the child's birth certificate. Unmarried fathers who are not so registered, but who wish to obtain parental responsibility, will still have to acquire it (see below). It should be noted, however, that *all* fathers, with or without parental responsibility, have a duty to maintain their children (see Chapter 14) and also have a right to apply for s.8 orders (see 12.4).

Parents of a void marriage both have parental responsibility, provided at the time of the child's conception, or at the time of the marriage, if later, either or both of them reasonably believed that the marriage was valid (s.1 Legitimacy Act 1976). Parents who marry after the birth of a child are treated as if they were married to each other at the time of the child's birth (s.2 LA 1976) and therefore both have parental responsibility. An unmarried father without parental responsibility can therefore acquire parental responsibility by marrying the mother of his child.

The following persons also have parental responsibility: a guardian (s.5(6) CA 1989); a person in whose favour a residence order is made, but only while the order is in force (s.12 CA 1989); and a person who adopts a child (see Chapter 17). A local authority also possesses a limited sort of parental responsibility when a child is in its care (s.33(3)), or when an emergency protection order is made (s.44(4)(c)).

More than one person can have parental responsibility for the same child at the same time (s.2(5)), and parental responsibility does not terminate because another person subsequently acquires it (s.2(6)). Neither is it lost when a child goes into local authority care. Parental responsibility also continues after divorce or relationship breakdown.

The Exercise of Parental Responsibility

Persons with parental responsibility can act independently of each other in meeting that responsibility, unless any Act of Parliament, including the Children Act, requires the consent of more than one person in any matter affecting the child (s.2(7)), or where the court has decided otherwise. For example, the consent of both parents with parental responsibility is required for one of them to remove the child from the UK, and both parents with parental responsibility must consent to their child's adoption, unless their consent is dispensed with. The court has also held that certain other important decisions about children should not be taken unilaterally, e.g. to change a child's education arrangements (see *Re G (Parental Responsibility: Education)* [1994] 2 FLR 964). However, in some circumstances the consent of both parents with parental responsibility will be insufficient on its own, as the court's consent will be required (e.g. in the context of serious medical treatment, such as sterilisation of a child).

A parent is prohibited from exercising parental responsibility in a way which is incompatible with a court order made under the Children Act 1989 (s.2(8)). It would, for instance, be contempt of court for a parent to remove a child from the care of a local authority or refuse to allow a child to emigrate with a parent in breach of a s.8 specific issue order. Where those sharing parental responsibility cannot agree on a particular course of action, then an application can be made for a s.8 order under the Children Act 1989 (see 12.4), if it cannot be settled by any other means.

A person with parental responsibility cannot surrender or transfer any of that responsibility, but may arrange for some or all of it to be met by one or more persons acting on his or her behalf (s.2(9)), and that person includes someone else with parental responsibility (s.2(10)). Thus it is possible to place the child with someone acting *in loco parentis* (e.g. childminder, babysitter, friend, or relative), or someone else with parental responsibility (e.g. the other parent, or a grandparent with parental responsibility under a residence order). However, as a person with parental responsibility cannot escape liability under the criminal or civil law by delegating responsibility to another person (s.2(11)), the onus is on parents to make proper arrangements for their children.

When a child is in care, the local authority can determine the extent to which the parents may meet their parental responsibility (s.33(3)(b)), but local authorities are required to work in partnership with parents (see Chapter 16).

11.7 Unmarried Fathers and Parental Responsibility

In discussions leading up to the Children Act 1989 there was reluctance to give unmarried fathers automatic parental responsibility, as rapists and fathers who had conceived a child during a casual relationship would have parental responsibility and this might be detrimental to some mothers and children. Since the implementation of the Children Act, however, there has been increasing criticism of the fact that unmarried fathers do not possess automatic parental responsibility. With increasing numbers of couples choosing to cohabit and increasing numbers of children being born outside marriage, it has generally been felt that the law discriminates against unmarried fathers and is also contrary to the best interests of their children. Indeed many unmarried fathers are unaware of the fact that they possess no parental responsibility. They only discover it on relationship breakdown. The lack of automatic parental responsibility for unmarried fathers has also caused problems in other areas of the law, notably in cases of child abduction (see Chapter 15).

As a result of the considerable dissatisfaction about the position for unmarried fathers, in March 1998 the Lord Chancellor's Department published a Consultation Paper (*1. Court Procedures for the Determination of Paternity. 2. The Law on Parental Responsibility for Unmarried Fathers*, see www.open.gov/lcd) in which it discussed giving unmarried fathers 'automatic' parental responsibility. However, the view taken was that it would be wrong to give all unmarried fathers automatic parental responsibility, and a compromise was reached. As a result, the Government is planning to amend the legislation governing birth registration so that any father named on the birth register jointly with the mother will have automatic parental responsibility. In fact, the Maternity and Parental Leave etc Regulations 1999 which came into force at the end of 1999 already make provision for this by providing that an unmarried father may qualify for parental leave if he has responsibility for a child under the Children Act 1989 or by being registered as the child's father under s.10(1) or s.10A(1) of the Births and Deaths Registration Act 1953.

Acquiring Parental Responsibility

An unmarried father who does not have 'automatic' parental responsibility can acquire it by:

- making a 'parental responsibility agreement' with the mother on a prescribed form (s.4);

- applying for a court order giving him parental responsibility (s.4);
- applying for a s.8 residence order (see 12.4) when the court must at the same time make a s.4 order;
- becoming the child's guardian on the mother's death (see 11.5 above);
- adopting the child (see Chapter 17); or
- marrying the mother.

Once a father has acquired parental responsibility he has all the rights of a married father. Thus, for example, he can consent or refuse to consent to adoption, make decisions about the child's education and appoint a guardian.

Acquiring Parental Responsibility by Agreement with the Child's Mother

Unmarried fathers can acquire parental responsibility by making an agreement with the mother (see s.4 Children Act 1989). They can do this without judicial or local authority scrutiny as to whether or not they are a suitable father. The agreement is made on a special form which must be signed by both parties, witnessed and registered in the Principal Registry of the Family Division. Where a child is in care, the local authority cannot prevent the child's mother entering into a parental responsibility agreement with the father, even though a person with parental responsibility must not act incompatibly with a care order (s.2(8)) and a local authority can determine the extent to which parents meet their responsibilities (s.33(3)(b)) (see *Re X Parental Responsibility Agreement: Children in Care)* [2000] 1 FLR 517, where the Court of Appeal so held, on the basis that a parental responsibility agreement does not of itself depend on the exercise of parental responsibility, and is an act done by parents in unison, rather than a unilateral exercise of a mother's parental responsibility). A parental responsibility agreement can be revoked by the court (see below).

Acquiring Parental Responsibility by Applying for a Parental Responsibility Order

An unmarried father may apply to the court for a parental responsibility order. Orders are in fact commonly made (7798 orders were made in 1998, see *Judicial Statistics 1998*, published by the Lord Chancellor's Department). The application is governed by the principle that the welfare of the child is the court's paramount consideration (s.1(1)) (see *Re G (A Minor)(Parental Responsibility Order)* [1994] 1 FLR 504). The no-delay principle applies (s.1(3)), and the no-order presumption (s.1(5)). However, the court is unlikely to apply the no-order presumption, because it takes the view that a parental responsibility order confers an important status on a father. When deciding whether or not to make an order, the court will take into account all the circumstances of the case, but Balcombe LJ in *Re H (Minors)(Local Authority: Parental Rights)(No 3)* [1991] Fam 151 said that the following factors are particularly important:

- the degree of commitment which the father has shown towards the child;
- the degree of attachment which exists between the father and the child; and
- the father's reasons for applying for the order.

These factors have been applied in many cases (see, for example, *Re CB (A Minor)(Parental Responsibility Order)* [1993] 1 FLR 920, *Re G (A Minor)(Parental Responsibility Order)* [1994] 1 FLR 504, *Re E (Parental Responsibility: Blood Tests)* [1995] 1 FLR 392). However, the Court of Appeal has more recently stated (see *Re H (Parental Responsibility)* [1998] 1 FLR 855) that Balcombe LJ's list of factors is not an exhaustive list. The court must take into account all the relevant circumstances and, applying the welfare principle in s.1(1) of the Children Act, decide whether a parental responsibility order is in the child's best interests. Thus, even though the above three factors are satisfied in a particular case, the court may decide that there are other factors which tip the balance against making the order.

As the court has taken the view that a parental responsibility order confers an important status on a father, an order will not usually be refused unless it is clearly contrary to a child's welfare. Good reason will therefore need to be shown why an order should not be granted. Thus, an order may be granted even though there may be a problem enforcing the rights which arise as a result of acquiring parental responsibility (*Re C (Minors)(Parental Rights)* [1992] 2 All ER 86), or where there is acrimony between the parents (*Re P (A Minor)(Parental Responsibility Order)* [1994] 1 FLR 578), or where parental responsibility cannot be exercised (see *Re H (A Minor)(Parental Responsibility)* [1993] 1 FLR 484). Furthermore, failure to provide maintenance will not of itself provide a reason for refusing an order (*Re H (Parental Responsibility: Maintenance)* [1996] 1 FLR 867). In *Re S (Parental Responsibility)* [1995] 2 FLR 648, the Court of Appeal stressed that, as a parental responsibility order granted an important status, it was wrong to place undue and false emphasis on the rights, duties and powers comprised in parental responsibility, because any abuse of its exercise could be controlled by making a s.8 order (see 12.4).

Despite the willingness of the courts to make parental responsibility orders, because of the important status it confers, the court may refuse to make an order where it would be contrary to the best interests of a child. Thus, there is no presumption that a devoted father will necessarily obtain an order (see *Re H (Parental Responsibility)* [1998] 1 FLR 855, where an order was refused as the father had injured his son and the child of a former partner). In *Re P (Parental Responsibility)* [1998] 2 FLR 96, the Court of Appeal refused to make an order as the father had been found to be in possession of obscene photographs of young children. As the father posed a risk to the child, the Court of Appeal refused to make an order even though any potential abuse of parental responsibility could be controlled by making a s.8 order. In *M* v. *M (Parental Responsibility)* [1999] 2 FLR 737, an application was refused because the father was held to be incapable of exercising parental responsibility (he had suffered serious brain damage in a motorcycle accident). Wilson J took the view that Balcombe LJ's third factor above (reasons or motivation for applying for the order) presupposed that a father was capable of reason, and ss.4(1) and 3(1) presupposed that a father who is granted parental responsibility is capable of exercising rights, performing duties and wielding powers in relation to the child. It is perhaps questionable, however, whether this decision was correctly decided. Why should the ability to exercise parental responsibilities be a prerequisite for an order? After all, the Court of Appeal has frequently stressed that granting an order gives the father an important status. Furthermore, orders have been granted where a father cannot exercise parental responsibility (for instance where he is in prison). Indeed Wilson J in *M* v. *M* stressed the importance of the child growing up in the knowledge of her father and his love for her, but nevertheless refused the order.

Although the courts have frequently stressed the importance of granting parental responsibility orders because of the important status an order gives unmarried fathers, Douglas (1998) has questioned whether it is the function of these orders to grant such a status. She says that by virtue of s.1 of the Family Law Reform Act 1987 (see 10.5) any references to a parent in the Children Act are to be construed without regard to that person's marital status, and for that reason she says that obtaining parental responsibility, by agreement or order, means 'exactly what it says – it gives the father the rights, duties, powers, responsibilities and authority – not status – conferred by law upon a parent (s.3(1)).' Douglas argues that the fact that parental responsibility can be removed (see below), and yet a father remains a father, emphasises that parental responsibility has nothing to do with status but with parental rights and responsibilities. Furthermore, in support of her argument, it can be added that unmarried fathers, with or without parental responsibility, already possess the status of fatherhood or parenthood, by virtue of their right as parents to apply for s.8 orders under the Children Act 1989 without the need to have parental responsibility.

Parental Responsibility via a Residence Order

An unmarried father can also acquire parental responsibility by applying for a s.8 residence order (see 12.4), when the court at the same time must make a s.4 order giving him parental responsibility (s.12(1)).

Parental Responsibility is not Necessarily Permanent

Parental responsibility obtained by unmarried fathers, whether by agreement or by court order, unlike that possessed by married fathers, is not necessarily permanent. It can be revoked by the court on an application by any person with parental responsibility for the child, or by the child himself, provided the child has the court's permission to apply for revocation, which it can grant if the child has sufficient understanding to make the application (s.4(3) and (4)). When deciding whether to terminate parental responsibility, the child's welfare is the court's paramount consideration (s.1(1)) and the court must apply the no-delay principle (s.1(2)). There are very few reported cases where responsibility has been revoked. However, one such case was *Re P (Terminating Parental Responsibility)* [1995] 1 FLR 1048, where a parental responsibility agreement was terminated by the court on the mother's application, as the child had suffered extreme injuries at the hands of her father. However, Singer J was keen to stress that such an application should not be used as a weapon by a dissatisfied mother of a non-marital child.

11.8   Non-Parents and Parental Responsibility

Sometimes persons who are not the child's natural parent may wish to obtain parental responsibility. They can do this by obtaining a s.8 residence order (see 12.4) or by adopting a child (see Chapter 17). If they wish to acquire it by applying for a residence order, they may need the permission of the court to apply. However, the disadvantage of parental responsibility obtained by this route is that parental responsibility lasts only for the duration of the residence order. If two people wish to obtain parental responsibility jointly, they may apply for a joint (i.e. shared) residence order. This is sometimes useful for cohabiting couples in the context of adoption because joint applications for adoption by cohabitants are not permitted. Thus, in *Re AB (Adoption: Joint Residence)* [1996] 1 FLR 27, the male cohabitant applied for an adoption order and he and his partner applied for a joint residence order. By this route they both acquired parental responsibility for the adopted child. In the public law context, if a care order is made (see 16.5), the local authority acquires parental responsibility for the child, although it is a limited type of responsibility. Furthermore, it does not terminate the parental responsibility of parents.

11.9   What is Parental Responsibility?

Section 3(1) of the Children Act 1989 defines parental responsibility as:

> 'all the rights, duties, powers, responsibilities and authority which by law a parent of a child has in relation to the child and his property.'

This definition is unhelpful, however, as it fails to define the precise nature of parental responsibility. The nature and scope of parental responsibility can only be deduced by looking at statute and case-law.

Despite the emphasis on parental responsibility rather than rights, parents do possess parental rights, notably against third parties and the State. They have, for instance, a right as a parent to bring proceedings under the Children Act 1989, not a parental responsibility to do so. Section s.3(1) itself (see above) mentions the word 'rights' and in *Gillick* (see 10.3) Lord Scarman, while recognising that the term 'responsibility' was a more appropriate term than 'rights', nevertheless stated that parental rights clearly existed but that the law had never treated such rights as 'sovereign or beyond review and control.' Parents do have rights, but they are not absolute. The scope and nature of any right depend on the right in question, the age and maturity of the child and all the circumstances of the case. Furthermore, the court can override parental rights. In *Re Z (A Minor)(Freedom of Publication)* [1997] Fam 1, [1996] 1 FLR 191, Sir Thomas Bingham MR said that if the court's judgment 'is in accord with that of the devoted and responsible parent, well and good. If not, then it is the duty of the court ... to give effect to its own judgment.' Thus the court can restrain a parent from doing, or not doing, any act which might adversely affect the child's welfare. For example, in *A* v. *M (Family Proceedings: Publicity)* [2000] 1 FLR 562, Charles J granted an injunction to stop the mother publishing information about what had happened in court proceedings involving herself, the father and the child (see also *Re W (A Minor)(Wardship: Freedom of Publication)* [1992] 1 FLR 99).

Although there is no statutory list of parental responsibilities or rights, parents do have the following rights and responsibilities:

(i) A Right to the Physical Possession of the Child

The criminal and civil law relating to child abduction (see Chapter 15), and the restriction under s.13 of the Children Act 1989 on a child subject to a residence order being removed out of the UK show that parents do have a right to the physical possession of the child. This is also emphasised by the fact that, under the Children Act, a parent can ask a local authority to hand the child back if the child is not subject to a care or emergency protection order. Indeed, one of the central policy aims of the Children Act is that children who are accommodated in care under a voluntary arrangement under Part III of the Act can be taken back by a parent at any time. The right to physical possession of a child also includes the right to decide where the child lives. Thus, for example, when a child is accommodated in local authority care under a voluntary arrangement, a local authority may not place the child in accommodation against parental wishes (see *R* v. *Tameside Metropolitan Borough Council ex parte J* [2000] 1 FLR 942).

(ii) *A Right and Duty to Have Contact with the Child*

The s.8 contact order (see 13.4) and the presumption of reasonable contact when a child is in local authority care (see 16.6) indicate that parents have a right of contact, even though it is never an absolute or fundamental right in the human rights' sense (see *Re KD (A Minor) (Ward: Termination of Access)* [1988] AC 806). A right of contact is always subject to the welfare of the child and can be terminated in private and in public law proceedings. The law encourages parent–child contact, as parents are considered to be the primary care-givers and maintaining contact is considered to be beneficial for a child. If contact is not maintained when a child is in care, then the chances of reha-bilitation are reduced. Although the law encourages contact, the case-law has emphasised that contact is a right of the child (*M* v. *M* [1973] 2 All ER 81). For this reason, contact is also a parental duty.

(iii) *A Right and a Duty to Educate the Child*

A parent has a duty to ensure that a child between the ages of five and sixteen receives 'efficient, full-time education suitable to his age, ability and aptitude, either by regular attendance at school or otherwise' (ss.35 and 36 Education Act 1944). A parent who fails to ensure the child's education (whether at home or at school) can be prosecuted (ss.39 and 40 EA 1944), and a local education authority can obtain an education supervision order under s.36 of the Children Act when a child fails to attend school. Parents have a right to choose which school their child attends, and education authorities must comply with parental wishes unless this would be prejudicial to efficient education or to an efficient use of resources (s.76 EA 1944; s.6 EA 1980). Parents have a right of appeal against a refusal of a place at a chosen school (s.7 EA 1980). Parents must also be provided with information about schools, e.g. curriculum, discipline, school policy etc. A parent also has a right to withdraw a child from religious educa-tion (s.9(3) Education Reform Act 1988) or from some sex education classes (s.17A ERA 1988), except where it is part of the National Curriculum.

(iv) *A Right to Choose the Child's Religion*

Parents have a right to choose the child's religion, or decide that the child should have no religion, at least until the child becomes '*Gillick*-competent'. For instance, they can choose to remove their child from religious instruction and school assemblies. The importance of religion is also reflected in statutory pro-visions relating to fostering and adoption placements, as the local authority must take into consideration the child's religious beliefs and religious background.

(v) A Right and a Duty to Consent to Medical Treatment

The *Gillick* case (see 10.3) did not remove the right (and duty) of parents to consent to the child's medical treatment. In fact the DHSS circular, which was the
object of Mrs Gillick's wrath, stated that doctors should act on the presumption
that parents should be consulted before contraceptives were prescribed. Where a
child is not a mature minor (is not *Gillick* competent), parental consent to medical treatment is needed, and even where a child is *Gillick* competent, the child's
wishes can be overridden by the child's parents and by the court.

However, parental rights in medical matters are not absolute. The parental
right to make a decision about a child's medical treatment can be overridden if
contrary to the child's best interests. Indeed, where there is a dispute between
parents and doctors about appropriate medical treatment, the court may have
to decide the matter, and, can where necessary, override the wishes of parents
and allow the medical profession to determine the treatment (see, for example,
Re MM (Medical Treatment) [2000] 1 FLR 224). In *Re C (HIV Test)* [1999]
2 FLR 1004, for example, the parents' refusal to have their baby tested for
HIV (the mother was HIV positive) was overridden by the court. The local
authority was granted a specific issue order so that the test could be carried
out, despite the parents' argument that it was an affront to their parental autonomy and that there was no value in having the baby tested. The Court of
Appeal said that the child might be at risk if there was ignorance about her
medical condition and that the degree of intrusion by the HIV test was slight.
However, although the child's welfare is always the court's paramount consideration in cases like this, the court will also put into the balancing exercise the
impact on parents of making a decision about medical treatment which is contrary to their wishes. For example, in *Re T (Wardship: Medical Treatment)*
[1997] 1 FLR 502, the fact that the parents did not wish to care for their child
who needed a life-saving liver transplant was taken into account, and the court
under its inherent jurisdiction, applying the welfare principle, refused to overrule the parents' refusal to consent.

Where an operation is a serious one, such as sterilisation, the court rather
than the parents may have to decide the matter. The Official Solicitor has stated
that sterilisation of a child in virtually all cases requires the prior sanction of a
High Court judge and that the preferred course of action is to apply under the
inherent jurisdiction or in wardship, because of procedural and administrative
difficulties which attach to applications for s.8 specific issue orders *(Practice
Direction: Official Solicitor: Sterilisation)* [1993] 2 FLR 222) (although an
application by way of a specific issue order was allowed in *Re HG (Specific
Issue Order: Sterilisation)* [1993] 1 FLR 587). The leading authority on sterilisation of a child is *Re B (A Minor)(Wardship: Sterilisation)* [1988] AC 199,
where the House of Lords in wardship authorised the sterilisation of a mentally

retarded 17-year-old girl child. By contrast, however, in *Re D (A Minor) (Wardship: Sterilisation)* [1976] Fam 185, sterilisation was refused, because the court felt the girl might at a later date be able to give informed consent to the operation. Consent of the court is not necessarily required, however, where sterilisation is needed for therapeutic reasons (*Re E (A Minor)(Wardship: Medical Treatment)* [1993] 1 FLR 386). It has recently been held that a dispute about circumcision is also one of the exceptional cases where a disagreement between those who possess parental responsibility must be determined by the courts (see *Re J (Specific Issue Orders: Child's Religious Upbringing and Circumcision)* [2000] 1 FLR 571).

Sometimes, the court will be faced with difficult and harrowing decisions about whether to order life-saving treatment for a child (see particularly *Re A (Conjoined Twins: Medical Treatment)* [2001] 1 FLR 266). In *Re B (A Minor)(Wardship: Medical Treatment)* [1990] 3 All ER 927, the court ordered that a small baby born with Down's syndrome be given a life-saving operation to remove an intestinal blockage, although the parents had refused to consent to the operation. In *Re J (A Minor)(Wardship: Medical Treatment)* [1991] Fam 33, on the other hand, the Court of Appeal dismissed an appeal by the Official Solicitor against a decision of the High Court in wardship where the judge had ordered that a severely disabled baby should not be reventilated if his breathing stopped. In some cases the courts have overruled the refusal of Jehovah's Witnesses to consent to their child's medical treatment (see, for example, *Re R (A Minor)(Blood Transfusion)* [1993] 2 FLR 757), but as Jehovah's Witnesses are now permitted to consent to blood transfusions and medical treatment in life-threatening cases without the fear of being excommunicated, these cases are now less likely to arise.

(vi) A Right to Consent to the Child's Marriage

Where a child is aged over 16 but under 18, parents and others with parental responsibility must give their consent to the child's marriage, although failure to do so is unlikely to invalidate it (see 2.2).

(vii) A Right and Duty to Choose the Child's Surname

A child by convention takes the father's surname, not the mother's, although this is not compulsory. A parent can choose any surname for the child. However, where a residence order is in force, the child's surname cannot be changed without the written consent of all those with parental responsibility, or with the permission of the court (see 13.5).

(viii) A Right to Consent to the Child's Adoption

Under the Adoption Act 1976, parents, except unmarried fathers without
parental responsibility, have a right to consent to their child's adoption,
although consent may be dispensed with on certain grounds (see Chapter 17).

(ix) A Right and a Duty to Discipline the Child and to Administer Reasonable Punishment

While a parent probably has a right and a duty to discipline a child, a parent
must only inflict reasonable punishment, otherwise he or she may be guilty of
a criminal offence under the Offences Against the Person Act 1861, the
Criminal Justice Act 1988, or the Children and Young Persons' Act 1933. An
assault is also a tort under the civil law, so that an aggrieved child can sue for
damages. However, the Government is currently in the process of reforming
the law (see 10.1).

(x) Other Rights

Parents have other rights. They can administer the child's property and enter
into contracts on the child's behalf. They have a right to appoint a guardian for
the child (see 11.5 above). They also have rights to appear before the courts
for orders in respect of their children, and a right to apply to the Child Support
Agency for arrangements to be made in respect of child support.

Summary

1 The Government has expressed its commitment to supporting parents.
2 There is a judge-made presumption of law that the best person to bring up a child
  is the child's natural parent. This approach is also enshrined in the Children Act
  (see Chapter 12).
3 Some couples may have to resort to assisted reproduction techniques or to surrogacy to have a child. The Human Fertilisation and Embryology Act 1990 governs
  assisted reproduction. Under the Surrogacy Arrangements Act 1985, it is a criminal offence to make surrogacy arrangements on a commercial basis.
4 Married commissioning parents of a surrogacy arrangement and married parents
  of a child conceived by assisted reproduction can apply for a 'parental order' under
  s.30 of the Human Fertilisation and Embryology Act 1990, which is an order for a
  child to be treated in law as a child of the parents' marriage.
5 A child born of married parents is presumed to be the child of the husband.
  The same presumption does not apply to unmarried parents. If there is a need
  to establish paternity, the court can direct that a blood test take place (s.20 of
  the Family Law Reform Act 1969), but the consent of the person who must submit
  to the blood test (if aged 16 and over) is needed. In the case of a child aged

under 16, the consent of the person with care and control of the child is required (s.21). The court will usually order a blood test, unless it is not in the best interests of the child concerned. However, if an adult refuses consent, the court can draw an inference that he is the father.

6 Step-parents and foster-parents have obligations to children in their care, and rights to bring proceedings under the Children Act 1989.

7 A guardian can be appointed for a child privately or by the court (ss.5 and 6 Children Act 1989).

8 Parents (but not an unmarried father) have parental responsibility (ss.2 and 3 Children Act 1989), but an unmarried father can acquire parental responsibility under s.4 of the Children Act by agreement with the mother, or by applying for a court order. Another option is for the unmarried father to apply for a s.8 residence order (see 12.4 and 13.3), when the court must at the same time grant him parental responsibility. The Government, however, is proposing to introduce new legislation which will give unmarried fathers parental responsibility if they are registered on their child's birth certificate.

9 Parents have certain rights and duties at common law and under statute, but parental rights are not absolute. Serious and irreversible operations on the child (e.g. sterilisation) need the consent of the court. Where a parental dispute about a child cannot be settled, then an application can be made for a s.8 specific issue order (see 12.4). Where a parent wishes to prevent the other parent doing something, then an application can be made for a s.8 prohibited steps order (see 12.4).

Further Reading and References

Bainham, Day-Slater and Richards, *What is a Parent? A Socio-Legal Analysis*, Hart Publishing, 1999.

Barton and Douglas, *Law and Parenthood*, Butterworths, 1995.

Bridge, 'Parental powers and the medical treatment of children', in Bridge (ed.), *Family Law Towards the Millennium: Essays for P. M. Bromley*, Butterworths, 1997.

Bridge, 'Religion, culture and conviction: the medical treatment of children' [1999] CFLQ 217.

Douglas, *Law, Fertility and Reproduction*, Sweet & Maxwell, 1991.

Downie, 'Consent to medical treatment – whose views or welfare?' [1999] Fam Law 818.

Downie, *'Re C (HIV) Test* – The limits of parental autonomy' [2000] CFLQ 197.

Eekelaar, 'Are parents morally obliged to care for their children?' (1991) OJLS 340.

Eekelaar, 'Parental responsibility: state of nature or nature of the state?' (1991) JSWFL 37.

Eekelaar and Sarcevic (eds), *Parenthood in Modern Society*, Martinus Nijhoff, 1993.

Lind, 'Perceptions of sex in the legal determination of fatherhood – *X, Y and Z* v. *UK*' [1997] CFLQ 401.

Sharp, 'Paternity testing – Time to update the law' [2000] Fam Law 560.

Website

Parentline Plus (provides help and support for parents; leaflets and information available, and also a helpline for parents called 'Parentline'): www.parentlineplus.org.uk/

Questions

1 Are cohabiting parents discriminated against compared with their married counterparts? If so, how?
2 Is the sterilisation of a child ever justified?

12   The Children Act 1989

12.1   The Children Act 1989

The Children Act 1989 consolidated much of both the private and public civil law applicable to children. The fusion of private and public law in the Act was largely accidental. The Law Commission happened to be examining the private law relating to children (*Report on Guardianship and Custody*, Law Com No 172, 1988) at the same time as the Government was examining the public law relating to children (*The Law on Child Care and Family Services*, Cm 62, 1987).

In addition to consolidating the law, the Children Act introduced important new principles and policies. Government reports and public inquiries relating to the management of child abuse by social workers and other agencies had a considerable influence on these changes of philosophy. Of particular importance was *The Report of the Inquiry into Child Abuse in Cleveland 1987* (Cm 412, 1988), which had severely criticised the over-zealous intervention of the local authority in cases of actual and suspected child abuse in Cleveland. The Report had an important influence on the public law provisions of the Children Act, particularly in respect of emergency protection for children and the need for inter-agency co-operation. The *Gillick* case (see 10.3) also had a significant impact, by giving children of sufficient age and understanding the right to bring proceedings under the Act and to have their views taken into account by the court. The concept of parental responsibility (see 11.6) was also introduced by the Act (partly as a result of *Gillick*), in order to stress the positive ongoing nature of parental involvement in bringing up children and to remove the adversarial undertones of the word 'rights'. The emphasis in the Act is on self-determination for both parents and children, with a policy of minimum State intervention. The court under the no-order presumption in s.1(5) can make orders only where it is better to do so than making no order at all, and local authorities must work in partnership with parents, with court orders being sought and made only in the last resort. As far as the public law is concerned, the aim of the Act was to restrict intervention into family life by courts and local authorities unless really necessary for the child's welfare.

Other major aims of the Act were to provide a flexible court structure and a flexible range of orders available in all family proceedings involving children. Applications under the Act can therefore be brought in magistrates' family proceedings courts, county courts and the High Court, but provision is made for cases to be transferred between these courts in urgent or serious cases, or where proceedings should be consolidated. Certain family members are also given greater rights under the Act, e.g. unmarried fathers can acquire parental responsibility and third parties such as grandparents can apply for private law orders with the permission of the court.

The Children Act has generally been considered to be a 'successful' Act, although some have criticised it for failing to put children's interests sufficiently to the fore (see Freeman, 1998). One problem, however, is that proceedings under the Act are often subject to considerable delay. Proceedings can be complex and protracted. Furthermore, with the coming into force of the Human Rights Act 1998 (see 1.5), human rights' arguments before the courts are likely to add to the complexity and time it takes for cases to be heard.

12.2   An Overview of the Act

The parts of the Children Act 1989 which are most relevant to family lawyers are Parts I to V, although Part XII (Miscellaneous and General) is also important because it contains the interpretation section (see s.105) for earlier Parts of the Act. The remaining Parts of the Act deal with such matters as community and voluntary homes, the registration of children's homes and private fostering arrangements. The Act also contains several important schedules, which must not be overlooked – in particular, Schedules 1 to 3 (see below).

Parts I to V deal with the following matters:

- **Part I ('Introductory')**: welfare principle, and other principles applicable in proceedings under the Act (s.1); parental responsibility (ss.2–4); appointment of guardians (ss.5–6); and welfare reports (s.7).

- **Part II ('Orders with Respect to Children in Family Proceedings')**: private law orders (residence, contact, specific issue and prohibited steps orders, see s.8); powers of the court in respect of these orders (ss.9–14); orders for financial relief for children (s.15); and family assistance orders (s.16).

- **Part III ('Local Authority Support for Children and Families')**: local authority services for children in need, their families and others (ss.17–19); the provision of accommodation for children (ss.20 and 21); the duties of local authorities in relation to children looked after by them (ss.22 and 23); advice and assistance for children (s.24); secure accommodation for children (s.25); case reviews (s.26); co-operation between local authorities (s.27); and consultation with local education authorities (s.28).

- **Part IV ('Care and Supervision')**: care orders; supervision orders; education supervision orders (ss.31–40); and provision in respect of guardians *ad litem* (ss.41 and 42).

- **Part V ('Protection of Children')**: child assessment orders (s.43); emergency protection orders (ss.44 and 45); police removal of children (s.46); local authority duty to investigate (s.47); power to assist in discovery of children (s.48); abduction of children in care (ss.49 and 50); and refuges for children at risk (s.51).

Schedules 1 to 3 deal with the following matters:

- **Schedule 1 ('Financial Provision for Children')**: orders for financial relief for children (para. 1); orders for financial relief for persons aged over 18 (para. 2); provision relating to the courts' powers to make these orders etc. (paras. 3–14); and local authority contribution to a child's maintenance (para. 15).

- **Schedule 2 ('Local Authority Support for Children and Families')**: provision of services for families (Part I, paras. 1–11); children looked after by local authorities (Part II, paras. 12–20); and contribution towards maintenance of children looked after by local authorities (Part III, paras. 21–25).

- **Schedule 3 ('Supervision Orders')**: powers of supervisor, psychiatric and medical examination and treatment (Part I, paras. 1–5); duration of supervision orders, information to be given to supervisor etc. (Part II, paras. 1–11); and education supervision orders (Part III, paras. 12–21).

12.3   The General Principles

The general principles of the Children Act 1989 are laid down in Part I.

(a) The Welfare of the Child

Section 1(1) provides:

'When a court determines any question with respect to—
(a) the upbringing of a child; or
(b) the administration of a child's property or the application of any income arising from it,
the child's welfare shall be the court's paramount consideration.'

The child's welfare is the paramount consideration in both private law proceedings (Part II) and in public law proceedings for care and supervision orders (Part IV) and for emergency protection orders (Part V). The welfare principle does not, however, apply to an application for permission to apply for a s.8 order (see 12.6) and to applications for financial relief under s.15 and Sched. 1 of the Act (see 14.3).

(b) The Statutory Checklist (s.1(3))

Section 1(3) of the Act contains a statutory checklist of factors which the court must have regard to when deciding whether to make, vary or discharge a s.8 order in contested proceedings (s.1(4)(a)), or to make, vary or discharge a care or supervision order under Part IV of the Act (s.1(4)(b)). The checklist does not apply to emergency proceedings under Part V, because consideration of all the factors in the checklist would inhibit emergency action.

Under the s.1(3) checklist, the court must have regard in particular to:

'(a) the ascertainable wishes and feelings of the child concerned (considered in the light of his age and understanding);
(b) his physical, emotional and educational needs;
(c) the likely effect on him of any change in his circumstances;
(d) his age, sex, background and any characteristics of his which the court considers relevant;
(e) any harm which he has suffered or is at risk of suffering;
(f) how capable each of his parents, and any other person in relation to whom the court considers the question to be relevant, is of meeting his needs;
(g) the range of powers available to the court under this Act in the proceedings in question.'

This list is not exclusive. Other factors may be taken into account. In *B* v. *B (Residence Order: Reasons for Decision)* [1997] 2 FLR 602, the Court of Appeal said that, although it is not always necessary or appropriate for a judge to go through the checklist item by item, it does represent an extremely useful and important discipline for judges to ensure that all the relevant factors and circumstances are considered and balanced.

As far as factor (a) is concerned, in private law proceedings the child's wishes are ascertained by the court welfare officer. In public law proceedings they are ascertained by the child's guardian *ad litem* (for judicial guidance on ascertaining a child's wishes, see Wall J in *B* v. *B (Minors)(Interviews and Listing Arrangements)* [1994] 2 FLR 489). The functions of the court welfare officer and guardian *ad litem* are similar but not identical (*Re S (A Minor)(Guardian ad Litem/Welfare Officer)* [1993] 1 FLR 110). Each has a duty to report to the court and to consider the welfare and best interests of the child and may be cross-examined on their report, but, unlike the court welfare officer, a guardian *ad litem* is a party to the proceedings and is present in court to represent the child (see 10.6). The child's religious and cultural heritage can be taken into account under factor (d) of the checklist (see *Re P (Section 91(14) Guidelines) (Residence and Religious Heritage)* [1999] 2 FLR 573, where a s.8 residence order was made in favour of Roman Catholic foster parents, even though the child's Orthodox Jewish parents objected). Factor (g) enables the court to consider whether any other power available under the Children Act should be used. In some cases the child's welfare may be better promoted by making a different order or making no order at all. (For further discussion of the factors in the checklist, see Chapter 13 in the context of residence and contact disputes.)

(c) *The No-Order Presumption (s.1(5))*

The no-order presumption was introduced by the Children Act as part of the general policy of the Act to place the primary responsibility for children on their parents, with court orders being made in the last resort. Section 1(5) provides:

> 'Where a court is considering whether or not to make one or more orders under this Act with respect to a child, it shall not make the order or any of the orders unless it considers that doing so would be better for the child than making no order at all.'

The presumption has two main aims. One is to discourage unnecessary court orders being made. The other is to ensure that orders are granted only where they will positively improve a child's welfare and not simply because the grounds are made out. The no-order principle is based on a recognition that court orders often exacerbate problems rather than solve them. On divorce, for example, orders may increase hostility between the parties, with harmful repercussions for their children. In some circumstances it may therefore be better to make no order at all. In the public law context, where the emphasis is on local authorities working with other agencies in voluntary partnerships with parents to promote the welfare of children, it may also be better not to make an order. However, the no-order presumption will never be allowed to prevail over a child's welfare. Thus in *B* v. *B (A Minor)(Residence Order)* [1992] 2 FLR 327, for example, an application by a grandmother for a residence order was refused at first instance on the basis of the no-order presumption, but the Court of Appeal allowed her appeal as the order gave her parental responsibility and also gave the child security.

(d) *The 'No-Delay Principle' (s.1(2))*

The Children Act recognises that delay is harmful for a child. Section 1(2) provides:

> 'In any proceedings in which any question with respect to the upbringing of a child arises, the court shall have regard to the general principle that any delay in determining the question is likely to prejudice the welfare of the child.'

In order to avoid delay, the progress of cases is determined by the court, which for this purpose must draw up a timetable for s.8 order proceedings (s.11(1)) and for care and supervision proceedings (s.32(1)).

The court can give directions and the rules of court make provision to avoid delay. Children's issues must be determined as soon as possible, so that minimum disruption is caused to the child's life and the child is not left in limbo. To avoid delay, proceedings can be transferred vertically or laterally between magistrates' family proceedings courts, county courts and the High Court. Parties to pending proceedings under the Children Act and under the High Court's inherent jurisdiction are required to provide a 'time estimate' in order to facilitate the listing and disposal of children's cases in the most effective way (*Practice Direction: Children Act 1989: Hearings Before High Court Judge – Time Estimates*) [1994] 1 FLR 108). Despite these provisions, delay is still a problem in many courts, and the implementation of the Human Rights Act 1998 (see 1.5) is likely to make proceedings even more protracted.

12.4   Section 8 Orders under the Children Act 1989

Section 8(1) of the Children Act makes provision for the following flexible range of private law orders, which are available in all courts in all family proceedings:

(a) a residence order;
(b) a contact order;
(c) a prohibited steps order;
(d) a specific issue order.

Residence and contact orders are the orders most commonly sought and made, as the following 1998 statistics for s.8 orders made in private law proceedings in all tiers of court show (*Judicial Statistics 1998*, Lord Chancellor's Department, www.open.gov.uk/lcd/):

	Applications withdrawn	Orders refused	Orders of no-order	Orders made
Residence	5 051	865	1 689	30 398
Contact	8 385	1 911	3 298	49 313
Prohibited steps	890	211	281	5 213
Specific issue	436	121	161	2 318

When considering whether to make any s.8 order, the court must apply the welfare principle in s.1(1), and, in contested proceedings, it must apply the s.1(3) checklist when making, varying or discharging any s.8 order (s.1(4)(a)). The no-delay principle (s.1(2)) and the no-order presumption (s.1(5)) must also be applied. Parents (whether married or unmarried, and with or without parental responsibility), and guardians, have an automatic right to apply for these orders, but other persons, including children, need the court's permission to do so (see 12.6 below).

(For further discussion of residence and contact orders, see Chapter 13, 'Children on Family Breakdown'.)

(a) Residence Order

A residence order is an order

> 'settling the arrangements to be made as to the person with whom the child is to live.'

Residence orders are often applied for on family breakdown to settle a dispute about where the child should live (see 13.3). They were introduced by the Children Act in 1991 to replace the old custody order. This was done to remove the claim right implicit in, and the adversarial undertones of, the word 'custody'. The emphasis is on residence rather than custody and is intended to reinforce the fact that both parents have a continuing role to play in relation to their children. With a residence order, it is a question of where the child should live, and not to whom the child belongs.

The making of a residence order does not affect the parental responsibility of any other person who possesses such responsibility (s.2(1)). Thus both parents with parental responsibility retain it whether or not a residence order is made in favour of one of them. A residence order does, however, provide a means for persons without parental responsibility to acquire it, but only for the duration of the order (s.12(2)). However, such parental responsibility does not include the right to give or refuse consent to adoption, or to appoint a guardian (s.12(3)). Where the court makes a residence order in favour of a father without parental responsibility, the court must also make a s.4 parental responsibility order (see 11.7) giving him such responsibility (s.12(2)).

The court can make a 'shared' (i.e. 'joint') residence order in favour of two or more persons who live in different households (s.11(4)) (see 13.3). In this way, two (or more) persons can acquire parental responsibility for a child (see, for example, *Re A (Adoption: Joint Residence)* [1996] 1 FLR 27). A residence order made in favour of one parent with parental responsibility (or both parents) ceases to have effect if the parents live together for more than six months (s.11(5)).

Once a residence order has been made, there are restrictions on changing the child's surname and taking the child out of the UK (s.13(1) and (2), and see 13.3). Where urgent action is required, a residence order may be granted *ex parte* (i.e. without the other party being given notice of proceedings) (see, for example, *Re G (Minors)(Ex Parte Interim Residence Order)* [1993] 1 FLR 910 and *Re P (A Minor)(Ex Parte Interim Residence Order)* [1993] 2 FLR 915). The court also possesses wide powers to attach conditions to residence orders (see s.11(7), and also 13.3).

Special restrictions apply, however, to residence orders when a child is in local authority care. A residence order is the only s.8 order that can be made in respect of a child in care (s.9(1)). If any of the other s.8 orders (contact, prohibited steps and specific issue orders) could be made, it would undermine a local authority's statutory powers. However, although a residence order can be made in respect of a child in care, it cannot be applied for, or made in favour of, a local authority (s.9(2)), as it would allow local authorities to gain parental responsibility by other means than a care order. However, local authorities with permission of the court may apply for s.8 specific issue and prohibited steps orders, and may also with the court's permission seek to invoke the inherent jurisdiction of the court (see 12.8). As a residence order automatically brings a care order to an end (s.91(1)), a person who has no right to apply to discharge a care order (see s.39(1)) can apply for a residence order as a means of discharging a care order.

(b) Contact Order

A contact order is an order

'requiring the person with whom a child lives, or is to live, to allow the child to visit or stay with the person named in the order, or for that person and the child otherwise to have contact with each other.'

The Children Act introduced the concept of 'contact' to replace that of 'access'. It did so in order to stress the importance of children maintaining links with parents and other family members on family breakdown. The change of terminology was intended to shift the emphasis from the adult to the child. Contact orders are often applied for on family breakdown, usually by fathers (see 13.4). The court has a wide discretion to insert directions and conditions into an order (s.11(7), and see 13.4).

As far as local authorities are concerned, a contact order cannot be made in respect of a child in local authority care and cannot be applied for by, or be made in favour of, a local authority (s.9). Contact in care is governed by s.34 of the Children Act (see 16.6).

(c) Prohibited Steps Order

A prohibited steps order is an order

'that no step which could be taken by a parent in meeting his parental responsibility for a child, and which is of a kind specified in the order, shall be taken by any person without the consent of the court.'

This order, like the specific issue order below, gives the court powers similar to those which before the Children Act were available only to the High Court in wardship (see 12.9 below). A prohibited steps order is a flexible order, rather like an injunction, which can be used in a wide range of different circumstances, e.g. to restrain a parent taking the child out of the UK, to restrain a person from associating with a child, or to restrain a person from unilaterally making a decision about a child. In *Re G (Parental Responsibility: Education)* [1994] 2 FLR 964, for example, a mother sought an *ex parte* prohibited steps order to prevent her husband sending their son away to boarding-school, but her application was refused. A prohibited steps order cannot be made, however, to achieve the same result which could be achieved by a residence or contact order, and cannot be made in any way denied to the High Court under its inherent jurisdiction under s.100(2) (s.9(5)). As a prohibited steps order is an order prohibiting 'a step which could be taken by a parent in meeting his parental responsibility' for the child, it cannot be used to restrict anything other than some aspect of parental responsibility. Thus, for example, it cannot be used to restrict publicity about a child since this is not within the scope of parental responsibility. Restrictions on publicity in order to protect children are dealt with by the High Court in wardship (see 12.9 below). Neither can a prohibited steps order be used to prevent parents having contact with each other, as it has been held that contact is not an aspect of parental responsibility (*Croydon London Borough Council v. A (No 1)* [1992] 2 FLR 341). It has also been held that a prohibited steps order cannot be made to oust a parent from the family home (see *Nottinghamshire County Council v. P* [1993] Fam 18, [1993] 2 FLR 134 and *Re D (Prohibited Steps Order)* [1996] 2 FLR 273).

(d) Specific Issue Order

A specific issue order is an order

'giving directions for the purpose of determining a specific question which has arisen, or which may arise, in connection with any aspect of parental responsibility for a child.'

This order can be made to settle any dispute which has arisen, or may arise, in respect of the exercise of parental responsibility. It can be used, for example, to settle a dispute arising in respect of a child's education or medical treatment, a decision to move the child abroad, or a change of the child's surname. A specific issue order cannot, however, be made to deem a child to be in need for the purposes of Part III of the Children Act, as this is not an 'aspect of parental responsibility' for the purposes of s.8 (see *Re J (Specific Issue Order: Leave to Apply)* [1995] 1 FLR 669, where it was held that the appropriate remedy is judicial review). Before the Children Act came into force, disputes about a child which involved an aspect of parental decision-making were settled by making the child a ward of court when the court under its wardship jurisdiction would decide what was in the child's best interests (see 12.9 below). Now, however, a specific issue order can be used instead. Thus, for example, in *Re HG (Specific Issue Order: Sterilisation)* [1993] 1 FLR 587, parents were granted a specific issue order so that their 18-year-old daughter could be sterilised. In *Re J (Specific Issue Orders: Child's Religious Upbringing and Circumcision)* [2000] 1 FLR 571, a Muslim father sought specific issue orders requiring his son to be brought up in the Muslim religion and to be circumcised. His applications failed. In *Re K (Specific Issue Order)* [1999] 2 FLR 280, a father sought a specific issue order requiring the child, a boy aged 9, to be informed about his paternity and about his father's existence. However, the order was refused, for although a child has a right to know the truth about his paternity, his welfare was the paramount concern.

Like a prohibited steps order, a specific issue order cannot be used in place of a residence or contact order, or to order a child to be placed or accommodated in the care of, or under the supervision of, a local authority which is denied to the High Court under the exercise of its inherent jurisdiction by virtue of s.100(2) (s.9(5)). However, a local authority may obtain the permission of the court to apply for a specific issue order to deal with a difficult issue. Thus, in *Re R (A Minor)(Blood Transfusion)* [1993] 2 FLR 757, a local authority obtained a specific issue order to authorise the use of blood products for the treatment of a baby who suffered from leukaemia but whose parents had refused to give consent as they were Jehovah's Witnesses. In *Re C (HIV Test)* [1999] 2 FLR 1004, a local authority obtained a specific issue order to have a baby tested for HIV after her parents had refused to allow this. However, when a child is in local authority care, only a residence order may be made in respect of the child, so that any decision about medical treatment cannot be decided by an application for a specific issue order. Instead, a local authority must apply to the court for permission to invoke the inherent jurisdiction of the court (see 12.9 below).

12.5   In What Proceedings can Section 8 Orders be Made?

Section 8 orders can be made in any family proceedings on an application, or of the court's own motion (s.10(1) and (2)).

'Family proceedings' for the purposes of the Children Act 1989 include the following proceedings (s.8(3)):

- *Wardship proceedings and* parens patriae *proceedings under the inherent jurisdiction of the High Court* (see 12.9);
- *Proceedings under the following statutes*: the Matrimonial Causes Act 1973; the Adoption Act 1976; the Domestic Proceedings and Magistrates' Courts Act 1978; Part IV of the Family Law Act 1996; Part III of the Matrimonial and Family Proceedings Act 1984; and s.30 of the Human Fertilisation and Embryology Act 1990;
- *Proceedings under Parts I, II and IV of the Children Act 1989* (see 12.2 above).

Thus a s.8 order can be applied for, or made of the court's own motion, in many different civil proceedings involving children, not just proceedings under the Children Act but, for instance, in divorce proceedings, in adoption proceedings and in proceedings for a non-molestation order or occupation order in domestic violence cases.

12.6   Who can Apply for Section 8 Orders?

Certain persons have an automatic right to apply for a s.8 order, but others can only apply with the court's permission.

(a) Applicants for Any Section 8 Order

Parents (with or without parental responsibility), guardians, and persons with a residence order in their favour with respect to the child may apply for any s.8 order, as may certain persons prescribed by rules of court, and other persons who have been given permission by the court (s.10(4)). Local authorities cannot apply for any s.8 order if the child is in care (s.9(1) and (2)).

Applications for Permission to Apply

Parents and guardians are automatically entitled to apply for any s.8 order, but other persons must seek permission of the court to apply.

Where an application is made for permission to apply for a s.8 order by a person other than the child, the court must in particular consider (s.10(9)):

- the nature of the proposed application;
- the applicant's connection with the child;
- any risk of the proposed application disrupting the child's life to such an extent that the child would be harmed; and

- (where the child is being looked after by a local authority) the local authority's plans for the future and the wishes and feelings of the child's parents.

Applications for permission to apply for s.8 orders are not governed by the welfare principle (see *Re A and W (Minors)(Residence Order: Leave to Apply)* [1992] Fam 182, [1992] 2 FLR 154). In *Re M (Minors)(Contact: Leave to Apply)* [1995] 2 FLR 98, the Court of Appeal held that an application for permission to apply will be refused if the application is frivolous or vexatious, or otherwise an abuse of the court. Ward LJ said that the case must disclose a real prospect of success, and the applicant must satisfy the court that there is a serious issue to be tried and a good arguable case (see also *Re M (Care: Contact: Grandmother's Application for Leave)* [1995] 2 FLR 86). In *G* v. *F (Contact and Shared Residence: Applications for Leave)* [1998] 2 FLR 799, permission to make applications for contact and a shared residence order was granted to a lesbian couple.

Applications by Foster-Parents

A local authority foster-parent may seek permission to apply for a s.8 order, provided he or she is, or was, within the last six months, a local authority foster-parent. In addition, a foster-parent must have local authority consent to make the application, and the foster-parent must either be a relative of the child, or have had the child living with him or her for at least three years preceding the application (s.9(3)) (see, for example, *C* v. *Salford City Council and Others* [1994] 2 FLR 926, where local authority foster-parents were granted permission by the court to apply for a residence order). In *Gloucestershire County Council* v. *P* [1999] 2 FLR 61, the Court of Appeal held that in exceptional circumstances the court acting of its own motion under s.10 may make a residence order in favour of foster-parents, even though they are disqualified by s.9(3) because they have failed to obtain local authority consent. However, the Court of Appeal stressed that a foster-parent application made without the support of the local authority would be subject to careful scrutiny.

Applications by Children

To apply for a s.8 order, a child must first of all obtain the permission of the court, which it *may* grant if the child has sufficient understanding to make the proposed application (s.10(8)). Thus, even if the child has sufficient understanding, the court retains a discretion whether or not to grant permission, and when exercising this discretion can take into account the likely success of the proposed application (Booth J in *Re SC (A Minor)(Leave to Seek Residence Order)* [1994] 1 FLR 96, and Johnson J in *Re H (Residence Order: Child's*

Application for Leave) [2000] 1 FLR 780). Applications by children for permission to apply for a s.8 order are heard in the High Court (*Practice Direction: Children Act 1989: Applications by Children* [1993] 1 FLR 668). There is some conflict in the case-law, however, as to whether or not the child's welfare is paramount when the court is considering the application for permission to apply for a s.8 order. In *Re C (A Minor)(Leave to Seek Section 8 Orders)* [1994] 1 FLR 26, Johnson J applied the welfare principle, but in *Re SC (A Minor)(Leave to Seek Residence Order)* [1994] 1 FLR 96, Booth J said that the child's welfare was not paramount. In *Re C (Residence) (Child's Application for Leave)* [1995] 1 FLR 927, Stuart-White J considered this divergence of judicial opinion, and concluded that the child's welfare is an important, but not a paramount, consideration, and this approach was adopted by Johnson J in *Re H (Residence Order: Child's Application for Leave)* [2000] above.

(b) Applicants for a Residence or Contact Order

In addition to those persons above who may apply for a residence or contact order, the following may apply for a residence or contact order without the need to obtain the court's permission to do so (s.10(5)): a step-parent; a person with whom the child has lived for at least three years (this need not be continuous, but must have begun not more than five years before, or ended more than three months before, the application); a person who has the consent of a person (or persons) with a residence order in their favour with respect to the child; a person who has local authority consent where the child is in care and/or the consent of any person having parental responsibility for the child; and any other person prescribed by the rules of court.

12.7   Jurisdiction to Make Section 8 Orders

Jurisdiction to make s.8 orders is governed by the Family Law Act 1986. The court has jurisdiction if on the date of the application the child is habitually resident in England and Wales, or is present in England and Wales, and is not habitually resident in any other part of the UK (s.2(2)). Habitual residence is not defined in the 1986 Act but principles on habitual residence are laid down in the case-law (see *Re J (A Minor)(Abduction: Custody Rights)* [1990] 2 AC 562, *sub nom C* v. *S (A Minor)(Abduction: Illegitimate Child)* [1990] 2 FLR 442 in Chapter 15). In several cases the courts have had to decide whether the English or the Scottish courts have jurisdiction to make the order (see, for example, *Re M (Minors)(Residence Order: Jurisdiction)* [1993] 1 FLR 495 and *D* v. *D (Custody Jurisdiction)* [1996] 1 FLR 574). The court may refuse jurisdiction where public policy considerations prevail over the child's welfare (for example, in the immigration context, see *Re M (A Minor)(Immigration: Residence Order)* [1993] 2 FLR 858). It can also refuse to hear the application if the matter has already been determined in proceedings outside England and Wales (s.5(1) FLA 1986) and may on application stay the proceedings if proceedings relating to the same matters are continuing outside England and Wales, or it would be more appropriate for those matters to be dealt with outside England and Wales (s.5(2)) (see *Re S (A Minor)(Stay of Proceedings)* [1993] 2 FLR 912, *Re F (Residence Order: Jurisdiction)* [1995] 2 FLR 518 and *Re S (Jurisdiction to Stay Application)* [1995] 1 FLR 1093).

12.8   Other Orders under the Children Act 1989

A wide range of orders other than s.8 orders can be made under the Children Act 1989. These are classified here as: (a) private law orders; (b) public law orders; and (c) 'hybrid orders' (orders which cut across both the private and public law domains). More information on these orders can be found in other chapters.

(a) Private Law Orders

(i) *Parental Responsibility Order (s.4)*   An unmarried father who has no parental responsibility can acquire it by applying for a parental responsibility order (see 11.6).

(ii) *Order Appointing a Guardian for the Child (s.5)*   The court can appoint a person to be a guardian of a child (see 11.5).

(iii) *Orders for Financial Relief (s.15)*   The court can make orders for financial relief for children, provision for which is laid down in Sched. 1 to the Children Act (see 14.3).

(b) Public Law Orders

(i) *Care and Supervision Orders (s.31)*   Where a child is suffering, or is likely to suffer, significant harm, the court can, if certain threshold criteria are satisfied and the child's welfare requires it, make a care order placing the child in the care of a local authority, or a supervision order placing the child under the supervision of a local authority officer or probation officer (see 16.5).

(ii) *Child Assessment Order (s.43)*   Where there is reasonable cause to suspect a child is suffering, or is likely to suffer, significant harm and an assessment of the child's health and development or the way in which the child is being treated is needed, the court can make a child assessment order (see 16.7).

(iii) Emergency Protection Order (s.44)   Where there is reasonable cause to believe that a child is likely to suffer significant harm, the court can in certain circumstances make an emergency protection order, which authorises the removal from, or retention of the child in, certain accommodation (see 16.7).

(iv) Order for Contact with a Child in Care (s.34)   Where a child is in local authority care, the authority must allow parents and certain other persons reasonable contact with the child, and the court can make orders in respect of such contact (see 16.6).

(v) Education Supervision Order (s.36)   Where a child of compulsory school age is not being properly educated, the court can on the application of a local education authority make an education supervision order in favour of that authority (see, for example, *Essex County Council* v. *B* [1993] 1 FLR 866).

(c) 'Hybrid' Orders

The term 'hybrid' orders has been used here to classify those orders which cut across the boundaries of private and public law.

(i) Family Assistance Order (s.16)   The aim of this order is to provide expert advice and assistance for a family for a short-term period in exceptional circumstances. It can be made on an application, or by the court of its own motion in any family proceedings (see 12.5 above). The effect of an order is to require a probation officer or local authority officer (e.g. social worker) to be made available to advise, assist and (where appropriate) befriend any person named in the order. As the local authority must agree to making an officer available (s.16(7)), an order will not be made if the local authority decides it does not wish to allocate resources to the matter. Only the following persons can be named in an order: a parent or guardian; any person with whom the child is living or who has a contact order in force with respect to the child; or the child (s.16(2)). An order can be made whether or not another order is made in the proceedings (s.16(1)), but it must be made only in exceptional circumstances and only where every person named in the order (other than the child) has consented to the order being made (s.16(3)). The order lasts for a period of up to six months (s.16(5)). Where a family assistance order and a s.8 order are both in force with respect to a child, the probation officer or local authority officer involved can ask the court to vary or discharge the s.8 order (s.16(6)). Although the aim of a family assistance order is 'to provide short-term help to a family, to overcome their problems and conflicts associated with their separation and divorce' (para. 2.50, *Children Act 1989: Guidance and Regulations,*

Vol. 1: Court Orders, HMSO, 1991), it may be used in other contexts. Thus in *Re E (Family Assistance Order)* [1999] 2 FLR 512, a family assistance order was made requiring the local authority to supervise contact with a mother who had been convicted of the father's manslaughter and detained under the Mental Health Act 1983.

There has been some criticism of the order. Trinder and Stone (1998) have called it a 'curious beast' and Sturgeon-Adams and James (1999) have argued that there is a need for clarification, as there is no shared understanding of family assistance orders, in particular what constitutes exceptional circumstances.

(ii) Order that a Local Authority Investigate the Child's Circumstances (s.37)
Where in any family proceedings a question arises in respect of the child's welfare and it may be appropriate for a care or supervision order to be made (see 16.5), the court may direct that a local authority undertake an investigation into the child's circumstances (s.37(1)) (see, for example, *Re L (Section 37 Direction)* [1999] 1 FLR 984 and *Re CE (Section 37 Direction)* [1995] 1 FLR 26).

(iii) Order for a Welfare Report (s.7)   When considering any question with respect to a child under the Children Act, the court may ask a probation officer, or a local authority officer, to arrange to make a welfare report on such matters relating to the child as are required to be dealt with in the report.

(iv) Order Restricting an Application to the Court (s.91(14))   When disposing of an application under the Children Act (whether or not it makes an order), the court may order that no application for an order under the Act of any specified kind may be made with respect to the child by any person named in the order without the court's permission (s.91(14)). The aim of a s.91(14) order is to prevent unnecessary and disruptive applications which may be detrimental to a child's best interests. In most cases the order is used to control persons who have made repeated and unreasonable applications, or who are likely to act unreasonably in the future. However, in exceptional cases it may be made in respect of a first application (see *Re Y (Child Orders: Restricting Applications)* [1994] 2 FLR 699, where a s.91(14) order was made in respect of a father who had killed the mother in front of the children but who sought a contact order or discharge of a care order).

In exercising its discretion under s.91(14) the welfare principle applies. However, the court will carry out a balancing exercise between the child's welfare and the litigant's right of unrestricted access to the courts, and the degree of restriction will be proportionate to the degree of harm which it is intended to avoid (see *Re M (Section 91(14) Order)* [1999] 2 FLR 533). The court can lift a s.91(14) order where an applicant can show a need for renewed judicial investigation (see *Re A (Application for Leave)* [1998] 1 FLR 1).

The courts are greatly aware of the severity of making a s.91(14) order. In *B* v. *B (Residence Order: Restricting Applications)* [1997] 1 FLR 139, the Court of Appeal held that the power to make an order must be exercised with great care as it represents a substantial interference with the principle of public policy that all citizens enjoy a right of unrestricted access to the courts. The cases emphasise that it is a Draconian order of last resort, which should not be made unless there is a clear evidential basis for doing so (see *Re R (Residence: Contact: Restricting Applications)* [1998] 1 FLR 749, *Re G and M (Child Orders: Restricting Applications)* [1995] 2 FLR 416 and *Re N (Section 91(14) Order)* [1996] 1 FLR 356).

With the implementation of the European Convention of Human Rights (see 1.5), the English courts will have to ensure that s.91(14) orders do not infringe art. 6 of the Convention (the right to have access to the courts). However, in *Re P (Section 91(14) Guidelines)(Residence and Religious Heritage)* [1999] 2 FLR 573, the Court of Appeal held that, as a s.91(14) order is only a *partial* restriction on disallowing claims before the court, it did not infringe the Human Rights Act 1998 and art. 6 of the Convention. However, the Court of Appeal stated that, because of the severity of the order, it should specify what types of applications are restricted and for how long.

12.9 Wardship and the Children Act 1989

The essence of wardship is that once a child becomes a ward of court, the situation is frozen, and the court itself stands *in loco parentis* for the child, so that no important step in the child's life can be taken without the court's consent. Wardship is part of the inherent jurisdiction of the court, and is of ancient origin. It goes back to the time when the King in his role as *parens patriae* (parent or protector of the realm) owed a duty to his subjects to protect their persons and their property. (This *parens patriae*, or inherent jurisdiction of the High Court, is sometimes used today, not only to protect children, but to protect adults who do not have the capacity to consent to medical treatment because of some mental disability.) Responsibility for the exercise of the *parens patriae* jurisdiction eventually moved from the King to the Lord Chancellor, then into the Chancery Division and finally into the Family Division of the High Court. Wardship is only one of the court's inherent powers and the High Court can also make orders under its general inherent jurisdiction.

Procedure in Wardship

The wardship procedure is governed by the Supreme Court Act 1981. Only the High Court has jurisdiction to ward a child, who becomes a ward as soon as the application is made, but ceases to be a ward if an application to hear the case is not made within 21 days of the initial application (s.41(1) and (2) SCA 1981). The Official Solicitor is usually appointed as the child's guardian *ad litem*, and is responsible for making enquiries, preparing reports and giving the child a voice in the proceedings. The judge must decide first of all whether the High Court should exercise its jurisdiction in wardship. In some cases the court may decide it has no jurisdiction to make the child a ward of court (see below). Once the court has decided it has jurisdiction, it can exercise a wide range of powers. It can make any s.8 order, or make a direction under s.37 CA 1989 that a local authority make enquiries about the child, or make a financial provision order under Sched.1 to the CA 1989, or appoint a guardian, or grant an injunction. In wardship proceedings, the welfare of the child is the court's paramount consideration where the child's upbringing or the administration of the child's property are in issue (s.1(1) CA 1989).

In the private law context, although there is no express prohibition in the Children Act against private individuals using wardship, it is likely to be resorted to only in rare cases, and even then jurisdiction may be declined by the courts. Not only is wardship expensive, but the s.8 specific issue and pro-hibited steps orders (see 12.4) allow all courts to make flexible orders similar to those that were once only available in wardship. Since the Children Act came into force, wardship exists only as a residuary jurisdiction providing a safety net for complex and difficult cases.

One of the main reforms of the Children Act 1989 was to restrict the use of wardship by local authorities. Consequently, wardship cannot be used by a local authority to place a child in its care or under its supervision (s.100(2)(a)). Before the Children Act came into force, local authorities regularly used ward-ship as a means of taking children into care, instead of using the statutory pro-cedures which were then available. This was expensive and time-consuming. However, a local authority can, with permission of the court, invoke the court's inherent jurisdiction (s.100(2), see below).

The Inherent Jurisdiction

Apart from wardship, the High Court also has a general inherent power to protect children which is exercisable whether or not the child is a ward of court. The inherent jurisdiction is sometimes used by local authorities who wish to settle a question about a child in care, because a child in care cannot be made a ward of court (s.100(2)(c)). Care orders and wardship are mutually exclusive, as a care order brings wardship to an end (s.91(4)). However, a local authority who wishes to invoke the inherent jurisdiction must seek prior permission of the court (s.100(3)). Sometimes local authorities have sought permission to invoke it where children in care need medical treatment. Thus, for example, in *Re W (A Minor)(Medical Treatment: Court's Jurisdiction)* [1993] Fam 64, [1993] 1 FLR 1 (see Chapter 11), a local authority applied under s.100(3) and (4) for permission to arrange medical treatment for a 16-year-old anorexic girl in its care who was refusing treatment. The Court of Appeal unanimously gave its consent under the inherent jurisdiction, holding that the jurisdiction extended beyond the powers of a natural parent, and stating that the High Court's inherent jurisdiction in relation to children is equally exercisable whether or not the child is a ward of court. In *Re RJ (Fostering: Person Disqualified)* [1999] 1 FLR 605, an interim care order was discharged and the children made wards of court under s.100(4) in order to maintain the status quo pending a full hearing. The inherent jurisdiction has also been used to fill in gaps in the adoption legislation (see 17.4) and was recently used in an abduction case where the child was outside the scope of the Hague Convention on abduction because she was aged over 16 (see 15.7). There is no need, however, for a local authority to seek permission to invoke the inherent jurisdiction under s.100 of the Children Act when applying for an injunction to protect a child in care (see *Re P (Care Orders: Injunctive Relief)* [2000] 2 FLR 385, and also 16.9).

Proceedings under the inherent jurisdiction are 'family proceedings' for the purpose of the Children Act (see 12.5 above), so that the High Court can make any s.8 order in the proceedings, except where the child is in care, when only a residence order may be made. As a s.8 order cannot be made in favour of a local authority on an application by a local authority when a child is in care (s.9(1) and (2)), the inherent powers of the court must be invoked to resolve questions about children in care. Although the inherent jurisdiction exists whether or not the child is a ward of court, it is only likely to be used in unusual cases such as *Re W* above. In *Re O (A Minor) (Medical Treatment)* [1993] 2 FLR 149, Johnson J held that the inherent jurisdiction was the most appropriate legal framework in which to consider a contested issue relating to emergency medical treatment for a child, and ordered that the child be given a blood transfusion despite the objections of the parents who were Jehovah's Witnesses. An interim care order, an emergency protection order or a specific issue order were not appropriate. Even where a local authority has parental responsibility, his Lordship said that the consent of the court would be needed in such a case. The following are other examples of local authorities using the inherent jurisdiction: *Re S (A Minor)(Medical Treatment)* [1993] 1 FLR 376 (for permission to permit a blood transfusion to be given to a child whose parents were Jehovah's Witnesses); *Re J (A Minor)(Medical Treatment)* [1992] 2 FLR 165 (for guidance on the treatment of a severely handicapped child); *Re M (Care: Leave to Interview Child)* [1995] 1 FLR 825 (to ask whether it should permit a solicitor to interview two boys in care concerning a rape).

Limits to Wardship and the Inherent Jurisdiction

The High Court may refuse to exercise its jurisdiction in wardship or under its general inherent jurisdiction where other interests prevail over the child's welfare. The High Court has, for example, refused to hear wardship applications in immigration cases on the basis that wardship cannot be used to deprive the Secretary of State of those powers conferred on him by the Immigration Act 1971 (see, for example, *Re F (A Minor)(Immigration: Wardship)* [1990] Fam 125 and *R v. Secretary of State for Home Department ex parte T* [1995] 1 FLR 293). It has also held that it cannot ward an unborn child because it would place an unjustifiable fetter on the rights of a mother (*Re F (In Utero)* [1998] Fam 122). Applications have sometimes been made under the inherent jurisdiction to protect a child from intrusions by the media or from the publication of harmful material (see, for example, *Re Z (A Minor)(Freedom of Publication)* [1997] Fam 1, [1996] 1 FLR 191 and *Nottingham City Council v. October Films Ltd* [1999] 2 FLR 347). However, the court may refuse to make an order on the ground that freedom of speech and freedom of publication must prevail over a child's welfare. In *Re X (A Minor)(Wardship: Jurisdiction)* [1975] Fam 47, the Court of Appeal refused to grant an injunction on the application of the child's step-father to prevent the publication of a book which contained references to the salacious behaviour of the ward's deceased father which might harm her if the book ever came to her knowledge. In *R (Mrs) v. Central Independent Television plc* [1994] Fam 192, Waite LJ said:

> '[N]o child, simply by virtue of being a child, is entitled to a right of privacy or confidentiality. That is true of a ward of court (or a child in respect of whom the inherent jurisdiction is otherwise invoked) as of any other child ....'

Summary

1 The Children Act 1989 has consolidated most of the civil law relating to children, with the notable exceptions of adoption law (see Chapter 17) and the law on education.
2 Part I lays down the general principles of the Act. Part II makes provision for private law orders. Parts III–V make provision in respect of the powers and duties of local authorities in respect of the care and protection of children.
3 The following general principles of the Act are laid down in s.1: the welfare principle (s.1(1)); the no-delay principle (s.1(2)); the statutory checklist (s.1(3)); and the no-order presumption (s.1(5)). The checklist must be applied in contested s.8 order proceedings and in care and supervision proceedings under Part IV of the Act (s.1(4)).
4 Different orders can be made under the Children Act, but of particular importance in private law proceedings are the range of orders laid down in s.8, namely: residence order; contact order; prohibited steps order; and specific issue order.

5 Section 8 orders can be made on application, or by the court of its own motion, in any family proceedings. Some persons have an automatic right to apply but other persons, including the child, need the permission of the court to make an application. The court has jurisdiction to make s.8 orders if the child is habitually resident or present in England and Wales and is not habitually resident in any other part of the UK (s.2 Family Law Act 1986).

6 Other orders which can be obtained under Part II of the Children Act 1989 are: parental responsibility orders (s.4); orders appointing a guardian (s.5); and orders for financial relief (s.15 and Sched. 1). The court can make a range of public law orders, in particular care and supervision orders, and orders needed for the emergency protection of children. The court can also make a range of 'hybrid' orders (orders which cut across private and public law), namely: family assistance order (s.16); order that a local authority investigate the child's circumstances (s.37); order for a welfare report (s.7); and a s.91(14) order restricting an application to the court.

7 Under the wardship jurisdiction, children can be made wards of court, but the Children Act has cut back the use of wardship, particularly by local authorities. Children can in certain cases be protected under the court's inherent (*parens patriae*) jurisdiction.

Further Reading and References

Bailey-Harris, Barron and Pearce, 'Settlement culture and the use of the 'no order' principle under the Children Act 1989' [1999] CFLQ 53.

Bainham, *Children – The Modern Law*, 2nd edn, Family Law (Jordans), 1998.

Davis and Pearce, 'On the trail of the welfare principle' [1999] Fam Law 144.

Davis and Pearce, 'A view from the trenches – practice and procedure in section 8 applications' [1999] Fam Law 457.

Freeman, 'The next Children's Act' [1998] Fam Law 341.

Sturgeon-Adams and James, 'Assisting families – section 16 orders under the Children Act 1989' [1999] Fam Law 471.

Trinder and Stone, 'Family assistance orders – Professional aspiration and party frustration' [1998] CFLQ 291.

Website

Children Act Reports 1995–99: available at www.open.gov.uk/

Questions

1 How might the Children Act 1989 be considered a successful Act? Does it protect the rights of children sufficiently?

2 The family assistance order is not regularly ordered by the courts. Why do you think this is?

13 Children on Family Breakdown

13.1 Children on Family Breakdown

In this chapter, residence and contact arrangements for children on the breakdown of their parents' relationship are considered, whether their parents are married or unmarried. The law applicable to disputes about children on family breakdown is laid down in the Children Act 1989 (see further in Chapter 12). However, the legal requirements for the supervision of arrangements for children whose parents divorce are also laid down in s.41 of the Matrimonial Causes Act 1973 and in the Family Proceedings Rules 1991.

Research (for example, by Richards, and Rodgers and Pryor) has shown that children can suffer considerable emotional trauma when their parents break up. They may suffer fear, anger, withdrawal, grief and guilt. Their educational development may suffer. They are more likely to become delinquent, and their own marital and cohabitation relationships are often more likely to break down. They also often suffer financially, as they tend to grow up in households with lower incomes, poorer housing and greater financial hardship. Because of children's vulnerability at the time of family breakdown, a major policy aim of divorce law has been to provide protection for children (see Chapter 7). It attempts to do this by requiring the court to consider divorcing parents' future arrangements for their children and by attempting to reduce the hostility and bitterness between divorcing parents by encouraging them to reach agreement about ancillary matters. However, while such provision exists to protect the children of divorcing parents, nothing exists for the children of cohabiting parents. This is a matter of some concern, as many couples choose to cohabit and many cohabitation relationships break down. However, it could be argued that the mechanisms in place for supervising arrangements for the children of divorcing couples are so inadequate that the children of cohabiting couples whose relationships break down are in fact in no worse a position.

Not only has there been criticism of the procedure for considering post-divorce arrangements for children, but there has also been criticism of the law's failure to allow children to participate in the divorce process, both in court proceedings and in mediation sessions. As the law now stands, children are not represented in the divorce process and are not permitted to become involved in mediation. Concern has shifted somewhat from discussions about the harm which children suffer on divorce to discussion about children's active participation in the process.

On family breakdown, disputes often arise in respect of residence and contact arrangements for children. If such a dispute arises, however, it is best for all concerned if the parties try to settle the dispute, with or without the assistance of mediators or lawyers, because bringing a case to court is costly, time-consuming, unpredictable and traumatic for all concerned. Even if a case is brought to court, the judge may apply the 'no-order presumption' (see 12.3) and refuse to make the order sought or make a different one altogether. If couples do decide to seek legal advice, then they will find that many lawyers adopt a conciliatory approach. Many solicitors in fact belong to the Solicitors' Family Law Association whose Code of Practice encourages settlement, particularly where children are concerned. Some couples may find it useful to seek the assistance of a mediator to help them reach agreement (see 1.3). Because conciliatory approaches are favoured, any statement made by either party in conciliation or mediations sessions is inadmissible in court proceedings under the Children Act 1989, except where a statement indicates that the maker of the statement has caused or is likely to cause serious harm to a child (*Re D (Minors)(Conciliation: Privilege)* [1993] 1 FLR 932).

When parental relationships break down, parents have continuing parental responsibility (see 11.6), so that parental rights and duties continue. Of particular importance is the duty of parents to provide financial support for their children, whether the parents are married or unmarried, and whether or not they have parental responsibility. Where a parent fails to provide financial support, or insufficient financial support, an application can be made to the Child Support Agency and in some cases to the courts (see Chapter 14).

13.2 The Duty to Children in Divorce Proceedings

A major policy aim of divorce law is to protect the interests of children. One way in which the law aims to do this is by requiring the petitioner to file a form called a Statement of Arrangements for Children giving details of the proposed arrangements for the children, e.g. accommodation, education, child care, maintenance, health and contact (r.2.2 FPR 1991). The Statement must be signed by the petitioner and, if possible, agreed with by the respondent, and must state whether the petitioner intends to apply for any s.8 order under the Children Act (see 12.4 and below). There is usually no need for parents to attend court. The procedure is essentially an administrative exercise.

Section 41(1) of the Matrimonial Causes Act 1973 (the divorce legislation) requires the district judge to examine the Statement of Arrangements for Children and to consider whether (in the light of arrangements made or proposed to be made) the court should exercise any of its powers under the Children Act 1989 with respect to any of the children. (For the courts' powers under the Children Act, see Chapter 12.) The court's duty under s.41 applies to any child of the family aged under 16, unless it directs otherwise (s.41(3)). 'Child of the family' includes a non-marital child of one or both parties and any other child treated by the parties as a child of the family (but not including a local authority foster-child) (s.52). The district judge must therefore consider arrangements for natural and adopted children, privately fostered children and step-children. In *Re A (Child of the Family)* [1998] 1 FLR 347, the Court of Appeal had to consider whether a 17-year-old girl brought up by her divorcing grandparents was a 'child of the family'. The Court of Appeal held that the question of whether a child has been treated as a child of the family was to be judged by an objective test. On the facts she was held to be a child of the family, as the grandparents were her primary carers, and their long-term commitment went beyond the ties that grandparents normally had with their grandchildren.

In most cases the district judge will be satisfied that the court need not exercise any of its powers under the Children Act, and will certify to that effect. If not satisfied, he can direct that further evidence be filed, or order a welfare report, or order that one or both of the parties attend before him. In exceptional circumstances, where the child's interests require it and the court is not able to exercise any of its powers under the Children Act without further consideration of the case, the district judge can direct that the decree of divorce should not be made absolute (s.41(2) MCA 1973). In practice, the court usually accepts the statements on the form and makes no further enquiries before granting the final divorce decree. Even if there is a disputed issue, the court will not usually delay the divorce, as it will usually take the view that any disputed matters can be dealt with at a subsequent hearing.

Had the new divorce law in Part II of the Family Law Act 1996 been implemented (see 7.5), the court would have been unable to grant a divorce unless the parties had made arrangements for the future, which would have included satisfying the requirements relating to the welfare of any children. The duties and powers of the court laid down in s.41 above would, however, have remained the same, except that amendments would have been made requiring the child's welfare and the following checklist of factors to be taken into account by the court when considering whether there were any circumstances requiring it to exercise any of its powers under the Children Act. The checklist would have required the court to consider:

'(a) the wishes and feelings of the child considered in the light of his age and understanding and the circumstances in which those wishes were expressed;

(b) the conduct of the parties in relation to the upbringing of the child;

(c) the general principle that, in the absence of evidence to the contrary, the welfare of the child will be best served by—

(i)   his having regular contact with those who have parental responsibility for him and with other members of his family; and

(ii) the maintenance of as good a continuing relationship with his parents as possible; and

(d) any risk to the child attributable to—

(i)   where the person with whom the child will reside is living or proposes to live;

(ii) any person with whom that person is living or with whom he proposes to live; or

(iii) any other arrangements for his care and upbringing.'

When considering whether to use its powers under the Children Act, and, if so, in what manner, the divorce court would also have had to exercise its powers in accordance with general principles laid down in Part I of the 1996 Act (see 7.5).

The shelving of the new divorce law (and now its permanent demise) has been seen by some as a retrograde step for children, as important initiatives on how to address the needs and interests of children have been lost (see Smart, 1999). In addition to the changes to s.41 referred to above, the proposed information meetings (see 7.6) would have provided an opportunity for parents to consider how their children might feel about divorce, and for children themselves to be provided with information, helplines and support. In addition, parenting plans were proposed to encourage parents to think about parenting after divorce.

Even though the new divorce law has not been implemented, the Government is still considering the possibility of reform. Indeed, the Government has recently expressed concern that too many divorcing couples are locked in dispute about contact with their children. Consequently, the Government is considering the possibility of refusing a divorce until the parties have sorted out proper arrangements for their children (*The Times*, 25 May 2000). The great disadvantage of such a proposal, however, is that spouses who do not wish to divorce might use this as a delaying tactic and a bargaining chip.

13.3   Residence

The two main areas of dispute which often arise in respect of children on family breakdown are with whom the child should live, and who should have contact. Where parents cannot agree on other matters (e.g. education, medical treatment, taking a child out of the UK, or changing the child's name), an application can be made for a s.8 prohibited steps or specific issue order (see 12.4). Sometimes it will be necessary to apply for maintenance or finance and property orders for children (see Chapter 14).

(a) The Residence Order (For more detail, see also Chapter 12)

Before the Children Act 1989 came into force in 1991, parental disputes about children on family breakdown were resolved in custody proceedings, in which the court would usually make a sole or joint custody order and grant care and control to one parent (usually the mother) and access to the other (usually the father). In its *Report on Guardianship and Custody* (Law Com No 172, 1988), the Law Commission criticised the concepts of custody, care and control and access. The term 'custody' was criticised because it created a parental claim right, which increased hostility and bitterness between the parties by creating winners and losers, and this was considered to have detrimental consequences for children. The residence order was therefore introduced by s.8 of the Children Act 1989 to place the emphasis on the child's living arrangements and not on which parent had a greater claim to the child. Parents have responsibilities for their children, not claims to them.

Where there is a dispute on family breakdown about with whom the child shall live, the court may make a residence order which is defined in s.8(1) as:

> 'an order settling the arrangements to be made as to the person with whom a child is to live.'

Parents must be advised, however, that the court has a discretion to do what is best for the child's welfare, and may not make the order applied for (s.1(5)) or may make a different s.8 order (s.10(1)(b)). Furthermore, it may direct that a welfare report on the child be carried out (s.7) or direct that a local authority investigate the child's circumstances (s.37). Parents, whether married or unmarried and with and without parental responsibility, can apply for a residence order. Other persons can too, provided they have the prior permission of the court (see 12.6).

(b) Shared Residence

A residence order can be made in favour of two or more persons who do not live together and can specify the periods during which the child is to live in the different households concerned (s.11(4) CA 1989). However, there has been judicial reluctance to make residence orders in favour of two or more persons (a 'shared residence order') because of the insecurity it might create for the child. The courts would only make them in exceptional circumstances (see *A* v. *A (Minors)(Shared Residence Order)* [1994] 1 FLR 669). Today, however, the courts are likely to be more willing to make a shared order, provided an applicant can show a positive benefit why such an order should be made, and there are no concrete issues between the parties still needing to be resolved (e.g. about contact and education) (Butler-Sloss LJ in *A* v. *A*). However, the court will not usually make a shared order unless there is a high degree of co-operation between the parties, but if there is such co-operation then a shared order would seem unnecessary because of the no-order presumption in s.1(5). However, a shared residence order can be useful because it confers parental responsibility on a person who does not possess it (see, for example, *Re AB (Adoption: Joint Residence)* [1996] 1 FLR 27). In *Re H (Shared Residence: Parental Responsibility)* [1995] 2 FLR 883, a shared residence order was made as it was considered to be of practical therapeutic importance, because it conferred parental responsibility on the step-father. In *Re WB (Residence Order)* [1995] 2 FLR 1023, on the other hand, the court refused to make a shared order as it would give the unmarried father parental responsibility which would be likely to foment disputes which would be contrary to the children's welfare. Each case depends on its own facts.

(c) How the Court Exercises its Power to Make Residence Orders – the Welfare Checklist

When determining whether or not to make a residence order, the court has wide discretionary powers, but must apply the welfare principle (s.1(1)), the no-delay principle (s.1(2)) and the no-order presumption (s.1(5)). In contested proceedings it must also apply the following factors laid down in the s.1(3) 'welfare checklist' (see 12.3):

Factor (a) in the checklist requires the court to consider the child's wishes in the light of his or her age and understanding. Where the child is intelligent and mature enough to make an informed decision, the child's wish to live with a particular parent may determine the matter, all other things being equal. However, some proponents of children's rights believe that children's wishes are not being sufficiently heard on family breakdown.

Factor (b) requires the court to consider the child's physical and emotional needs. However, the court will not necessarily make the order in favour of the wealthier parent. As Lindley LJ said in *Re McGrath (Infants)* [1893] Ch 143, 'the welfare of the child is not to be measured by money alone nor by physical comfort only.' As far as needs are concerned, however, the courts have held that it is usually better for a young child, particularly a young baby, to be brought up by a mother, but this is not a principle, or a presumption, but merely a consideration (see Butler-Sloss LJ in *Re S (A Minor)(Custody)* [1991] 2 FLR 388, and also *Re A (A Minor)(Custody)* [1991] 2 FLR 394, where Butler-Sloss LJ stated that where children were very young, the unbroken relationship of mother and child would be difficult to displace, unless the mother was unsuitable to care for them). In *Brixey* v. *Lynas* [1996] 2 FLR 499, the 'maternal preference factor' was endorsed by the House of Lords in an appeal from Scotland, and Lord Jauncey cited with approval Butler-Sloss LJ's words in *Re S (A Minor)(Custody)* and *Re A (A Minor)(Custody)* above – that mothers are by nature generally better fitted than fathers to provide for the needs of very young children, but stressed that this is only a consideration. In *Re W (Residence)* [1999] 2 FLR 390, the Court of Appeal said that the emotional and psychological attachment of a child to the parent is a consideration of very great importance to be included in the balancing exercise. The flexibility and availability of the primary carer were important considerations, particularly where the child was young and required constant and consistent care.

Factor (c) in the checklist requires the court to consider the likely effect on the child of a change of circumstances. This factor is the same as the 'continuity of care' or 'status quo' factor which was an important consideration before the Children Act introduced the checklist. In *D* v. *M (Minor)(Custody Appeal)* [1982] 3 WLR 891, Ormrod LJ stated:

> 'it is generally accepted by those who are professionally concerned with children that, particularly in the early years, continuity of care is a most important part of a child's sense of security and that disruption of established bonds is to be avoided whenever it is possible to do so.'

The court may therefore be unwilling to disturb arrangements which have satisfactorily been in place for some time. In many cases this will mean the child remaining with the mother. But this is not necessarily so. Thus, for example, in *Re B (Residence Order: Status Quo)* [1998] 1 FLR 368, the Court of Appeal held that the status quo prevailed over the maternal preference factor, and allowed the father's appeal against the residence order made in favour of the child's mother. The father had cared for the eight-year-old child since the child was aged two. The court may also be unwilling to disturb existing arrangements by splitting up brothers and sisters. It may also be concerned about disruptions to schooling arrangements and the possibility of a child losing contact with friends and relatives if an existing residence arrangement is changed.

Factor (d) requires the court to take into account the age, sex, background and any of the child's characteristics that it considers relevant. Under this section, the child's religious preferences, racial and cultural background, health and disabilities will be considered.

Factor (e) requires the court to consider any harm the child has suffered or is at risk of suffering. This will include emotional or physical harm. If there has been sexual abuse or violence in the home, the court is unlikely to make a residence order in favour of the perpetrator of the abuse or violence. Living with a parent with extreme religious views will not necessarily result in a residence order not being made in favour of that person. Thus in *Re R (A Minor) (Residence: Religion)* [1993] 2 FLR 163, a residence order was made in favour of the father after the mother's death, even though he was a member of the Exclusive Brethren, an extreme religious sect in which members are not allowed to mix socially with anyone not in the fellowship. However, the court also made a supervision order in favour of the local authority (see 16.5). Where a mother lives with a lesbian partner after relationship breakdown with the child's father this will not necessarily result in a residence order being made in favour of the child's father, despite concerns that such children might develop emotional problems and be stigmatised by their peers and others (see *C v. C (A Minor)(Custody: Appeal)* [1991] 1 FLR 223 and *B v. B (Minors)(Custody, Care and Control)* [1991] 1 FLR 402). Where the court is concerned about making a residence order because there is a risk of harm, it may make an interim residence order, or back up a residence order with another order, such as a specific issue or prohibited steps order, a family assistance order, or a s.37 direction for a local authority to investigate the case. In *Re H (A Minor)(Section 37 Direction)* [1993] 2 FLR 541, an interim residence order was made in favour of a lesbian couple where the child was not their own but where the natural parent had agreed to them bringing up the child. A supervision order and a s.37 direction that the local authority investigate the case were also made.

Factor (f) of the checklist requires the court to consider how capable each parent is of meeting the child's needs. Under this section, the court might consider, for example, whether a parent can provide accommodation, love, emotional security, intellectual stimulation and care during working hours.

Factor (g), the last factor in the checklist, requires the court to consider the range of powers available to it under the Children Act (see Chapter 12). As proceedings for a residence order are themselves family proceedings (s.8(3)), the court can make other orders on application, or of its own motion, e.g. any other s.8 order; a s.16 family assessment order; an order appointing a guardian; or a s.37 direction that a local authority investigate the child's circumstances (for more on all these orders, see Chapter 12).

Each case, however, will turn on its own facts. In some cases matters will be so finely balanced that the court will have to make a difficult and often harrowing decision. The court welfare report, prepared by the court welfare officer and giving an independent assessment of the case, is important, particularly where a case is finely balanced. Judges are extremely dependent on the contributions of court welfare officers who will have visited the child's home and seen children and parents in the home-environment. For this reason, judges are not entitled to depart from the recommendations of the court welfare officer without giving reasons (see *Re W (Residence)* [1999] 2 FLR 390).

Where a judge has misgivings about a court welfare officer's report, then the court must explore these misgivings with the court welfare officer in the witness box (*Re A (Children: 1959 UN Declaration)* [1998] 1 FLR 354, followed in *Re W (Residence)*, above).

Although the Children Act aims to get rid of the idea that parents are winners and losers by placing the emphasis on residential arrangements for the child and on continuing joint parental responsibility, the non-residential parent may consider himself or herself a loser, particularly as contact arrangements are often difficult to sustain and many parents (particularly fathers) eventually lose contact with their children. Furthermore, as judges have a wide discretion to make orders, any appeal against a residence order is likely to be unsuccessful. Thus, for example, in *Re R (Residence Order: Finance)* [1995] 2 FLR 612, the mother's appeal against a shared residence order was dismissed, even though the judge had taken into account financial considerations, which are not expressly provided for in the s.1(3) checklist.

13.4   Contact

Where there is a dispute about contact with the child on family breakdown and the dispute cannot be settled without going to court, then an application may be made for a contact order under the Children Act 1989. (For more on contact orders, see Chapter 12.) A contact order is defined in s.8(1) as:

> 'an order requiring the person with whom a child lives, or is to live, to allow the child to visit or stay with the person named in the order, or for that person and the child otherwise to have contact with each other.'

Prior to the Children Act, a parent would apply for an 'access' order. The change of terminology to 'contact' was considered to be more child-centred, as it ordered the residential parent to allow the child to have contact with a named person, rather than allowing a parent to have a right of access to a child. It was children, not parents, who had a right of access (Wrangham LJ in *M* v. *M* [1973] 2 All ER 81).

Parents, with or without parental responsibility, have an automatic right to apply to the court for a contact order. Other persons, such as grandparents and other family members, can apply, and so can the child, provided he or she has the prior permission of the court (see 12.6).

When considering whether to make a contact order and, if so, in what manner, the court must apply the welfare principle (s.1(1)), the no-order presumption (s.1(5)) and in a contested application the s.1(3) welfare checklist. In *Re M (Contact: Welfare Test)* [1995] 1 FLR 274, Wilson J said it was helpful to cast the relevant principles on contact into the framework of the s.1(3) welfare checklist and ask whether the fundamental emotional need for every child to have an enduring relationship with both of his parents was outweighed by the depth of harm which, in the light, *inter alia*, of his wishes and feelings, the child would be at risk of suffering by virtue of a contact order. The court might decide not to make an order under the s.1(5) 'no-order presumption', but as contact is a right of the child it is unlikely to do so.

As contact is considered to be beneficial for the child, the case-law has created a presumption in favour of contact. In *Re W (A Minor)(Contact)* [1994] 2 FLR 441, Sir Stephen Brown P said at 447 that it is 'quite clear that contact with a parent is a fundamental right of a child, save in wholly exceptional circumstances.' The same approach is adopted in art. 9(3) of the UN Convention on the Rights of the Child 1989, which provides that 'States Parties shall respect the right of the child...to maintain personal relations and direct contact with both parents on a regular basis, except if it is contrary to the child's best interests.'

In *Re H (Minors)(Access)* [1992] 1 FLR 148, Balcombe LJ said that the question to be asked when considering cessation or resumption of access (now contact) is whether there are any cogent reasons why the child should not have access, not whether or not access is beneficial for the child (see also *Re H (Contact Principles)* [1994] 2 FLR 969). In *Re R (A Minor)(Contact)* [1993] 2 FLR 762, Butler-Sloss LJ stated that it 'is a right of a child to have a relationship with both parents wherever possible' and that 'in general the parents with whom the child does not live has a continuing role to play, which is recognised by s.2(1) of the Children Act 1989.' The decision whether or not to grant contact is therefore child-centred. As the welfare of the child is the court's paramount consideration, parental interests are only relevant in so far as they impact on the child's welfare. In most cases, the court will decide that it is almost always in the child's best interests for contact with a parent to be maintained. It has been held, however, that the court should take a medium-term and long-term view of a child's development and should not accord excessive weight to short-term problems (Sir Thomas Bingham MR in *Re O (Contact: Imposition of Conditions)* [1995] 2 FLR 124 at 129).

Thus the court is unlikely to deprive a child of parental contact unless there are cogent reasons against it. Even where the child has no biological relationship with a parent, a contact order may be made (e.g. in favour of a step-father, see *Re H (Minor)(Contact)* [1994] 2 FLR 776). Because of the importance of a child knowing his or her natural parent, contact may be ordered even though a father is absent, for instance in prison (see *Re R (A Minor)(Contact)* [1993] 2 FLR 762 and *A v. L (Contact)* [1998] 1 FLR 361). The presumption in favour of contact with a natural parent is not, however, adopted by the courts in applications by other family members, for example grandparents (see *Re A (Section 8 Order: Grandparent Application)* [1995] 2 FLR 153). In *Re W (Contact: Application by Grandparent)* [1997] 1 FLR 793, Hollis J stated that, while grandparents have a very great role to play in the life of children, particularly young children, they must remember that they are grandparents, not parents. Hollis J said that their influence could be extremely beneficial to children provided it was exercised with care and not too frequently.

Different sorts of contact can be ordered, depending on the circumstances. Section 8(1) provides that the child can visit, stay or otherwise have contact with the parent or other named person. In most cases, direct contact (visiting or staying contact) will be ordered, unless there are cogent reasons to the contrary affecting the child's welfare (e.g. where there is violence as in *Re D (Contact: Reasons for Refusal)* [1997] 2 FLR 48). Sometimes, however, the court will order indirect or supervised contact (the word 'otherwise' in s.8(1) allows the court to do this). The court can specify what arrangements are to take place, for instance, by making a direction in the order that there be 'indirect contact' by letter, birthday and Christmas cards or telephone (see s.11(7) and *Re O (Contact: Imposition of Conditions)* [1995] 2 FLR 124). In *Re P (Contact: Indirect Contact)* [1999] 2 FLR 893, indirect contact was ordered as the father was a former drug addict who had just been released from prison. Letters may be transmitted via the court welfare service (see *Re M (A Minor)(Contact: Conditions)* [1994] 1 FLR 272). Where there is a risk that contact may harm the child, the court may decide that supervised contact in the presence of a third party is best (see, for example, *Re P (Contact: Supervision)* [1996] 2 FLR 314). In exceptional cases, the court may decide to make a s.16 family assistance order (see 12.7) to protect the child and provide counselling and advice for the family (see *Re L (Contact: Transsexual Applicant)* [1995] 2 FLR 438 and *Re F (Minors)(Denial of Contact)* [1993] 2 FLR 677). In *Re E (Family Assistance Order)* [1999] 2 FLR 512, a family assistance order was made requiring the local authority to supervise contact, despite the cost, as it was vital that the child remain in touch with the mother, even though she had been convicted of the father's manslaughter and detained under the Mental Health Act 1983.

Problems with Contact

Contact arrangements on family breakdown sometimes cause problems. Contact arrangements often break down. They may break down unintentionally or one parent may refuse to co-operate with the arrangements. Sometimes they break down because of hostility to contact by mothers even though breach of a contact order is contempt of court and can ultimately result in imprisonment (see *F* v. *P (Contact: Committal)* [1998] 2 FLR 237, where a mother was imprisoned for failing to comply with an order for supervised contact). Some mothers, however, are hostile to contact for quite genuine reasons. Some fear the children will suffer violence if they are allowed to have contact. In recent years, in fact, there has been increasing concern about violence and contact, and criticism has been made of the presumption in favour of contact and the rigid enforcement of contact orders because of the risk of exposing some children to violence (see below). Smart and Neale (1997) have criticised the way in which the courts have given short shrift to contact where there is a risk of violence and have stated that 'the public and judicial treatment of contact has taken on a rigid and dogmatic form, which is becoming a harmful trend in family law' (p.332).

The courts have generally taken the view that, if contact is deemed to be in the best interests of the child, then contact orders should be enforced even where a parent (usually the mother) is strongly against the order. The courts have been concerned to see that contact is not thwarted by the behaviour of residential parents. Thus in *Re H (A Minor)(Contact)* [1994] 2 FLR 776, Butler-Sloss LJ stated that it was important that there should not be 'a selfish parents' charter', whereby a parent could make so much fuss about contact that it could prevent the court from ordering it. Where there has been hostility to contact, indirect contact, supervised contact and a contact order with conditions imposed under s.11(7) have provided solutions (see, for example, *Re O (Contact: Imposition of Conditions)* [1995] 2 FLR 124). Only in exceptional circumstances has the court refused contact. Contact was refused, for example, in *Re J (A Minor)(Contact)* [1994] 1 FLR 729, where the Court of Appeal upheld a decision that a contact order be refused because the mother's hostility to the father caused the child stress. However, Balcombe LJ emphasised the exceptional nature of the case and said that judges should be very reluctant to allow the implacable hostility of one parent to deter them from making a contact order where they believed the child's welfare required it (see also *Re D (A Minor)(Contact: Mother's Hostility)* [1993] 2 FLR 1).

In more recent cases, however, the courts have increasingly realised that mothers may have quite genuine reasons for being hostile to contact (see Hale J in *Re D (Contact: Reasons for Refusal)* [1997] 2 FLR 48). For this reason the term 'implacable hostility', which was often used by the courts, is now considered inappropriate. Indeed, in *Re H (Contact: Domestic Violence)* [1998] 2 FLR 42, the Court of Appeal said that, although the term 'implacable hostility' was often used as an 'umbrella term', a distinction should be drawn between cases where there was no good reason for hostility (in which the court would be very reluctant to deny contact) and cases where hostility was based on genuine and rational fear (in which the court would have to ask whether contact would be in the child's best interests).

Contact and Domestic Violence

In the last few years there has been increasing concern about the problem of contact and domestic violence, and some disquiet about the approach of the courts which was that domestic violence on its own could not constitute a bar to contact, but was simply one fact in a very complex equation (see *Re H (Contact: Domestic Violence*, above). In English law there is no presumption against contact where there is domestic violence, although such a presumption exists in other legal systems. In the English courts, contact orders have been granted in favour of fathers, even where there have been allegations of violence. As a result, there has been concern that the courts have created too high a threshold for a denial of contact. In *Re M (Contact: Family Assistance: McKenzie Friend)* [1999] 1 FLR 75, for example, the mother's genuinely held fears about contact were sufficiently serious on the facts to justify indirect, not direct, contact, but the Court of Appeal continued to stress that contact ought not to be denied unless there was evidence that continuation of contact would seriously interfere with the child's welfare.

In 1999, a report by Radford (*Unreasonable Fears? Child Contact in the Context of Domestic Violence: A Survey of Mothers' Perception of Harm*) was published by the Women's Aid organisation. The Report provided evidence of physical and sexual abuse of children as a result of contact being ordered, and stated that changes in court practice were overdue (see also 'Domestic Violence Research' [2000] Fam Law 156). The Report recommended the introduction of a rebuttable presumption against residence, and direct or unsupervised contact in cases where there was a risk of violence. It also recommended better monitoring of practice and better provision for representation of children in court proceedings.

In June 1999 a Consultation Paper (*Contact Between Children and Violent Parents: The Question of Parental Contact in Cases Where There is Domestic Violence*) was published by the Children Act Sub-Committee of the Advisory Board on Family Law. The Paper proposed guidelines for good practice rather than legislative amendment. In April 2000 a Report based on the responses to the Consultation Paper was presented to the Lord Chancellor (*Report to the Lord Chancellor on the Question of Parental Contact in Cases Where There is Domestic Violence*, Lord Chancellor's Department, www.open.gov/lcd). According to the Report, those who had responded to the Consultation Paper had acknowledged that contact and domestic violence was not being fully or appropriately handled by the courts, and that something needed to be done. The principal recommendation of the Report was that guidelines for good practice should be laid down, preferably in the form of a Practice Direction. It also recommended the need for professionals involved to be better informed and to have continuous training in the matter. However, the Children Act Sub-Committee was not in favour of a legislative presumption against contact in cases involving domestic violence, as there is in some countries.

The Report was considered by the Court of Appeal in *Re L (Contact: Domestic Violence); Re V (Contact: Domestic Violence); Re M (Contact: Domestic Violence); Re H (Contact: Domestic Violence)* [2000] 2 FLR 334 (see the case-note by Kaganas at [2000] CFLQ 311). In each case the father's application for direct contact had been refused against a background of domestic violence between the parents, and each father had appealed. The Court of Appeal stated that family judges and magistrates needed to have a heightened awareness of the existence and consequences for children of exposure to violence between their parents or other partners. The Court of Appeal refused to accept, however, that there should be a presumption of no contact on proof of domestic violence, but said that domestic violence was a factor in the balancing exercise of discretion carried out by the judge applying the welfare principle (s.1(1)) and the welfare checklist (s.1(3)). Where domestic violence was proved, then the court would have to weigh the seriousness of domestic violence, the risks involved and the impact on the child against the positive factors, if any, of contact. The Court of Appeal also held that the ability of an offending parent to recognise his or her past conduct, and to be aware of the need to change and to make genuine efforts to do so, would be likely to be an important consideration when performing the balancing exercise. As far as the right to family life under art. 8 of the European Convention for the Protection of Human Rights was concerned, the Court of Appeal held that, where there was a conflict between the rights and interests of a child and those of a parent, the interests of the child had to prevail under art. 8(2) of the Convention (see 1.5).

As a result of concerns expressed about contact and violence, the courts will now take allegations of violence in contact cases more seriously, and may order indirect or supervised contact, or, in an extreme case, refuse to order contact at all (see, for example, *Re M (Contact: Violent Parent)* [1999] 2 FLR 321 and also *Re K (Contact: Mother's Anxiety)* [1999] 2 FLR 703, where indirect contact was ordered because the father's violence had caused the mother anxiety which had been passed on to the child). Until fairly recently, the courts have been too much concerned with the benefits for children of bringing them up with a positive image of their father at the expense of exposing children to violence. Too little weight had been given to the need for fathers to change their behaviour and demonstrate their fitness to exercise their parental functions. The courts have now adopted a principle, however, that where there is domestic violence, a father will have to show a future track record of proper behaviour, including taking up the offer of indirect contact, before successfully gaining direct contact (see dicta of Wall J in *Re O (Contact: Imposition of Conditions)* [1995] 2 FLR 124, approved by Cazalet J in *Re S (Violent Parent: Indirect Contact)* [2000] 1 FLR 481).

13.5 Changing a Child's Surname

Where parents are married at the time of their child's birth, the duty to provide information for birth registration purposes under the Births and Deaths

Registration Acts 1953 and 1994 lies on both parents. However, where parents are unmarried at the time of their child's birth, only the mother has a duty to register the birth, although the unmarried father may be entered on the register of births if the mother consents or there is a court order in force. Where the child is legitimated by the parents' subsequent marriage, the parents must re-register the child's birth (s.9 Legitimacy Act 1976).

As far as changing a child's surname is concerned, it can be changed by a person with parental responsibility for the child, provided all other persons with parental responsibility have consented to it. Verbal consent is sufficient. If consent is not forthcoming, then the dispute can be settled by bringing proceedings under the Children Act 1989 (see *Re PC (Change of Surname)* [1997] 2 FLR 73 and *Re T (Change of Surname)* [1998] 2 FLR 620). Where a residence order is in force, however, the position is different, for s.13(1)(b) of the Children Act provides that the *written* consent of all those with parental responsibility is needed for a change of surname, otherwise the permission of the court is required. Written consent is also required of all those with parental responsibility if the child is in local authority care (s.33(7), and see *Re S (Change of Surname)* [1999] 1 FLR 672).

An intractable dispute about a child's surname can be settled by making an application for a specific issue order (see 12.4), or, if a residence order is in force, by making an application under s.13. The welfare of the child is the court's paramount consideration (s.1(1) CA 1989). In an application by way of a specific issue order, the court must also have regard to the s.1(3) welfare checklist (see s.1(4)). Although the Children Act does not mandate the court to consider the checklist in an application under s.13, the court is likely to perform the same sort of exercise. Changing a child's surname is considered to be a serious issue. The welfare of the child, not the wishes of the parents, will be the court's paramount concern. In *Re C (Change of Surname)* [1998] 2 FLR 656, the Court of Appeal held that there is a heavy responsibility on those who seek to effect a change of name, as a matter of prudence if not of direct law, to take the issue to the court and to appreciate that good reasons have to be shown before the judge will allow a change of name. In *Re W; Re A; Re B (Change of Name)* [1999] 2 FLR 930, Butler-Sloss LJ said that changing the child's name based on the fact that the child and the applicant parent do not have the same name will generally not carry much weight. Her Ladyship also said that, when the applicant is an unmarried father, the court will consider his commitment to the child, the quality of the contact and the existence or otherwise of a parental responsibility order.

In *Dawson* v. *Wearmouth* [1999] AC 308, [1999] 1 FLR 1167, the mother, without consulting the child's unmarried father, had registered the child's name in her former husband's name. The unmarried father applied for a specific issue order (as no residence order was in force). The House of Lords dismissed the unmarried father's appeal, holding that the Court of Appeal had correctly applied the relevant provisions of the Children Act in the exercise of its discretion to refuse to make an order. The House of Lords held that the welfare of the child, not the rights of parents, was the overriding concern. For this reason, it held that the father's argument that his right to respect for his family life under art. 8 of the European Convention had been infringed had no basis.

13.6 Removing a Child out of the UK

On relationship breakdown, one parent may wish to leave the UK with the child. In this situation, the consent of all those with parental responsibility is needed, otherwise a parent commits a criminal offence (see 15.5). If a residence order is in force, the position is different, for the child cannot be removed from the UK (except for a period of less than one month, s.13(2)) without the *written* consent of all those with parental responsibility, or if this is not forthcoming then without the court's permission (s.13(1)(b)). (See further, 15.4.)

13.7 Are Children Adequately Protected on Family Breakdown?

In the UK, about one in three children under the age of 16 experiences their parents' divorce. It has always been an important policy objective of divorce law to protect children (see Chapter 7). However, the law is considered to be inadequate in this respect. A primary concern is that the process by which the divorce court looks at arrangements for children under s.41 of the Matrimonial Causes Act 1973 is unsatisfactory, because district judges rarely take action after scrutinising the details about arrangements for children. One of the main reasons for this is because they do not consider there is much they can usefully do to remedy any problems they have identified (see the research by Murch *et al.*, and see [1999] Fam Law). It is generally felt that better mechanisms are needed to identify children who are at risk, and the recent concerns about contact and domestic violence (see above) highlight this. Another matter of some concern is children's lack of participation in the divorce process. Had the new divorce law under Part II of the Family Law Act 1996 come into force, modest changes to the law relating to children on divorce would have been made. Amendments to s.41 MCA would have been made by s.11 (see 13.2) and s.64 would have introduced the possibility of separate representation for children. Many feel there is a pressing need for continuing debate about what is to be done for children on divorce, particularly now that Part II of the Family Law Act has not been implemented (see, for example, Timms, 1999).

Another concern is whether society is failing in its responsibility to children by having no provision in place to protect the children of unmarried parents whose relationship breaks down. Cohabitation breakdown is probably more common than marriage breakdown, resulting in large numbers of children of unmarried parents experiencing family breakdown. If the welfare of children is a primary concern, then the different treatment of children on family breakdown depending on whether their parents are married or unmarried, is an arbitrary one. Although it is possible to justify non-intervention by the State in respect of cohabitants themselves on the basis of freedom of choice and autonomy rights, the same arguments cannot be used to justify the approach that the State has adopted towards the children of unmarried parents.

Summary

1 Many children suffer when their parents' relationships break down.
2 Where the parents are divorcing, the district judge under s.41 of the Matrimonial Causes Act 1973 must consider the proposed arrangements for the children, and consider whether to exercise his or her powers under the Children Act 1989. In exceptional circumstances, a decree absolute of divorce can be postponed so that arrangements for the children can be given further consideration. Had the new divorce law come into force under Part II of the Family Law Act 1996, the court would have been unable to grant a divorce unless the parties had made arrangements for the children, and s.11 of the 1996 Act would have required the judge to consider a checklist of factors, such as the child's wishes, and the conduct of the parties in relation to the child's upbringing, and also stressing the importance of contact.
3 Both parents retain parental responsibility for their children on relationship breakdown.
4 Maintenance for children on family breakdown can be sought from the Child Support Agency (and in some cases in the courts), and lump sum and property orders can be sought from the courts (see Chapter 14).
5 Where there is a dispute about with whom a child should live on family breakdown, or who should have contact, it is better for parents to settle the dispute either on their own or with the help of a mediator or lawyer.
6 Disputes about which parent the child should live with on family breakdown can be settled by making an application for a s.8 residence order under the Children Act 1989 (see also Chapter 12). The principles in s.1 of the Children Act 1989 apply, namely the welfare principle (s.1(1)), the no-delay principle (s.1(2)), the welfare checklist (s.1(3)) and the no-order presumption (s.1(5)). Maintaining the status quo will be particularly important. The court also takes the view that young children, particularly babies, should live with their mother. A shared residence order can be made in certain circumstances (s.11(4)). Once a residence order is made, no person can change the child's surname or remove the child from the UK without the *written* consent of all those with parental responsibility, or otherwise with the permission of the court (s.13(1)). However, the person in whose favour the residence order is made can take the child out of the UK for a period of up to one month without the consent of all those with parental responsibility (s.12(2)).
7 The child has a right to contact. Any dispute about contact can be settled by making an application for a s.8 contact order under the Children Act 1989. There

is a presumption of parental contact unless there are cogent reasons against it. The court must apply the welfare principles (see above). Direct contact, indirect contact (e.g. by letters, birthday cards, photographs etc.) and supervised contact are possible options for the court. Hostility to contact by the residential parent has sometimes caused difficulties for the court, and recently concern has focused on the problem of contact and domestic violence.

8 Other disputes can be settled by an application for a s.8 specific issue or prohibited steps order (see Chapter 12).

9 A dispute about the child's surname can be decided by making an application for a specific issue order (see Chapter 12), or, if a residence order is in force, by making an application under s.13.

10 A parent who wishes to remove the child from the UK and take up residence abroad may have to obtain the court's permission if the other parent refuses to consent to such removal (see 15.4).

11 There has been some criticism of what is considered to be inadequate provision for the supervision of arrangements for children on divorce. There is also concern that the law is failing children of unmarried parents because there is no provision whereby parental arrangements on family breakdown are looked at unless an unmarried parent applies to the court for a residence or contact order, or any other s.8 order.

Further Reading and References

Advisory Board on Family Law Sub-Committee, *A Consultation Paper on Contact between Children and Violent Parents: The Question of Parental Contact in Cases where there is Domestic Violence*, The Stationery Office, 1999.

Bailey-Harris and Pearce, 'From utility to rights? The presumption of contact in practice' [1999] Int J of Law, Policy and the Family 111.

Bainham, 'Contact as a fundamental right' (1995) 54 CLJ 255.

Barnett, 'Disclosure of domestic violence by women involved in child contact disputes' [1999] Fam Law 104.

Bond, 'Reconstructing families – Changing children's surnames' [1998] CFLQ 17.

Bridge, 'Shared residence in England and New Zealand – a comparative analysis' [1996] CFLQ 12.

Cantwell, Roberts and Young, 'The presumption of contact in private law – an interdisciplinary issue' [1999] Fam Law 227.

Elliott and Richards, 'Children and divorce: educational behaviour, before and after parental separation' [1991] IJLF 258.

Elliott and Richards, 'Parental divorce and the life chances of children' [1991] Fam 481.

Hayes, '*Dawson* v. *Wearmouth* – What's in a name? A child by any other name is surely just as sweet?' [1999] CFLQ 423.

Hoyal, 'Children and violence in their homes' [1999] Fam Law 367.

Humphreys, 'Judicial alienation syndrome: failure to respond to post-separation violence' [1999] Fam Law 313.

Ingman, 'Contact and the obdurate parent' [1996] Fam Law 615.

Jolly, 'Implacable hostility, contact, and the limits of the law' [1995] CFLQ 228.

Kaganas, '*Re L (Contact: Domestic Violence); Re V (Contact: Domestic Violence); Re M (Contact: Domestic Violence); Re H (Contact: Domestic Violence)*: Contact and domestic violence' [2000] CFLQ 301.

Kaganas and Day-Slater, 'Contact and domestic violence – the winds of change' [2000] Fam Law 630.

Kaye, 'Domestic violence, residence and contact' [1996] CFLQ 285.

Masson, 'Thinking about contact – a social or legal problem?' [2000] CFLQ 15.

Murch *et al.*, *Safeguarding Children's Welfare in Uncontentious Divorce: A Study of Section 41 of the Matrimonial Causes Act 1973*, see also at [1999] Fam Law 682.

Perry, 'Safeguarding children's welfare in non-contentious divorce' (2000) 63 MLR 177.

Rhoades, 'Child law reforms in Australia – a shifting landscape' [2000] CFLQ 117.

Richards, 'Children and parents and divorce', in Eekelaar and Sarcevic (eds), *Parenthood in Modern Society – Legal and Social Issues for the Twenty-First Century*, Martinus Nijhoff, 1993.

Richards, 'Private worlds and public intentions – the role of the State at divorce', in Pearl and Pickford (eds), *Frontiers of Family Law, Part I*, John Wiley, 1993.

Richards, 'Divorcing children: roles for parents and the State', in Maclean and Kurczewski (eds), *Families, Politics and the Law*, Clarendon Press, 1994.

Richards, 'But what about the children? Some reflections on the divorce White Paper' [1995] CFLQ 223.

Rodgers and Pryor, *Divorce and Separation: The Outcomes for Children*, Joseph Rowntree Foundation, 1998 (www.jrf.org.uk).

Smart, 'Shelving Part II of the Family Law Act – Shelving children?' [1999] Fam Law 801.

Smart and Neale, 'Arguments against virtue – must contact be enforced?' [1997] Fam Law 332.

Smart and Neale, *Family Fragments*, Polity, 1999.

Smart and Neale, ' "It's my life too" – Children's perspectives on post-divorce parenting' [2000] Fam Law 163.

Timms, 'Children and family breakdown' [1999] Fam Law 679.

Trinder, 'Competing constructions of childhood – Children's rights and children's wishes in divorce' [1997] JSWFL 291.

Websites

Families Need Fathers (organisation which believes in the right to a loving relationship with both parents; information on law and research, including links to Acts of Parliament): www.fnf.org.uk/

Gingerbread (support organisation for lone-parent families, information on law, etc.): www.gingerbread.org.uk/

Shared Parenting Information (aims to promote responsible shared parenting after separation and divorce; research, information and resources available): www.spig.clara.net/

Questions

1 Is the law failing the children of cohabiting couples and divorcing couples on family breakdown?
2 Is there really any realistic way in which arrangements for children on family breakdown can be adequately monitored and supervised?

14   Child Support and Financial Provision and Property Orders for Children

14.1   Finance and Property for Children

All parents, whether married or unmarried and whether or not they have parental responsibility, have a duty to provide financial support for their children, and this obligation continues when parental relationships break down. This maintenance duty is recognised in art. 27(3) of the UN Convention on the Rights of the Child 1989, which provides that 'States Parties shall take all appropriate measures to secure the recovery of maintenance for the child from the parents.'

Financial provision for children may take the form of maintenance (a regular contribution to the upkeep of a child) or a capital sum. Transfers of property orders can also be made for children. Parents may make their own informal arrangements about financial provision or make a written agreement to that effect. The divorce court also has jurisdiction to make consent orders on divorce (and on nullity or separation) (see 9.8) which can contain an agreed provision in respect of child maintenance or other financial provision. If parents cannot reach agreement about child maintenance, an application can be made to the Child Support Agency (see below), except where there are special circumstances, in which case an application can be made to the court. The Agency can only make decisions about maintenance; applications for lump sums or property orders for children must be made to the court (see below).

As far as ownership of property is concerned, a child cannot own a legal estate in land (s.1(6) Law of Property Act 1925), but can own land in equity under a trust. Thus, in *Kingston-upon-Thames Borough Council* v. *Prince* [1999] 1 FLR 593, a 13-year-old girl, on the death of her grandfather with whom she had lived for three years, was held to be a secure tenant in equity of the council house which her grandfather had held under a secure tenancy. However, the Court of Appeal held that until she reached majority, the legal estate would be held on trust by her mother.

14.2   Child Support Maintenance via the Child Support Agency

Maintenance for children ('child support') may be sought by making an application to the Child Support Agency which has powers and duties under the Child Support Acts 1991 and 1995, and under regulations made under those Acts. The Agency has a useful website and national enquiry line (see end of chapter). Parents are not obliged to apply. They can, if they wish, make their own arrangements about child maintenance, although any written agreement about maintenance is void if it purports to oust the jurisdiction of the Agency. Divorcing parents can choose if they wish to have a maintenance agreement incorporated into a court order known as a consent order (see 9.8).

(a) The Development of the Law

The Child Support Act 1991 came into force on 5 April 1993. Before that date, child maintenance applications were heard by the courts which had wide discretionary powers to make periodical payments orders for children according to the circumstances of each case. In 1990, however, the Conservative Government published a White Paper, *Children Come First* (Cm 1264), criticising the discretionary court-based system and making proposals for a new child maintenance system run by a Government agency (the Child Support Agency) which would be responsible for calculating maintenance by using a mathematical formula, and for collecting and enforcing payment. The Government's proposals for reform arose because of the following concerns:

- the wide discretion of the courts was resulting in arbitrary and unpredictable awards of child maintenance being granted;
- many fathers (in breach of their parental responsibility) were failing to fulfil their maintenance obligations because of problems of disclosure and enforcement;
- lone mothers were being caught in the poverty trap;
- the rise in the divorce rate and the growth of one parent families had resulted in women, in particular, being increasingly dependent on state benefits;
- as many fathers were not paying maintenance, even when ordered to do so, the cost was being imposed on the state in the form of welfare benefits, and consequently on the taxpayer;
- the welfare needs of children were not being sufficiently protected;
- court proceedings were slow and costly.

The Government concluded that the child maintenance system was unnecessarily fragmented, uncertain, inconsistent, slow and ineffective, and proposed the introduction of a new system based on child support systems in Australia and the USA. As a result of these recommendations the Child Support Act 1991 was rapidly passed, removing child maintenance from the courts into the Child Support Agency. The Government in its White Paper emphasised that the new Act was based on a recognition that children have a right to be maintained, and that parents, not the state, have a responsibility to maintain them.

Perhaps not unexpectedly, there was immediate and intense hostility to the reforms. Many fathers in particular felt that the system was grossly unfair in that they were being made to pay much higher levels of maintenance than under the discretionary court-based system. Step-fathers felt especially aggrieved, as the amount of maintenance they were required to pay made it difficult for them to support their new families. Another concern was that maintenance assessments were unfair because they failed to take account of 'clean break' arrangements made on divorce before the Act had come into force (see 9.4). Many men said they would not have agreed to make a clean break settlement had they realised that their maintenance payments calculated by the Agency would be so high. In *Crozier* v. *Crozier* [1994] Fam 114, for example, a father applied to have a clean break order made on divorce set aside or varied, so that he could recover his half-share of the former matrimonial home which he said he would never have agreed to transfer to his wife had he known that the maintenance assessment calculated by the Agency was going to be so high. His application failed. Another absurdity of the child support system was demonstrated in *Phillips* v. *Pearce* [1996] 2 FLR 230. Here the mother was forced to apply to the court for a lump sum for the child under Sched. 1 to the Children Act 1989 (see below) because, although the father lived in a house worth £2.6 million and owned and controlled a company, the child support officer, applying the formula, had found that he had no actual income and accordingly could not make maintenance payments.

Changes since the introduction of the system have, however, mitigated to some extent the hardships and anomalies created by the child support provisions. Thus, in February 1994, as a result of the criticisms of the system, minor changes were made to the formula. In January 1995 the Government published another White Paper, *Improving Child Support* (Cm 2745), in which it proposed further changes. Some of these changes came into effect in April 1995. The remainder of the White Paper's proposals were enacted in the Child Support Act 1995, which provided for a 'departures' system to enable the Agency to depart from the formula where the assessment had produced unfair results.

Despite the fact that the orginal scheme has been much amended, dissatisfaction has continued. In fact, the child support scheme is considered to be one of the worst disasters of British social policy. As a result of continuing dissatisfaction, amendments to the scheme are again proposed, in particular to simplify the way in which maintenance is calculated. No doubt dissatisfaction will continue to be voiced.

(b) The Child Support Agency

The child maintenance system is administered under the Child Support Acts 1991 and 1995 by the Child Support Agency which is staffed by Department of Social Security decisions makers (DMs) (formerly called child support officers), whose duty is to assess maintenance according to a mathematical formula on the basis of information supplied by parents, employers, the Department of Social Security (DSS), the Inland Revenue, courts and local authorities. The Agency manages the scheme for people living in England, Scotland, Wales and Northern Ireland.

Besides assessing, reviewing and arranging child support payments, the Agency's other principal activities include: tracing and contacting non-resident parents; sorting out paternity disputes; collecting and passing on maintenance payments and taking action to enforce payment; dealing with applications for 'departures' from the normal assessment formula; preparing and presenting appeals to be heard by the independent Child Support Appeal Tribunal Service; and working with the Benefits Agency, where clients receive social security, to ensure correct payments and protect against fraud.

Most of the decisions of the Agency are non-discretionary but some discretionary decisions may be made, e.g. whether a caring parent in receipt of benefits should authorise the Agency to act (s.6), whether it should make a reduced benefit direction (s.46), and whether it should make an interim assessment. When exercising any discretionary power, Agency decision makers must take account of the welfare of any child likely to be affected (s.2).

The Agency has jurisdiction to make a maintenance assessment, if the person with care, the non-resident parent and the child are habitually resident in the UK (s.44(1)). However, habitual residence here means something different from habitual residence in other areas of the law, as an emphasis is given to the nature and degree of residence in the UK and the intentions for the future (see decision of the Child Support Commissioner, CCS/7395/1995). If a party is not habitually resident in the UK, any dispute about child maintenance will have to be settled by an application to the court. In other words an application will have to be made under the Matrimonial Causes Act 1973 (if the parties are divorcing), or otherwise under Sched. 1 to the Children Act 1989 (see further below).

(c) The Basic Principles and Concepts

Each parent of a 'qualifying child' is responsible for paying child maintenance (s.1(1)) and this responsibility is met when the 'non-resident parent' pays child maintenance, as assessed by the Agency, to the 'qualifying child'.

A '**parent**' is a person who is in law the mother or father of the child (s.54). The term 'parent' also includes an adoptive parent, and a person who is a parent by virtue of a parental order made under s.30 of the Human Fertilisation and Embryology Act 1990. However, a step-parent is not a parent for the purposes of child support, and neither is a guardian or any person who has parental responsibility by virtue of a residence order.

A child is a '**qualifying child**' if at least one of his or her parents is a non-resident parent (s.3(1)) and the child is (s.55): aged under 16; aged 16 to under 19 and receiving full-time non-advanced education; or aged 16 to under 18 and registered for work or youth training. A child who is, or has been, married (even if the marriage was void or annulled) is not a 'child' for this purpose (s.55(2)). A child who falls outside the definition of 'qualifying child' may, however, be entitled to maintenance by court order.

A parent is a '**non-resident parent**' if he or she is not living in the same household as the child, and the child has his or her home with the 'caring parent' (s.3(2)). Both parents can be non-resident parents. The word 'household' is not defined in the legislation – reference will have to be made to case-law – but it is possible to have two households under one roof.

A person is a '**caring parent**' if the child has his or her home with that person and he or she usually provides day-to-day care for the child (whether exclusively or in conjunction with another person) (s.3(3)). A caring parent can thus include a parent, a guardian, a person with a residence order in his or her favour with respect to the child, a relative, or a friend. Local authorities and local authority foster-parents do not, however, qualify as persons with care (s.3(3)(c) CSA 1991).

For the purpose of child support, parents fall into two categories: those who are on welfare benefits, and those who are not. The rules differ for each category. Thus, caring parents not in receipt of welfare benefits can choose whether or not to apply to the Agency. However, caring parents in receipt of certain welfare benefits (e.g. Income Support, Family Credit (Working Families' Tax Credit), Disability Working Allowance (Disabled Person's Tax Credit) or income based Jobseeker's Allowance), or whose partner is in receipt of such benefit, authorise the Agency to seek child support against the non-resident parent, unless it can be shown that the caring parent or child will suffer harm or undue distress (s.6(2) and (3)). A caring parent on benefit is obliged to provide specified information without unreasonable delay so that maintenance can be recovered (s.6(6)). Failure to co-operate may result in a caring parent suffering a benefit penalty (s.46).

Applications for child support may be made by caring parents or non-resident parents (s.4(1)) who can also apply for collection and enforcement (s.4(2)). Once the Agency has made a maintenance assessment, the non-resident parent must make the required payment of child support, and by doing so is taken to have met his or her maintenance responsibility (s.1(2) and (3)).

Disputes abouzt Parentage

Parentage is assumed where a child is adopted, or a parental order has been made under s.30 of the Human Fertilisation and Embryology Act 1990, or where there has been a declaration of parentage. Where there is a dispute about parentage (usually paternity), the Agency or the caring parent can apply to the court for a declaration as to parentage (see ss.26 and 27 CSA 1991). Voluntary DNA testing is available from the Agency. The court can also order blood tests under s.20 of the Family Law Reform Act 1969 (see 11.4).

(d) Calculating Child Support: The Formula

The formula for calculating child support is laid down in Sched. 1 to the Child Support Act 1991 and in regulations. For the purpose of calculating child support, the income of both parents is taken into account. The formula and regulations are complex, and the allowances and rates which apply are amended from time to time. Advice should be sought from the Agency (for contact details, see end of chapter).

Making a calculation under the formula requires the following steps to be completed:

(i) The Child's Maintenance Requirement

The first step is to work out the child's 'maintenance requirement', in other words how much child support is needed for the day-to-day cost of maintaining each child. This requirement is based on Income Support rates and depends on the age of the child. The maintenance of each child is aggregated, as the maintenance requirement is worked out per family.

(ii) Calculating Maintenance

The next step is to calculate the non-resident parent's income and basic outgoings. If the non-resident parent is in receipt of Income Support or income-based Jobseeker's Allowance (or his partner is), there is no need to calculate his income and outgoings. If the non-resident parent (or his partner) is in receipt of one or other of these benefits, he pays nothing if he is sick, disabled or has dependent children in his household, but otherwise pays an amount equivalent to the minimum amount of child maintenance which is deducted from his benefit. If the non-resident parent is not receiving Income Support or income-based Jobseeker's Allowance, the following steps must be taken to calculate how much maintenance should be paid.

Step 1: Net Income

The first step is to calculate the net income of the non-resident parent. Net income is earnings after tax and National Insurance have been paid, and half of any superannuation or pension contributions, plus any social security or other benefits – but not Child Benefit, Attendance Allowance and Disability Living Allowance – have been deducted. Income from capital, such as building society interest or rents from properties and other sources, are also included as income, but earnings and income from a partner do not count as income.

Step 2: Exempt Income

The non-resident parent's 'exempt income' must be calculated, in other words his or her minimum day-to-day living expenses. This includes a personal allowance and an allowance for any children of the non-parent who live with him or her (including children of a new marriage or other relationship). Exempt income also includes rent or mortgage costs, net of any Housing Benefit, and any property and capital transfers to the parent with care of the child and/or the child that were transferred under a court order or written maintenance agreement made before 5 April 1993. Special rules apply to such property and capital transfers. Transfers for spousal maintenance are ignored, except where they make provision for child maintenance. With other transfers, it is assumed where the parents were married that half of the value of the asset was made for the parent and half for the children. Where parents are not married, it is assumed that the total amount of the transfer was for the children. If the transfer concerns a property, its value is calculated after deducting any outstanding mortgage or charge. Travel to work costs in excess of 150 miles per week (as the crow flies) are also included as exempt income, except where the employer provides transport or pays the travel costs, or the non-resident parent is self-employed.

Step 3: Assessable Income

The next step is to calculate the non-resident parent's 'assessable income' (income available for the payment of child support). Assessable income is calculated by deducting exempt income from net income. Child support is only paid out of assessable income.

Step 4: The Maintenance Assessment

The final step is to work out how much of the assessable income should be paid as child support. Non-resident parents must pay 50 pence in every £1 of assessable income until the basic 'maintenance requirement' is met. The non-resident parent keeps the other 50 pence in every £1 for himself or herself.

The following examples (based on weekly amounts) are taken from a Child Support Agency leaflet, *For Parents who Live Apart*, which can be accessed via the Agency's website (see end of chapter):

If the basic maintenance requirement for the children is £87.40, the non-resident parent would need £174.80 assessable income to pay this in full. This is because the non-resident parent pays 50 pence in each £1 of his assessable income for child maintenance, and keeps the other 50 pence for himself.

If, on the other hand, the basic maintenance needed for the children is £103.20 and the non-resident parent's assessable income is £180, the most he will be required to pay is £90 towards the child maintenance needed (50 per cent of the £180, keeping the other 50 per cent for himself).

Protected Income

The maintenance assessment includes a safeguard known as 'protected income' to ensure that non-resident parents and any second family have enough to live on. A calculation is therefore made in all cases to ensure that non-resident parents (and any second family of the non-resident parent) retain more money than they would get if they were receiving Income Support or income-based Jobseeker's Allowance. Generally, non-resident parents are not expected to pay more than 30 per cent of their net income in child support, or more than 33 per cent if they are paying any arrears, or up to 40 per cent if they have failed to make or keep to an agreement to pay child support.

What if the Non-Resident Parent has Money Left Over?

Where, after paying the required basic maintenance, a non-resident parent has assessable income remaining from which no child maintenance has been deducted, he is required to carry on paying child support, but at the rate of 15 pence in each extra £1 if there is one child, 20 pence in each extra £1 if there are two children, and 25 pence in the £1 if there are three or more children. The aim of this additional amount is to make parents with higher incomes pay proportionately more child support so that their children can enjoy their higher standard of living. However, there is a 'ceiling' on the amount payable (see below). The Agency leaflet referred to above gives the following example:

If the non-resident parent has assessable income of £200 and the basic child maintenance needed is £87.40, he pays 50 pence in the £1 until he has covered that £87.40, which uses up £174.80 of his assessable income.

(Box Continued)

This means he has £25.20 assessable income left over. If he has three or more children he pays 25 pence in each £1 out of the remaining £25.20 which means he pays an extra £6.30 on top of the £87.40 basic maintenance needed.

A Maximum Level of Child Support

There is a maximum level above which child support ceases. The maximum payable depends on the non-resident parent's circumstances. However, a caring parent may apply to the court for an order to 'top up' the amount payable as the result of an Agency assessment (see s.8).

A Minimum Level of Child Support

There is a specified minimum level of child support. Thus, if the assessment is less than the specified sum, a non-resident parent will only be required to pay that sum, unless he is sick, disabled, a prisoner, has dependent children living with him, or his income is less that the specified sum, in which case he can choose to pay nothing at all.

Special Circumstances – 'Departures Directions'

Where either parent considers that his or her circumstances are special, he or she can apply for a 'departures direction' (see below).

(e) Shared Care

Where a child spends at least 104 nights a year with a non-resident parent, the parent who provides the lesser amount of care is treated as the non-resident parent, but liability is reduced where the non-resident parent is providing a significant amount of care for the child.

(f) Impact of Child Maintenance on Welfare Benefits

Where one parent (or both) is in receipt of either Working Families' Tax Credit or Disabled Person's Tax Credit, any child maintenance received is not taken into account when working out the claim for either of these Tax Credits. However, where the parent with care (or a person living with that parent) claims Income Support or income-based Jobseeker's Allowance, any child maintenance received will reduce that benefit by the same amount. Since

7 April 1997, persons with care who stop getting Income Support or income-based Jobseeker's Allowance when they (or any partner) return to work, receive a Child Maintenance Bonus. This is a tax-free lump-sum based on the amount of child maintenance which has been paid for their child.

(g) *Reviews and Appeals*

A maintenance assessment is reviewed every two years, although an applicant can request further reviews where there has been a change of circumstances, or if he or she wishes to challenge the decision of an Agency decision maker. Appeals against an assessment are to another decision maker and then to a tribunal, although appeals on points of law are to the Child Support Commissioner and then, with permission, to the Court of Appeal.

(h) *Enforcement and Collection of Maintenance*

Where applicants for child maintenance are in receipt of welfare benefits, maintenance is usually collected by the Agency. Applicants not in receipt of benefits may choose whether or not to use the Agency's collection service. The Agency has various enforcement and collection mechanisms. It puts pressure on non-resident parents to supply information, and to do so promptly, by giving them the right to qualify for eight weeks' deferral of liability if within four weeks of being issued with the maintenance enquiry they provide the Agency with certain information (e.g. name, address, confirmation of being the parent etc.). If the enquiry form is not returned within four weeks, maintenance is normally payable from the date the form was issued. If the non-resident parent does not reply promptly and fully, the Agency can make an interim maintenance assessment which is usually higher than a normal assessment. This interim assessment remains payable until the information for a full assessment is provided.

Payment of maintenance is made weekly or monthly, or at some other agreed interval. The non-resident parent may pay direct to the person with care, or pay through the Agency by direct debit, standing order or deductions from salary. The Agency can require payment to be made by standing order and can order the payer to open a bank account for this purpose (s.29). Where a parent falls into arrears, it can send an arrears notice to the defaulting payer and attempt to negotiate an arrears agreement. The Agency can order that deductions from earnings be made (s.31). If payment is not made, a 'liability' order can be sought from the magistrates' court (s.33), which may be enforced by distress (s.35), or in the county court by garnishee proceedings or a charging order (s.36), and in the last resort by imprisonment (s.40). The High Court has no power to make a 'freezing order' (*Mareva* injunction) to prevent the disposal of assets, as it has no jurisdiction over the substantive claim, as the Child Support Act 1991 provides a complete code for assessing and enforcing the financial responsibilities of parents (*Department of Social Security* v. *Butler* [1996] 1 FLR 65).

(i) Modifications to the Formula and 'Departures' from the Formula

In 1995, in response to criticisms of the child support scheme (in particular the inadequacy of the formula), the Government published a White Paper, *Improving Child Support* (Cm 2745), recommending changes to the system. As a result of the recommendations, new regulations came into force on 18 April 1995 and the Child Support Act 1995 was passed, making further changes. These changes did not radically alter the scheme but made refinements to the way in which maintenance is assessed. However, these refinements did not staunch the constant flow of criticisms.

In April 1995, changes to the formula were made in order to: cap child maintenance at 30 per cent of income; introduce an allowance for unusually high travel-to-work costs; allow 100 per cent housing costs for second families; and reduce the maximum payable under the formula. Two new interim maintenance assessments were introduced (for self-employed and wealthier non-resident parents), as well as two-yearly instead of annual reviews.

In April 1996, after widespread publicity about the inflexibility of the formula, a 'departures' scheme was implemented under the Child Support Act 1995. This allows a non-resident or caring parent to apply for a 'departures direction' (a variation of the formula), which the Agency has a discretion to grant where an applicant can show:

- high costs incurred in travelling to work;
- high costs incurred by a non-resident parent in maintaining contact with his children;
- costs arising from the disability of the applicant or of a dependant of the applicant;
- costs incurred in supporting a step-child;
- debts outstanding from before the family separated (excluding gambling debts, fines, unpaid legal cost, and credit card debts);
- pre-April 1993 financial commitments from which it is impossible or unreasonable to withdraw;
- a pre-April 1993 clean break property or capital settlement;
- a diversion of income;
- a lifestyle inconsistent with declared income;
- any asset(s) capable of providing income (or higher income);

- housing costs in the formula are unreasonably high (or a new partner is able to contribute to them);
- travel-to-work costs in the formula assessment are unreasonably high, or the parent can afford to pay them.

However, while the departures scheme has injected some flexibility and greater fairness into the system, it has created uncertainty and complexity, which is what the Government hoped to get away from when it moved child support from the courts into the Agency.

Making a Complaint

Any person dissatisfied with the service provided by the Agency can make a complaint to the Agency. If still not satisfied, a complainant can write to the Independent Case Examiner, whose duty it is to investigate the complaint, but who has no power to consider a complaint involving child support law (e.g. if the complainant considers that a maintenance assessment is wrong). The Case Examiner will not investigate the matter unless the Agency has first been given the opportunity to put things right, or if the complaint is being investigated by the Ombudsman (Parliamentary Commissioner for Administration). The Agency can make special payments to persons who have suffered financial loss, inconvenience, or whose health has been affected as a result of a mistake and/or delay by the Agency. Independent advice about child maintenance can be sought from Citizens' Advice Bureaux, MPs and solicitors. Appeals against a maintenance assessment are also available (see above).

(j) The Role of the Courts

The court retains jurisdiction to decide maintenance matters where a court order in respect of child maintenance or a child maintenance agreement made before 5 April 1993 is still in force, provided the parent concerned is not in receipt of welfare benefits. Thus the court still has jurisdiction to vary or discharge such an order (see 9.11). However, the court cannot discharge an order so that an application can be made to the Agency (s.8(4), and see *B* v. *M (Child Support: Revocation of Order)* [1994] 1 FLR 342).

Under the Child Support Act 1991, the court retains a residual jurisdiction to make maintenance orders where:

- parents have made a consent order which incorporates an agreement about child maintenance (s.8(5));
- additional maintenance is required after a maximum assessment has been made by the Agency (s.8(6));

- maintenance is required to meet the expenses of education or training for a trade, profession or vocation (s.8(7));
- maintenance is needed for a disabled child (s.8(8));
- a child does not come within the definition of a 'qualifying child' in s.55, e.g. a step-child;
- maintenance is required against the caring parent (s.8(10));
- the Agency cannot make a maintenance assessment, for example, because a parent or child is not habitually resident in the UK;
- a court order is needed to give effect to a written maintenance agreement made before April 5 1993.

(k) *Proposals for a New Scheme*

Despite numerous modifications to the child support scheme since its introduction in 1993, there has continued to be dissatisfaction, in particular about delays and errors of calculation. The inflexibility and complexity of the formula, the size of assessments and their impact on second families have all been criticised. Enforcing payments has also caused problems. According to the 1999 White Paper below, only about 40 per cent of fathers pay everything that is due and 30 per cent pay nothing at all.

Because of continuing dissatisfaction with the scheme, the Government has proposed improvements to the system, in particular to simplify and speed up the calculation of maintenance. In 1998 it published a Green Paper, *Children First: A New Approach to Child Support* (Cm 3992), followed in 1999 by a White Paper, *A New Contract for Welfare: Children's Rights and Parents' Responsibilities*, Cm 4349. (Both these papers can be accessed at the DSS website, see end of chapter.)

In its White Paper, the Government acknowledged that the child support system had failed to improve the position of children living apart from their parents, and that the system was too complex. According to the Government, not only is it difficult for parents to understand, but it requires a substantial amount of information to be provided. It is also prone to errors, and constantly needs altering to reflect changes. The Government has therefore decided to abolish the current system and replace it with 'a simple and more deliverable system focused on the needs of children and good, responsible parents' (Introduction, para. 9). It believes this will benefit both parents and children. Parents will be able to see more clearly how much maintenance is due, and children will receive maintenance more quickly and more regularly (Introduction, para. 11).

The proposed reforms were included in the Child Support, Pensions and Social Security Bill, which had its second reading in Parliament at the beginning of 2000, but the new scheme is not likely to be in place before late 2001 at the earliest.

The new scheme proposes the following changes:

A Simple System for Calculating Maintenance   The main change will be the introduction of a new and simple system for calculating maintenance. Under the reforms, non-resident parents will be required to pay maintenance as follows:

Number of children	Proportion of non-resident parent's net income (%)
One	15
Two	20
Three or more	25

Maintenance will be reduced if a non-resident parent is caring for the child, or has a low income. Where there are second families (step-parents and children) the non-resident parent's income will be reduced by the same percentages. The new rates will produce a slightly lower average weekly liability for non-resident parents in work than under the current system. Changes will also be made as to what counts as income, to make income calculations simpler. The earnings of parents with care will be excluded from the calculation of child support, and the Government does not plan to set a maximum liability under the new scheme. Where information to make an assessment is not available, a default rate may be introduced to get maintenance flowing.

A Child Maintenance Premium   The Government proposes to introduce a 'child maintenance premium' for families on Income Support. Under the current system, any maintenance paid to a parent reduces Income Support pound for pound, so that the poorest families see no direct advantage from child support. The introduction of a child maintenance premium will allow non-resident parents on Income Support and income-based Jobseeker's Allowance to keep the first £10 a week of any maintenance paid. The Government expects the introduction of the child maintenance premium at least to double the proportion of lone parents on benefits who are receiving maintenance without asking the taxpayer to provide any more money. The Government also plans to ignore any child maintenance paid when calculating Working Families' Tax Credit.

A Tougher Sanctions Regime   A tougher sanctions regime is proposed to ensure that non-resident parents cannot avoid their responsibilities. The new reforms include: the introduction of criminal sanctions; automatic deductions from earnings for non-resident parents who miss payment by other means; late payment penalties; using tax information to work out the liability of self-employed persons who do not co-operate; simplification of the rules on paternity to bring them into line with other paternity provisions; and strengthening the power of inspectors to obtain information from unco-operative parents. The Government also proposes to look at other ways of making sure that child support is paid promptly and regularly.

A New Child Support Service   The Government proposes to change the way in which the scheme works. The Agency will be radically reformed so that maintenance will be calculated and paid more quickly. Contact with parents will be mainly by telephone, but parents will be able to have face-to-face interviews with Agency staff where appropriate. A substantially greater proportion of the Agency's resources will be used to ensure that maintenance is paid regularly and promptly, and parents will be sent regular statements of accounts.

Other Changes

Exceptional Cases   The White Paper recognises (at Chapter 6, para. 2) that there will always be 'truly exceptional cases' where a non-resident parent has particular difficulty in paying child support (e.g. where the cost of maintaining a child or keeping in touch is higher than normal). Although the 'departures' system will continue, the circumstances in which the Agency will have a discretion to depart from the formula will be restricted to clearly exceptional – and clearly defined – cases. Thus, the Government proposes to allow the child support assessment to be lowered where the non-resident parent has certain specified and clearly exceptional expenses, and the rates to be raised where they clearly result in an unreasonably low level of maintenance liability.

Maintenance liability will be lowered only for clear child-centred reasons, and, as with the current 'departures' scheme, will only be varied if it is just and equitable to do so. The person considering an exceptional case will have to decide whether the standard rate produces an unfair result. To obtain a reduction in maintenance liability, a non-resident applicant will have to show that exceptional expenses are needed for:

- keeping in touch with the children;
- supporting a severely disabled child in his second family;
- paying off debts incurred for the child's benefit when the parents were living together; or
- paying to maintain the child while away at school (but not including tuition fees).

A reduction may also be possible if the non-resident parent transferred property or capital to the parent with care before April 1993 to help support the child, or if he is paying the mortgage on the former home and has transferred all the equity to his former partner. As with the current 'departures' system, the Government intends to provide a threshold for expenses below which there will be no possibility of lowering the rates. However, a non-resident parent's application for a variation will be considered only if he or she is paying maintenance regularly.

In exceptional cases, parents with care will be able to apply to the Agency for an increase in the child support rate when maintenance liability assessed at the basic rate is clearly unfair. The circumstances where this is likely to apply are where a non-resident parent: has deliberately diverted income to reduce his child support liability; enjoys a lifestyle which is inconsistent with the income used to calculate child support; or has significant income from investments, or could realise significant income from investments if he chose to do so.

Contact and Shared Care   The Government proposes to make changes in respect of contact and shared care because of its stated commitment 'to an active family policy which integrates all activities that affect the family – including maintenance and contact' (Chapter 6, para. 7). The Government White Paper refers to research evidence by McClean and Eekelaar (1997) which shows that non-resident parents who have regular contact with their children are more likely to pay maintenance. In order to promote contact, the Government proposes to modify child support rates where both parents are substantially involved in caring for their children. Thus child support will be reduced by one-seventh for every night that a child spends with the non-resident parent. A non-resident parent on benefit will be exempt from the £5 minimum payment when he cares for the child for at least one night a week. Special provision will also be made for parents who have exactly equal care.

Collecting Maintenance   The Government intends to provide 'a simple and streamlined process for collecting child support' (White Paper, Chapter 8). Several changes are proposed, including a late payment penalty of up to 25 per cent of money that is overdue. The Government is also considering other sanctions to ensure payment (e.g. withdrawal of driving licences and passports).

The Role of the Courts   Under the proposals, the court will retain its role in dealing with written maintenance agreements and court orders, but the Government is determined to ensure that there will be no 'two-tier' child maintenance service with rich parents opting out of the child support rates (para. 18). Parents wishing to transfer to a child support assessment will have to give at least two months' notice (which will allow parents and their lawyers to renegotiate new voluntary agreements, if appropriate). Furthermore, if private payment arrangements break down, the Agency assessment will replace the court order (para. 23).

14.3 Court Orders for Children During Their Parents' Marriage

Magistrates' courts (under the Domestic Proceedings and Magistrates' Courts Act 1978) and county courts (under s.27 Matrimonial Causes Act 1973) can on the application of a married parent make orders for periodical payments (maintenance) and/or lump sums to or for the benefit of a child of the family (including a step-child and privately fostered child). The exercise of the court's powers under these provisions is discretionary, but the court must apply certain statutory criteria when exercising its discretion. These criteria are the same as those applied by the divorce court when making orders in favour of children (see below), except that magistrates' courts must also consider whether they should exercise any of their powers under the Children Act 1989 (s.8 DPMCA 1978) (see Chapter 12).

14.4 Court Orders for Children in Divorce Proceedings

Under s.23 of the Matrimonial Causes Act 1973 (see Chapter 9), the divorce court can make periodical payments and lump sum orders for children (including step-children and non-marital children of one or both parties, s.52(1)). It can also make the following property adjustment orders to or for the benefit of children under s.24 of the Act: a transfer of property; a settlement of property; an order varying any ante-nuptial settlement; and a post-nuptial settlement for the benefit of the child. The court can also make an order for sale (s.24A). Orders under the 1973 Act can be made for: a child aged under 18; or a child who is, or will be, receiving instruction at an educational establishment or undergoing training for a trade, profession or vocation (whether or not the 'child' will be in gainful employment); or a child who has special circumstances (s.29(1) and (3)).

When exercising its discretion to decide whether to make an order and in what manner, the court must consider all the circumstances of the case, including (s.25(3)):

(a) the financial needs of the child;
(b) the income, earning capacity (if any), property and other financial resources of the child;
(c) any physical or mental disability of the child;
(d) the manner in which he or she was being and in which the parties to the marriage expect him or her to be educated or trained; and
(e) factors (a), (b), (c) and (e) of the checklist in s.25(2) of the 1973 Act which apply to the child's divorcing parents (see 9.4).

Where the court is exercising its powers against a party to the marriage in favour of a child of the family who is not a child of that party (e.g. in respect of a step-child), the court must also have regard to the following (s.25(4)):

(a) whether that party assumed any responsibility for the child's maintenance, and, if so, the extent to which, and the basis upon which, that party assumed such responsibility and the length of time for which that party discharged such responsibility;
(b) whether in assuming and discharging such responsibility that party did so knowing that the child was not his or her own; and
(c) the liability of any other person to maintain the child.

14.5   Financial Provision under the Children Act 1989

Under s.15 and paras. 1 and 2 of Sched. 1 to the Children Act 1989, the court has jurisdiction to make orders for financial provision (including property orders) for children aged under 18, and also for children aged over 18 in certain circumstances. It can make these orders on an application. It can also make them of its own motion (i.e. without an application having been made) when it is making, varying or discharging a residence order (para. 1(6)), or where the child is a ward of court (para. 1(7)).

(i) Orders under Paragraph 1

On the application of a parent, guardian or any person with a residence order in his or her favour, the court can make orders for periodical payments, lump sums and settlement and transfers of property against one or both parents (including a step-parent). Except for a settlement of property, which can only be made for the benefit of a child, the orders may be made directly to the child, or to the applicant for the benefit of the child. Only unsecured periodical payments and lump sum orders can be made in magistrates' courts, but the whole range of orders can be made in county courts and the High Court.

(ii) Orders under Paragraph 2

The court has jurisdiction to make periodical payments and lump sum orders for a child aged over 18 against one or both parents (but not step-parents or foster-parents – para. 16). The court can make these orders on the application of a child aged over 18 who is, will be, or (if an order were made) would be, receiving instruction at an educational establishment or undergoing training for a trade, profession or vocation (whether or not while in gainful employment).

The court can also make an order where special circumstances exist which justify it making an order. However, an application is not possible if an order for periodical payments was in force in favour of the applicant immediately before he or she reached the age of 16 (para. 2(3)). Furthermore, the court cannot make an order if the applicant's parents are living with each other in the same household (para 2(4)).

(iii) How the Court Exercises its Discretion

When exercising its discretion to make orders under paras. 1 and 2, and if so in what manner, the court must have regard to all the circumstances, including (para. 4(1)):

(a) the income, earning capacity, property and other financial resources of the parties;
(b) the financial needs, obligations and responsibilities which the parties are likely to have in the foreseeable future;
(c) the financial needs of the child;
(d) the income, earning capacity (if any), property and other financial resources of the child;
(e) any physical or mental disability of the child; and
(f) the manner in which the child is being, or is expected to be, educated or trained.

Where the court is exercising its powers under para. 1 against a person who is not the child's mother or father (e.g. in the case of a step-parent), the court must also consider (para 4(2)):

(a) whether that person has assumed responsibility for the child's maintenance and, if so, the extent to which and basis on which that responsibility was assumed and the length of the period during which he met that responsibility;
(b) whether he did so knowing that the child was not his child;
(c) the liability of any other person to maintain the child.

The child's welfare is a relevant, but not the paramount consideration, as the paramountcy principle in s.1(1) of the Children Act 1989 does not apply to a child's 'upbringing', which is defined in s.105(1) as excluding questions of maintenance. The no-order presumption in s.1(5) does not apply (*K* v. *H (Child Maintenance)* [1993] 2 FLR 61). As a general principle, it is rare for an order to be made to last beyond a child's majority or beyond the end of full-time education. Orders will not ordinarily be made after the child has reached independence (see *A* v. *A (Financial Provision)* [1994] 1 FLR 657, where Ward J refused to make a property adjustment order for the benefit of a child).

In *T* v. *S (Financial Provision for Children)* [1994] 2 FLR 883, the father's appeal against a *Mesher*-type property adjustment order (see 9.5) was allowed so that the property would revert to the father and not to the children when the youngest child reached the age of 21. Johnson J, citing dicta of Booth J in *Kiely* v. *Kiely* [1988] 1 FLR 248, stated that the provisions of Sched. 1 were to make financial provision for children as children or dependants, unless the children's circumstances were special or unusual. In *Re G (Children Act 1989, Schedule 1)* [1996] 2 FLR 171, it was held that the court has jurisdiction to make an order under Sched. 1 against a bankrupt father. In *J* v. *C (Child: Financial Provision)* [1999] 1 FLR 152, an unmarried mother sought orders for the child under para. 1 after the father had won £1.4 million on the national lottery. Hale J said that the child was entitled to be brought up in circumstances which bore some sort of relationship to the father's current resources and present standard of living, and it was irrelevant that he had not wanted the child. Furthermore, public policy required that where a parent could provide resources which excluded the need for a child to be supported by public funds, he or she should be obliged to do so. In the circumstances, Hale J held that it was appropriate to make an order requiring the father to purchase a four-bedroomed house for the child to live in with her mother, which would be held on trust for the child's benefit throughout her dependency and would revert to her father when she reached the age of 21 or finished full-time education, whichever was the later. Capital provision was also ordered to pay for a car, furniture and chattels.

(iv) Variation and Discharge of Periodical Payments

Periodical payments made under Sched. 1 can be varied or discharged on the application of any person by or to whom payments were required to be made (paras. 1(4) and 2(5)).

Summary

1 All parents (married and unmarried and with or without parental responsibility) have a duty to maintain their children, and all children have a right to be maintained.

2 If a parent fails to provide maintenance, an application can be made for child support from the Child Support Agency, which has power under the Child Support Acts 1991 and 1995 to calculate and enforce child maintenance payments. The amount of maintenance payable is calculated by a mathematical formula. However, some limited discretion has been introduced by the 'departures' system. There are proposals to change the law to make the system simpler and quicker, by introducing a fixed sum payable in all cases depending on the number of children who need maintenance.

3 In certain cases (e.g. school fees cases, or where a child is disabled, or where the parents are wealthy), maintenance can be sought in the courts.
4 During marriage, parents may seek periodical payments (maintenance) and lump sums for children from the magistrates' family proceedings courts under the Domestic Proceedings and Magistrates' Courts Act 1978. The same orders for children (and also property adjustment orders) can be sought during marriage from county courts and the High Court under s.27 of the Matrimonial Causes Act 1973. Periodical payments orders, lump sum orders and property adjustment orders can be sought for children on divorce (nullity and judicial separation) under Part II of the Matrimonial Causes Act 1973.
5 Orders for financial relief (periodical payments, lump sums, settlements and transfers of property) can be sought under para. 1 of Sched. 1 to the Children Act 1989 by parents, guardians and persons with a residence order in their favour. Children aged over 18 can apply under para. 2 for periodical payments and lump sums against their parents.

Further Reading and References

Barton, 'Third time lucky for child support?' [1998] Fam Law 668.
Cooke, 'Children and real property – trusts, interests and considerations' [1998] Fam Law 349.
Davis, Wikely and Young, *Child Support in Action*, Hart Publishing, 1998.
McClean and Eekelaar, *The Parental Obligation – A Study of Parenthood Across Households*, Hart Publishing, 1997.
Morgan, '*Kingston upon Thames Borough Council* v. *Prince* – Children are people too' [2000] CFLQ 65.

Website

The Child Support Agency: www.dss.gov.uk/csa/ The Agency also has a national enquiry line: 0845 7133 133.

Questions

1 What arguments are there in favour of returning child maintenance to the courts? What arguments are there against it?
2 Are the proposed reforms of child support maintenance likely to increase public confidence in the child support system?

15   Child Abduction

15.1   The Problem of Child Abduction

Child abduction is a distressing consequence of family breakdown. It is also a widespread problem resulting not only from world-wide increases in family breakdown, but also from the growth in international marriages and the greater and easier movement of persons. At the international level, two Conventions exist to combat child abduction: the Hague Convention on the Civil Aspects of International Child Abduction 1980 (the 'Hague Convention') and the European Convention on Recognition and Enforcement of Decisions Concerning Custody of Children 1980 (the 'European Convention'). The UK is party to both Conventions which are effective in the UK by virtue of the Child Abduction and Custody Act 1985, the schedules to which contain the texts of the Conventions.

At the national level, the Child Abduction Act 1984 makes child abduction a criminal offence, and the Family Law Act 1986 facilitates the return of children abducted within the UK. Furthermore, where there is a residence order in force (see 12.4), the Children Act 1989 prohibits the removal of a child from the UK without the written consent of all those with parental responsibility, or otherwise the consent of the court (s.13(1)(b)), although the person with the residence order can take the child out of the UK for up to one month (s.13(2)). There are also restrictions on taking children in local authority care out of the UK. Section 8 orders can also be made under the Children Act 1989 to prohibit abduction or to settle a dispute about taking a child abroad (see 12.4). Most of the reported case-law on abduction, however, involves 'incoming' abductions, in other words abductions from other countries into the UK. How 'outgoing' cases of abduction from the UK will be dealt with depends on whether or not the child has been abducted to a Convention country. Where a child is abducted out of the UK to a non-Convention country, return of the child will depend on that country's law. In many cases effecting the return of a child is difficult, and sometimes impossible.

Information and advice on child abduction can be obtained from the Child Abduction Unit of the Official Solicitor's Department, based in the Lord Chancellor's Department (see its website at the end of this chapter), which is the Central Authority in England and Wales for co-ordinating cases of child abduction and for making administrative arrangements to secure the return of children. Where a child has been abducted to a Convention country, the Lord Chancellor's Department can seek the child's voluntary return by liaising with the Central Authority in that country, and where necessary institute legal proceedings. Where a child has been abducted to a non-Convention country, the Child Abduction Unit can provide advice, and so can the Consular Department of the Foreign and Commonwealth Office. Reunite (the National Council for Abducted Children) can also provide information and assistance on abduction (see its website at the end of the chapter).

15.2 Tracing a Child

Tracing a child can be a distressing and lengthy process. Furthermore, the longer it takes to trace a child, the more settled the child will become in his or her new environment, so that effecting return may become even more difficult. There are various ways of tracing a child. Where a child has been abducted within or into the UK, information which may help in tracing a child can be obtained from Government Departments, e.g. from the DSS, the Passport Office, the NHS Central Register and the Ministry of Defence (when forces' personnel are involved). Where a child has been abducted from the UK to a foreign country, the Foreign and Commonwealth Office and foreign Embassies can help. In order to help trace a child, the court can also make orders requiring a person to disclose information about a child (see below).

15.3 Preventing Abduction

Where there is a risk of abduction, preventative measures must be urgently taken, as once a child has left the UK, the chances of finding and returning that child are much more difficult. Where there is a danger of removal, a parent must be vigilant, and should consider taking the following steps:

(a) Police Assistance: The 'All Ports Warning'

As child abduction is a criminal offence, a parent, or any other person, who believes that a child has been, or may be about to be, abducted can inform the police. The police have various powers. They can arrest any person who is abducting or is suspected of abducting a child. They can also bring into effect the 'All Ports Warning System', whereby details about the child and the abductor are sent by the police national computer to immigration officers at ports and airports across the country, who assist the police in trying to prevent the child leaving the country. A port alert is only instituted, however, if the police consider an application is *bona fide*. Thus, there must be a real and imminent actual or threatened removal. The person seeking assistance will be required to provide the police with as much information as possible, e.g. about the child, the abductor, the likely time of travel, the port of departure etc.

(b) Court Order

Where there is a risk of abduction, it may be advisable to obtain a court order. A court order is useful for several reasons. Not only is breach of an order contempt of court, but it may be useful if a parent wishes to institute proceedings or seek the help of various agencies abroad. Furthermore, although an order is not necessary to institute a port alert (see above), it is useful because it provides evidence of a genuine risk of abduction. Court orders can also make provision for the surrender of passports (s.37 Family Law Act 1986).

A useful range of orders is available under s.8 of the Children Act 1989 (see 12.4), in particular the prohibited steps order and specific issue order. These orders can be made even if a child has already been abducted, but the court may be reluctant to do so where there are likely to be problems enforcing the order abroad (*Re D (Child: Removal from Jurisdiction)* [1992] 1 WLR 315). An alternative to a s.8 order is to apply to have the child made a ward of court (12.9, and see, for example, *Re B (Child Abduction: Wardship: Power to Detain)* [1994] 2 FLR 479). Where urgent action is needed, the court can make an order without the other person being given notice of the proceedings, and consequently not being present in court. An order made in this way is called an *ex parte* order (see, for example, *Re B (A Minor)(Residence Order: Ex Parte)* [1992] Fam 162). Such orders have been held not to be in breach of art. 6 of the European Convention on Human Rights (right to a fair trial) (*Re J (Abduction: Wrongful Removal)* [2000] 1 FLR 78).

The court has other powers. Under its inherent jurisdiction (see 12.9) and under statute, the court can order a person to disclose a child's whereabouts (s.33 Family Law Act 1986 and s.24A Child Abduction and Custody Act 1985, and see *Re B (Abduction: Disclosure)* [1995] 1 FLR 774 and *Re H (Abduction: Whereabouts Order to Solicitors)* [2000] 1 FLR 766).

An unmarried father without parental responsibility whose child has been, or is about to be, abducted is in a particularly precarious position and should consider acquiring parental responsibility (see 11.6 and 11.7) and/or a residence order (see 12.4). However, it is advisable to have parental responsibility backed up with a s.8 specific issue or prohibited steps order preventing the child's removal from the UK (see 12.4).

(c) Passport Control

A restriction on the child's or the likely abductor's passport can impede abduction. A parent can write to the Passport Department of the Home Office to object to the child being issued with a passport without the permission of the court, or the consent of every person with parental responsibility. Where a child has a UK passport, or is included on a parent's UK passport, the court can order the surrender of that passport where an order restricting removal is in force (s.37 FLA 1986, and see *Re A (Return of Passport)* [1997] 2 FLR 137). The court can order the surrender of a non-UK passport under its inherent jurisdiction (see 12.8, and see also *Re A-K (Foreign Passport: Jurisdiction)* [1997] 2 FLR 569). The passport can be ordered to be surrendered to the court or to a solicitor. As any s.8 order can contain conditions or directions, a s.8 order can be made conditional on a suspected abductor depositing his or her passport with a solicitor.

15.4   Removing a Child Lawfully from the UK

Sometimes on family breakdown, one parent may wish to take the child out of the UK. A parent (or any other person) can do this lawfully, provided the removal of the child is not prohibited by statute or by court order, and provided all those with parental responsibility agree to it. However, where a residence order or care order is in force, the child cannot be taken out of the UK for more than one month without the written consent of all those with parental responsibility or with the permission of the court (ss.13(1) and 33(7) CA 1989).

Sometimes, however, on family breakdown one parent may wish to take the child out of the UK but the other parent objects, perhaps because of the difficulty of maintaining contact, or because there is a risk that the child will not be returned. Where parents cannot resolve the matter themselves, then an application will have to be made for the court to give its permission to the child's removal. An application can be made under the Children Act 1989 for a s.8 specific issue or prohibited steps order, or, where a residence order is in force, by an application under s.13(1) of the Children Act.

In any application for permission to take the child out of the UK, the court applies the welfare principle in s.1 of the Children Act 1989 (and the welfare checklist in s.1(3) if the application is by way of a s.8 specific issue or prohibited steps order). As a general rule, however, the court will usually grant permission for the child and the 'custodial' parent to leave the UK, for there is a presumption in favour of a reasonable and properly thought out application, unless the wish to leave is clearly incompatible with the child's welfare (*Poel v. Poel* [1970] WLR 1469, endorsed by the Court of Appeal in *Re H (Application to Remove from Jurisdiction)* [1998] 1 FLR 848). Thus, if a custodial parent takes a reasonable decision to leave the UK (e.g. to marry a foreigner or because job prospects abroad are better), the court will not usually interfere with that decision, unless it is clearly contrary to the child's best interests. The rationale for this presumption is that if permission is refused, the applicant may convey his or her resentment to the child, which will be contrary to the child's welfare. In some cases the court has refused the applicant permission to leave the UK, as it did in *Re C (Leave to Remove from Jurisdiction)* [2000] 2 FLR 457, where the judge felt that the presumption in favour of the mother's reasonable wish to go to Singapore, where her new husband had a job, was outweighed by the fact that the move would severely limit the child's contact with the father. The judge so held even though it was likely to lead to the break-up of the mother's marriage, as she had told the court that she would not leave the child in England if she were refused permission to go to Singapore. The mother appealed to the Court of Appeal, which by a majority upheld the decision of the judge on the basis that it was wrong to interfere with a discretionary decision made at first instance unless such a decision was plainly wrong or the judge had failed to take into account relevant matters. However, Thorpe LJ dissented on the basis that the judge had failed to reflect on the consequences for the child of refusing to allow the mother to leave the UK. (For other cases where permission to leave the UK was refused, see *MH* v. *GP (Child: Emigration)* [1995] 2 FLR 106, *Re K (A Minor)(Removal from Jurisdiction)* [1992] 2 FLR 98, *M* v. *A (Wardship: Removal from Jurisdiction)* [1993] 2 FLR 715 and *Re T (Removal from Jurisdiction)* [1996] 2 FLR 252.)

Permission to leave the UK has been granted in many cases because of the presumption in favour of allowing a reasonable and properly worked out application (see, for example, *Re K (Application to Remove from Jurisdiction)* [1998] 2 FLR 1006 and *Re M (Leave to Remove Child from Jurisdiction)* [1999] 2 FLR 334). However, the presumption has been criticised for placing too great an emphasis on the interests of applicants and too little emphasis on the welfare principle. Kirkconel (1999), for example, has argued in favour of an approach which would require an applicant parent to prove that the plans to leave the UK are not merely reasonable but are also positively beneficial to the child. This would create a higher threshold than at present.

Whether the court will grant an applicant permission to leave the UK will depend on the facts of the case, but the following factors are likely to be particularly important: housing and education arrangements; contact arrangements; likely cultural difficulties for the child; the bond that the child has with his or her parents; and whether refusal will damage the 'custodial' parent's relationship with the child. The child's wishes may also be important. Thus, in *M* v. *A (Wardship: Removal from Jurisdiction)* [1993] 2 FLR 715, the mother's application to take the children to Canada was refused as her plans were not reasonable and did not accommodate the needs and wishes of the children, who did not wish the status quo to be changed. However, each case is decided on its own facts. Indeed, in *Re H (Application to Remove from Jurisdiction)* [1998] 1 FLR 848, Thorpe LJ warned against regarding previous decisions as anything other than illustrations of the exercise of discretion.

With the coming into force of the Human Rights Act 1998, some parents have argued that giving the 'custodial' parent permission to leave the UK with the child is a breach of the other parent's right to family life under art. 8 of the European Convention for the Protection of Human Rights. However, such an argument is likely to fail, as it did in *Re A (Permission to Remove Child from Jurisdiction: Human Rights)* [2000] 2 FLR 225, where it was held that the test in *Poel* v. *Poel* (see above) was not in conflict with the European Convention. The Court of Appeal held that, while art. 8 undoubtedly gave the father a right to family life, art. 8(1) gave the mother a right to a private life, and art. 8(2) required the court to balance such rights when they were in conflict. The father's appeal was dismissed as the court had balanced the interests of the parties carefully and conscientiously. Buxton LJ in fact doubted whether difficult balancing questions like this fell within the scope of the Human Rights Convention at all.

If the court grants the applicant permission to take the child out of the UK, there are various practical safeguards which the court can put in place. It can, for example, impose conditions, or require undertakings to be made to the court, or require the parties to enter into a notarised agreement containing provisions about returning the child. It can also require 'mirror' orders (orders equivalent to English orders) to be applied for in a foreign court. In *Re A (Security for Return to Jurisdiction)(Note)* [1999] 2 FLR 1, the parties were required to swear on the Holy Qur'an before a Shariah Court in order to ensure that the children would be returned from Saudi Arabia. In *Re S (Removal from Jurisdiction)* [1999] 1 FLR 850, the mother was permitted to go to Chile with the children, but only on condition that she placed £130 000 in the father's solicitors' bank account pending authentication of an English contact order by the Chilean court. Practical steps like these are particularly important when a child is being taken to a country which is a non-Convention country. Cases which require the court to consider a foreign legal system, and which may require mirror orders to be made, are heard in the High Court and with oral evidence being given in order to assess the reliability and credibility of the person wishing to take the child out of the UK (see *Re K (Removal from Jurisdiction: Practice)* [1999] 2 FLR 1084).

15.5 Illegal Removal: The Criminal Law

A person who abducts, or attempts to abduct, a child may commit a criminal offence under: (a) the Child Abduction Act 1984; or (b) the common law.

(a) Child Abduction Act 1984

Persons 'connected with the child' (s.1) and 'other persons' (s.2) can commit a criminal offence under the Child Abduction Act 1984.

(i) Persons 'Connected with the Child'

Under s.1 of the Child Abduction Act 1984 it is an offence for a person 'connected with a child' under the age of 16 to take or send the child out of the UK without the 'appropriate consent'. A person 'connected with a child' is: a parent (including an unmarried father if there are reasonable grounds for believing he is the father); a guardian; any person with a residence order in their favour; and any person with custody of the child (s.1). 'Appropriate consent' means the consent of: the mother; the father (with parental responsibility); a guardian; any person with a residence order in force in their favour; and any person with custody of the child (s.1(2)(a)). 'Appropriate consent' can also include the court's consent where such consent is required under Part II of the Children Act 1989. Thus, the court's consent is required where a residence order is in force (s.1(2)(b) and (c)). But, a person with a residence order does not commit the criminal offence of abduction if the child is taken out of the UK for less than one month, except where this is in breach of another s.8 order (s.1(4)).

However, a person has a defence to the offence of child abduction if he or she: (a) believed that the other person consented to the abduction or would have consented had he or she been aware of all the circumstances; or (b) has been unable to communicate with the other person despite taking reasonable steps to do so; or (c) the other person has unreasonably refused consent (s.1(5)). Defence (c) does not apply if the person who refused consent has a residence order in their favour, or the person taking or sending the child out of the UK has done so in breach of a court order (s.1(5A)).

(ii) 'Other Persons'

Under s.2, a person who is not 'connected with the child' (see above) commits the offence of child abduction if, without lawful authority or reasonable excuse, he or she takes or detains a child under the age of 16 so as to remove the child from the lawful control of any person having lawful control of the child, or so as to keep the child out of the lawful control of any person entitled to lawful control (s.2(1)). An unmarried father without parental responsibility comes under s.2, unless he is the child's guardian, or has a residence order in his favour, or has custody of the child. An unmarried father, however, has a defence if he can prove that he is the child's father, or that at the time of the alleged offence he reasonably believed he was the child's father (s.2(3)(a)). It is also a defence if the accused believed that at the time of the alleged offence the child had attained the age of 16 (s.2(3)(b)).

(b) The Common Law Offence of Kidnapping

A person who abducts a child unlawfully may commit the common law offence of kidnapping (see, for example, *R* v. *D* [1984] AC 778). Where the child is under 16 and the person removing the child is a person 'connected with' the child under s.1 of the Child Abduction Act 1984 (see above), the consent of the Director of Public Prosecutions is needed to bring a prosecution (s.5 CAA 1984). The offence of kidnapping may be useful where an abduction involves a child aged 16 and over, as children over 16 do not come within the scope of the 1984 Act above.

15.6 Child Abduction within the UK

Under the Family Law Act 1986, court orders relating to children made in one part of the UK can be recognised and enforced in another part. Thus, for example, a s.8 order made under the Children Act 1989 in a court in England and Wales can be registered in and enforced by the Scottish and Northern Ireland courts. Once registered, the court in that part of the UK has the same powers of enforcement as if it had made the original order. However, a parent and any other interested party can object to enforcement on the ground that the original order was made without jurisdiction, or, because of a change of circumstances, the original order should be varied. Although the court in the other part of the UK can stay proceedings or dismiss the application (ss.30 and 31), it is likely to enforce the order. Under the 1986 Act, the court has other powers which may be useful in abduction cases. It can order disclosure of a child's whereabouts (s.33), order recovery of a child (s.34), restrict removal of a child from the jurisdiction (s.35) and order the surrender of passports (s.37).

15.7 International Child Abduction: The Hague Convention

The UK is a Contracting State to the Hague Convention on the Civil Aspects of International Child Abduction 1980, which was implemented into UK law by Part I of the Child Abduction and Custody Act 1985. The text of the Convention is laid down in Sched. 1 to the 1985 Act and a list of Contracting States is available on the websites at the end of this chapter.

The primary aim of the Hague Convention on abduction is to secure the prompt return of children wrongfully removed to or retained in a Contracting State, and to ensure that rights of custody and rights of access arising under the law of one Contracting State are respected in another (art. 1). The Convention works by establishing a network of Central Authorities who have duty to 'co-operate with each other and promote co-operation amongst the competent authorities in their respective States to secure the prompt return of children and to achieve the other objects of this Convention' (art. 7). Central Authorities have various responsibilities, which include discovering the abducted child's whereabouts, preventing further harm to the child by taking provisional measures, securing the child's voluntary return, exchanging information, providing information etc. The Central Authority in England and Wales is the Lord Chancellor's Department, but the Official Solicitor's Department within that Department is responsible for managing abduction.

The Hague Convention is concerned with breaches of custody *rights*, not custody *orders*, and in this respect is quite different from the European Convention on Abduction (see below). Applications under the Hague Convention are heard by the High Court (s.4 CACA 1985), which can also make declarations that removal or retention of a child outside the UK is wrongful under art. 3 of the Convention (see below). The Hague Convention takes precedence over the European Convention. Thus, if Hague Convention and European Convention proceedings are both brought, the Hague application must be heard first (s.16(4)(c) CACA 1985). As decisions under the Hague Convention are not decisions on the merits of a custody issue (art. 19), the resolution of Convention proceedings does not determine the child's long-term future. This will be done in the court of the child's habitual residence (if a return order is made), or in the court in England and Wales. The central question in Convention proceedings is whether a child should be returned to the court of his or her habitual residence, not whether a child should be returned to a particular person.

As speed is of the essence in abduction cases, the proceedings are summary in nature, so that the court will not, for example, investigate the marital situation of parents or examine the welfare of the child (Sir Stephen Brown P, *Re D (Abduction: Custody Rights)* [1999] 2 FLR 626). Because of the summary nature of proceedings, cases are heard and decided on the basis of written evidence, although oral evidence can be admitted in exceptional circumstances (see, for example, *Re M (Abduction: Leave to Appeal)* [1999] 2 FLR 550, where oral evidence was allowed as there was a considerable degree of violence against the mother by the father). As proceedings are summary, legal advisers are required to ensure that the issues are succinctly defined and that the evidence is confined to the issues (Connell J, *Re S (Abduction: Intolerable Situation: Beth Din)* [2000] 1 FLR 454). In exceptional circumstances, a child can be granted leave to be joined as party to the proceedings (see *Re HB (Abduction: Child's Objections) (No 2)* [1998] 1 FLR 564) and the court can order that a child be separately represented (see *Re T (Abduction: Appointment of Guardian ad Litem)* [1999] 2 FLR 796).

As the underlying purpose of the Hague Convention is that abducted children should be returned, there is a presumption in favour of summary return, but the presumption is greater in the first 12 months after removal or retention as the court must return the child during that period, unless a defence is successful (see art. 12). Specific defences are laid down in art. 13 (see below), but these are interpreted strictly so as not to defeat the Convention's general policy aims. Other defences can be argued, e.g. that an abduction was not wrongful because the applicant possessed no rights of custody capable of being breached, or because the child's habitual residence is no longer the country from which he or she was removed.

Because the Convention is an international legal instrument, Lord Browne-Wilkinson said in *Re H (Minors)(Abduction: Acquiescence)* [1998] AC 72, [1997] 1 FLR 872 that it was important for it to be construed uniformly in Contracting States. To this end, the Hague Conference on private international law has established a database of leading Convention case-law in Contracting States called the International Child Abduction Database (INCADAT).

As far as use of the Convention is concerned, it is interesting to note that the Convention has not been used as originally anticipated by its framers. When originally negotiated, the typical scenario envisaged was of fathers snatching their children. In practice, however, more than two-thirds of abductions are by mothers abducting their children because of domestic violence (McClean, 1997).

(a) The Scope of the Convention: 'Habitual Residence' and 'Rights of Custody'

The Convention can be invoked in respect of a child aged under 16, who was habitually resident in a Contracting State immediately before any breach of a custody or access right (art. 4) and who has been wrongfully removed to or retained in another Contracting State. If by the time of the hearing the child has reached the age of 16, the High Court can consider the case under its inherent jurisdiction (see *Re H (Abduction: Child of 16)* [2000] 2 FLR 51).

(i) Habitual Residence Habitual residence is an important concept in the Convention. First, it is the connecting factor which determines whether the child comes within the scope of the Convention. Secondly, it establishes whether there has been wrongful removal or retention under art. 3(a), because if a child has been abducted from a Contracting State which is no longer his or her habitual residence, then there can be no wrongful removal or retention.

The leading case on habitual residence is *Re J (A Minor)(Abduction: Custody Rights)* [1990] 2 AC 562, *sub nom C* v. *S (A Minor)(Abduction)* [1990] 2 FLR 442. In this case an unmarried mother brought the child to England from Australia without the unmarried father's permission, whereupon he promptly obtained Australian court orders giving him sole custody and guardianship of the child, and a declaration that the removal was wrongful under art. 3 of the Hague Convention. He subsequently applied to the English court for the child's return under the Hague Convention, but his application was refused on appeal by the House of Lords because there had been no wrongful removal or retention under the Convention. There was no wrongful removal because as an unmarried father he possessed no custody rights capable of being breached at the time when the mother left Australia. Neither was there wrongful retention, despite the Australian custody order, as the House of Lords held that the child had ceased to be habitually resident in Australia before the custody order had been made. Their Lordships held that the mother possessed a unilateral right to determine the child's place of habitual residence (because the father had no custody rights), and that her settled intention to come to England had terminated the child's habitual residence in Australia. Had the father possessed rights of custody at the time of the child's removal from Australia, then the outcome of the case would have been quite different.

In *Re J, sub nom C* v. *S*, Lord Brandon, who gave the leading opinion, laid down the following rules in respect of habitual residence, and these have been applied in subsequent cases:

- habitual residence is primarily a question of fact to be decided by reference to all the circumstances of the case;
- the habitual residence of a young child in the physical care of a parent with sole parental responsibility is the same as that parent's habitual residence, but where both parents have parental responsibility neither of them can unilaterally change the child's habitual residence by removing or retaining the child wrongfully and in breach of the other parent's rights;
- while a person can cease to be habitually resident in country A in a single day, an appreciable period of time and settled intention is needed before a person can become habitually resident in country B.

In *Re A (Abduction: Habitual Residence)* [1998] 1 FLR 497, it was held that a short visit to a country does not start a period of habitual residence running. Thus, in *Re A*, a three-week visit to Greece for what was akin to a holiday was not an 'appreciable period of time' to create a new habitual residence. (For other cases on habitual residence, see, for example, *Re V (Abduction: Habitual Residence)* [1995] 2 FLR 992, *Re M (Abduction: Habitual Residence)* [1996] 1 FLR 887 and *Re A (Abduction: Habitual Residence)* [1996] 1 FLR 1.)

(ii) Wrongful Removal and Retention   In addition to the requirement of habitual residence, there must be a wrongful removal to, or wrongful retention in, a Contracting State. Wrongful removal and wrongful retention are mutually exclusive concepts (*Re H; Re S (Minors)(Abduction: Custody Rights)* [1991] 2 FLR 262). A wrongful removal occurs when a child is wrongfully removed

from his or her place of habitual residence in breach of a right of custody. Thus, there would be a wrongful removal if a parent removed a child from England and Wales without the consent of the other parent. A wrongful retention, on the other hand, occurs when at the end of a period of lawful removal, a parent refuses to return a child.

Article 3 provides that removal and retention are 'wrongful' where:

'(a) [the removal or retention] is in breach of rights of custody attributed to a person, an institution or any other body, either jointly or alone, under the law of the State in which the child was habitually resident immediately before the removal or retention; and

(b) at the time of removal or retention those rights were actually exercised, either jointly or alone, or would have been so exercised but for the removal or retention.'

Rights of custody include 'rights relating to the care of the person of the child and, in particular, the right to determine the child's place of residence' (art. 5(a)). A person can apply for a declaration that removal or retention of the child is wrongful under art. 3 of the Convention (see art. 15 and section 8 CACA 1985).

'Rights of Custody'

To come within the Convention, there must be a breach of a 'right of custody', otherwise the removal or retention of a child is not wrongful. However, the term 'right of custody' has been broadly and purposively interpreted by the English courts in order to give effect to the spirit and purpose of the Convention. Thus, the English courts have interpreted custody rights to include both legal and factual custody. In other words, where a person is exercising rights of a parental or custodial nature, this will constitute factual (*de facto*) custody. In this way, unmarried fathers without legal custody have been held to have custody rights for the purposes of the Convention, despite *Re J, sub nom C* v. *S* (above), where the House of Lords held that the unmarried father had no rights of custody and therefore fell outside the scope of the Convention. It has also been held that, even where removal of a child is not wrongful within art. 3, because the applicant has no custody rights which have been breached, the retention of a child may become wrongful if an order granting rights of custody is made with which such retention is incompatible (*Re S (Custody: Habitual Residence)* [1998] 1 FLR 122, which distinguished *Re J, sub nom C* v. *S (A Minor)* above).

The leading case on factual custody being sufficient for Convention purposes is *Re B (A Minor)(Abduction)* [1994] 2 FLR 249. Here the facts were almost identical to those in *Re J, sub nom C* v. *S (A Minor)* (above), except that there had been some subterfuge and dishonesty by the mother. However, although the unmarried father, like the father in *Re J*, possessed no legal custody rights under Australian law, the Court of Appeal nevertheless held that he possessed *de facto* custody rights (he had cared for the child), and these rights were sufficient to bring him within the scope of the Convention. Consequently, the removal and retention of the child were held to be wrongful, and the child was ordered to be returned to Australia. Waite LJ said that, as the purposes of the Convention were partly humanitarian, the expression 'rights of custody' should be construed in the sense that would best accord with that objective, which in most cases would involve giving the term the widest sense possible. Thus, in *Re B*, the majority of the Court of Appeal held that parental rights of an inchoate nature were sufficient to create rights of custody. Peter Gibson LJ, however, dissented, for while he felt sympathy for the father's plight, he held that it was impossible for the Court of Appeal to depart from the approach adopted by the House of Lords in *Re J, sub nom C* v. *S* above, as the facts of *Re B* were virtually the same. It is difficult not to agree with Peter Gibson LJ's reasoning, but at the same time it is suggested that the House of Lords took a wrong turn in *Re J, sub nom C* v. *S* by failing to adopt a purposive approach to rights of custody and thereby failing to comply with the underlying policy of the Hague Convention, which is for Contracting States to work together to effect the return of abducted children.

However, despite the decision of the House of Lords in *Re J, sub nom C* v. *S*, the courts have adopted the majority approach of the Court of Appeal in *Re B* above, so that unmarried fathers and other persons without legal custody have been held to have custody rights for the purposes of the Convention (see, for example, *Re O (Child Abduction: Custody Rights)* [1997] 2 FLR 702, where a grandparent was held to have custody rights). Rights of custody have also been held to arise where there is no legal or *de facto* custody right, but there is a right of veto on the child's removal (see *C* v. *C (Minor: Abduction: Rights of Custody Abroad)* [1989] 2 All ER 465). Removal or retention of a child has also been held to be wrongful where it breaches a 'right of custody' possessed by the court. Thus, in *Re H (Abduction: Rights of Custody)* [2000] 1 FLR 374, an unmarried mother abducted a child from Ireland and brought him to England. The unmarried father, who had an interim order for access (contact), applied for the child's return under the Hague Convention, but his application was dismissed as he possessed no custody rights to bring him within the Convention. However, the House of Lords held that a court is 'an institution or other body' to which rights of custody can be attributed within the meaning of art. 3. It said that 'rights' should be given a wide interpretation and that the power to determine a child's place of residence can itself be characterised as a right. The House of Lords held that rights of custody are conferred on the court when the application is served, and, unless the proceedings are stayed, the court is continuously involved until the application is disposed of. The child was therefore ordered to be returned to Ireland on the basis of the Irish court possessing rights of custody.

Rights of access do not amount to 'rights of custody' for the purpose of the Convention. For this reason, in *S* v. *H (Abduction: Access Rights)* [1998] Fam 49, [1997] 1 FLR 971, Hale J refused to order the child's return to Italy, as the unmarried father applicant has no rights of custody under Italian law or under the Convention. Although he had a right to watch over the child's education and living conditions and had rights of access, and despite the need to construe the Convention broadly and purposively, Hale J nevertheless held that the Convention drew a clear distinction between rights of custody and rights of access. Access rights can, however, be enforced in other ways under the Convention (see p.308 below).

Rights of Custody and English Unmarried Fathers

As we have seen above, unmarried fathers are sometimes in a vulnerable position because they have no custody rights to bring them within the Convention. Unmarried fathers who live in England and Wales may also find themselves in a vulnerable position if they have no parental responsibility for their child. However, the English courts have taken a broad view of 'custody rights', and in the case of *Re W; Re B (Child Abduction: Unmarried Father)* [1999] Fam 1, [1998] 2 FLR 146, Hale J defined the situations where the courts would permit an unmarried father to come within the scope of the Hague Convention. In *Re W: Re B*, two unmarried fathers applied to the High Court for declarations under s.8 of the Child Abduction and Custody Act 1985 that their children had been wrongfully removed or wrongfully retained under the Hague Convention. Hale J held that in the case of an unmarried father whose child is habitually resident in England and Wales, removal of a child is wrongful for Hague Convention purposes if:

- an unmarried father has parental responsibility;
- a court order is in force prohibiting removal;
- relevant proceedings (see below) are pending in England and Wales;
- an unmarried father is the primary carer of the child, at least if the mother had delegated such care to him; or
- the court is actively seized of proceedings to determine rights of custody (in which case, removal will be in breach of the rights of custody attributed to the court provided the proceedings remain pending).

Hale J said that 'relevant proceedings' for the purpose of these rules were proceedings for residence, parental responsibility, or prohibiting removal of a child. And proceedings were 'pending' if interim orders had been made and directions given for a full hearing, but not where proceedings had merely been issued. (For cases where unmarried fathers have been granted declarations of wrongful removal, see *Re J (Abduction: Declaration of Wrongful Removal)* [2000] 1 FLR 78 and *Re C (Abduction: Wrongful Removal)* [1999] 2 FLR 859, and see also *Practice Note: Hague Convention – Application by Fathers without Parental Responsibility) 14 October 1997* [1998] 1 FLR 491).

(b) Return of Children

A person (institution or other body) claiming that a child has been removed or retained in breach of a right of custody can apply to the Central Authority of the child's habitual residence or to the Central Authority of any other Contracting State for assistance in securing the child's return (art. 8). The Central Authority of the State where the child is present must take all appropriate measures to effect the voluntary return of the child (art. 10). If this is not possible, then court proceedings can be brought.

As the Convention is based on a presumption that abducted children should be returned to their place of habitual residence, so that the court in that country can decide on the child's future, the court hearing the application for return *must* return the child if the application is made during the first 12 months after wrongful removal or retention (art. 12). After that 12-month period, the court must also order return, unless the child is 'settled in its new environment' (art. 12) or one of the art. 13 defences below is proved. The duty under art. 12 to return a child is subject, however, to any defence being successful (see below). Because speed is of the essence in abduction cases, judicial and administrative authorities in a Contracting State must act expeditiously in proceedings for the return of a child (art. 11).

Undertakings

Instead of making an order for the child's return, the English courts have sometimes adopted the practice of accepting undertakings from parties to Hague Convention proceedings (e.g. to return the child, to provide accommodation, to pay travel costs and maintenance). However, the Court of Appeal has warned that undertakings 'must not be used by parties to try to clog or fetter, or, in particular, to delay the enforcement of a paramount decision to return the child' (Butler-Sloss LJ in *Re M (Abduction: Undertakings)* [1995] 1 FLR 1021). The problem with undertakings, however, is that while they are familiar to English courts, they are not easily understood by foreign courts and enforcement abroad may be difficult.

(c) Defences to an Application for Return of a Child

A person who has taken the child from a foreign country and brought the child to England and Wales has several defences available. One defence is to argue that the case does not come within the scope of the Convention, either because the applicant has no custody rights capable of being breached, or because the country from which the child was taken is no longer the child's country of habitual residence. Other defences are, however, expressly laid down in the Convention. Thus, art. 12 allows a person to argue that the child should not be returned because the child is settled in his or her new environment (but only in cases where the child has been in England and Wales for more than 12 months after the alleged wrongful removal or retention). Article 13 in particular, however, lays down several defences to a return application.

Article 13 provides that, notwithstanding art. 12 which requires mandatory return within the first 12 months, a judicial or administrative authority is not bound to return the child if the person opposing the child's return establishes that:

'(a) the person ... having the care of the person of the child was not actually exercising the custody rights at the time of removal or retention, or had consented to or had subsequently acquiesced in the removal or retention; or

(b) there is a grave risk that his or her return would expose the child to physical or psychological harm or otherwise place the child in an intolerable situation.'

Article 13 also provides that:

'The judicial or administrative authority may also refuse to order the return of the child if it finds that the child objects to being returned and has attained an age and degree of maturity at which it is appropriate to take account of its views.'

These defences, however, are rarely successful, because to allow them to succeed would undermine the principles of the Convention, which are to effect the return of abducted children and to promote and respect comity between Contracting States. The courts have constantly emphasised that the underlying thesis of the Convention is that the welfare of children is best determined by the courts of their habitual residence (see, for example, Ward LJ in *Re C (Abduction: Grave Risk of Psychological Harm)* [1999] 1 FLR 1145). In *Re E (A Minor) (Abduction)* [1989] 1 FLR 135, Anthony Lincoln J stated that:

'there is a very heavy burden indeed upon a person alleged to have abducted a child in bringing himself or herself within the provisions of Article 13, and the court should hesitate very long before it grants what is in effect an exemption from the urgency which is a characteristic of this Convention and the Act incorporating it.'

The right to family life under art. 8 of the European Convention for the Protection of Human Rights (see 1.5) has also been used as a justification for ordering a child's return (see *Re F (Abduction: Child's Right to Family Life* [1999] Fam Law 806, where Cazalet J said that the court would be failing to have respect for the child's right for family life under the European Convention if it overrode the arrangements made by the Portuguese court which had provided for contact between the two siblings concerned).

Once a defence under art. 13 has been proved, the court has a discretion whether or not to order the child's return. In most cases, however, the court will refuse to order return once a defence has been successfully made out. Only in exceptional cases will it order return if a defence is successful. An exceptional case where the court refused to order return, despite a defence having been made out, was *Re D (Abduction: Discretionary Return)* [2000] 1 FLR 24. Here Wilson J found that the mother had consented to the children's removal and that the children were settled in England with their father, but nevertheless ordered their return to France, as the French court was already seized of the issue and it was a better forum in which to resolve the question of residence. The principles of comity and appropriate forum justified ordering the children's return, despite the successful defence.

The Defences

(i) Consent   Consent for the purposes of art. 13(a) is a question of fact. It must be real, positive and unequivocal, but can be inferred from conduct in the absence of a written or express statement (see *Re C (Abduction: Consent)* [1996] 1 FLR 414, *Re K (Abduction: Consent)* [1997] 2 FLR 212, *Re R (Abduction: Consent)* [1999] 1 FLR 828 and *Re M (Abduction: Consent: Acquiescence)* [1999] 1 FLR 171). The evidence in support of consent must be clear and cogent. The principles that apply to acquiescence (see below) also apply to consent. A consent defence can also be raised under art. 3 of the Convention – in other words, that there was no breach of a custody right because the other party consented to the child leaving the country. In *Re O (Abduction: Consent and Acquiescence)* [1997] 1 FLR 924, Bennett J held that, where a wronged parent had *prima facie* given consent but asserted it had been vitiated by duress, deceit or some other vitiating factor, then the matter fell within art. 3. Once consent is established, the court has a discretion whether or not to order a child's return, but in most cases it does not do so (see above).

(ii) Acquiescence Acquiescence under art. 13(a) is commonly argued. The leading case is *Re H (Minors)(Abduction: Acquiescence)* [1998] AC 72, *sub nom Re H (Abduction: Acquiescence)* [1997] 1 FLR 872. Here the parents were married and were strict Orthodox Jews living in Israel. The mother moved the children to England without the father's consent, whereupon he contacted the Beth Din (a religious court) in Israel, which told him not to take part in English proceedings. Later on, however, after the Israeli Beth Din had authorised him to take whatever steps he thought fit, he immediately invoked Hague Convention proceedings (but six months after the children's removal from Israel). The mother argued that the father had acquiesced in the children's removal by failing to make a prompt application. The High Court ordered the children's return to Israel, but the Court of Appeal allowed the mother's appeal, on the basis of the father's acquiescence, applying *Re A (Minors)(Abduction: Custody Rights)* [1992] Fam 106, *sub nom Re A (Minors)(Abduction: Acquiescence)* [1992] 2 FLR 14. In *Re A*, the Court of Appeal had applied an objective test to the question of acquiescence, and had held that acquiescence could be signified by a single act or communication, even though that act or communication appeared to be at variance with the general course of a parent's conduct. It had held that, although there could be an element of subjective analysis (e.g. the court could inquire into the state of the aggrieved parent's knowledge of his or her rights under the Convention), the court was not permitted to give undue emphasis to these subjective elements (see also *Re AZ (A Minor) (Abduction: Acquiescence)* [1993] 1 FLR 682). However, in *Re H* the House of Lords overruled the test of acquiescence laid down by the Court of Appeal in *Re A*, and ordered the summary return of the children to Israel, as it was clear that the father had not acquiesced in their retention in England.

Lord Browne-Wilkinson, who gave the leading opinion in *Re H*, laid down a subjective test for acquiescence, and stated the following principles:

'1. For the purposes of art. 13, the question of whether the wronged parent has "acquiesced" in the removal or retention of the child depends on his actual state of mind.

2. The subjective intention of the wronged parent is a question of fact for the trial judge to determine in all the circumstances of the case, the burden of proof being on the abducting parent.

3. The trial judge, in reaching his decision on that question of fact, will no doubt be inclined to attach more weight to the contemporaneous words and actions of the wronged parent than to his bare assertions in evidence of his intention. But that is a question of the weight to be attached to evidence and is not a question of law.

4. There is only one exception. Where the words or actions of the wronged parent clearly and unequivocally show and have led the other parent to believe that the wronged parent is not asserting or going to assert his right

to the summary return of the child and are inconsistent with such return, justice requires that the wronged parent be held to have acquiesced.'

The court must therefore establish whether the wronged parent has actually acquiesced as a matter of fact, and, if so, then go on to consider whether or not the case falls within the exception in point 4, above. However, this exception is a narrow one and is unlikely to be relevant in most cases, as the external facts of the case are usually unlikely to be in conflict with the wronged parent's subjective intent (see dicta of the Court of Appeal in *Re D (Abduction: Acquiescence)* [1998] 2 FLR 335, and *P* v. *P (Abduction: Acquiescence)* [1998] 2 FLR 835). However, in *Re D (Abduction: Acquiescence)* [1998] 1 FLR 686, a father was held to have acquiesced under point 4, above, as he had consented to the jurisdiction of the court in Wales and had consented to the making of full and final residence orders.

Acquiescence is therefore a question of fact in each case. It has been held that an application for custody in the child's country of habitual residence is a strong indication that there is no acquiescence (*Re A and Another (Minors: Abduction)* [1991] 2 FLR 241 and *Re F (A Minor) (Child Abduction)* [1992] 1 FLR 548). Making long-term plans for contact may indicate acquiescence (*Re S (Abduction: Acquiescence)* [1998] 2 FLR 115), and so may bringing proceedings for contact in the English courts, even though brought in ignorance of the Convention (see *Re B (Abduction: Acquiescence)* [1999] 2 FLR 818, where Kirkwood J said the case fell in the exception in point 4, above). Acquiescence does not require an applicant to have specific knowledge of the Convention (*Re AZ (A Minor)(Abduction: Acquiescence)* [1993] 1 FLR 682). A willingness to be involved in negotiations to sort out what is best for a child and the parties does not necesssarily amount to acquiescence, even if no agreement is reached (*Re I (Abduction: Acquiescence)* [1999] 1 FLR 778), as the Court of Appeal has held that negotiations at the early stage of a difficult broken relationship are to be encouraged (*P* v. *P (Abduction: Acquiescence)* [1998] 2 FLR 835). Once acquiescence is established, the court has a discretion whether or not to order the child's return, but it most cases it does not do so (see above).

(iii) Grave Risk of Physical or Psychological Harm   The court may refuse to order the child's return if there is a grave risk that return would expose the child to physical or psychological harm, or otherwise place the child in an intolerable situation (art. 13(b)). The burden of establishing this defence, as under art. 13(a), is a heavy one. There must be clear and compelling evidence of a grave risk of harm or other intolerability, which must be substantial, not trivial, and of a severity which is much more than the inevitable disruption, uncertainty and anxiety which inevitably follow the return of a child to his or her country of habitual residence (see *Re C (Abduction: Grave Risk of*

Psychological Harm) [1999] 1 FLR 1145). A high degree of intolerability must be established (see Balcombe LJ in *Re A (Minors)(Abduction: Custody Rights)* [1992] Fam 106 and Sir Stephen Brown P in *B* v. *B (Abduction)* [1993] 1 FLR 238). The courts constantly emphasise that to refuse to order return would defeat the underlying purpose of the Convention and be contrary to international relations.

In *N* v. *N (Abduction: Article 13 Defence)* [1995] 1 FLR 107, where the defence failed and the children were ordered to be returned to Australia, Thorpe J said that the court is entitled to weigh the risk of psychological harm of return against the psychological harm of refusing return, although in exercising its discretion due weight must be given to the primary purpose of the Convention, which is to ensure the swift return of abducted children. His Lordship stated that the child's welfare is an important, but not a paramount, consideration, and stressed that abducting parents should not be empowered to defeat the Convention by manipulation or even by the expression of genuine fears and sincerely held feelings. It has also been held that the court should not allow the defence to succeed where the applicant has created the psychological condition. In *Re C (A Minor)(Abduction)* [1989] 1 FLR 403, at 410, Butler-Sloss LJ said that 'if the grave risk of psychological harm to a child is to be inflicted by the conduct of the parent who abducted him, then it would be relied on by every mother of a young child who removed him out of the jurisdiction and refused to return him'. A defence based on an argument that ordering a child's return will separate siblings will not necessarily constitute psychological harm (see *Re C (Abduction: Grave Risk of Physical or Psychological Harm)* [1999] 2 FLR 478). Indeed, the courts have recognised that some psychological harm to a child is inherent in any abduction case (Lord Donaldson MR in *Re C (A Minor)(Abduction)* [1989] 1 FLR 403, and see *E* v. *E (Child Abduction: Intolerable Situation)* [1998] 2 FLR 980). In *Re S (Abduction: Intolerable Situation: Beth Din)* [2000] 1 FLR 454, a mother argued that if the children were ordered to be returned to Israel, it would result in an intolerable situation under art. 13(b), as women who were orthodox Jews were discriminated against under Israeli religious law and this would result in her rights and those of the children being breached under art. 8 of the European Convention for the Protection of Human Rights (the right to family life). However, Connell J refused to accept this argument. (For rare cases where the defence has succeeded and the court has refused to order return, see, for example, *Re F (Child Abduction: Risk if Returned)* [1995] 2 FLR 31, *Re L (Child Abduction)(Psychological Harm)* [1993] 2 FLR 401 and *Re M (Abduction: Psychological Harm)* [1997] 2 FLR 690.)

(iv) Child Objects to Being Returned The court may refuse to order return if the child objects to being returned and has attained an age and degree of maturity at which it is appropriate to take account of the child's views (art. 13).

As with other defences, a parent asserting this defence has a heavy burden to discharge. The court has a discretion as to the amount of weight to be given to the child's views, but will refuse to order return only in exceptional circumstances, as to do otherwise would undermine the policy of the Convention. There is no fixed age below which a child's objections will not be taken into account. In fact, the views of children as young as seven have been taken into account, but this age is on the borderline (see *Re K (Abduction: Child's Objections)* [1995] 1 FLR 977). As Hague Convention proceedings are summary and speed is of the essence, the court will usually refuse to hear oral evidence in respect of a child's wishes (see *Re K (Abduction: Child's Objections)* [1995], above). If the court is put on inquiry that a child objects to being returned, the court welfare officer performs the dual role of assessing whether the child has sufficient maturity and of conveying the child's views to the court.

The court will be 'vigilant to ascertain and assess the reasons for the child not wishing to return to the parent living in the State of habitual residence' (Butler-Sloss LJ in *Re M (A Minor)(Child Abduction)* [1994] 1 FLR 390). Although art. 12 requires the child to be returned to the state of habitual residence and not to the person requesting the child's return, the court can consider the child's reasons for objecting to return to the parent rather than to the state (*Re M (A Minor)(Child Abduction)* [1994] 1 FLR 390, disapproving *B* v. *K* [1992] 2 FCR 606). In an exceptional case, a child may be made a party to a Convention application (see *Re M (A Minor)(Abduction: Child's Objections)* [1994] 2 FLR 126, where the dispute was between the mother and child, not the mother and father). There may be difficulties enforcing orders where a child has strong objections to being returned. Thus, in *Re HB (Abduction: Children's Objections)* [1998] 1 FLR 422, an 11-year-old girl had strong objections to being returned to Denmark, but the High Court nevertheless ordered her return. However, she refused to board the plane. Subsequently, after having been granted permission to be joined as party to Hague Convention proceedings, the Court of Appeal held that the court was no longer bound to order her return, as 12 months had passed for the purposes of art. 12 (see above), and because of her strong objections to return.

(For cases where children have not been returned because of their objections, see: *S* v. *S (Child Abduction: Child's Views)* [1992] 2 FLR 492, *B* v. *K (Child Abduction)* [1993] 1 FCR 382, *Re R (A Minor: Abduction)* [1992] 1 FLR 105, *Re B (Abduction: Children's Objections)* [1998] 1 FLR 667, and *Re T (Abduction: Child's Objections to Return)* [2000] 2 FLR 193.)

(d) Access (Contact) Rights

Although art. 21 of the Hague Convention provides that access rights may be secured, this confers no power on the courts to determine access matters, or to recognise or enforce foreign access orders. It merely provides for executive co-operation between Central Authorities for the recognition and enforcement of such access rights as national laws allow. Thus in England and Wales the Child Abduction Unit of the Lord Chancellor's Department will provide assistance in finding a solicitor, help with legal aid, and help institute proceedings for s.8 orders under the Children Act 1989 (see *Re G (A Minor)(Hague Convention: Access)* [1993] 1 FLR 669 and *Practice Note: (Child Abduction – Lord Chancellor's Department)* [1993] 1 FLR 804). If an access order is in force, an application can be made to have it recognised and enforced in the English court under the European Convention (see below, and also *Re A (Foreign Access Order: Enforcement)* [1996] 1 FLR 561).

Because concern has been voiced about the difficulty of enforcing access rights at international level, a new Convention aimed at guaranteeing access is being completed by the Council of Europe. There has also been strong support for the Hague Conference on Private International Law investigating the feasibility of adding a Protocol to the Hague Convention on Abduction to deal more specifically with the protection of access rights.

15.8   International Child Abduction: The European Convention

The European Convention on the Recognition and Enforcement of Decisions Concerning Custody of Children 1980 (the 'European Convention') was implemented into UK law by Part II of the Child Abduction and Custody Act 1985. The text of the Convention is laid down in Sched. 2 to the 1985 Act. A list of Contracting States can be found on the websites at the end of this chapter.

Under the European Convention a custody decision given in a Contracting State must be recognised and, where it is enforceable in the State of origin, made enforceable in every other Contracting State (art. 7). Like the Hague Convention, the European Convention creates an international network of Contracting States who must work together to effect the return of abducted children but, unlike the Hague Convention, it deals with the enforcement of custody orders rather than custody rights.

In practice, however, the Convention is rarely invoked because it has largely been superseded by the Hague Convention (see 15.7 above), because the Hague Convention takes precedence over it, and because (with the exception of Iceland) all Contracting States to the European Convention are now Contracting States to the Hague Convention. However, despite the fact that the European Convention is rarely invoked, it remains useful for enforcing access (contact) orders, particularly as access rights are given much less recognition than custody rights under the Hague Convention.

The European Convention deals with the recognition and enforcement of custody decisions where there has been 'improper removal of a child', by allowing any person who has obtained a custody decision in a Contracting State to apply to a Central Authority in another Contracting State to have that decision recognised or enforced in that State (art. 4). The Convention applies to custody decisions made before or after the child's wrongful removal across an international frontier from one Contracting State to another (art. 12). A 'custody decision' is a decision made by any judicial or administrative authority relating to the care of a child, including a right to determine the child's place of residence or a right of access to the child (art. 1(c)).

'Improper removal' is defined as 'the removal of a child across an international frontier in breach of a decision relating to his custody which has been given in a Contracting State and which is enforceable in such a State' and includes: '(i) the failure to return a child across an international frontier at the end of a period of the exercise of the right of access to this child or at the end of any other temporary stay in a territory other than that where the custody is exercised' and '(ii) a removal which is subsequently declared unlawful within the meaning of article 12' (art. 1(d)).

Decisions on access, and custody decisions dealing with access, can also be recognised and enforced under the Convention subject to the same conditions which apply to custody decisions, but the competent authority of the State addressed may fix the conditions for the implementation and exercise of the right of access, taking into account, in particular, undertakings given by the parties on this matter (art. 11). Where there is no decision as to access or where recognition or enforcement of a custody decision has been refused, the Central Authority of the State addressed may apply to its own competent authorities for a decision on the right of access if the person claiming a right of access so requests (art. 11(3)). In *Re A (Foreign Access Order: Enforcement)* [1996] 1 FLR 561, an order was made giving recognition to a French access order and making it enforceable in England.

A person wishing to have a custody or access decision recognised or enforced in another Contracting State may apply to the Central Authority in any Contracting State (art. 4) (in England and Wales, the Lord Chancellor's Department), which must take various appropriate steps without delay. These steps include instituting proceedings, discovering the child's whereabouts, securing the recognition or enforcement of the decision, securing delivery of the child to the applicant where enforcement is granted, and informing the requesting authority of the measures taken and their results (art. 5).

Before a custody decision made in another Contracting State can be recognised and enforced in England and Wales it must be registered (ss.15(2)(b) and 16 CACA 1985). An application for registration can be made to the High Court by any person who has rights under the custody decision. The High Court can refuse to register a decision, thereby refusing recognition and enforcement, on certain procedural and/or substantive grounds (see below) or where an application for the child's return is pending under the Hague Convention (s.16(4) CACA 1985). In no circumstances may the original foreign custody decision be reviewed as to its substance (art. 9(3)).

Grounds for Refusal to Register an Order

Under arts. 9 and 10 of the European Convention, the court can on certain grounds refuse to register an order, and thereby fail to recognise and enforce it. However, it is unlikely to do so, as the aim of the European Convention, like that of the Hague Convention, is to foster international co-operation to effect the return of abducted children.

Article 9 lays down certain procedural grounds for refusing to register an order, namely: (a) where the decision was made in the absence of the defendant or his lawyer, and they were not given sufficient notice of the proceedings; (b) where the decision was made in the absence of the defendant or his or her lawyer, and the competence of the authority giving the decision was not based on the habitual residence of the defendant, the parents, or the child; and (c) where the decision is incompatible with a decision made in the State addressed before the child's removal, unless the child has had his or her habitual residence in the territory of the requesting State for one year before his or her removal.

Article 10 lays down certain substantive grounds which allow the court to refuse to register an order, namely: (a) where the effects of the decision are manifestly incompatible with the fundamental principles of family and child law in the State addressed; (b) where the effects of a custody decision are no longer in accordance with the child's welfare owing to a change of circumstances, including the passage of time, but not a mere change of the child's residence after an improper removal; (c) where at the time proceedings were instituted in the State of origin, the child was a national of, or habitually resident in, the State addressed; and (d) if the decision is incompatible with a decision given in the State addressed. Where the court is considering whether to refuse to register an order on the basis of (b) above (no longer in accordance with the child's welfare etc.), it must ascertain the child's views (unless impracticable to do so, having regard to his age and understanding), and it may request appropriate enquiries to be carried out (art. 15(1)).

A recent example of the use of the European Convention is *Re L (Abduction: European Convention: Access)* [1999] 2 FLR 1089. In this case the children's grandparents applied for an access order to be enforced in England, after the children had been taken from France. However, they were unsuccessful, as there had been a change of circumstances so that the access order was no longer appropriate under art. 10(b) above. It had been made by the French court on the basis that the children would be living in France, but they were now living in England. Although the English court had jurisdiction under art. 11(2) to vary the order, Bennett J felt that variation was not appropriate in the circumstances.

15.9   International Child Abduction: Non-Convention Cases

Some children are brought into England and Wales from countries which are not Hague or European Convention Contracting States. In such cases a person who wishes to have the child returned will have to apply to the High Court, which has a wide discretion in non-Convention cases. Thus, unlike Hague Convention proceedings, it can order the child's summary return or investigate the merits of the case.

A few years ago the approach of the High Court was to apply the general principles of the Hague Convention, including the art. 13 defences, fairly closely, so that the presumption was much more strongly in favour of ordering a child's return (see, for example, *Re M (Abduction: Non-Convention Country)* [1995] 1 FLR 89 and *D* v. *D (Child Abduction: Non-Convention Country)* [1994] 1 FLR 137). However, this approach has changed. It has been held that the governing principle in non-Convention cases is that the welfare of the child is the court's paramount consideration, and that it is incorrect to apply the Hague Convention, and cases heard under it, by too strict an analogy (see *Re P (Abduction: Non-Convention Country)* [1997] 1 FLR 780, *Re JA (Child Abduction: Non-Convention Country)* [1998] 1 FLR 231 and *T* v. *T (Child Abduction: Non-Convention Country)* [1998] 2 FLR 1110). However, there remains a general presumption, as there does under the Hague Convention, that it is normally in a child's best interests to return the child to his or her country of habitual residence, so that custody matters can be decided there. In *Re M (Abduction: Peremptory Return Order)* [1996] 1 FLR 478, where the children were ordered to be returned to Dubai, Waite LJ stated that underlying the whole purpose of the peremptory return order is 'a principle of international comity under which judges in England will assume that facilities for a fair hearing will be provided in the court of the other jurisdiction'. His Lordship said that very exceptional circumstances would be needed to depart from that general principle. Each case turns on its own facts, but in exercising its discretion to decide whether to order a child's return a particularly important consideration will be whether the court of the child's habitual residence possesses and applies a welfare principle in children's cases (see, for example, *Re Z (Non-Convention Country)* [1999] 1 FLR 1270, where the child was ordered to be returned to Malta, as the Maltese court would regard the child's welfare as the paramount consideration).

Although the child's welfare is the court's paramount consideration in non-Convention cases, the court will look at welfare in the context of the child's cultural background. In *Re E (Abduction: Non-Convention Country)* [1999] 2 FLR 642, Thorpe LJ said that 'what constitutes the welfare of the child must be subject to the cultural background and expectations of the jurisdiction striving to achieve it.' His Lordship said that, if international child abduction was to be dealt with effectively, the courts had to show respect towards a variety of concepts of child welfare, deriving from different cultures and traditions. It was not possible to regard welfare as an absolute standard. Applying the welfare principle to the facts, the mother was ordered to return the children to the Sudan even though under Islamic law she was disqualified from obtaining custody. Thorpe LJ felt that, as there was no investigation into the family justice systems operating in Hague Convention countries, and no criticism of those systems was permitted in litigation, it was unwise in non-Convention cases to permit abducting parents to criticise the standards of the family justice system in their own country of habitual residence, save in exceptional circumstances, e.g. where there was persecution, or ethnic, sex or other discrimination. The application of Muslim law in this case was appropriate and acceptable, and a solution to the issue according to local law was capable of being in the best interests of the children. Thus, even in non-Convention cases, return of the child is usually the preferred outcome of the court.

15.10   International Child Abduction: The Future

Although the Hague and European Conventions have helped facilitate the return of abducted children, child abduction remains a world-wide problem. Tracing a child is difficult and expensive, and many countries are not parties to the Conventions. Islamic countries have, for instance, refused to sign the Convention, so that there is no reciprocal provision in place to cope with abductions. A major problem is that, even if legal proceedings can be instituted in non-Convention countries, the courts in those countries may not order the child's return. Unlike courts having jurisdiction under the Conventions, which must apply uniform principles of law, the courts in non-Convention countries can only apply their own legal principles. Thus, a mother whose child has been abducted to Saudi Arabia, for instance, will have to apply for her child's return in the courts in that country, where Shariah law will be applied. Furthermore, in Muslim countries only a father has rights in his child, so that an application by a mother to have her child returned may be unlikely to succeed.

In 1990 the House of Commons established a working party on abduction, which made certain recommendations, which included granting legal aid to help mothers fight their cases in foreign courts, marking children's passports in cases of family dispute, and appointing a Children's Commissioner to take up cases with foreign courts and governments and to intercede on behalf of children. The working party also recommended that the courts should be more willing to listen to parents who showed that there was a threat of abduction, and police and courts should be quicker to respond. In 1996, in advance of the review of the Hague Convention by a Special Commission of the Hague Conference, the Lord Chancellor's Department issued a Consultation Paper on international child abduction. Some of the topics raised for consultation were the extent to which the wishes of children should be taken into account, the problem of enforcing return orders and undertakings, the safety of children returning to their country of habitual residence, the need for a code of practice, the need to encourage mediation and the setting up of an international panel of arbiters to resolve disputes. The development of mediatory approaches to divorce may help to reduce abduction, but with increasing family breakdown the chances are that child abduction is likely to remain a serious and distressing problem.

Summary

1 Child abduction is a world-wide problem, caused by increasing family breakdown. Advice on child abduction can be sought from the Child Abduction Unit, which is based in the Official Solicitor's Department at the Lord Chancellor's Department (see website below).
2 A child can be lawfully taken out of the UK provided there is no court order prohibiting removal and every person with parental responsibility consents. If consent is not forthcoming, a s.8 specific issue order can be sought under the Children Act 1989 (see 12.4). Where a residence order is in force, there is an automatic prohibition against removing a child from the UK for more than one month unless all those with parental responsibility give written consent to the removal, or the court grants permission (s.13 CA 1989).
3 The following steps can be taken to prevent abduction: court order; passport control; and police assistance, including an 'All Ports Warning'.
4 Child abduction is a criminal offence under the Child Abduction Act 1984. Abduction can also constitute the criminal offence of kidnapping.
5 The Family Law Act 1986 enables a court order made in one part of the UK to be enforced in another part.
6 The Hague Convention (to which the UK is a party) enables Contracting States to work together to return children wrongfully removed from their country of habitual residence or wrongfully retained in another Contracting State, subject to certain defences, but defences are rarely successful. Once a defence is made out, the court must then go on to consider whether it is in the child's best interests to order return.
7 The European Convention (to which the UK is a party) enables custody decisions (and access orders) made in one Contracting State to be recognised, registered and enforced in another, when the child has been improperly removed, subject to certain defences. As the Hague Convention takes precedence over the European Convention, the latter is hardly used and there are few reported cases.

8 Where a child is wrongfully brought into England and Wales from a country which is not a party to the Hague or European Convention, the High Court will decide whether the welfare of the child requires it to order the child's return. However, there is a presumption in favour of return unless such return is contrary to the child's best interests.
9 Although the law gives more protection to abducted children than it once did, many problems still remain.

Further Reading and References

Beaumont and McEleavy, *Hague Convention on International Child Abduction*, Oxford University Press, 1999.
Hutchinson, Roberts and Setright, *International Parental Child Abduction*, Family Law, 1998.
Kirkconel, 'Removing children from the jurisdiction' [1999] Fam Law 333.
McClean, 'International child abduction – some recent trends' [1997] CFLQ 387.
Muirhead, 'Sending children back under the Hague Convention – Are current practices wide of the rules?' [1998] Fam Law 769.

Websites

The Child Abduction Unit (based in the Official Solicitor's Department of the Lord Chancellor's Department) (information and guidance about child abduction, details about the Hague and European Conventions, list of contracting states, and a link to the Foreign and Commonwealth Office): www.offsol.demon.co.uk/caumenu.htm
Reunite (National Council for Abducted Children) (information and research on child abduction, including a list of the Hague and European Convention Contracting States): www.reunite.org/

Questions

1 Would the case of *Re J (A Minor), sub nom C* v. *S (A Minor)* (1990) be decided any differently today? If so, why?
2 What opportunities are there for using human rights' arguments in child abduction cases, as a result of the coming into force of the Human Rights Act 1998?

16 Child Protection

16.1 Responsibility for Child Protection

One of the main philosophies of the law relating to children is that parents, not the State, have primary responsibility for their children, and this is reflected in the law governing child protection which is laid down in the Children Act 1989. Sometimes, however, when parents fall down in their responsibilities, the State intervenes. Criminal sanctions may be imposed on parents who harm children and the civil law also provides protection in various ways. Thus injunctions can be obtained to protect children from violence (see Chapter 6) and parents can be required to pay maintenance for their children (see Chapter 14). Sometimes, however, a child is suffering, or is at risk of suffering, such harm that the State has a duty to intervene to provide parents with advice and assistance, and in serious cases to remove children temporarily or permanently from their parents by court order. This duty to protect children is also laid down in art. 18(2) of the UN Convention on the Rights of the Child 1989, which requires Member States to 'render appropriate assistance to parents and legal guardians in the performance of their child-rearing responsibilities' and to 'ensure the development of institutions, facilities and services for the care of children.'

The State's function to protect children is entrusted to local authorities, who have statutory duties and powers to ensure that parents and other persons fulfil their responsibilities to children. Each local authority carries out its obligations by means of its Social Services Department whose social workers have various duties and powers laid down by statute and regulation, e.g. to provide assistance to children in need, to investigate cases where children are, or may be, suffering harm, to inspect various persons and premises, and to keep registers and records about problem families. Local authority powers and duties are laid down in the Children Act 1989 and in regulations. Part III of the Children Act makes provision in respect of local authority support for children and families. Parts IV and V make provision for compulsory intervention by local authorities when it becomes necessary for a local authority to apply for a court order to protect a child. In certain situations, local authorities can also apply to invoke the inherent jurisdiction of the High Court (see 12.9). Local authorities have other duties towards children under the Children Act, for example, in respect of the provision, registration and inspection of community and voluntary homes, the inspection and supervision of foster-parents and their homes, and the protection of children accommodated for long periods in health and educational establishments. However, only local authority duties and powers under Parts III, IV and V of the Act are considered here.

As far as attitudes to State intervention by local authorities are concerned, they are often ambivalent. Local authority social workers are in an invidious position, because they must tread a fine line between taking sufficient steps to protect children, while ensuring that they are not over-zealous in their task of child protection, and thereby too intrusive into family life. Under art. 8 of the European Convention for the Protection of Human Rights, a person has a right to a private and a family life and there must be no interference by a public authority with the exercise of those rights, except such as is in accordance with the law and is necessary for the protection of the rights and freedoms of others. Local authorities are public authorities for the purposes of the Human Rights Act 1998 (see 1.5), and must therefore exercise their powers and duties in ways which comply with the European Convention on Human Rights. Local authorities are required to bear in mind the principles underpinning the right to family life in art. 8 of the Convention (see, for example, Local Authority Circular, Care Plans and Care Proceedings under the Children Act 1989, LAC (99) 29). They must therefore recognise that it is generally in the best interests of children to remain in their own families. However, when parents fall down in their duties to their children, local authorities must intervene.

In the past, social workers have sometimes been criticised for being too interventionist, and at other times for not being interventionist enough. In the Maria Colwell case, for instance, where Maria Colwell was tragically killed by her step-father after suffering months of horrendous abuse, the social services department involved was criticised for failing to intervene despite receiving reports about Maria's suffering (see the *Report of the Committee of Inquiry into the Care and Supervision Provided in Relation to Maria Colwell*, 1974). However, in the Cleveland affair in the late 1980s, on the other hand, social workers were criticised for being too interventionist and too intrusive into family life, when more than one hundred children suspected of being sexually abused were taken away from their homes on the evidence of two paediatricians without other agencies being consulted. The report of the public enquiry set up in the aftermath of the Cleveland affair (*Report of the Enquiry into Child Abuse in Cleveland 1987*, Cm 412, 1987), which was chaired by Butler-Sloss LJ, recommended *inter alia* better inter-agency co-operation to protect children and better safeguards for parents and children where emergency intervention was needed. In fact the *Cleveland Report* had a considerable impact on the Children Act 1989, in particular on its aim to achieve the right balance between family autonomy and State intervention, in other words between necessary and unnecessary intervention. The *Gillick* case also had a strong influence on the Children Act (see 10.3), in that the wishes of children with sufficient maturity should be taken into account. Both the *Maria Colwell*

Report and the *Cleveland Report* had stressed the importance of listening to the voices of children, but whether the Children Act has succceeded in actually doing this as much as proponents of children's rights would have liked is open to doubt.

Despite the need to respect the right to family life, there will be some cases where it will be necessary to remove a child from home and place him or her in local authority care. However, taking a child into care can create its own set of problems, as children in care fare less well socially and educationally than other children. Many turn to crime. Some children have even suffered abuse at the hands of those who work in the care system (see the Waterhouse Report, *Lost in Care*, The Stationery Office, 2000). However, proposals have been made to ensure that children in care are better protected from harm, for instance by allowing them to have access to an independent visitor and an advocate, and, where necessary, the courts. The *Waterhouse Report* also emphasised the importance of listening to children (just as the *Cleveland Report* above had done), and recommended the creation of an independent children's commissioner. The Government has now confirmed that the post of Children's Rights Director will be created as part of the National Care Commission. Furthermore, the Government has also recently proposed that there should be a greater emphasis on placing children in care for adoption, so that they can reap the benefits of living in a permanent family (see 17.13).

16.2   Policies and Principles in the Children Act 1989

The Children Act 1989 is based on the following general principles which govern the practice of child protection:

- the welfare of the child is the paramount consideration;
- children should be brought up within their own families where possible;
- where children are in need, parents should be provided with support to help them bring up their children;
- children should be protected by effective intervention where they are suffering or are likely to suffer significant harm;
- courts should ensure that delay is avoided;
- courts should only make an order if it is better than making no order at all;
- children should be informed about plans for themselves, and should be given the opportunity to participate in decisions about themselves; and
- parents continue to have parental responsibility when a child is in local authority care, and should therefore be kept informed about and be permitted to participate in decisions about their children.

The general policy of the Children Act is therefore on keeping children within their families, with parents, not the State, having primary responsibility for them. Local authorities must provide help and assistance for families and children in need, with intervention by court order only in the last resort. The Children Act reinforces this policy of non-intervention in several ways. Under the no-order presumption, the court must not make an order unless making an order is better for the child than making no order at all (s.1(5)), and local authorities must work in partnership with parents to promote and safeguard the welfare of children to prevent them being taken into care. Furthermore, as removing a child from his or her parents is considered to be a serious matter, it can only be effected by a court order on proof that a child is suffering, or is likely to suffer, significant harm. This is quite different from the law before the Children Act came into force, when a local authority could acquire parental rights in respect of a child merely by passing an administrative resolution without the need to go to court. However, despite the importance of parents being the primary caretakers, there is some concern that the Children Act's emphasis on minimum State intervention has gone too far and that the child protection system is failing to protect abused and neglected children (see 'Failing Children Act' [2000] 527).

In proceedings under the Children Act, the child's welfare is the court's paramount consideration (s.1(1)), and in care and supervision proceedings (but not emergency protection proceedings) the court must apply the welfare checklist in s.1(3) (see 12.3). The court must also bear in mind the principle that delay is detrimental to a child (s.1(2)) and must apply the no-order presumption in s.1(5). An important change introduced by the Children Act was to cut back the use of wardship jurisdiction by local authorities (see 12.9). Prior to the Children Act, local authorities often used wardship as a way of taking children into care instead of using the statutory procedures that were then available.

16.3 The Practice of Child Protection

Local authority social services departments are responsible for the task of child protection, whether this involves support for children in need, or more drastic intervention where children are at risk of harm. The Children Act 1989 lays down the legal duties and powers for social services departments, but rules of practice are laid down in *Working Together to Safeguard Children: A guide to inter-agency working to safeguard and promote the welfare of children* (Department of Health, 1999, available on its website, see end of chapter). The status of these rules of practice is that, although they do not have the full force of law, they must be complied with unless local circumstances indicate that there are exceptional reasons justifying a variation. The Government has also laid down a set of objectives for social services working to protect children (see *The Government's Objectives for Children's Social Services*, Department of Health, 1999, also available on its website, see end of chapter).

Working Together to Safeguard Children establishes two key policy objectives governing good social work practice: the importance of inter-agency co-operation and the importance of encouraging partnership and participation with parents. The importance of inter-agency co-operation was one of the recommendations made by the Cleveland Enquiry (see above). Social workers are required to consult teachers, the police, doctors, probation officers and other people involved with the child and to consider their views. Inter-agency co-operation is facilitated by the Area Child Protection Committee (ACPC), which deals with general issues (e.g. planning, training, procedure and policy), and by the local Child Protection Conference (CPC), which decides what inquiries, assessment and/or invention are needed in respect of a child, including whether to put the child on the child protection register. As part of this emphasis on inter-agency co-operation, s.27 of the Children Act provides that local authorities, local education authorities, local housing authorities and local health authorities (or National Health Service Trusts) have a right to request help from each other and a reciprocal duty to provide it, except where this is incompatible with their own statutory obligations. Under s.27, for example, a social services department could ask a local housing department to provide accommodation for a child leaving care, and the housing department would be obliged to assist. Courts and local authorities must also work together and give each other mutual respect.

An important task for social services departments is to decide whether a child is a 'child in need' or is a child suffering, or at risk of suffering, harm. In the latter case, more drastic intervention and protection are likely to be needed. Once a local authority has been alerted about a child, it will conduct an initial assessment, although the assessment may be extremely brief if the criteria for initiating child protection inquiries are satisfied (see *Framework for Assessing Children in Need and their Families*, Department of Health, 2000, available on its website, see end of chapter). If at the initial assessment it is evident that the child is suffering, or is likely to suffer, significant harm, then the local authority is under a duty to make such inquiries as it considers necessary to enable it to decide whether to take any action to safeguard or promote the child's welfare (s.47(1)). This will mean visiting the child to make an assessment, unless there is already sufficient information available (s.47(4)). However, if access to the child is thwarted and the local authority is concerned about the child, then it will have to consider applying for an emergency protection order (see below).

If, following initial inquiries, the child is found not be at risk of harm, social services will still consider whether the child and his or her family need ongoing support, and it can, if appropriate, put in place various protective plans without the need to hold a child protection conference (see below). However, if it is established that the child is, or is at risk of, suffering significant harm, then social services will convene a child protection conference, a multi-agency meeting, at which information will be assessed and plans made to safeguard and promote the child's welfare. If the child is, or will be, at risk, the child's name is placed on the child protection register under the category of physical, emotional or sexual abuse, or neglect. Following the decision to register the child, the conference must next formulate a child protection plan, which may mean initiating care proceedings. A key worker for the child must also be appointed. Regular reviews must be carried out, and if the child is no longer at risk of significant harm, the child will be de-registered. If the initial assessment reveals a likelihood of serious immediate harm, emergency protection measures will have to be taken. The general approach adopted in *Working Together*, however, is one of minimum state intervention. Thus putting the child's name on the child protection register and initiating care proceedings are steps taken only in the last resort. Only in exceptional cases is there compulsory intervention by social services.

As a key principle of good practice is the promotion of positive partnerships between families and the State, parents and families are encouraged to participate in the decision-making process. Thus, only in exceptional circumstances will parents be excluded from meetings, and, if they are excluded, they must be allowed to express their views in other ways. Families are also encouraged to participate actively in the decision-making process through the use of Family Group Conferences (FGCs), through referral to advice and advocacy services, and through the sharing of information to help them understand the child protection process. However, despite the emphasis on parental involvement, Lindley and Richards (2000, at p.213) state that 'it remains the case that parents whose children are the subject of compulsory intervention by the state are inevitably unequal partners in the process,' and that while the guidance improves the position of parents 'by raising the expectation that they should be encouraged and empowered to participate, ... it does not create a "right" for them to be involved or represented.'

16.4 Local Authority Support for Children and Families

Under Part III of the Children Act 1989, local authorities have a duty to provide support for children in need and their families. In this context, 'family' means more than just parent(s) and children, as it includes any person with parental responsibility for a child in need or any other person with whom the child is living (s.17(10)). Services can only be provided, however, where they are necessary to safeguard or promote the welfare of a child in need (s.17(3)). Part III duties include the provision of services (ss.17–19) and the provision of accommodation (ss.20 and 21). Local authorities have duties to children 'looked after' by them (ss.22 and 23) and must provide advice and assistance (s.24), and in some cases provide secure accommodation (s.25). Local authorities must hold case-reviews, co-operate with each other and consult education authorities (see ss.26–30). Schedule 2 to the Children Act lists the services which local authorities can supply for children in need and their families (see below). It should be noted, however, that the welfare principles in s.1 of the Children Act do not apply to Part III duties and powers (see *Re M (Secure Accommodation Order)* [1995] 1 FLR 418).

The provision of support for families and children under Part III of the Children Act may obviate the need to bring care or supervision proceedings. Help and support for the child in his or her own home is the preferred option, with compulsory intervention by court order only in the last resort. The Children Act Guidance and Regulations (*Family Support, Day Care and Educational Provision for Young Children*, Vol. 2, para. 1.2, Department of Health, 1991) provides that:

> '[T]he best place for the child to be brought up is usually in his own family, and ... the child in need (who includes the child with disabilities) can be helped most effectively if the local authority, working in partnership with parents, provides a range and level of services appropriate to the child's needs.'

However, although the Children Act lays down a duty to safeguard and promote the welfare of children, the provision of services is only a discretionary matter. In fact, it is important when reading the Children Act to distinguish between statutory duties and statutory discretions. Sometimes the Act uses the word 'shall'. Sometimes it uses the word 'may' or the words 'shall, so far as is reasonably practicable.' Sometimes the provisions in Part III often merely require a local authority to take 'reasonable steps' to provide such services 'as is appropriate.' The provision of services is therefore ultimately a question of local authority policy and depends on the allocation and availability of resources, which are often limited. Challenges in respect of Part III provision can be made by bringing a complaint to a Complaints Panel or by bringing an application for judicial review (see 16.10 below). However, because of the decision in *R* v. *Gloucestershire County Council ex parte Barry* [1997] AC 584, where it was held, in the context of the community care legislation, that 'need' is a relative concept and that local authority resources are a relevant consideration, successful challenges by way of judicial review against local authorities in respect of children in need are likely to be difficult (see Hogg, 2000). Although there are various remedies for challenging local authority action or inaction under Part III (see 16.10), it is not possible to force a local authority to act by applying for a s.8 specific issue under the Children Act (see 12.4, and also *Re J (Leave to Apply for a Specific Issue Order)* 1995] 1 FLR 669).

Local authorities have various duties to children in need, but they include in particular the following duties:

- to safeguard and promote the child's welfare (s.22(3));
- to consult the wishes and feelings of the child, his or her parents, any person who has parental responsibility for the child, and any other person whom the local authority considers relevant (s.22(4));
- to provide accommodation (s.23(2));
- to maintain the child (s.23(1)(b), s.29);
- to promote contact (Sched. 2, para. 4);
- to provide 'after care' for children who leave care (s.24(1)).

Other duties are listed in Part II of Sched. 2 to the Children Act.

(a) Who is a 'Child in Need'?

Local authorities' duties towards children under Part III of the Children Act 1989 are towards children in need. A child is in need if (s.17(10)):

'(a) he is unlikely to achieve or maintain, or to have the opportunity of achieving or maintaining, a reasonable standard of health or development without the provision for him of services by a local authority under [Part III];

(b) his health or development is likely to be significantly impaired, or further impaired, without the provision for him of such services; or

(c) he is disabled.'

A child is 'disabled' for the purposes of s.17(10) if he is blind, deaf or dumb, or suffers from mental disorder of any kind, or is substantially and permanently handicapped by illness, injury or congenital deformity or such other disability as may be prescribed. 'Development' means physical, intellectual, emotional, social or behavioural development, and 'health' means physical or mental health (s.17(11)).

(b) The Part III General Duty

The general duty of local authorities under Part III is laid down in s.17(1) which provides that:

'It shall be the general duty of every local authority (in addition to the other duties imposed on them by [Part III of the Act]) –

(a) to safeguard and promote the welfare of children within their area who are in need; and

(b) so far as is consistent with that duty, to promote the upbringing of such children by their families, by providing a range and level of services appropriate to those children's needs.'

Section 17(2) provides that for the purpose principally of facilitating the discharge of their general duty under this section, every local authority shall have the specific duties and powers set out in Part I of Sched. 2 to the Children Act.

(c) Services for Children in Need

The general duty of local authorities laid down in s.17(1) above is facilitated by the performance of specific duties and powers laid down in Part I of Sched. 2 (s.17(2)), e.g. the identification and assessment of children in need, advertising available services, keeping a register of and providing services for disabled children, preventing neglect and abuse, providing accommodation for those who are ill-treating, or are likely to ill-treat, children, in order to reduce the need for criminal or civil proceedings, reintegrating children in need with their families, promoting contact between a child and his family, etc. Where a child in need is living with his or her family, appropriate services must be provided, e.g. advice, activities, home help, travelling assistance and assistance to enable the child and his or her family to have a holiday. Local authorities must establish 'family centres', where children, parents, those with parental responsibility or carers can go for advice, guidance, or counselling, and for various social and cultural activities. Local authorities must also, when making day-care arrangements or recruiting local authority foster-parents, consider the different racial groups to which children belong. Services under Part III can be of assistance in kind or exceptionally in cash (s.17(6)). Conditions can be imposed as to repayment of cash, unless a person is receiving Income Support or Family Credit (s.17(7)). Before providing assistance or imposing conditions, the financial means of the child and his or her parents must be considered (s.17(8)). Local authorities have a duty to facilitate the provision of similar services by others bodies such as voluntary organisations (e.g. NSPCC and Dr Barnados) and may delegate their powers to other bodies (s.17(5)).

(d) Provision of Day Care

Local authorities must provide appropriate day care for pre-school children in need, and they can if they wish provide it for children who are not in need (s.18(1)(2) and (4)). School-children in need must be provided with care or supervised activities outside school hours or during school holidays (s.18(5)) and children not in need may be provided with care or supervised activities (s.18(6)). The Act contains lengthy provisions for the review of day care, in particular in respect of child-minders.

(e) The Provision of Accommodation

An important duty of local authorities under Part III is the duty to provide accommodation for children in need (ss.20–25). Some families may need help, for instance, when a parent dies or a parent is ill, or for some other reason cannot care for a child. Section 20(1) provides that every local authority must provide accommodation for any child in need aged under 16 within its area who appears to require accommodation as a result of:

'(a) there being no person who has parental responsibility for him;

(b) his being lost or having been abandoned; or

(c) the person who has been caring for him being prevented (whether or not permanently, and for whatever reason) from providing him with suitable accommodation or care.'

Accommodation must also be provided for a child aged 16 or over if a local authority considers the child's welfare is likely to be seriously prejudiced if accommodation is not provided (s.20(3)). Accommodation in a community home can be provided for someone aged 16 to 21 if it would safeguard or promote his or her welfare (s.20(5)). In *Re T (Accommodation by Local Authority)* [1995] 1 FLR 159, a girl aged 17 was refused accommodation by the director of social services even though the local authority's complaints panel had upheld her complaint. Her application for judicial review was allowed, as the director of social services had erred in considering only her past circumstances and not considering whether to exercise the s.17 powers to such a degree as to avoid serious prejudice to the girl's welfare in the future.

However, a local authority is under no duty to provide accommodation under s.20 if any person with parental responsibility objects, and that person is willing and able to provide accommodation or able to arrange it (s.20(7)). The only exception is where a person with a residence order or who has care of the child under a court order agrees to the child being accommodated by the local authority (s.20(9)). Any person with parental responsibility for the child may remove the child from local authority accommodation at any time without giving notice (s.20(8)), except where the child is aged 16 or over and he or she agrees to being provided with accommodation (s.20(1)). As the arrangement is voluntary, the local authority must comply with the wishes of persons with parental responsibility, unless the child is suffering, or is likely to suffer, significant harm, in which case an application for a care or supervision order or emergency protection order may be necessary. Decisions about where the child should live remain with parents, not the local authority, as one aspect of parental responsibility is the right to decide where a child should live. In *R* v. *Tameside Metropolitan Borough Council ex parte J* [2000] 1 FLR 942, the parents of a seriously disabled 13-year-old girl successfully challenged by way of judicial review a local authority's decision to move their daughter from a residential home into foster-care. Scott Baker J said that a local authority which accommodates a child pursuant to s.20 is able to exercise mundane day-to-day powers of management in respect of a child, but a move of the kind envisaged went much further and trespassed into the kind of decision-making that was ultimately exercised by persons with parental responsibility. In respect of a child accommodated under Part III of the Children Act, a local authority has no power to move the child to different accommodation where it is contrary to parental wishes. The only way in which a local authority can override parental wishes is by bringing care proceedings in respect of the child or taking emergency action.

Before providing accommodation, a local authority must, so far as is reasonably practicable and consistent with the child's welfare, ascertain the child's wishes about the provision of accommodation and give due consideration to those wishes having regard to the child's age and understanding (s.20(6)). The local authority must also draw up a written care plan for the child (Arrangements for Placement of Children (General) Regulations 1991). Once a child is being accommodated by the local authority, the child is described as being 'looked after' by the local authority, whereupon it has certain statutory duties in respect of that child (ss.23–30). Children who are in care under a court order are also described as being 'looked after' and similar duties are owed to them under the same provisions.

Accommodation can be provided by the local authority by placing the child with another family, with a relative, with some other suitable person, or in a children's home (s.23(2)). Any family member, relative and any other person providing accommodation for a child is described as being a local authority foster-parent (s.23(3)), and arrangements for fostering and supervision and inspection of foster parents and their premises must be carried out by the local authority (see Arrangements for Placement of Children (General) Regulations 1991; Foster Placement (Children) Regulations 1991). There are also provisions in the Children Act governing accommodation in children's homes.

16.5 Care and Supervision Proceedings

Voluntary arrangements provided under Part III of the Children Act 1989 may not work in some cases, or it may come to the notice of a local authority that a child is being, or is at risk of being, harmed. In such circumstances a local authority may have to intervene by bringing proceedings for a care or supervision order under Part IV of the Act, or by taking emergency action under Part V.

A care order places a child in the care of a designated local authority. A supervision order places a child under the supervision of a designated local authority or a probation officer. A care order is a stronger and more serious order than a supervision order, and is only made in preference to a supervision order if it is really necessary for the child's protection (*Re B (Care or Supervision Order)* [1996] 2 FLR 693). The court has the power to make a different order from that applied for (see *Re C (Care or Supervision Order)* [1999] 2 FLR 621, where a supervision order was made when the local authority had requested a care order), but the court has stressed that there must be cogent and strong reasons to force upon a local authority the more Draconian care order (see Hale J in *Oxfordshire County Council v. L (Care or Supervision Order)* [1998] 1 FLR 70). As Part IV proceedings are 'family proceedings' for the purposes of the Children Act (s.8(3)), the court can make a s.8 order instead of a care or supervision order, either on an application or of its own motion (12.4, and see also *Re K (Care Order or Residence Order)* [1995] 1 FLR 675). The court has jurisdiction to hear an application for a care or supervision order if the child is habitually resident or resident in England and Wales (ss.1 and 3 Family Law Act 1986, and see *Re R (Care Order: Jurisdiction)* [1995] 1 FLR 711). However, the court has no jurisdiction to do so once the child has reached the age of 17 (s.31(3)).

If the court makes a care order, it cannot dictate how the local authority should implement it (*Re T (A Minor)(Care Order: Conditions)* [1994] 2 FLR 423), as to do so would circumscribe the wide discretionary powers entrusted to local authorities by Parliament. However, there are limits on local authorities' powers. Thus, for instance, the court has no inherent jurisdiction (see 12.8) to grant an injunction in relation to the exercise by a local authority of its statutory powers (e.g. to restrain a parent from going within a certain distance of where a child in care lives, see *Devon County Council v. B* [1997] 1 FLR 591).

One criticism sometimes made by the courts is that there is nothing in the Children Act which allows the court to compel a local authority to institute care or supervision proceedings. All the court can do is make a direction under s.37 (see 12.8) that a local authority investigate the child's circumstances. Judicial concern has been voiced about the court's lack of power to compel a local authority to take action (see Stephen Brown P in *Nottinghamshire County Council v. P* [1994] Fam 18, at 43). The position was different before the Children Act came into force, as the divorce court and the High Court in wardship could make care or supervision orders in exceptional circumstances, even though there had been no application for such an order.

(a) Who can Apply for Care and Supervision Orders?

Only local authorities or bodies authorised by the Secretary of State can institute care or supervision proceedings. The National Society for the Prevention of Cruelty to Children (NSPCC) is the only 'authorised' body (s.31(9)), but in practice most applications are brought by local authorities as they have a duty to investigate cases where children are suffering, or are at risk of suffering, significant harm (ss.37 and 47). Parents, guardians, friends, relatives and children cannot apply for an order, but as local authorities have a duty to investigate any reported harm, a parent, relative or child can give a social services department details of any harm or suspected harm, whereupon the local authority must make enquiries, provide assistance under Part III of the Children Act or, where necessary, institute care or supervision proceedings under Part IV, or take emergency action under Part V.

(b) The 'Two-Stage Exercise'

When deciding whether or not to make a care order or supervision order, the court performs a two-stage exercise. At the first stage (the 'threshold stage'), the court must be satisfied that one (or more) of the 'threshold criteria' laid down in s.31(2) is proved (see below). This inquiry 'has to be treated as a clinical issue of fact, determined in the light of the circumstances prevailing when the process was initiated' (Waite LJ in *Re S (Discharge of Care Order)* [1995] 2 FLR 639 at 643, referring to *Re M (A Minor)(Care Order: Threshold Conditions)* [1994] 2 AC 424, see below). Once the threshold stage is crossed, the court at the second stage (the 'welfare stage') must apply the welfare test (s.1(1)), the welfare checklist (s.1(3)) and the no-order presumption (s.1(5)) (see 12.3) to decide whether or not to make a care or supervision order. The threshold stage is, as its name says, only a threshold, so that even if it is crossed, the court need not make a care or supervision order and may even decide to make a different order. As care and supervision proceedings are family proceedings, it might decide instead to make a residence order (see 12.4). However, if the court decides to make a residence order, it must also make an interim supervision order, unless the child's welfare is safeguarded without such an order (s.38(3)). In *Lancashire County Council* v. *B* [2000] 1 FLR 583, the House of Lords stated that it by no means follows that because the threshold conditions are satisfied, the court will proceed to make a care or supervision order. Whether it does so will depend on a detailed assessment of the child's welfare in all the circumstances of the case.

Thus, whether or not a care order or a supervision order, or no order at all, will be made depends on the facts of each case. Expert evidence is important and the court will also consider the recommendations of the child's guardian *ad litem*. The facts of earlier cases do not necessarily create precedents for later cases. In *Re SH (Care Order: Orphan)* [1995] 1 FLR 746, for example, a care order was made in respect of an orphaned boy, but no order was made in respect of orphaned children in *Birmingham City Council* v. *D* and *Birmingham City Council* v. *M* [1994] 2 FLR 502, as they were satisfactorily accommodated in care under Part III of the Act.

(c) The 'Threshold Criteria' for making a Care or Supervision Order

At the 'threshold' stage, the court must be satisfied (s.31(2)):

'(a) that the child concerned is suffering, or is likely to suffer, significant harm; and
(b) that the harm, or likelihood of harm, is attributable to—
   (i) the care given to the child, or likely to be given to him if the order were not made, not being what it would be reasonable to expect a parent to give him; or
   (ii) the child's being beyond parental control.'

Significant harm is an important concept in the Children Act (see ss.31, 43 and 44), but the word 'significant' is not defined. Whether harm is 'significant' depends on all the circumstances of the case. In the DHSS, *Review of Child Care Law – Report to Ministers of an Interdepartmental Working Party* (1985) at 15.15, the Government stated:

'We consider that, having set an acceptable standard of upbringing for the child, it should be necessary to show some *substantial* deficit in that standard. Minor short-comings in the health care provided or minor deficits in physical, psychological or social development should not give rise to compulsory intervention unless they are having, or are likely to have, serious and lasting effects upon the child.'

The Department of Health's *Guidance*, Vol. 3 suggested that harm may be 'significant' if it is likely to have a 'serious and lasting' effect on the child. The word 'care' in s.31(2)(b)(i) is also vague and is also not defined in the Act. However 'care' will include both physical and emotional care.

Section 31(9) defines 'harm' as ill-treatment or the impairment of health (physical or mental) or development (physical, intellectual, emotional, social or behavioural), and provides that 'ill-treatment' includes sexual abuse and forms of ill-treatment which are not physical. Abandonment of a child can constitute 'ill-treatment' under s.31(9) (*Re M (Care Order: Parental Responsibility)* [1996] 2 FLR 84). Where the question of harm suffered by a child turns on the child's health or development, his or her health or development must be compared with that which could reasonably be expected of a similar child (s.31(10)). In *Re O (A Minor)(Care Proceedings: Education)* [1992] 1 WLR 912, where a care order was made in respect of a 15-year-old girl who had continually played truant, Ewbank J held that 'a similar child' meant a child of equivalent intellectual and social development. As far as lack of parental control is concerned (see s.31(2)(b)(ii)), it does not matter whether the child is beyond parental control because of the fault of the parent(s) or of the child (*Re O*, above); and harm, or likelihood of harm, attributable to the child's being beyond parental control is capable of describing a state of affairs in the past, the present or the future (Stuart-White J in *M* v. *Birmingham City Council* [1994] 2 FLR 141).

(d) When must the Threshold Conditions be Satisfied?

In *Re M (A Minor)(Care Order: Threshold Conditions)* [1994] 2 AC 424, the House of Lords had to consider when the threshold conditions in s.31(2) have to be satisfied. At first instance, Bracewell J made a care order in respect of M (a four-month-old child whose mother had been murdered in his presence), holding that the relevant date for 'is suffering' in s.31(2)(a) is the period immediately before the process of protecting the child had been put in motion. On appeal, the Court of Appeal substituted the care order with a residence order, holding that the threshold criteria had not been satisfied on the relevant date, namely the date when the case came before the court for disposal. The father of the child appealed to the House of Lords, which allowed his appeal and restored the care order, holding that nothing in s.31(2) required that the satisfaction of the threshold principles was to be disassociated from the time when the local authority made the application. As the relevant date was the date upon which the local authority had initiated protective proceedings, the court had jurisdiction to make the care order.

(e) The Standard of Proof in Care Proceedings

In *Re H (Minors)(Sexual Abuse: Standard of Proof)* [1996] AC 563, *sub nom Re H and R (Child Sexual Abuse: Standard of Proof)* [1996] 1 FLR 80, the House of Lords laid down the standard of proof which applies to the threshold test in s.31(2), Here the local authority applied for care orders in respect of three girls (aged 13, 8 and 2), after the eldest daughter (aged 14) alleged she had been sexually abused by her mother's cohabitant. He was charged with rape but was acquitted. The applications for care orders were dismissed, as the threshold conditions in s.31(2) were not satisfied. It could not be established to the requisite high standard of proof that the 14-year-old daughter's allegations were true. The House of Lords, by a majority, held that the standard of proof in cases involving the care of children was the ordinary civil standard of balance of probability, but that the more improbable the event, the stronger the evidence had to be before, on the balance of probability, the occurrence of the event would be established. Lord Nicholls said that a conclusion that a child is suffering, or is likely to suffer, harm 'must be based on facts, not just suspicion.'

The House of Lords unanimously rejected, however, a submission that 'likely' in the phrase 'likely to suffer harm' meant 'probable', but held that 'likely' meant likely 'in the sense of a real possibility, a possibility that cannot sensibly be ignored having regard to the nature and gravity of the feared harm in the particular case' (Lord Nicholls).

Re H was applied in *Re M and R (Child Abuse: Evidence)* [1996] 2 FLR 195, where the Court of Appeal held that at both the threshold stage and the welfare stage it was not open to the court to find children were at risk of sexual abuse on the basis of a mere suspicion of sexual abuse in the past. The Court of Appeal held that factor (e) in the welfare checklist in s.1(3) of the Children Act (any harm which the child is suffering or is at risk of suffering, see 12.3) dealt with actual harm or risk of harm and not with possibilities, so that there was no justification for the proposition that, because the child's welfare was the paramount consideration, the standard of proof for establishing harm could be less than the balance of probabilities. (For another application of *Re H*, see *Re P (Sexual Abuse: Standard of Proof)* [1996] 2 FLR 333.)

McCafferty (1999) has criticised the decision in *Re H* for creating a complicated standard of proof for allegations of serious abuse. He says that the decision is wrong because it has had the effect of taking the non-intervention principle enshrined in the Children Act too far, particularly in the light of art. 3 of the European Convention on Human Rights (right not to be subject to inhuman and degrading treatment) and its interpretation by the Court of Human Rights in *A* v. *United Kingdom (Human Rights: Punishment of Child)* [1998] 2 FLR 959 (see 10.4). McCafferty argues that the child's welfare should be paramount not just at the second stage (the welfare stage), but also at the threshold stage. Hemingway and Williams (1997) have also criticised the decision in *Re H*. They claim that its reasoning is flawed and that as a result of the decision there is a real danger that some children will not be afforded the protection they deserve.

(f) The Natural Parent Presumption

Sometimes the court will have to decide which of two persons shall look after the child under a care order. Where one of these persons is the child's natural parent, the court will first consider the natural parent as the potential carer, and then go on to decide whether there are any compelling factors that displace the presumption that a child has a right to be brought up by his or her natural parent(s). The Court of Appeal applied this rule in *Re D (Care: Natural Parent Presumption)* [1999] 1 FLR 134, where it ordered a child to be placed with his father under a care order rather than with his grandmother, even though this would separate him from his elder siblings who were living with their grandmother. The Court of Appeal held that the judge had erred in failing to give sufficient weight to the presumption in favour of the father and had given too much weight to the sibling relationship, but it did acknowledge that there might be other cases where the presumption in favour of a natural parent might give way to the rule that it is best to keep siblings together wherever possible. It should also be mentioned that the natural parent presumption is one of the reasons for the need to satisfy the threshold criteria. In this way, intrusive State intervention is avoided and the right to family life not breached.

(g) Shared Care and the Threshold Criteria

In *Lancashire County Council* v. *B* [2000] 1 FLR 583, the House of Lords had to decide how the threshold criteria should be applied to a child who had been harmed (child A) but whose care had been shared by a number of people (here the child's parents and a childminder). In this case A, a young baby, had suffered harm as a result of being shaken, but it could not be established whether the parents of child A or the childminder (the mother of child B) were responsible. In the Court of Appeal it was held that the threshold criteria in s.31(2)(b)(i) were satisfied in respect of child A, but not in respect of child B (because she had suffered no harm), even though it was unclear whether the parents or the childminder were responsible for child A's injuries.

The parents of A appealed to the House of Lords, arguing first that the harm suffered to their child had to be attributable to their care, and secondly that the continuation of the care proceedings infringed their right to family life under art. 8 of the European Convention on Human Rights. The House of Lords unanimously dismissed their appeal, as the threshold conditions had been met. Lords Nicholls, Slyn, Nolan and Hoffman said that, under s.31(2)(b)(i), the court had to be satisfied that the harm suffered by the child was attributable to 'the care given to the child,' and that this normally referred to the care given by parents or other primary carer. However, their Lordships held that different considerations applied in cases of shared care where the child suffers harm but the court is unable to identify which of the carers provided the deficient care. They said that the words 'care given to the child' embraced the care given by any of the carers and that the threshold conditions could be satisfied where there was no more than a possibility that the parents were responsible for inflicting the injuries. This interpretation, their Lordships said, was necessary to permit the court to intervene to protect a child at risk where the individual responsible for harming the child could not be identified. Lord Clyde, however, said that s.31(2)(b)(i) simply defined the standard of care and did not require the identification of the person who caused the harm. His Lordship said that no restriction limiting the subsection's scope to care given by particular kinds of people could be read into it. The House of Lords stressed that in cases of this kind the fact that the parents had not been proved to be responsible for the child's injuries could be taken into account at the 'welfare stage' after the threshold conditions have been met. The House of Lords also held that there had been no breach of art. 8, as the steps taken by the local authority had been those reasonably necessary to pursue the legitimate aim of protecting the child from injury.

The *Lancashire* case generated some critical academic comment. Hayes (2000) argued that, as child B had been left unprotected, the decision could lead to some children at risk being left unprotected by the law, as it would make it 'easier for a local authority to satisfy the threshold criteria in respect of a child who has suffered harm than it is to satisfy the criteria on the basis of "likely" harm' (p.264). Hall (2000) questioned how the decision squared with the decision in *Re H (Minors)(Sexual Abuse: Standard of Proof)* (above), where the House of Lords had held that significant harm had to be based on a real possibility of risk, not mere suspicion. In the *Lancashire* case, the threshold conditions in respect of child A were met even though it was not clear which person had caused the harm. (See also the case-note by Perry [2000] CFLQ 301.)

(h) Considering the Local Authority's Care Plan

The local authority is required to draw up a care plan (see Arrangements for Placement of Children (General Regulations) 1991) which it should draw up in as objective manner as possible and in neutral and unemotive language (Wall J in *Re DH (A Minor)(Child Abuse)* [1994] 1 FLR 679, at 687). A care plan includes information about the aim of the plan, a timetable of arrangements, the child's needs, including contact, the views of others, placement details, and management and support to be provided by the local authority. Local authorities are also required to take into account the provisions of the European Convention on Human Rights (see 1.5), in particular art. 8 which guarantees a right to family life (see *Care Plans and Care Proceedings under the Children Act 1989*, LAC (99)29). The care plan is considered by the court at the second stage of the proceedings (the welfare stage), once the threshold conditions have been met. The court must carefully scrutinise the plan in order to be satisfied that giving parental responsibility to the local authority will not do more harm than good for the child's welfare (see Hale J in *Berkshire County Council* v. *B* [1997] 2 FLR 171). If the court considers that the care plan is not in the child's best interests, or more information is needed, it can refuse to make a care order, or it can make an interim order. In *Re J (Minors)(Care: Care Plan)* [1994] 1 FLR 253, Wall J stressed that the care plan is an extremely important document and that it should accord, if possible, with *The Children Act 1989 Guidance and Regulations: Family Placements*, vol. 3, chap. 2, para. 2.62. His Lordship said that in care proceedings a proper balance should be struck between the need for a local authority to satisfy the court about the appropriateness of the care plan and the avoidance of an over-zealous investigation into matters within the administrative discretion of the local authority. He said at 261:

> 'A properly constructed care plan is not only essential to enable the court to make its decision based on all the known facts; it will or should have been compiled either in consultation with the parents and other interested parties, including where appropriate the child or children involved, or at the very least after taking their views and wishes into account. It will thus enable the other parties to focus on the relevant issues. Much court time and costs may thereby be saved.'

The court expects a local authority to pay due regard to the function of the judge in giving judgment on the care plan after its careful appraisal, even though statutory responsibility for a child remains solely with the local authority (not the court) once a care order is made (Thorpe LJ in *Re CH (Care or Interim Care Order)* [1998] 1 FLR 402, at 410).

Although the court must consider the care plan, it has no power to impose conditions on a care order in respect of the child's accommodation arrangements or direct how the local authority should look after the child (*Re T (A Minor) (Care Order: Conditions)* [1994] 2 FLR 423 and *Re S and D (Children: Powers of Court)* [1995] 2 FLR 456). Thus, the court has no power to add a direction to a care order directing that a guardian *ad litem* be allowed to continue his or her involvement with a child (*Kent County Council* v. *C* [1993] 1 FLR 308). Neither has the court power to impose conditions on an interim order (e.g. in respect of a residential assessment of a mother and child, see *Re M (Interim Care Order: Assessment)* [1996] 2 FLR 464). Once a care order is made, statutory responsibility for the child passes to the local authority, and the court has no power (unless expressly provided by statute) to interfere with the wide discretionary powers entrusted to local authorities by Parliament (*A* v. *Liverpool City Council* [1982] AC 363).

If the court does not agree with the care plan, it can refuse to make a final care or supervision order (*Re T (A Minor) (Care Order: Conditions)*, above), but it often makes an interim care order even though it is not completely happy with the plan (*Re L (Sexual Abuse: Standard of Proof)* [1996] 1 FLR 116, approving Wall J's views in *Re J (Minors) (Care: Care Plan)*, above). Cases where it is appropriate to refuse to make an order are rare (*Re T (A Minor)(Care Order: Conditions)*, above). Before making a care order, the court must consider the arrangements that the local authority has made, or proposes to make, in respect of contact with the child (see 16.6 below), and invite the parties to the proceedings to comment on those arrangements (s.34(11)).

(i) Care Order or Supervision Order?

Although the threshold criteria for both a care order and a supervision order are the same, the two orders are 'wholly and utterly different', and a supervision order will 'not in any sense be seen as a sort of watered down version of a care order' (Judge Coningsby QC in *Re S (J) (A Minor)(Care or Supervision Order)* [1993] 2 FLR 919 at 950, cited by Dillon LJ in *Re V (Care or Supervision Order)* [1996] 1 FLR 776 at 788). As a care order is the most Draconian order that can be made under the Children Act, it is made only in preference to a supervision order where the stronger order is necessary for the child's protection (Hale J in *Re O (Care or Supervision Order)* [1996] 2 FLR 755, and see also *Re B (Care or Supervision Order)* [1996] 2 FLR 693 and *Oxfordshire County Council v. L (Care or Supervision Order)* [1998] 1 FLR 70). In *Re O (Care or Supervision Order)* above, Hale J said that it is right to approach the question of the child's interests from the point of view of the non-intervention principle in s.1(5) of the Children Act (see 12.2), and the court should start from the premise that less, rather than more, intervention is generally in a child's best interests. Although the court should be slow to impose the Draconian solution of a care order where lesser intervention is appropriate, Hale J held that the court must give very cogent reasons if it decides to make a different order from that requested. In *Re K (Supervision Orders)* [1999] 2 FLR 303, Wall J said that a supervision order should only be made if the child needs more protection than can be given voluntarily by the local authority.

(j) The Effect of a Care Order

A care order has various legal effects. Once it is made, the child is described as being 'looked after' by the local authority, whereupon it has various duties and powers in respect of the child. The court no longer monitors the administrative arrangements for the child and has no say in these arrangements unless there is an application before the court (Butler-Sloss LJ in *Re B (Minors)(Care: Contact: Local Authority's Plan)* [1993] 1 FLR 543 at 548). The guardian *ad litem*'s involvement in the case also terminates on the making of the care order (*Kent County Council v. C* [1993] Fam 57, [1993] 1 FLR 308).

A care order imposes a duty on the local authority to receive and keep the child in its care (s.33(1)), and under s.22 the local authority has a general duty to safeguard and promote the child's welfare. A care order also gives the local authority parental responsibility for the child, and the power to determine the extent to which the child's parent(s) or guardian may meet their parental responsibility where needed to safeguard and promote the child's welfare (s.33(3) and (4)). Although the local authority has parental responsibility, it has no power to consent or refuse to consent to adoption, or to appoint a guardian or to change a child's religion (s.33(6)). Neither has it power to prevent an unmarried mother entering into a parental responsibility agreement with the child's father (*Re X (Parental Responsibility Agreement: Children in Care)* [2000] 1 FLR 517), although it can apply for a parental responsibility agreement or order to be brought to an end (see s.4(3)). Parents do not lose parental responsibility while a care order is in force and there is a presumption of reasonable contact between the child, parents and other persons (see 16.6 below). Thus, a parent remains entitled to do what is reasonable in all the circumstances for the purpose of safeguarding and promoting the child's welfare (s.33(5)), and retains any right, duty, power and responsibility in relation to the child and his or her property under any other enactment (s.33(9)), e.g. to make decisions about education and medical treatment. While a care order is in force, the child's surname cannot be changed and the child cannot be removed from the UK without the written consent of all those with parental responsibility, or otherwise with the permission of the court (s.33(7)). However, a local authority is permitted to take the child out of the UK for up to one month (s.33(8)(a)) and can under Sched. 2, para. 19 arrange (or assist in arranging) for the child to live outside England and Wales subject to the court's approval. A care order discharges any s.8 order, a supervision order and a school attendance order, and also terminates wardship (s.91). A care order remains in force until the child reaches 18, unless brought to an end earlier (s.91(2)).

(k) The Effect of a Supervision Order

A supervision order, unlike a care order, does not give a local authority parental responsibility, but places the child under the supervision of a designated local authority or a probation officer (s.31(1)(b)). Thus, safeguarding the child's interests remains the primary responsibility of the parents. As Bracewell J said in *Re T (A Minor)(Care or Supervision Order)* [1994] 1 FLR 103, the nature of a supervision order is to help and assist a child where the parents have full responsibility for care and upbringing. With a supervision order, the local authority merely assists and befriends the child (s.35(1)(a) and (b)), and the operation of any conditions or undertakings depends on parental agreement (see *Re B (Supervision Order: Parental Undertaking)* [1996] 1 FLR 676). A supervisor can, however, apply to have the supervision order varied or discharged where the order is not complied with, or a supervisor considers that the order is no longer necessary (s.35(1)(c)). Parts I and II of Sched. 3 to the Children Act list more specific powers in respect of supervision, e.g. the supervisor can give directions that the child live in a certain place, attend at a certain place and participate in certain activities. A supervision order can require a child to have a medical or psychiatric examination, but only with the child's consent if the child has sufficient understanding to make an informed decision, and only if satisfactory arrangements have been, or can be, made for the examination. A supervision order can be made in the first instance for up to one year, but the supervisor can apply to have the order extended for up to three years (Sched. 3, para. 6). The court has no power to impose conditions on a supervision order (*Re V (Care or Supervision Order)* [1996] 1 FLR 776, followed in *Re S (Care or Supervision Order)* [1996] 1 FLR 753).

(l) Interim Care and Supervision Orders

Before the final hearing, the court will often make a series of interim care or supervision orders under s.38 of the Children Act. The purpose of interim orders is to enable the court to maintain the status quo pending the final hearing, and for it to obtain any information needed about the child before it makes its final decision. Interim care or supervision orders can be made where care and supervision proceedings are adjourned (e.g. for inquiries or reports to be made), or where the court makes a s.37(1) order directing a local authority to investigate the child's circumstances (s.38(1)). However, an interim order can only be made if there are reasonable grounds for believing that the threshold criteria for making a care or supervision order are satisfied (s.38(2)). An interim order must be used for its intended purpose; it cannot be used to provide the court with continuing control over a local authority (see *Re L (Sexual Abuse: Standard of Proof)* [1996] 1 FLR 116 and *Re J (Minors)(Care: Care Plan)* [1994] 1 FLR 253). Although an interim order is a 'holding' order, it is regarded as a form of care order, so that once it is made, care of a child passes to the local authority and the manner in which the child is cared for passes out of the court's control. For this reason the court has no more power to impose conditions on an interim order than it has on a final order, except in respect of medical or psychiatric assessment (see below, and also *Re L (Interim Care Order: Power of Court)* [1996] 2 FLR 742).

If the court decides to make a residence order in care or supervision proceedings, an interim supervision order must also be made, unless the child's welfare is otherwise satisfactorily safeguarded (s.38(3)). There is no limit on the number of interim orders that can be made but, as delay is detrimental to the child (s.1(2)) and it is important to for a final decision to be made, interim orders are of limited duration (s.38(4) and (5)). They are effective for the period specified in the order but in any event are limited to eight weeks at the first instance and four weeks in subsequent orders (s.38(4)). There must always be good reason for the continuation of an interim care order (*C* v. *Solihull Metropolitan Borough Council* [1993] 1 FLR 290 and *Hounslow London Borough Council* v. *A* [1993] 1 FLR 702).

(m) Directing a Medical, Psychiatric or Other Examination or Assessment

The court can impose on an interim care or supervision order a direction ordering (s.38(6)) or prohibiting (s.38(7)) a medical, psychiatric or other examination or assessment. The court can name the person who is to perform the examination or assessment, but will not do so if that person is unwilling to carry out the assessment, as that would be contrary to the best interests of the child (see *Re W (Assessment of Child)* [1998] 1 FLR 630). In *Re C (Interim Care Order: Residential Assessment)* [1997] AC 489, [1997] 1 FLR 1, the House of Lords held that s.38(6) and (7) should be construed purposively, as the purpose of these provisions was to enable the court to obtain the information it needed to decide what final order to make, even though control over the child in all other respects was vested in the local authority. 'Other assessment' could therefore include assessment of a mother and child at a residential unit, despite the local authority objecting to it on the grounds of cost and the risk to the child if rehabilitation with the mother was to take place, and even though the assessment involved an assessment of the parent as well as the child.

In *Re M (Residential Assessment Directions)* [1998] 2 FLR 371, a mother applied for a direction under s.38(6) that she be assessed at a clinic to see whether her parenting problems could be ameliorated. Holman J, applying *Re C* above, granted the direction and said that although the welfare principle in s.1(1) of the Children Act does not apply to a direction application, a direction must not be contrary to a child's best interests and must be necessary to enable the court to decide whether to grant an application. Even if these requirements are satisfied, his Lordship said that the court retains an overall discretion as to whether it is appropriate to give the direction. In *Re B (Psychiatric Therapy for Parents)* [1999] 1 FLR 701, a direction was given under s.38(6) that parents receive a therapeutic programme which might prevent their child being adopted, but the local authority objected to this. The direction was overturned by the Court of Appeal, which held that 'assessment' under s.38(6) did not include treatment or therapy. The Court of Appeal stressed that, as the successful operation of the Children Act depended crucially on inter-disciplinarity and partnership, the circumstances in which a judge finds himself or herself in conflict with a responsible local authority should be restricted to an absolute minimum.

Although a child with sufficient understanding to make an informed decision can refuse to consent to an examination or assessment (s.38(6)), the court under its inherent jurisdiction (see 12.9) can override a child's refusal to submit to such an examination or assessment, even if the child has sufficient understanding for the purpose of s.38(6) (*South Glamorgan County Council v. W and B* [1993] 1 FLR 574).

(n) Discharge and Variation of Care and Supervision Orders

A care order can only be discharged, as variation would undermine a local authority's responsibility for a child. Application for discharge can be made by any person with parental responsibility, the child or the local authority (s.39(1)). A child does not need the prior permission of the court to make an application for discharge (*Re A (Care: Discharge Application by Child)* [1995] 1 FLR 599). Persons who do not have the requisite parental responsibility to apply for discharge can apply for a residence order which (if granted) discharges the care order (s.91(1)). Applications for discharge of care orders are usually made by local authorities who at every statutory case conference must consider whether to apply to discharge the order (Review of Children's Cases Regulations 1991). Instead of discharging a care order, the court can substitute it with a supervision order, and do so without the need to satisfy the significant harm test in s.31(2) (s.39(4) and (5)).

In an application for discharge, the court applies the s.1 welfare principle and the s.1(3) welfare checklist. A party does not have to satisfy the court that the threshold conditions for a care order no longer apply (see *Re S (Discharge of Care Order)* [1995] 2 FLR 639). In an appropriate case the court can discharge a care order and make the child a ward of court (12.9, and see also *Re RJ (Fostering: Person Disqualified)* [1999] 1 FLR 605). A further application to discharge a care order or to substitute a supervision order cannot be made for six months after the disposal of the original application for discharge, except with the court's permission (s.91(15)).

A supervision order can be varied or discharged on the application of any person with parental responsibility for the child, the child or the supervisor (s.39(2)). A supervision order can also be varied on an application by a person with whom the child is living, if the original order imposes a requirement which affects that person (s.39(3)). When exercising its powers, the court applies the welfare principle in s.1(1) of the Children Act, and the other s.1 provisions (see 12.3). A further application for discharge or variation of a supervision order cannot be made for six months after the original application, except with the court's permission (s.91(15)).

(o) Procedure in Care and Supervision Proceedings

Care or supervision proceedings normally commence in the magistrates' family proceedings court, but they can be transferred to a county court or the High Court (to consolidate proceedings or in urgent or serious cases), or transferred to another magistrates' family proceedings court (to consolidate proceedings or in urgent cases). An application for a care or supervision order can be made in care and supervision proceedings or in any family proceedings (s.31(4)) (for the definition of 'family proceedings', see 12.5). In addition to the local authority, the child and any person with parental responsibility are automatically parties to the proceedings, although other persons can apply to be joined (r.7 Family Proceedings Courts (Children Act 1989) Rules 1991). (See also 10.5 on representation of children.) Although fathers without parental responsibility have no right to be joined as a party to proceedings, they are entitled to notice of proceedings and are likely to be given permission by the court to take part. In *Re B (Care Proceedings: Notification of Father without Parental Responsibility)* [1999] 2 FLR 408, Holman J said that if an unmarried father wished to participate in care proceedings, he should be permitted to do so unless there is some justifiable reason to the contrary. Other persons without parental responsibility, on the other hand, must show justifiable reason why they should be made a party. Holman J also stated that a father without parental responsibility who showed an interest in seeking to participate in care proceedings and applying for orders himself was entitled to be seen by, and investigated by, the child's guardian *ad litem*. Any failure to allow an unmarried father without parental responsibility to participate in proceedings could be a breach of a right to family under art. 8 of the European Convention for the Protection of Human Rights. In *McMichael* v. *UK* [1995] 20 EHRR 205, the Court of Human Rights had held that failure to allow an unmarried father without parental responsibility to participate in a Scottish children's hearing was a breach of art. 8.

(p) *Appointment of a Guardian* ad Litem

In care and supervision proceedings, the court must appoint a guardian *ad litem* for the child, unless a guardian is not needed to safeguard the child's interests (s.41(1)). A guardian *ad litem* is usually a qualified social worker selected from a local authority panel of guardians *ad litem* who must be independent of the parties to prevent a conflict of interest arising. Besides having a general duty to safeguard the interests of the child in the manner prescribed by the rules of court (s.41(2)(b)), a guardian has specific duties, e.g. to ascertain the child's wishes and whether the child has sufficient understanding, to investigate all the circumstances, to interview people involved, to inspect records and to appoint professional assistance. The guardian has a right to examine and copy local authority records relating to a child, which can be admitted in evidence (s.42). This includes the minutes of any child protection conference and any report compiled by an area child protection committee (*Re R (Care Proceedings: Disclosure)* [2000] 2 FLR 751). When the investigation has been completed, the guardian *ad litem* must make a written report advising what should be done in the best interests of the child. The report (unless the court directs otherwise) must be filed at the court seven days before the hearing date, and copies served on all the parties. This report usually has a considerable influence on the court.

The guardian must appoint a solicitor to act for the child (if not already appointed), and must give instructions on the child's behalf, except where the child is capable of giving instructions and those instructions conflict with those of the guardian (when the solicitor must take instructions from the child) (rr.1(3) and 12(1)(a) Family Proceedings Courts (Children Act 1989) Rules 1991, and see *Re H (A Minor)(Care Proceedings: Child's Wishes)* [1993] 1 FLR 440).

(q) Appeals

Any party to the original proceedings for a care or supervision order can appeal against the making of, or refusal to make, a care or supervision order (including an interim order). Appeals from the magistrates' family proceedings court are to the High Court and from the county court and High Court to the Court of Appeal. Appeals against care orders are decided under the principle laid down by the House of Lords in *G* v. *G (Minors)(Custody Appeal)* [1985] 1 WLR 647, (1985) FLR 894. Thus the appellant is not entitled to a rehearing, and the appeal court will not interfere with a discretionary decision made by a lower court, unless the judge has erred in law, or is under a misapprehension of fact, or the decision is outside a band of reasonable discretion within which reasonable disagreement is possible. This rule applies to all appeals, whether heard by the Court of Appeal or not (see *Re S (Local Authority: Care Appeals)* [1997] 2 FLR 856, where Cazalet J stated that the principle in *G* v. *G* applied and that an appeal from a district judge is not to take the form of a new hearing but is dealt with in the same way as the Court of Appeal would deal with an appeal against the decision of a circuit judge).

16.6   Contact in Care

As a general rule, all children, whether or not in care, have a right to contact, so that cogent reasons are required for terminating contact between a child and his or her family (Balcombe LJ in *Re J (A Minor)(Contact)* [1994] 1 FLR 729 at p.735). Article 9(3) of the UN Convention on the Rights of the Child 1989 provides that 'States Parties must respect the right of the child who is separated from one or both parents to maintain personal relations and direct contact with both parents on a regular basis, except if it is contrary to the child's best interest.'

Children in care, like all other children, therefore have a right to contact, and there is a presumption that contact will be allowed. Maintaining contact is particularly important for children in care as it improves the chances of them being rehabilitated with their families. For this reason, s.34(1) of the Children Act creates a presumption of contact by providing that a local authority must (subject to the provisions of s.34) allow a child in care reasonable contact with the following persons: parents; guardian; a person with a residence order in his or her favour; and a person who has care of the child under an order made under the High Court's inherent jurisdiction (see 12.8). 'Reasonable' contact does not mean contact at the discretion of the local authority but contact which was agreed between the authority and the parents, or otherwise contact which is objectively reasonable (*Re P (Minors)(Contact with Children in Care)* [1993] 2 FLR 156).

Orders under s.34 can be made on application, or by the court of its own motion, when it is making a care order or in any family proceedings in connection with a child in care (s.34(5)). Orders can be made when the care order is made or at a later date (s.34(10)). Before making a care order, the court is required to consider the arrangements the local authority has made, or proposes to make, for contact and must invite the parties to the proceedings to comment on these arrangements (s.34(11)). Orders made under s.34 can be varied or discharged on the application of the local authority, the child, or any person named in the order (s.34(9)). The court can impose conditions on any s.34 order (s.34(7)). The principles which the court must apply when exercising its powers to make orders under s.34 are those laid down in s.1 of the Children Act (see 12.2), namely the welfare paramountcy principle (s.1(1)), the welfare checklist (s.1(3)), the no-delay principle (s.1(2)) and the non-intervention principle (s.1(5)).

There are two sorts of orders which can be made under s.34: (i) an order in respect of contact; and (ii) a s.34(4) order authorising a local authority to refuse contact.

(i) An Order in Respect of Contact

Under s.34(2), the court, on the application of the local authority or the child, has the power to make such order as it considers appropriate in respect of the contact which is to be allowed between the child and any named person. The court has no power under this section to make an order prohibiting the local authority from permitting parental contact with a child (*Re W (Section 34(2) Orders)* [2000] 1 FLR 502). Under s.34(3), the court may also make the same sort of order on an application by any person who has a right to reasonable contact under s.34(1) (see above), or by any person who has been granted permission to apply. Although a grandparent, a relative or a friend of a child are not allowed contact with a child as of right (unless they have a residence order in their favour, or an order made under the High Court's inherent jurisdiction), they may seek the prior permission of the court to apply for contact with the child in care (s.34(3)(b)). As the special position of relatives and friends and other persons connected with the child is recognised and protected by Sched. 2, para.15 of the Children Act, contact between the child and his or her relatives is assumed to be beneficial. For this reason, local authorities are required to file evidence to justify why it is not consistent with the child's welfare to promote such contact (see *Re M (Care: Contact: Grandmother's Application for Leave)* [1995] 2 FLR 86). In *Re M*, it was also held that the same criteria apply to applications for permission to apply for an order under s.34(3) as apply to applications for permission to apply for a s.8 order (see 12.6). The court must also consider the nature of the contact being sought, the connection of the applicant to the child, any disruption to the child, and the wishes of the parents and the local authority.

In *Re D and H (Care: Termination of Contact)* [1997] 1 FLR 841, the Court of Appeal held that it was wrong to make an order under s.34(2) or (5) phasing out contact between a mother and her children when such an order was inconsistent with the local authority's recommendations in its care plan (see also *Re T (Termination of Contact)* [1997] 1 FLR 841). The court can under s.34, however, order that parents have contact with their children, even though the local authority's long-term care plan is eventually to terminate contact because the children are to be adopted (*Berkshire County Council* v. *B* [1997] 1 FLR 171).

(ii) A Section 34(4) Order Authorising a Local Authority to Refuse Contact

A local authority or child can apply under s.34(4) for an order permitting the local authority to refuse contact between the child and any person(s) entitled to reasonable contact under s.34(1) (see above). In such an application the court balances the presumption of contact against the child's long-term welfare and considers the question of contact in relation to the care plan for the child. However, a s.34(4) order terminating contact will not be granted while there remains a realistic possibility of rehabilitation or where there is no foreseeable need to terminate contact (*Re T (Termination of Contact: Discharge of Order)* [1997] 1 FLR 517).

The leading case on s.34(4) is *In Re B (Minors)(Termination of Contact: Paramount Consideration)* [1993] Fam 301, *sub nom Re B (Minors)(Care: Contact: Local Authority's Plans)* [1993] 1 FLR 543. Here the Court of Appeal held that, as the child's welfare is the paramount consideration, the court can require a local authority to justify its long-term plans for a child in care, even though it has parental responsibility for the child. And, if the benefits

of contact outweigh the disadvantages of disrupting any of the local authority's plans, then the court must refuse the local authority's application for the
s.34(4) order. Butler-Sloss LJ, however, held that while Parliament had given
the court, not the local authority, the duty to decide on contact between the
child and those named in s.34(1), the proposals of a local authority had to
command the court's greatest respect and consideration. Although the ultimate
decision about contact belongs to the court, not the local authority, where the
nature and extent of contact is an integral part of a local authority's care plan,
the court should not decide precisely what contact is reasonable (*Re S (A
Minor)(Care: Contact Order)* [1994] 2 FLR 222). The court has the power to
make an interim order under s.34(4) allowing the authority to terminate contact (*West Glamorgan County Council* v. *P* [1992] 2 FLR 369). If the court
refuses to make an order under s.34(4), a further application cannot be made
for six months except with leave of the court (s.91(17)).

Despite the presumption in favour of contact, a local authority can as a matter of urgency refuse contact for up to seven days without obtaining a court
order, provided such action is needed to promote the child's welfare (s.34(6)).
In such a case, written notice of the decision must be given to any child who
has sufficient understanding and to any person in respect of whom there is a
presumption of reasonable contact (r.2, Contact with Children Regulations
1991).

Human rights arguments were used by a mother in *In Re F (Minors)(Care
Proceedings: Contact)* 22 June 2000, *The Times*. She argued that the s.34(4)
order permitting the local authority to terminate contact with her three children was premature and also a breach of art. 6 (right to a fair trial) and art. 8
(right to family life) of the European Convention on Human Rights. She
argued that once the order had been made, the decision of the local authority
to terminate contact would be an administrative one against which she had no
meaningful remedy. Wall J dismissed her appeal as there was no possibility of
rehabilitation and adoptive placements were urgently required. Wall J said it
was a case where in the words of Butler-Sloss in *In Re B* (above), the care
plan was 'decisive of the contact application.' With regard to the human rights
challenge, Wall J said that while the Children Act had to be read and given
effect to in a way which was compatible with the European Convention on
Human Rights, it was for the English courts applying English criteria of fairness and justice to decide whether those rights had been breached. His
Lordship held that placing the children in care on the basis of a care plan,
which was for adoption with termination of contact on placement, was both
correct and proportionate in the circumstances.

A s.34(4) order can be discharged (s.34(9)) if it can be shown that there has
been a change of circumstances since the order was made and, if so, that discharge will promote the child's welfare (*Re T (Termination of Contact:
Discharge of Order)* [1997] 1 FLR 517). However, as one of the policies of

the Children Act is for local authorities to work in partnership with children and their families, the local authority and the person in whose favour the order was made can make an agreement about contact (instead of applying for variation or discharge), provided the child of sufficient understanding agrees (r.3 Contact with Children Regulations 1991).

16.7 Emergency Protection

Part V of the Children Act 1989 provides the legal framework for dealing with children who need protection in an emergency or otherwise. It does so by making provision *inter alia* for child assessment and emergency protection orders. These orders, however, are subject to certain safeguards, which were introduced as a result of the Cleveland Enquiry (see 16.1 above), in order to prevent unjustifiable State intrusion into family life. Thus, for instance, they are of short duration, and are open to challenge. In some cases, however, emergency action will be followed by an application for a care or supervision order.

Under Part V, local authorities also have various investigative duties when they are informed that a child who lives, or is found, in their area, is the subject of an emergency protection order or is in police protection (see below), or the local authority has reasonable cause to suspect that such a child is suffering, or is likely to suffer, significant harm (s.47(1)). Once a local authority has obtained an order under Part V, enquiries must be made to decide what action should be taken to safeguard or promote the child's welfare (s.47(2)).

Part V proceedings are not 'family proceedings' for the purposes of the Children Act (see s.8(4)), so that the court cannot make any s.8 order (see 12.4) on an application, or of its own motion, in the proceedings. When considering whether to make orders under Part V, the child's welfare is the court's paramount consideration (s.1(1)). The no-delay principle (s.1(2)) applies and the court can make an order only if it is better for the child than making no order at all (s.1(5)). However, the welfare checklist in s.1(3) does not apply, as to have to ascertain the child's wishes and feelings, needs etc. would be time-consuming and would defeat the whole purpose of an application under Part V, which is for immediate short-term emergency protection.

The following are available for emergency protection: (a) a child assessment order; (b) an emergency protection order; and (c) police protection.

(a) Child Assessment Order

Under s.43 of the Children Act, the court can make a child assessment order, which is an order requiring the child to be produced for the purposes of a medical or psychiatric assessment. The order permits intervention where the circumstances are not sufficiently urgent or serious enough to justify intervention by means of an emergency protection order. As the child remains at home, it is less severe than an emergency protection order.

A child assessment order can be made on the application of a local authority (or the NSPCC) but only if the court is satisfied that (s.43(1)):

'(a) the applicant has reasonable cause to suspect that the child is suffering, or is likely to suffer, significant harm;

(b) an assessment of the state of the child's health or development, or of the way in which he or she has been treated, is required to enable the applicant to determine whether or not the child is suffering, or is likely to suffer, significant harm; and

(c) it is unlikely that such an assessment will be made, or be satisfactory, in the absence of an order under this section.'

The court can treat the application as an application for an emergency protection order (s.43(3)). In fact, it is prohibited from making a child assessment order if the grounds for making an emergency protection order exist, and the court considers it ought to make an emergency protection order rather than a child assessment order (s.43(4)). A child assessment order must specify the date when assessment is to begin and must last no longer than seven days from that date (s.43(5)). Once an order is in force, any person in a position to do so is required to produce the child to the person named in the order and comply with any directions in the order (s.43(6)). The order authorises any person carrying out the assessment, or any part of the assessment, to do so in accordance with the terms of the order (s.43(7)). However, a child with sufficient understanding to make an informed decision may refuse to submit to a medical or psychiatric examination, or other assessment, regardless of any term in the order authorising assessment (s.43(8)) (but see *South Glamorgan County Council* v. *W and B*, at 16.5 above).

A child may be kept away from home (e.g. in hospital), but only where necessary for assessment and only in accordance with directions and for the period(s) of time specified in the order (s.43(9)). The order must contain directions about contact (s.43(10)). Before the application is heard, the local authority (or the NSPCC) must take reasonable practicable steps to ensure that notice of the application is given to: the child's parents; any person with parental responsibility; any person caring for the child; any person who has contact with the child either under a s.8 contact order or a s.34 order; and the child (s.43(11)). This notice requirement is to ensure, where possible, that the hearing takes place between the parties in order to prevent unjustifiable intervention. The rules of court make provision for variation and discharge (s.43(12)).

(b) Emergency Protection Order

The court has jurisdiction under s.44 to make an emergency protection order on the application of 'any person', but in practice it is usually a local authority. The court must be satisfied that there is reasonable cause to believe that the child is likely to suffer harm if: he or she is not removed to accommodation provided by or on behalf of the applicant; or he or she does not remain in the place in which he or she is being accommodated (s.44(1)(a)). The court may also make an order on the application of a local authority (or the NSPCC) if enquiries in respect of the child are being made under s.47(1)(b) and those enquiries are being frustrated by access to the child being unreasonably refused to a person authorised to seek access, and the applicant has reasonable cause to believe that access to the child is required as a matter of urgency (s.44(1)(b) and (c)).

In an emergency, the application can be heard by a single justice and may, with leave of the clerk of the court, be made without notice being given to the other party (or parties), although, wherever possible, proceedings must be heard *inter partes*. The order can be granted in the first instance to last for up to eight days, but a subsequent application can be made by a local authority (or the NSPCC), when the court can grant one extension of up to a further seven days, but only if there is reasonable cause to believe the child is likely to suffer significant harm if the order is not extended (s.45).

While an emergency protection order is in force it operates as a direction to any person who is in a position to do so to comply with any request to produce the child to the applicant (s.44(4)(a)). It authorises the child's removal to accommodation provided by or on behalf of the applicant and the child being kept there; or it prevents the child's removal from any hospital, or other place, in which he or she was being accommodated immediately before the order was made (s.44(4)(b)). It is a criminal offence intentionally to obstruct a person authorised to remove the child, or prevent the removal of the child (s.44(15)). The order gives the applicant limited parental responsibility (s.44(4)(c) and s.44(5)(b)). The applicant must comply with regulations made by the Secretary of State (s.44(5)).

While the order is in force, the applicant (usually the local authority) cannot remove the child from his or her home or retain him or her in a place for longer than is necessary to safeguard the child's welfare, and must return the child or allow him or her to be removed when safe to do so (s.44(10)). The child can be returned to the care of the person from whom he or she was removed or, if that is not reasonably practicable, then to a parent, a person with parental responsibility, or to such other person as the applicant with the agreement of the court considers appropriate, although while the order is in force the applicant can exercise his or her powers with respect to the child where it is necessary to do so (s.44(11) and (12)). The applicant must (subject to directions in the order as to contact and medical assessment or examination) allow the child reasonable contact with the following persons and any person acting on his or her behalf: parents; any other person with parental responsibility; any person with whom the child was living immediately before the order was made; and any person with a right to contact under a s.8 contact order or under a s.34 order (s.44(13)).

When an order is made, or at any time while it is in force, the court can give directions and impose conditions as to contact and/or may give directions with respect to the medical or psychiatric examination or other assessment of the child, which can include a condition that no examination or assessment be carried out unless the court directs (s.44(6), (8) and (9)). Where a direction as to medical or psychiatric examination or assessment is made, a child of sufficient understanding to make an informed decision may refuse the examination or assessment (s.44(6)). Directions in an order can be varied at any time (s.44(9)(b)).

There is no appeal against the making or refusal to make an emergency protection order, but an application can be heard to discharge an order 72 hours or more after it was made (s.45(9) and (10)). The following persons can apply for discharge: the child; his or her parent; any person who is not a parent but who has parental responsibility for the child; or any person with whom the child was living immediately before the order was made.

Emergency protection orders are granted in a wide range of different circumstances. In *Re O (A Minor) (Medical Treatment)* [1993] 2 FLR 149, for instance, an order was made in respect of a premature baby of Jehovah's Witnesses who required a blood transfusion. In *Re P (Emergency Protection Order)* [1996] 1 FLR 482, a local authority obtained an emergency protection order in respect of a child who had nearly died on two occasions (the paediatrician suspected the mother of attempting to suffocate the child), but the justices refused to extend the order when it fell to be renewed. Eventually, after the mother was diagnosed as having Munchausen's syndrome by proxy, a care order was made. In the care proceedings, Johnson J stated that the justices' refusal to extend the emergency protection order in the face of firm medical evidence indicating life-threatening abuse drew attention to the fact that the Children Act lacked any effective procedure by which a local authority could challenge that refusal. His Lordship said that consideration should be given to providing a mechanism for review, which would have to be one that operated very quickly.

(c) Police Protection

Under s.46, the police have various powers in emergency cases involving children. A constable who has reasonable cause to believe a child would otherwise be likely to suffer significant harm can remove the child to accommodation and keep the child there, or prevent a child being removed from any hospital or other place where he or she is being accommodated (s.46(1)). The local authority must be notified as soon as is reasonably possible and given reasoned details of steps taken and proposed to be taken, and details of where the child is accommodated. The child must also be notified of any plans, if capable of understanding them, as must parents, persons with parental responsibility and any person with whom the child was living. As soon as is reasonably practicable, an inquiry must be carried out by a designated officer (s.46(3)(e)). Once this inquiry is concluded, the officer conducting it must release the child unless there is reasonable cause for believing the child is likely to suffer significant harm (s.46(5)). A child cannot be kept in police protection for more than 72 hours, but during that time a designated officer can apply for an emergency protection order on behalf of a local authority, and must do what is reasonable in the circumstances to safeguard or promote the child's welfare, which includes allowing parents and other persons to have contact (if any) with the child as is both reasonable and in the child's best interests (s.46(6), (7) and (10)). While the child is in police protection, the constable or designated officer does not have parental responsibility but must do what is reasonable to safeguard or promote the child's welfare (s.46(9)(b)).

16.8   Excluding a Child Abuser from the Home

As the family environment is generally considered to be the best place in which to bring up a child, it is sometimes in a child's best interests to remove the abuser, not the child victim, from the home. Until the implementation of Part IV of the Family Law Act 1996 (see Chapter 6), local authorities had no power to remove an abuser from the home. Section 8 orders under the Children Act (see 12.3) could not be used. Thus, in *Nottinghamshire County Council* v. *P* [1994] Fam 18, a local authority's application for a specific issue order to exclude an abusing father was dismissed, and in *Re H (Prohibited Steps Order)* [1995] 1 FLR 638, the court held that it had no power to make a prohibited steps order against a mother to prohibit contact between an abusing father and his children.

This lack of power in the child care legislation to remove an abuser from the home was felt to be a lacuna in the law and, as a result of recommendations made by the Law Commission (*Domestic Violence and Occupation of the Family Home*, Law Com No 207, 1992, paras. 6, 15 and 16) and by the Government, amendments were made to the Children Act by s.52 and Sched. 6 of the Family Law Act 1996. These amendments give the court jurisdiction to include an exclusion requirement in an interim care order (s.38A) and an emergency protection order (s.44A), so that the abuser, rather than the child, can be removed from the home. The grounds for an interim care order or emergency protection order must be made out and there must be reasonable cause to believe that if the 'relevant person' is excluded from the home the child will cease to suffer, or cease to be likely to suffer, significant harm. The court must also be satisfied that another person living in the home (whether or not a parent) is able and willing to give the child the care which it would be reasonable to expect a parent to give him or her, and that that person consents to the exclusion requirement (s.38A(2)). The exclusion requirement may provide that the abuser leave the house, be prevented from entering the house and/or be excluded from a defined area around the house (s.38A(3)). A power of arrest may be attached to the exclusion requirement (s.38A(5)). The court may accept an undertaking from the abuser instead of making an exclusion requirement.

16.9   Local Authorities' Duties to Children 'Looked After' by Them

Local authorities have duties under the Children Act towards children 'looked after' by them, whether accommodated under a voluntary arrangement or under a care order (s.22(1)). A local authority must safeguard and promote the child's welfare and make such use of services available for children cared for by their own parents as appears reasonable in the case of the particular child (s.22(3)). Before making a decision about a child being looked after, or proposed to be looked after, the local authority must ascertain the wishes and feelings of the child, his or her parents, any other person with parental responsibility and any other relevant person (s.22(4)). It must also consider their wishes in respect of the child's religion, racial origin, and cultural and linguistic background (s.22(5)). It must advise, assist and befriend the child, with a view to promoting his or her welfare when he or she ceases to be looked after by them (s 24(1)). A local authority must encourage rehabilitation by allowing the child to live with his or her family, unless contrary to his or her welfare (s.23(6)), and ensure that the accommodation provided is near the child's home, and that brothers and sisters remain together (s.23(7)). A local authority's general duties to a child are facilitated by more specific duties, e.g. by the inspection of foster-parents, other persons with whom the child can be placed and children's homes. Local authorities also have a duty to promote contact (16.6 above, and see Sched. 2, para. 15(1) of the Children Act).

Where a child is subject to a care or supervision order, the local authority concerned can apply for an injunction ancillary to the care order which the court can grant under its inherent jurisdiction (now under s.37 of the Supreme Court Act 1981), without the need for the local authority to seek permission to apply to invoke the inherent jurisdiction under s.100 of the Children Act (see

Re P (Care Orders: Injunctive Relief) [2000] 2 FLR 385, where injunctions were granted on the application of a local authority requiring parents of a child in care under a care order to attend college without parental interference, and permitting the local authority to monitor the family).

16.10 Challenging Local Authority Decisions about Children

Sometimes, parents, relatives, the child, foster-parents and others may be dissatisfied with the action taken, or not taken, by a local authority. It may be possible to resolve a grievance informally, particularly as the policy of the Children Act is to encourage co-operation and agreement between all concerned, but if this is impossible, then the following procedures are available:

(a) Challenges under the Children Act 1989

One way of challenging a local authority is to appeal against a care or supervision order or apply to have it discharged (see 16.5 above). An application to discharge an emergency protection order can be made but not an appeal. A decision about contact with a child may be challenged by an application under s.34 (see 16.6 above). Another option is to apply for a s.8 residence order (see 12.3), which, if granted, automatically discharges a care order (s.91(1)). A child needs the permission of the court to apply for a s.8 order (see 12.6). However, the court is unlikely to grant an order, or grant permission to apply for it, where this will interfere with a local authority's plans. In *Re A and W (Minors)(Residence Order: Leave to Apply)* [1992] Fam 182 [1992], 2 FLR 154, a foster-mother applied for permission to seek a residence order as a means of challenging a local authority decision forbidding her to foster children. Permission was refused. The Court of Appeal held that the court had a duty to consider the local authority's plans for the child (s.10(9)(d)(i)), but as a local authority's general duty was to safeguard and promote the welfare of any child in care (s.22(3)), the court would not grant permission to depart from those plans which were intended for the welfare of the child. An application to challenge a local authority by applying to make a child in care a ward of court (see 12.9) cannot be made, as a child cannot be simultaneously a ward of court and in local authority care (ss.100(2)(c) and 91(4)). However, a complaint could be made to the Secretary of State, who has the power to declare a local authority to be in default, if it fails without reasonable cause to comply with a duty under the Children Act, and who can require compliance within a specified period (s.84).

(b) The Complaints Procedure

Where Part III powers and duties of local authorities are involved, a complaint may be made under the 'Complaints Procedure' which every local authority is required to establish (see s.26, and also Representations Procedure (Children) Regulations 1991, and Review of Children's Cases Regulations 1991). A complaint may be made by: a child being looked after by the local authority or a child in need; a parent; a person with parental responsibility; a local authority foster-parent; any person whom the local authority considers has sufficient interest in the child's welfare to warrant representation being considered; and a young person who considers he or she has been given inadequate preparation for leaving care or for after-care. The Complaints Procedure, however, has certain drawbacks. One is that wider family members cannot make representations, except at the discretion of the local authority. Another is that, although one member of the Complaints Panel must be independent of the local authority, impartiality may be difficult to maintain. A major drawback, however, is that the Complaints Procedure is only available in respect of Part III duties and powers, although the Department of Health *Guidance* suggests that local authorities should consider extending the procedure to cover other matters. In fact, many authorities have done so, which means that complaints can also be made in respect of Part IV and Part V powers and duties.

(c) An Action in Tort

An action in tort for negligence or for breach of a statutory duty can be brought against a local authority, but as the courts do not like to fetter and undermine the discretionary powers of local authorities, it is usually difficult to succeed. However, with the implementation of the Human Rights Act 1998 (see 1.5), the chances of succeeding have improved because the courts will now look at the merits of the case instead of striking the case out on the ground that a local authority owes no duty of care in negligence. Before the decision of the House of Lords in *Barrett* v. *Enfield London Borough Council* [1999] 3 WLR 79, the courts would usually strike out negligence actions against local authorities on the grounds of public policy, holding that the local authority owed no duty of care to the claimant. Thus in *X (Minors)* v. *Bedfordshire County Council and Related Appeals* [1995] 2 AC 633, [1995] 2 FLR 276, claims in negligence (and for breach of a statutory duty) brought against local authority social services departments in respect of their child care functions were struck out by the House of Lords on the grounds of public policy. However, in *Barrett* there was a sea change. Here the claimant had sued the local authority for damages in negligence for the way in which he had been looked after in care. His case failed in the Court of Appeal, where

X v. *Bedfordshire* was applied, but the House of Lords, allowing his appeal, refused to strike out the case on policy grounds and held that Mr Barrett should have the opportunity to have his case heard on its merits. The House of Lords in *Barrett* was influenced by *Osman* v. *UK* [1999] 1 FLR 193, where the European Court of Human Rights had held that to strike out a case on policy grounds, without hearing it on its merits, was a breach of art. 6 of the European Convention (right to a fair trial). With the implementation of the Convention in the UK under the Human Rights Act 1998, the House of Lords in *Barrett* was under considerable pressure to apply art. 6, although it did so somewhat reluctantly. Because of the expense and time involved in going to court, particularly now that the court will have to consider the merits of a case, a local authority may well settle the matter out of court.

(d) Application to the European Court of Human Rights

A parent or other aggrieved party, who has exhausted all the remedies available in the courts in the UK, can apply to the European Commission or Court of Human Rights in Strasbourg, alleging that the UK is in breach of the European Convention for the Protection of Human Rights, e.g. of the right to family life (art. 8) or the right to a fair hearing (art. 6), or some other fundamental human right (see, for example, *Gaskin* v. *UK* [1990] 12 EHRR 36, [1990] 1 FLR 167, where an action was brought by a person who had been in local authority care). Applications can take a considerable time before they are determined. Damages can be awarded at the discretion of the court.

(e) Challenges under the Human Rights Act 1998

Although it is still open to an individual to bring an action before the Commission and Court of Human Rights under the European Convention of Human Rights (see above), the implementation of the Convention into UK law under the Human Rights Act 1998 (see 1.5) means that there will be less reason to do so. This is because Convention rights are now directly enforceable in the UK. Local authorities are also 'public authorities' for the purposes of the Act, and must not act in a way which is incompatible with a Convention right (s.6 HRA 1998). Furthermore, any person who is a victim of an unlawful act (or proposed act) may bring proceedings against a local authority or may rely on the Convention right in any other legal proceedings (s.7). As a result of the Act, there is now much greater pressure on those engaged in child protection

354   *Children*

to ensure that they comply with the European Convention, and it is likely that human rights' arguments will be frequently used in, for instance, care and supervision proceedings. Challenges by way of judicial review against local authorities are also likely to be increasingly brought on the basis of breaches of human rights. The Human Rights Act also requires the courts in this country to take account of the decisions of the Commission and Court of Human Rights (s.2). Consequently, cases heard by the European Court or Commission in respect of child protection, such as *L* v. *UK* [2000] 2 FLR 322 (unsuccessful challenge under arts. 8 and 6 by mother against a supervision order) and *L* v. *Finland* [2000] 2 FLR 118 (successful challenge in respect of care orders under arts. 8 and 6), will have to be considered in similar cases coming before the English courts.

(f) Judicial Review

An application for the public law remedy of judicial review may be made against a local authority (or other public body, such as a government department, court or health authority) by an aggrieved family member, including a child. The application must be made to the Queen's Bench Division of the High Court (see s.29 Supreme Court Act 1981, and Ord. 53 of the Rules of the Supreme Court 1965 (SI 1965/1766)). The court can grant the following remedies: an order of *mandamus* (directing the respondent to take a particular course of action); an order of prohibition (prohibiting the respondent from taking a particular course of action); an order of *certiorari* (quashing the decision of the respondent); a declaration; and an injunction. Damages can be claimed, but they are rarely awarded for breaches of public law rights.

Strict rules, however, govern judicial review applications. Thus, before the application is heard on its merits, the applicant must seek permission to apply, which will be granted only if there is a reasonable chance of the court deciding that the local authority's decision was so unreasonable that no reasonable authority could have ever come to it (see, for example, Balcombe LJ in *R* v. *Lancashire County Council ex p M* [1992] 1 FLR 109). Permission to apply must also be sought promptly without delay, and within three months from the date on which the grounds for the application arose. Permission to apply will not be granted unless the applicant has a sufficient interest in the matter to which the application relates (this is not usually a problem where the issue involves family members). The grounds on which judicial review may be granted are: illegality, procedural impropriety (breach of the rules of natural justice), or irrationality (see per Lord Diplock, *Council of Civil Service Unions* v. *Minister for the Civil Service* [1985] AC 374). However, as judicial review is a discretionary remedy, even if the ground is made out, the court has a discretion to refuse a remedy.

However, where a local authority has wide discretion in a particular matter, it is difficult to succeed in an action by way of judicial review, and where there are other procedures available for challenging local authority action or inaction, the court will not grant judicial review without those procedures having been pursued first. Thus, for example, in *R* v. *Royal Borough of Kingston upon Thames ex p T* [1994] 1 FLR 798, an application for judicial review in respect of a local authority's obligations under Part III of the Children Act was refused, on the ground that a remedy had not been sought under the Complaints Procedure. A considerable disadvantage, however, of an application for judicial review is that, even if *certiorari* (the more likely remedy) is granted, the local authority only has an obligation to reconsider its original decision on its merits, and, provided the later decision is not illegal, procedurally improper or irrational, then it can come to the same decision as it did the first time.

There have been many applications for judicial review of action or inaction by local authorities in the context of their statutory duties towards children, for example placing a child's name on the child protection register (*R* v. *Hampshire County Council ex parte H* [1999] 2 FLR 359), and deregistering a foster parent (*R* v. *Avon County Council ex parte Crabtree* [1996] 1 FLR 502). In *R* v. *Cornwall County Council ex parte LH* [2000] 1 FLR 236, declarations were granted in judicial review declaring that a local authority had acted unlawfully in failing to allow the applicant's solicitor to attend a child protection case conference, and failing to supply the applicant with the minutes. In *R* v. *Tameside Metropolitan Borough Council ex parte J* [2000] 1 FLR 942, it was held that while a local authority accommodating children under s.20 of the Children Act is able to exercise mundane powers relating to the provision of accommodation, it cannot override the wishes of parents with parental responsibility. For this reason, the local authority could not place the child with foster-parents, against the wishes of her parents who wished her to remain at a residential school for disabled children.

With the coming into force of the Human Rights Act 1998 (see 1.5), which requires public authorities to comply with the European Convention on Human Rights, it is likely that applications for judicial review will increase and increasing numbers of applicants will use human rights' arguments before the court.

(g) Local Government Ombudsman

A complaint can be made to the Commissioner for Local Administration (the Local Government Ombudsman), who has a duty to investigate complaints of maladministration by local authorities, but this is a lengthy and limited remedy.

Summary

1 Local authorities have duties and powers under the Children Act 1989 to safeguard and promote the welfare of children. Local authorities must work in partnership with families and children, with compulsory intervention by court order in the last resort.
2 As local authorities are public authorities for the purposes of the Human Rights Act 1998, they must abide by the European Convention for the Protection of Human Rights (see 1.5).
3 Local authorities must co-operate with other professionals and other agencies in the task of child protection.
4 Under Part III of the Children Act, local authorities have a duty to provide services for children in need and also disabled children, including in particular the provision of day care and accommodation. A child 'accommodated in care' under a voluntary arrangement can be removed at any time.
5 Under Part IV, local authorities (and the NSPCC) can apply for care or supervision orders, which may be granted by the court if the 'threshold criteria' in s.31(2) are satisfied, and the court considers the child's welfare requires such an order to be made. In assessing welfare, the court must apply the welfare principle (s.1(1)), the no-delay principle (s.1(2)), the welfare checklist (s.1(3)) and the no-order presumption (s.1(5)). A care order gives the local authority parental responsibility for the child, but a parent does not lose parental responsibility. A supervision order puts the child under the supervision of a designated local authority officer or a probation officer. A care order can be discharged. A supervision order can be varied or discharged. There is a presumption of continuing reasonable contact between parents and others and the child in care, unless terminated or restricted by court order (s.34).
6 Under Part V of the Children Act, a child assessment order (s.43) and an emergency protection order (s.44) can be made where children need emergency protection. The police have powers to provide protection for children where they have reasonable cause to believe that a child is likely to suffer significant harm (s.46).
7 Local authorities have certain duties to children 'looked after' by them whether under a voluntary arrangement or under a court order.
8 Local authorities can be challenged under the Children Act complaints procedure or under the general law by bringing a tort action or by seeking judicial review. An application may also be made to the local ombudsman. Complaints can also be made to Strasbourg under the European Convention on Human Rights but only where remedies under English law have been exhausted. However, with the implementation of the Convention into English law by the Human Rights Act 1998 (see 1.5), applications to the European Commission or Court of Human Rights are likely to decline.

Further Reading and References

Fortin, 'Re D (Care: Natural Parent Presumption) – Is blood really thicker than water?' [1999] CFLQ 435.
Gillespie, 'The care plan' [1999] 4 Web JCLI (webjcli.ncl.ac.uk/1999/issue4/gillespie4.html).
Gillespie, 'Establishing a third order in care proceedings' [2000] CFLQ 239.
Hall, 'What price the logic of proof of evidence?' [2000] Fam Law 423.

Hayes, Mary, 'Child protection – From principles and policies to practices' [1998] CFLQ 119.

Hayes, John, 'The threshold test and the unknown perpetrator' [2000] Fam Law 260.

Hemingway and Williams, '*Re M and R: Re H and R*' [1997] Fam Law 740.

Hogg, 'Preferred option shortfall – children in need' [2000] Fam Law 114.

Kaganas, King and Piper (eds), *Legislating for Harmony: Partnership under the Children Act 1989*, Jessica Kingsley, 1995.

Keating, 'Shifting standards in the House of Lords: *Re H and Others (Minors)(Sexual Abuse: Standard of Proof)*' [1996] CFLQ 157.

King, 'The future of specialist child care mediation' [1999] CFLQ 137.

Levy (ed.), *Re-Focus on Child Abuse*, Hawksmere, 1994.

Lindley and Richards, 'Working Together 2000 – How will parents fare under the new child protection process?' [2000] CFLQ 213.

McCafferty, 'A duty to act – article 3 of the Human Rights Convention v. the non-intervention principle' [1999] Fam Law 717.

Mitchell, District Judge, 'Working together to safeguard children: child protection and assessment' [2000] Fam Law 501.

Mullender, 'Negligence, public authorities and policy-level decisions' [2000] 116 LQR 21.

Mullis, '*Barrett* v. *Enfield London Borough Council* – A compensation-seeker's charter?' [2000] CFLQ 185.

Perry, '*Lancashire County Council* v. *B*: Section 31 – threshold or barrier?' [2000] CFLQ 301.

Smith, 'Judicial power and local authority discretion – the contested frontier' [1997] CFLQ 243.

Thoburn, Lewis and Shemmings, *Paternalism or Partnership? Family Involvement in the Child Protection Process*, HMSO, 1995.

Wall, Judge of the Family Division, 'Concurrent planning – a judicial perspective' [1999] CFLQ 97.

Websites

Department of Health: www.open.gov.uk/doh (*The Government's Objectives for Children's Social Services* (1999), *Working Together to Safeguard Children* (1999) and *Framework for the Assessment of Children in Need and their Families* (1999) are available on this website).

NCH Action for Children/Solicitors' Family Law Association – Carelaw (developed by SFLA and NCH to provide accessible and up-to-date information for young people in care.): www.carelaw.org.uk/

NSPCC (National Society for the Protection of Cruelty to Children) (publications, research and information service.): www.nspcc.org.uk/

Questions

1 In what sorts of fact situations can you envisage persons challenging local authorities under the Human Rights Act 1998, and on what grounds?

2 In what sorts of fact situations can you envisage challenges being made against a local authority in tort or by way of judicial review?

3 The House of Lords on three occasions has had to rule on the 'threshold conditions' in s.31(2) of the Children Act. What are your views on these decisions?

17 Adoption

17.1 Introduction

Adoption of a child is effected by a court order known as an adoption order which extinguishes the parental responsibility of the natural parents and vests it in the adopters. The law of adoption is laid down in the Adoption Act 1976. The Children Act 1989 is also relevant; for, as adoption proceedings are family proceedings for the purposes of the Children Act, the court can, of its own motion or on an application, make any s.8 order in the adoption proceedings (see 12.3). Thus, for example, the court might consider it more appropriate to make a residence order instead of an adoption order (see, for example, *Re M (Adoption or Residence Order)* [1998] 1 FLR 570) or make a contact order to allow the child to have contact with a family member. The Adoption Rules 1984 govern procedure and the Adoption Agencies Regulations 1983 and various government circulars regulate practice.

There has been widespread discussion and consultation on adoption since 1989 when an inter-departmental review of adoption was commenced. Reforms of adoption law were proposed as a result of widespread dissatisfaction with the law. In 1992 a consultative document was published (*Review of Adoption Law: Report to Ministers of an Inter-Departmental Working Group*), which was followed in 1993 by a White Paper (*Adoption: The Future*, Cm 2288). The White Paper was in turn followed in 1996 by a consultative document (*Adoption: A Service for Children*) containing a draft Adoption Bill, which made fundamental changes to adoption law, including in particular a 'placement order' to replace the current freeing order, a new welfare principle and changes to the grounds for dispensing with agreement to adoption. However, as some of these reforms were controversial, the Bill was not introduced into Parliament before the Conservative Government fell from power. Since coming into power, the Labour Government has accepted the need to improve the law on adoption (see para. 1.5, p.6, *Supporting Families*, Home Office, 1998), and in July 2000 the Cabinet Office published a paper containing proposals for reform, and a White Paper on adoption was published in December 2000 (see 17.13). Reform is needed because adoption law does not harmonise with the Children Act 1989 and does not reflect the changes in adoption practice which have taken place.

The nature of adoption has changed significantly over the years. A significant change has been the decline in the number of adoptions. In 1968, for example, there were 24 800 adoptions, and in 1999 there were only 3962. The decline in adoption is due largely to the shortage of babies available for adoption, as a result of contraception, the legalisation of abortion, and the fact that single mothers are no longer under pressure to give up their babies. Another change in adoption has been the increasing numbers of older children who are adopted. Many adopted children are children who have been taken into local authority care and placed for adoption because rehabilitation with their own families is not possible. Some of these children have severe disabilities. Other changes have been an increase in inter-country adoptions and the trend towards 'open' adoption, whereby adopted children are sometimes allowed indirect or direct contact with their birth parents and other family members.

Adoptions are entered into for different reasons. Many adoptions are by persons who cannot have children of their own, although assisted reproduction techniques are now more commonly used. About half the number of adoptions are by relatives who seek adoption in order to cement family bonds. Step-parent adoptions (mainly by step-fathers) are particularly common, because of the increase in divorce and remarriage, but sometimes grandparents apply to adopt their grandchildren. These 'in family' adoptions, however, have disadvantages, and reforms have been discussed (see 17.13). However, as an alternative to adoption, some relatives might consider applying for a residence or contact order under the Children Act 1989 (see 12.4). Some adoptions are part of local authority care plans in respect of children in care. Some adoptions involve children from overseas.

17.2   Adoption Services and Placements

Adoption Agencies

It is a criminal offence to make private placements of children for adoption. Payment for adoption is also prohibited (see s.57), although payment can be retrospectively authorised by the court (see, for example, *Re ZHH (Adoption Application)* [1993] 1 FLR 83, *Re C (Adoption Application)* [1993] 1FLR 87 and *Re WM (Adoption: Non-Patrial)* [1997] 1 FLR 132).

Only adoption agencies can make arrangements and place children for adoption, unless the adopter is the child's relative or is acting under a High Court order (s.11). Only local authorities and approved voluntary adoption societies can act as adoption agencies. Local authorities have a statutory duty to establish and maintain an adoption service in their area, or ensure that such a service is provided by an approved adoption society (s.1). In practice, however, most local authorities act as adoption agencies and provide their own adoption service. The main function of adoption agencies is to screen prospective adopters and supervise placements. They must comply with the Adoption Agencies Regulations 1983, which includes setting up an adoption panel to consider and make recommendations about prospective adoptions and placements. When placing a child for adoption, an adoption agency must consider, so far as is practicable, the wishes of the child's parents or guardian about the child's religious upbringing (s.7). Although there is no duty under the Adoption Act for an adoption agency to consider a child's racial or cultural background, a local authority or voluntary organisation looking after a child must consider not only the child's religion, but the child's 'racial origin and cultural and linguistic background' (ss.22(5)(c) and 61(3)(c) CA 1989).

17.3   The Welfare of the Child

The welfare principle governing adoption is laid down in s.6 of the Adoption Act 1976 which provides that:

> 'In reaching any decision relating to the adoption of a child a court or adoption agency shall have regard to all the circumstances, first consideration being given to the need to safeguard and promote the welfare of the child throughout his childhood; and shall so far as practicable ascertain the wishes and feelings of the child regarding the decision and give due consideration to them, having regard to his age and understanding.'

The welfare principle applies to decisions made both by courts and adoption agencies. However, unlike the welfare principle in s.1(1) of the Children Act 1989, the child's welfare is the 'first', not 'paramount' consideration. The reason for this is that the interests of the birth parents and the birth family must be taken into account, not just the welfare of the child, particularly as adoption is a serious and, in most cases, an irrevocable step.

Sometimes a child's welfare will require the presumption in favour of natural parents to prevail. In *Re B (Adoption: Child's Welfare)* [1995] 1 FLR 895, for example, English foster-parents applied to adopt a young child from The Gambia whom they had been looking after under an informal fostering arrangement, but whose parents objected to her adoption. Wall J refused to make an adoption order, holding that it was logical that a different welfare test applied in adoption proceedings from that in the Children Act, because a different test needed to be applied to the making of an order which extinguished parental rights as opposed to one which regulated their operation. His Lordship said that in principle a child has a right, but not an absolute one, to be brought up by his or her parents in their way of life and in their religion. In a similar case, *Re M (Child's Upbringing)* [1996] 2 FLR 441, the court in wardship proceedings ordered a Zulu boy to be sent back to South Africa and not be adopted in England. Applying Lord Templeman's words in *Re KD*

(A Minor)(Ward: Termination of Access) [1988] AC 806 and those of Waite LJ in *Re K (A Minor)(Custody)* [1990] 2 FLR 64, the court held that there was a strong supposition that, other things being equal, it was in a child's best interests to be brought up by his natural parents.

Other considerations may also be relevant to the question of the child's welfare. Thus, the court may have to consider the fact that adoption can confer British nationality on a child (see *Re B (Adoption Order: Nationality)* [1999] AC 136, [1999] 1 FLR 907). When considering the child's welfare, the court will be very aware of the fact that adoption involves a change of status and is not just a question of where it is in the child's best interests to live (*Re M (Adoption or Residence Order)* [1998] 1 FLR 570). Other considerations may have to be taken into account, and may prevail over the child's welfare. Thus, for example, immigration policy can prevail (see, for example, *Re K (A Minor)(Adoption Order: Nationality)* [1994] 2 FLR 557).

The draft Adoption Bill 1996 proposed that the welfare principle be amended so that courts and adoption agencies would be required to give paramount, not first, consideration to the child during childhood and adulthood (cl.1(2)). It also proposed the introduction of a 'welfare checklist', like that in s.1(3) of the Children Act 1989, to help guide decision-making (cl.1(4)). These proposals have now been included in the Government's recent proposals for reform (see 17.13).

17.4 Freeing for Adoption

'Freeing for adoption' is a procedure which applies only to agency cases. It precedes the application for an adoption order, and sometimes even the placement of a child. The advantage of freeing is that it removes any anxiety about the birth parents withdrawing their agreement to the adoption, as once a freeing order is made, the parental agreement requirement is satisfied and parental responsibility for the child vests in the adoption agency.

Under the freeing procedure, an adoption agency applies to the court for a 'freeing order', which is an order declaring that the child is free for adoption (s.18(1)). The application can only be made if there has been parental agreement to the adoption, unless the child is in local authority care and the local authority is applying to dispense with such agreement (ss.18(1)(b) and (2A)). Agreement to freeing for adoption may, however, be dispensed with on certain grounds, in the same way as it can be in an application for an adoption order (see 17.7 below). The unmarried father without parental responsibility is not required to give his agreement to his child's adoption, but the court must none the less be satisfied that he does not intend to apply for a parental responsibility order or a residence order under the Children Act, or that such an application would be likely to be refused (s.18(7)). A mother's agreement to adoption is not effective unless it is given more than six weeks after the baby's birth (s.18(4)).

Before making a freeing order, the court must be satisfied that each birth parent has been given the opportunity to make a declaration that he or she does not wish to be involved in any future questions concerning the adoption (s.18(6)). Where there is no such declaration, then 12 months after the freeing order the adoption agency must inform each parent (if not already informed) as to whether or not the child has been adopted, or has his or her home with a person with whom he or she has been placed for adoption (s.19(2)). The welfare principle in s.6 (see 17.3 above) applies to a freeing application. Where the court is considering an application for a freeing order simultaneously with a care order, the application for the care order is the primary consideration (*Re D (Simultaneous Applications for Care Order and Freeing Order)* [1999] 2 FLR 49).

Effects of a Freeing Order

The main effect of a freeing order is that parental responsibility for the child vests in the adoption agency until an adoption order is made or until the freeing order is revoked (s.18(5)). Once a freeing order is made, the adoption agency must give first consideration to the child's welfare (s.6), monitor the child's care and hold six-monthly reviews if the child is not placed for adoption (r.13 Adoption Agencies Regulations 1983). Like an adoption order, a freeing order extinguishes: parental responsibility; any order made under the Children Act; and any maintenance obligation to the child existing under an agreement or court order but subject to a contrary intention or any maintenance obligation existing under a trust (ss.18(5) and 12(2)–(4)). As the effect of a freeing order is to remove the birth parent's status (s.18(5)), they need the prior permission of the court to make an application for a s.8 order under the Children Act (see *Re C (Minors)(Adoption: Residence Order)* [1994] Fam 1). Pending adoption, however, birth parents do not need the court's permission to apply for revocation of a freeing order. Pending adoption, however, the court can if appropriate make a contact order under s.8 of the Children Act so that contact can be maintained between the child and the birth parents, and the High Court under its inherent jurisdiction can reduce the amount of any contact as appropriate (see *Re C (Contact: Jurisdiction)* [1995] 1 FLR 777).

Revocation

If 12 months after a freeing order is made, an adoption order has not been made, and the child does not have his or her home with the person with whom he or she was placed for adoption, a birth parent can apply to have the freeing order revoked on the ground that he or she wishes to resume parental responsibility for the child (s.20(1)). Revocation is not, however, available to a parent who has made a declaration that he or she does not wish to be involved in any questions concerning the child (see s.18(6)). Where there is no parent available to revoke a freeing order, the High Court can in certain circumstances revoke it under its inherent jurisdiction (see *Re C (Adoption: Freeing Order)* [1999] Fam 240, [1999] 1 FLR 348, and see further below).

The effect of revocation is to extinguish the agency's parental responsibility and give it back to the child's birth mother and father (but not the unmarried father without parental responsibility). It also revives any parental responsibility agreement or order, and any appointment of a guardian (s.20(3)). However, revocation does not revive any order made under the Children Act (except in respect of parental responsibility and guardianship), and any maintenance obligation existing under an agreement or court order, and does not affect any parental responsibility held by an adoption agency after the freeing order was made (s.20(3A)) (i.e. the parental responsibility possessed by a local authority when a child is in care).

Problems with Freeing

The freeing procedure has not been entirely satisfactory, as the case of *Re G (Adoption: Freeing Order)* [1997] AC 613, [1997] 2 FLR 202 shows (see Richards, 1997). In *Re G*, the child, who had been in care from the age of 5, was freed for adoption at the age of 7. His mother had consented to the adoption and had made a declaration under s.18(6) that she did not wish to be involved in future questions concerning adoption. Eventually, as the boy had reached the age of 15 and had not been adopted, it was agreed that he remain in local authority care and that parental responsibility be shared between the local authority and his mother. However, there was no statutory mechanism available to revoke the freeing order, as the only person who can apply for revocation is a former parent who has not signed a s.18(6) declaration that he or she does not wish to be involved in the adoption (see s.20 and s.19(1)). Thus, neither the mother nor the local authority could apply for revocation, and, even if it could be revoked, it would have restored parental responsibility to the mother which was not what the local authority desired – it wished the child to remain in care. The House of Lords held that, as it could not have been the intention of Parliament to leave children in an adoptive limbo, because of a gap in the legislation, the court could grant the local authority permission to invoke the inherent jurisdiction under s.100 of the Children Act to fill the statutory gap and to revoke the freeing order in the best interests of the child. The court held that revocation would take effect on the making of a care order.

The inherent jurisdiction was also used to revoke a freeing order in *Re J (Freeing for Adoption)* [2000] 2 FLR 58. Here the local authority wished to revoke a freeing order within 12 months of it being made, as the adoption plan had been abandoned and the 12-month period had ceased to serve the child's best interests. It was also unlikely that the child's mother would apply for revocation. Black J held that the inherent jurisdiction could be used to supplement the powers of the court under the Adoption Act in order to protect the child. His Lordship held that nothing expressly prohibited the use of the inherent jurisdiction where an application for revocation under s.20 was not appropriate.

Because of general dissatisfaction with the freeing procedure, in particular the slowness and uncertainty it has created for children, some of whom are left in limbo by the process, the *Review of Adoption* recommended the introduction of adoption placement orders and agreements, instead of freeing for adoption. The Government's recent proposals for changes to the adoption law also recommend the same reforms.

17.5   The Adoption Order

Adoption is finalised by an adoption order, which gives the adopters parental responsibility for the child (s.12(1)). When deciding whether to make an adoption order, the court conducts a two-stage exercise. First, it considers whether adoption is in the child's best interest. If it is, it must then establish whether the relevant agreements to the adoption have been given or can be dispensed with (see 17.8 below). If the court decides that adoption is not in the child's best interests, then there is no need for the question of agreement to be considered. An adoption order cannot be made in respect of a child who is, or has been, married (s.12(5)), but it can be made in respect of a child who has been adopted on a previous occasion (s.12(7)).

Under the Adoption Agencies Regulations 1983, the adoption agency is required to provide the court with a report giving details of the adoption. In contested or complex cases, the court will appoint a guardian *ad litem* to investigate the case (r.18 Adoption Rules 1984). In deciding whether or not to make an adoption order, the court is required to apply the welfare principle in s.6, but it cannot make an order unless the adoption agency or local authority concerned has been given sufficient opportunities to see the child together with the applicant(s) in the home environment (s.13(3)). Furthermore, the court can refuse to make an adoption order where any money has been paid in respect of the adoption (see ss.57 and 24(2)), although the court does have the power to authorise illegal payments retrospectively (s.57(2)) (see *Re Adoption Application AA 212/86 (Adoption: Payment)* [1987] 2 All ER 826, *Re C (A Minor)(Adoption Application)* [1993] 1 FLR 87 and *Re MW (Adoption: Surrogacy)* [1995] 2 FLR 759). If an application for an adoption order is refused, an applicant cannot re-apply, unless the court which refused the application stated otherwise, or because of a change of circumstances or any other reason, the court hearing the re-application considers it proper to proceed (s.24(1)).

An adoption order may contain such terms and conditions as the court thinks fit (s.12(6)). However, as this may undermine the sense of security of the adopters and the child, the House of Lords in *Re C (A Minor)(Adoption Order: Conditions)* [1989] AC 1 held that terms and conditions should only be included in exceptional circumstances. In *Re C*, a condition was inserted to allow contact between an adopted child and her brother. However, since the implementation of the Children Act in 1991, there has been much less need to add terms and conditions to an adoption order, because the court has the power to make a flexible range of orders under s.8 of that Act (see 12.3). Thus in *Re S (A Minor)(Blood Transfusion: Adoption Order Conditions)* [1994] 2 FLR 416, for example, the Court of Appeal, applying *Re C*, refused to insert a condition in an adoption order in respect of blood transfusions where the adopters were Jehovah's Witnesses, as the matter could be dealt with later when the need arose (e.g. by making a specific issue order under s.8 of the Children Act). Because of the court's flexible power to make s.8 orders under the Children Act in adoption proceedings, the draft Adoption Bill 1996 did not give the court power to impose conditions on an adoption order. However, in order to prevent a s.8 order undermining an adoption, the Bill only allowed the court to make a s.8 contact order in conjunction with a placement order (cl.28(3)(a)).

An interim adoption order can be made, which has the effect of giving parental responsibility to the applicant(s) for a probationary period of up to two years and upon such terms as to the maintenance of the child and otherwise as the court thinks fit (s.25(1)). However, interim orders are rarely made, for where there is any doubt about the suitability of the adopter(s), or a chance that the child might be rehabilitated with his or her parents, the court can make a s.8 residence order which, unlike an adoption order, can be revoked if necessary. Another option would be for the court to consider making a family assistance order (see 12.8). Because interim orders are rarely made, and have little use, the draft Adoption Bill 1996 made no provision for them.

Although an adoption order is a final order which cannot be revoked (it can only be removed by a further adoption order), it may be discharged on appeal, or in very exceptional circumstances set aside. Thus in *Re M (Minors)(Adoption)* [1991] 1 FLR 458, an order was set aside owing to procedural irregularity – agreement to adoption had been given by mistake. In *Re K (Adoption and Wardship)* [1997] 2 FLR 221, an adoption order was also set aside and the case remitted for a rehearing, as the order was fundamentally flawed. The adopters had adopted a Bosnian baby, but had failed to comply with the procedural requirements in respect of an inter-country adoption (e.g. to appoint a guardian *ad litem*, to inform the baby's Bosnian guardian and to inform the Home Office). However, adoption orders are not set aside in every case where there is a mistake or some misapprehension. Thus, in *Re B (Adoption: Setting Aside)* [1995] 1 FLR 1, an application to set an adoption aside was made by a person who had been adopted and raised in the Jewish faith, but who had later discovered his natural father was an Arab and his mother a Roman Catholic. His application was refused.

Appeals

It is difficult to bring a successful appeal against a decision made in adoption proceedings, as the court has considerable discretion in these matters, and appeal courts are reluctant to interfere with discretionary decisions. In *Re O (Adoption: Withholding Consent)* [1999] 1 FLR 45, where an appeal was dismissed, Swinton Thomas LJ referred to the following words of Lord Reid in *O'Connor and Another* v. *A and B* [1971] 1 WLR 1277 at 1229:

'Adoption cases depend so much on general impression rather than the ascertainment of particular facts that when the judge at first instance has seen the parties an appeal court must be slow to reverse his decision unless he has misdirected himself as to the law or has otherwise clearly gone wrong.'

Effects of an Adoption Order

The effect of an adoption order is to terminate the child's legal relationship with his or her birth family and give him or her a new legal status. Where the adopters are married, the child must be treated in law as if he or she had been born of the adopters' marriage, whether or not he or she was born after the marriage was solemnised (s.39(1)(a)). In other cases, the child must be treated in law as if he or she had been born to the adopters in wedlock (but not as a child of any actual marriage of the adopter) (s.39(1)(b)). Thus the child is treated as a marital, not non-marital child. An adoption order extinguishes: any parental responsibility which any person had before the adoption order was made; any order made under the Children Act; and any maintenance obligation to the child existing under an agreement or court order, unless the agreement exists under a trust or the agreement states otherwise (s.12(3) and (4)). An adoption order automatically terminates any court order and discharges any care order (s.12(3)(a)).

An adopted child acquires British citizenship on adoption if the adoption order is made by a court in the UK, and the adopter is a British citizen (s.1(5) British Nationality Act 1981). Under the Immigration Rules, a child who has been adopted abroad or a child who is to be adopted in the UK can be admitted to the UK, but only at the discretion of the Home Secretary. Permission to enter is refused if the adoption has conferred, or will confer, no benefit on the child other than British citizenship. Thus, if the motive for adoption is to obtain British nationality and immigration rights, rather than to promote a child's welfare, an application will be refused. In *Re K (A Minor)(Adoption Order: Nationality)* [1994] 2 FLR 557, an adoption order in respect of a teenage girl from South Africa was discharged on the Home Secretary's appeal, as it was held that the benefits of adoption were minimal as compared to considerations of public policy. However, in *Re H (Adoption: Non-Patrial)* [1996] 2 FLR 187, an adoption order was granted in respect of a child from Pakistan despite the Home Secretary's refusal to allow the child to remain in the UK.

17.6 Qualifications for Adoption

(a) Who can be Adopted?

Only a child under the age of 18 who is not, or has not been, married can be adopted (s.72(1), s.12(5)). A child who has nearly reached majority can be adopted. Thus, in *Re D (Adoption: Foreign Guardianship)* [1999] 2 FLR 865, because of the legal, social and psychological advantages adoption gave her, an adoption order was made in respect of a 17-year-old girl who had been a Romanian orphan. A child who has already been adopted can be adopted again (s.12(7)). A child who is going to be adopted must have spent some time living with the applicant(s) before an adoption order is made. In the case of an 'in family' adoption (e.g. where the adoption involves a step-parent or a relative), or where the child was placed with the applicant(s) by an adoption agency or under a High Court order, an adoption order cannot be made unless the child is more than 9 weeks old and at all times during the preceding 13 weeks has had his or her home with the applicant(s) (s.13(1)). With other adoptions, the child must be at least 12 months old and must have lived with the applicant(s) at all times during the previous 12 months (s.13(2)). An adoption order cannot be made unless the adoption agency or local authority has been given sufficient opportunities to see the child with the applicant(s) in the home environment (s.13(3)). Parental agreement to the adoption must have been given or have been dispensed with (s.16) (see below), or the child must be free for adoption (see 17.4 above).

(b) Who can Adopt?

Joint and sole applications can be made.

(i) Joint Applications Only a married couple can make a joint application (s.14(1)), and each party must be at least 21 years old. However, in the case of

an adoption by a birth parent and a step-parent of the child, it is sufficient that the birth parent is aged 18 (s.14(1A) and (1B)). A cohabiting couple cannot make a joint application for adoption, but if both of them wish to acquire parental responsibility for the child, then one of them can apply for an adoption order and one or both of them apply for a joint s.8 residence order under the Children Act 1989 (see 12.4). The effect of a residence order is to give the applicant parental responsibility for the duration of the order. In *Re AB (Adoption: Joint Residence)* [1996] 1 FLR 27, an adoption order was made in favour of a foster-father with a joint residence order made in favour of himself and his female cohabitant. The draft Adoption Bill 1996 (rather surprisingly when cohabitation is so common) made no provision to allow cohabitants to make joint applications. The Government considered it better for children to be brought up in the security and stability of married relationships.

(ii) Sole Application   A sole application may be made for an adoption order, provided the applicant is at least 21 years old (s.15). A married person cannot make a sole application unless he or she satisfies the court that the other spouse cannot be found, or that they have separated permanently and are living apart, or that the other spouse is incapable of making an application owing to physical or mental ill-health (s.15(1)). The Act does not prohibit sole applications by homosexual persons whether living alone or otherwise. Thus in *Re W (Adoption: Homosexual Adopter)* [1998] Fam 58, [1997] 2 FLR 406, a lesbian woman who had been living in a long and stable relationship with a professional woman was granted an adoption order (see also *Re E (Adoption: Freeing Order)* [1995] 1 FLR 382, where the Court of Appeal upheld the judge's decision to dispense with the agreement of a mother who objected to her child being adopted by a single lesbian).

Suitability for Adoption

Adoption agencies are responsible for establishing whether prospective adopters are suitable for adoption. Each agency has its own policies and guidelines in respect of assessing suitability, but the age and the health of the applicant(s), and the home environment are important considerations. The adoption panel is responsible for making recommendations as to whether adoption is in the child's best interests, and as to the suitability of the applicants. The adoption agency is required to take into account the adoption panel's recommendations when making its decision (rr.10 and 11 Adoption Agencies Regulations 1983). Would-be adopters who are rejected for adoption can challenge the agency's decision by applying for judicial review on the ground, for instance, that the decision is unreasonable or unlawful, or there is some procedural impropriety (see, for example, *R v. Secretary of State for*

Health, ex p Luff [1992] 1 FLR 59, *R* v. *Lancashire County Council, ex p M* [1992] 1 FLR 109 and *R* v. *Lewisham London Borough Council ex p P* [1991] 2 FLR 185).

17.7   Agreement to Adoption

Once the court has decided that adoption is in the child's best interests, it must be satisfied before making an adoption (or freeing) order that each birth parent (or guardian of the child) freely and with full understanding of what is involved agrees unconditionally to the making of the order, or that their agreement can be dispensed with on any of the grounds laid down in ss.16(1) and 18(1) (see below). Agreement to adoption must exist at the time the order is made, but can be withdrawn at any time before then. For the purpose of agreement, a guardian is a person appointed under s.5 of the Children Act (see 11.5) and a parent is any person having parental responsibility for the child under the Children Act (s.72) (see 11.6). In the case of a baby, the mother's agreement cannot be obtained until at least six weeks after the child's birth (ss.16(4) and 18(4)).

The reporting officer (an independent social worker or probation officer appointed by the court from the Panel of Guardians *ad litem* and Reporting Officers) is responsible for ensuring that parental agreement is freely given and witnessing the formal agreement (s.61). The reporting officer can also provide the court with a report about the case. Although the contents of a guardian *ad litem*'s report about the child need not be disclosed to the child's birth parents in a contested application, the House of Lords has held that non-disclosure should be the exception, rather than the rule (*Re D (Adoption Reports: Confidentiality)* [1996] AC 593, [1995] 2 FLR 687).

The Unmarried Father and Adoption

Although an adoption agency does not need to obtain the agreement to the adoption of the unmarried father with parental responsibility (as he does not come within the definition of 'parent' in s.72), he is taken into account in several ways during the adoption process. First, before making a freeing order the court must be satisfied that the unmarried father without parental responsibility is not applying for an order which would give him parental responsibility, or that if he did so, he would be refused (s.18(7)). Secondly, he has a right to be heard on the merits of the adoption application where he is contributing to the child's maintenance, in which case he must be joined as a respondent (r.15(2)(h) Adoption Rules 1984). Thirdly, the court may allow him to participate in the proceedings under its discretionary powers to add anyone as a party (r.4(3)). His interests are also protected to some extent because the agency must deal with him as any other father 'so far as it is reasonably practicable and in the interests of the child' (r.7(3) Adoption Agencies Regulations 1983).

Despite these provisions, however, an unmarried father without parental responsibility is in a disadvantageous position, as the agency is not obliged to inform him that his child is going to be adopted and is not obliged to ascertain his wishes and feelings about the proposed adoption (see *Re P (Adoption: Natural Father's Rights)* [1994] 1 FLR 771). Neither is it mandatory for him to be joined as respondent to adoption proceedings (*Re C (Adoption: Parties)* [1995] 2 FLR 483). However, as a result of increasing recognition given to unmarried fathers (see 11.7), fathers without parental responsibility may have their wishes taken into account in certain circumstances. In *Re G (Adoption Order)* [1999] 1 FLR 400, the Court of Appeal held that a natural father lacking parental responsibility and the statutory right to refuse consent had to be evaluated on a wide spectrum. As the unmarried father in this case had been manifestly entitled to greater consideration than that given by the judge, the Court of Appeal allowed his appeal against the adoption order made in favour of the child's mother and her new husband. Furthermore, in *Keegan* v. *Ireland* (1994) 18 EHRR 342, the Irish authorities' failure to notify an unmarried father that his child had been placed for adoption was held to be a breach of the European Convention on Human Rights, even though the father had never lived with the child. Despite a change of attitude to unmarried fathers, it is advisable for an unmarried father who wishes to challenge the adoption of his child to obtain parental responsibility, if he does not already possess it (see 11.7).

Child's Agreement

The child's agreement to adoption is not required, although courts and adoption agencies must 'so far as practicable ascertain the wishes and feelings of the child regarding the decision and give due consideration to them, having regard to his age and understanding' (s.6).

17.8   Grounds for Dispensing with Parental Agreement

The court can dispense with the agreement of a parent or guardian in proceedings for an adoption order (s.16(2)) or a freeing order (s.18(1)) where (see s.16(2)) the parent or guardian concerned:

(a) cannot be found or is incapable of giving agreement;
(b) is withholding his or her agreement unreasonably;
(c) has persistently failed without reasonable cause to discharge his or her parental responsibility for the child;

(d) has abandoned or neglected the child;
(e) has persistently ill-treated the child; or
(f) has seriously ill-treated the child.

Agreement may not be dispensed with unless the child is already placed for adoption, or the court is satisfied that the child will be placed for adoption (s.18(3)).

As far as ground (a) (cannot be found) is concerned, the court will require all reasonable steps to have been taken to find the parent or guardian, and if one reasonable step is not taken then this ground may not be satisfied (see *Re S (Adoption)* [1999] 2 FLR 374, a decision of the Scottish court in respect of the identical provision under the Adoption (Scotland) Act 1978).

Agreement is most often dispensed with on ground (b) (withholding agreement unreasonably) and it is this ground which has produced most judicial discussion. The leading authority is *Re W (An Infant)* [1971] AC 682. Here the House of Lords held that the test of unreasonably withholding agreement is not one of culpability or of callous self-indifference, or of failure or probable failure of parental duty or of potential lasting damage to the child, but of reasonableness in all the circumstances. Their Lordships held that, although the child's welfare *per se* was not the test, the fact that a reasonable parent would consider the child's welfare made welfare a more or less relevant or decisive factor depending on how the reasonable parent would regard it. Reasonableness was to be judged by an objective test – whether a reasonable parent in the same circumstances would withhold consent, rather than whether the particular parent in question had reasonably done so. However, the House of Lords held that the court should not substitute its own view for that of the parent. The question to be asked was whether the decision of the parent in the particular case came within a band of reasonable decisions which a parent in the same position would make, taking account of all the circumstances. The question of reasonableness is judged at the time of the adoption proceedings (*Devon County Council* v. *B* [1997] 1 FLR 591). In adoption proceedings, therefore, the birth parents' wishes do not prevail, and the presumption in favour of natural parents is not an overriding factor (see *Re A (Adoption: Mother's Objections)* [2000] 1 FLR 665, where agreement was dispensed with).

In *Re F (Adoption: Freeing Order)* [2000] 2 FLR 505, the Court of Appeal had to consider whether consent to a freeing order was being unreasonably withheld, where a father of four children objected to the youngest child's adoption on the basis that it would isolate her and result in her suffering loss of meaningful contact with her older sisters. The judge at first instance held that adoption was in the child's best interests but refused to make the order on the basis that a reasonable parent would conclude that the advantages of adoption were outweighed by the loss of inter-sibling contact. Therefore the father's consent to a freeing order was not being unreasonably withheld. The guardian *ad litem*'s appeal against the freeing order was allowed by the Court of Appeal, which stated that the judgment in *Re C (A Minor)(Adoption: Parental Agreement: Contact)* [1993] 2 FLR 260 contained a useful and clear exposition of the approach to be taken. In *Re C*, it was held that the question to be answered by a judge considering whether a parent was withholding consent to a freeing order unreasonably was whether, having regard to the evidence and applying the current values of society, the advantages of adoption for the welfare of the child appeared sufficiently strong to justify overriding the views and interest of the objecting parent.

Whether the court will dispense with agreement on the ground that it is being unreasonably withheld depends on the facts of the case. Disagreement has been dispensed with, for example, where a parent has vacillated about agreement for some time (see *Re H (Infants)(Adoption: Parental Consent)* [1977] WLR 471), and where a parent has refused to give consent because of her suspicion and dislike of social services rather than her concern for the child (see *Re H (Adoption: Parental Agreement)* [1983] 4 FLR 614). In *Re E (Adoption: Freeing Order)* [1995] 1 FLR 382, the court dispensed with the birth mother's consent to the adoption of her child by a single lesbian woman. Applying the objective test of a hypothetical reasonable parent having regard to the needs of the child and taking into account expert evidence on lesbian parenting, the mother was unreasonably refusing consent. In *Re R (Adoption: Protection from Offenders Regulations)* [1999] 1 FLR 472, agreement was dispensed with even though the adoptive father had 20 years earlier been convicted of offences relating to children. The child was a Down's syndrome child whom the parents had rejected and had not seen since infancy. Sir Stephen Brown P held that hypothetical reasonable parents would not withhold consent where a child was a stranger to them, had special needs which they were unable to meet, had known no family other than the foster carers, and on whom she was wholly dependent. The court is unlikely to dispense with a birth parent's agreement to adoption by a step-parent (see 17.9 below), but it may do so in some circumstances (see *Re B (Adoption: Father's Objections)* [1999] 2 FLR 215, where it did so).

Whether or not agreement should be dispensed with on the ground that it is being unreasonably withheld involves a difficult task for the court (see *Re M (Adoption or Residence Order)* [1998] 1 FLR 570, where the Court of Appeal was divided on the issue of whether the child's wishes should prevail over parental wishes). The outcome of a case sometimes depends on whether the courts take a 'child-centred' or 'parent-centred' approach, and the case-law shows a certain ambivalence in this respect (see, for example, *Re H; Re W (Adoption: Parental Agreement)* (1983) FLR 614, *Re E (Minors)(Adoption: Parental Agreement)* [1990] 2 FLR 397 and *(Re C (A Minor)(Adoption: Parental Agreement: Contact)* [1993], see above). This ambivalence between welfare and parental wishes has been evident in proposed reforms. The *Review* recommended the retention of ground (a) above (parent cannot be found or is incapable of giving agreement). But it recommended that the other grounds be replaced by a single ground that the court must be satisfied that the advantages to the child of becoming part of a new family and having a new legal status are so significantly greater than the advantages to the child of any alternative option as to justify overriding the wishes of a parent or guardian (para. 12.6). The approach recommended in the *Review* was therefore parent-centred. It made it clear that the child's welfare should not be the court's paramount consideration when deciding whether to dispense with consent. However, the draft 1996 Bill took a more child-centred welfarist approach. It made the child's welfare the 'paramount' consideration, and provided that the court could dispense with consent, if (a) the parent or guardian could not be found or was incapable of giving consent, or (b) the court was satisfied that the welfare of the child required the consent to be dispensed with. The Government's recent proposals also recommend that the child's welfare should be the paramount consideration in adoption proceedings (see 17.13).

17.9   Adoptions by Step-parents and Relatives

Sometimes children are adopted by their relatives, and sometimes even by their own mother or father. Thus, in *B* v. *P (Adoption by Unmarried Father)* [2000] 2 FLR 717, an unmarried father was granted an adoption order after the mother had put the child up for adoption. Bracewell J granted the adoption order as she felt that this would give the child greater security and protection. Sometimes children are adopted by their birth parent when that parent remarries. In fact, increasing numbers of children live with step-parents. Some step-parents may wish to adopt their step-child in order to cement the family relationship and to show their commitment to the child. As married couples are required to make joint applications for adoption, the child's birth parent and the child's step-parent must both apply to adopt the child. Step-parent adoptions and adoptions by the child's relatives (such as a grandmother) are often unsatisfactory. First, they are highly artificial because with step-parent adoptions the child's birth parent must make an application. Secondly, an 'in family' adoption may terminate the child's legal relationship with the other birth parent and sever the child's social relationship with the birth parent and the other half of his or her birth family. The *Review of Adoption* expressed concern about step-parent adoptions. It said that where the prime motivation for adoption was to cement the family unit and put away the past, this might be confusing for a child and lead to identity problems, especially if the new marriage broke down, which was statistically not unlikely. It was also felt that the step-parent's own family might show little interest or involvement in the adopted child so that he or she would not only lose his or her birth family but fail to gain another.

The court is therefore likely to be cautious about granting an adoption order in a step-parent adoption for the reasons above, and it might consider that the matter is better dealt with by making an order under the Children Act. Thus it might decide instead to make a residence order in favour of a step-parent, which would have the effect of conferring parental responsibility on the step-parent (or other relative) for the duration of the order (see 12.4). In *Re PJ (Adoption: Practice on Appeal)* [1998] 2 FLR 252, at 260, Thorpe LJ said:

> 'Cautionary dicta are still apt since applications in step-parent adoptions may be driven or complicated by motives or emotions derived from conflict within the triangle of adult relationships. They may also be buoyed up by quite unrealistic hopes and assumptions as to the quality of the marriage replacing that into which the children were born.'

The court is unlikely to make an adoption order in the case of a step-parent adoption where the other birth parent objects to the adoption, but it may do so in some circumstances, as it did in *Re B (Adoption: Father's Objections)* [1999] 2 FLR 215. Here the Court of Appeal dispensed with the birth father's consent to adoption by the child's step-father, because the child, aged 12, wished to be adopted by his step-father and feared that his natural father might abduct him. Butler-Sloss LJ said it was unusual to dispense with agreement to a step-parent adoption, but nevertheless refused to consider an 'open' adoption (adoption with contact) on the facts, and an adoption order was made.

Because of criticisms of step-parent adoptions, the *Review of Adoption Law* (at para. 19.3) recommended that a new order should be introduced which would be available only to step-parents and which did not make the birth-parent an adoptive parent.

17.10   Adoption with Contact

Attitudes to contact after adoption have changed over the years. At one time, adoption was 'closed' in the sense that contact after adoption was not considered a possibility. It was best for the child that links with his or her family were severed for ever. However, it gradually became accepted that contact might be beneficial to children in exceptional cases. In later cases, however, it was sometimes considered beneficial if contact between children and their birth family was maintained whether or not the case was exceptional. As it is now older children who are often adopted, contact with the child's birth family may be in a child's best interests. In fact, according to a study by the Social Services Inspectorate (*Moving Goalposts*, SSI, 1995), in approximately 70 per cent of the adoptions in the areas studied some form of direct or indirect contact with the birth family was maintained.

Because contact is beneficial in some cases, before a child is placed for adoption the agency making the placement discusses the question of contact with the parties and the child and the form it might take. If contact is considered beneficial for a child, it will not necessarily result in direct contact, but indirect contact might be ordered, such as periodical reports about the child. In *Re O (Adoption: Withholding Consent)* [1999] 1 FLR 45, the child's unmarried father objected to the adoption. The court held that he was withholding his agreement unreasonably and an adoption order was made, but he was granted a parental responsibility order and provision was made for him to have direct contact with his child twice a year. In some cases the adoption agency may encourage the parties to draw up an agreement about future contact. Adopters who enter into an agreement about contact are not permitted to renege on an agreement without good reason. In *Re T (Adopted Children: Contact)* [1996] Fam 34, [1995] 2 FLR 792, the adopters reneged on their agreement to provide their adopted children's half-sister with annual reports about them. As a result, the half-sister was granted leave to apply for a contact order.

However, despite the possible benefits of contact, the court is unlikely to make a contact order against the wishes of adoptive parents, as this would undermine their parental responsibility and their autonomy to make decisions about the child, and would cause friction for all concerned. In some cases the court may apply the no-order presumption in s.1(5) of the Children Act (see 12.3) and consider that contact arrangements can be made informally without the need for an order (*Re T (Adoption: Contact)* [1995] 2 FLR 251).

The court can order contact by inserting a condition into an adoption order under s.12(6) of the Adoption Act (see *Re C (A Minor)(Adoption Order: Conditions)* [1989] AC 1 above), or by making a s.8 contact order under the Children Act either in separate proceedings or in the freeing or adoption proceedings, which are family proceedings for the purposes of the Children Act (see s.8(4)). The procedure which is usually used is to apply for a s.8 contact order. However, if adoption has already taken place, the birth parents and any other person will require the prior permission of the court to apply for a contact order (see 12.6). In most cases, however, leave is unlikely to be granted because of the permanent and final nature of adoption orders (see Thorpe J in *Re C (A Minor)(Adopted Child: Contact)* [1993] 2 FLR 431), except where there has been unacceptable behaviour. In *Re S (Contact: Application by Sibling)* [1999] Fam 283, [1998] 2 FLR 819, a 9 year-old girl, who wished to see her 7-year-old half brother, sought the court's permission to apply for a contact order, but the adoptive mother thought it would be wrong to disrupt her brother's upbringing. Charles J refused permission for the girl to apply for a contact order, stressing the finality and permanence of adoption orders and stating that issues such as contact should not be re-opened after an adoption order has been made unless there has been some fundamental change of circumstances. Contact was not in the best interests of her brother. Where a birth parent wishes to maintain contact, the court is likely to think seriously about whether an adoption order is appropriate at all. In *Re P (Adoption: Freeing Order)* [1994] 2 FLR 1000, the judge was held to be wrong in saying in a freeing application that the mother was unreasonably withholding her agreement to adoption while also saying that contact should be a precondition of adoption.

17.11   Registration of Adoption and Access to Birth Records and the Contact Register

At one time, adoption was seen as a secretive process in which it was thought best for children not to have contact with, or knowledge of, their birth parents. However, this view has changed, and it is now recognised that 'a child's knowledge of his or her background is crucial to the formation of a positive self-identity, and that adoptive families should be encouraged to be open about the child's adoptive status and the special nature of the adoptive relationship' (*Review*, para. 4.1). Thus, it is now possible for an adopted person to investigate his or her origins, and make contact with his or her birth family, if so desired.

Registration of Adoption

The Registrar General is responsible for maintaining an Adopted Children Register which provides proof by public record of adoptions (s.50(1)). It is open to public inspection (s.50(3)). On adoption, the child's birth certificate is replaced with a certified copy of the entry in the Register, which gives the child's names and is sufficient evidence of date and place of birth (s.50(2)). The court has no jurisdiction to restrict the information which must be placed in the Adopted Children Register, but the court under its inherent jurisdiction may prohibit the Registrar General providing details of the adoption to any applicant while the child is under the age of 18. Thus, in *Re X (A Minor) (Adoption Details: Disclosure)* [1994] 2 FLR 450, the local authority successfully invoked the inherent jurisdiction under s.100 of the Children Act to obtain a court order prohibiting the Registrar General from disclosing information in the Register to the child's natural mother as she might seek to trace the child which would cause the child distress and insecurity (see also *Re W (Adoption Details: Disclosure)* [1998] 2 FLR 625).

Birth Certificates

An adopted person over the age of 18 may obtain a copy of his or her original birth certificate from the Registrar General (s.51(1)). Before providing a copy, the Registrar General must first inform the applicant that counselling services are available at the General Register Office or from a local authority (s.51(3)). The Registrar General, however, retains a discretion to refuse to provide a copy, for example for reasons of public policy. In *R* v. *Registrar General ex p Smith* [1991] 2 QB 393, the Registrar General had refused to provide a Broadmoor patient with a copy of his original birth certificate, on the ground that his mother might be endangered if he were released. The prisoner's application for judicial review of the Registrar General's decision was refused.

Adoption Records

Adoption agencies are required to keep adoption records for 75 years. Local authorities who have supervised adoption placements and provided reports are not obliged to keep records but some do so. Some agencies and local authorities may be prepared to disclose information about an adoption. The Registrar General has a duty to keep records about the child. The court can in exceptional circumstances, where it is reasonable to do so, make orders requiring the Registrar General to disclose information about the child (s.50(5)). In *Re H (Adoption: Disclosure of Information)* [1995] 1 FLR 236, an order was granted authorising the Registrar General to provide information so that a 53-year-old adoptee with a treatable genetic disease could trace her brother so that he could be screened and treated if necessary. However, in *D* v. *Registrar General* [1997] 1 FLR 715, a birth mother's application for the Registrar General to disclose information to enable her to trace her child was refused, as the applicant had failed to make out a sufficient case to persuade the court of the reasonableness of the order sought. A natural parent who wishes to make even indirect inquiries about his or her adopted child must show circumstances of an exceptional nature and show that contact would result in some need or benefit to the adopted person. Strong emotional curiosity on the part of a natural parent is not sufficient to override the statutory duties of non-disclosure imposed on the Registrar General by s.50(5) of the Adoption Act (*Re L (Adoption: Disclosure of Information)* [1998] Fam 19).

Adoption Contact Register

The Registrar General is required to keep an Adoption Contact Register (s.51A). The purpose of the Register is to enable adopted children to register their wish to contact their relatives and for relatives to register details of an adopted person's birth. A fee is charged. Part I of the Register contains the names of adopted persons who have obtained a copy of their birth certificate and who wish to contact a relative. Part II contains the names and present addresses of relatives who would like to contact an adopted person. Where there is a match, the Registrar General gives the adopted person the relative's name and address, but no information is provided to the relative. Because of the distress that contact can cause, the draft Adoption Bill 1996 provided that adopted persons, birth parents and relatives could register their wish not to be contacted (cl.65).

17.12   Inter-Country Adoption

Over the years there have been increasing numbers of inter-country adoptions. Wars throughout the world, as well as poverty, have left large numbers of children abandoned and orphaned. However, although the adoption of children from abroad may give them a quality of life they did not possess in their country of origin, there has been concern that these adoptions exploit the needs of children, as they are too adult-centred. They may satisfy the needs of those who wish to adopt children but they fail to take account of the importance of children remaining in touch with their own cultural roots and their birth family. There is also the additional concern that such adoptions may have been arranged privately without the checks and safeguards which exist for adoptions under domestic law.

As a result of concerns about inter-country adoption, the Hague Convention on Inter-Country Adoption 1993 was passed, and is due to be implemented into UK law in January 2002 by the Adoption (Inter-country Aspects) Act 1999. Article 1 of the Convention provides that the aims of the Convention are:

'(1) to establish safeguards to ensure that inter-country adoptions take place in the best interests of the child and with respect for the child's fundamental rights as recognised by international law;

 (2) to establish a system of co-operation among Contracting States to ensure that those safeguards are respected and thereby prevent the abduction, the sale of, or traffic in children;

 (3) to secure the recognition in Contracting States of adoptions made in accordance with the Convention.'

The underlying rationale of the Convention is for Contracting States to work together to ensure that adoption is in the best interests of the child, and only after possibilities for placement of the child within the State of origin have been given due consideration (art. 4(b)). The aim is for children to stay within their own communities where possible. Where this is not possible, then the Convention makes provisions to regulate the adoption process. It does this by requiring Central Authorities to be established whose function is to work together to protect the child during the adoption process and to monitor the operation of the Convention. Central Authorities are responsible *inter alia* for exchanging information about the child, ensuring that the child is adoptable, that the relevant consents have been given after appropriate counselling and that they have not been induced by payment or compensation, and ensuring that the prospective adopters are eligible and suited to adopt the child. The Convention also provides for the automatic recognition in all Contracting States of adoptions certified by the Central Authority concerned as having been made in accordance with the Convention.

17.13   Adoption: The Future

Adoption has a continuing role to play, but reform of the law is needed to reflect the changes and trends which have occurred since the Adoption Act 1976 was passed.

In some situations, notably in the context of 'in-family' adoptions, particularly step-parent adoptions, changes are needed. Step-parent adoptions are common, owing to the high incidence of divorce and remarriage, but these adoptions are unsatisfactory because the child's own parent must apply to adopt the child, and because adoption may result in the child being separated from his or her birth parent and birth family. Reforms were proposed in the 1990s to reduce the need for step-parents to apply for adoption. The *Review* (at para. 19) recommended a new type of adoption order which could be granted to a step-parent but which would not make the birth parent an adoptive parent. It also recommended that a step-parent adoption order could be revoked where the marriage ended in divorce or in death. Under the recommendations, a step-parent would therefore be able to make a sole application for adoption. The proposals also aimed to reduce the need for step-parent adoption by allowing step-parents to share parental responsibility by an agreement made with both natural parents which would be registered with the court (draft Adoption Bill, cl 85).

Although a wholesale harmonisation of adoption law and the Children Act 1989 is not a good idea, because the underlying policies and principles of adoption are quite different from other areas of child law, some of the concepts in the Children Act could be integrated into a reformed adoption law. The introduction of a welfare checklist similar to that in s.1(3) of the Children Act might be beneficial, and possibly a 'no-delay' principle like that in s.1(2). It might be inappropriate, however, to introduce into adoption law a welfare test based on the paramountcy principle. Adoption is a serious step and parental interests need to be considered, as well as those of children.

An important reform which is overdue is the need to amend the law to give cohabiting partners the right to make joint applications for adoption. Under the current law, only one cohabitant can obtain an adoption order and the other must obtain parental responsibility by means of a residence order. This is unsatisfactory for children and discriminates against cohabitants. There is no reason why the right to make a joint application for adoption should not be available to cohabitants, whether they be heterosexual or homosexual partners. Another important reform which is needed is for children of sufficient age and understanding to be given a statutory right to consent to adoption, unless incapable of doing so. This would bring adoption law into line with the Children Act and other areas of the law. The provisions in respect of freeing for adoption also need to be reformed, in particular to rid the law of the gaps which result in some children becoming 'statutory orphans'.

It is now about 25 years since the Adoption Act 1976 was passed and there have been significant changes in adoption practice. Reform of adoption is considered to be long overdue. However, reform is now imminent. On 7 July 2000 the Prime Minister announced a series of measures to promote and speed up the adoption process, and also launched a consultation period on a range of proposals as part of a wide-ranging review of adoption (*The Prime Minister's Review of Adoption*, Cabinet Office, and see Barton, 2000). The Government said it intended to increase the adoption of children in local authority care and to introduce a wide-ranging strategy to deliver the service which children had a right to expect, and to put the needs and rights of children at the centre of the adoption process. The Government recommended the introduction of placement orders, and suggested proposals for an order which would be halfway between an adoption order and a residence order. The Government (para. 8.5) said that an intermediate legal status for children was needed which gave children greater security than long-term fostering without the absolute legal severance from the birth family associated with adoption. Such an order would also be useful in the context of 'in family' adoptions. A particularly radical proposal was the introduction of a new welfare principle which would make the child's welfare 'paramount' in adoption, as it is in the Children Act 1989. Currently, it is the 'first' consideration. In December 2000 the Government published a White Paper, *Adoption: A New Approach* (Cm 5017, Department of Health, and available on the DOH website). In the Foreword the Prime Minister, Tony Blair, said:

> 'Poor performance, widespread variations, unacceptable delays, agonisingly high hurdles for adopters to surmount – in far too many parts of the system, there is a lack of clarity, of consistency and of fairness. Most pressingly, children in an already vulnerable position are being badly let down.'

Because of the drawbacks of the current system, the Government proposes to modernise adoption and to introduce a new approach, above all because it wants to see vulnerable children safe in permanent families. In particular it wishes to improve the role of adoption in the context of children in local authority care, because it considers the child care system is failing children.

Too many children are being moved too often between placements, and are not being placed in permanent families. The process is slow, and there are wide variations in practice by local authorities. As part of is 'new approach' to adoption, the Government plans to invest money in improving the adoption service, and to increase the number of children in care who are adopted. It also intends to legislate to overhaul and modernise the legal framework for adoption. This will include the establishment of an adoption register (with details of all children waiting to be adopted and approved adoptive families), a new legal framework for adoption allowances, and an independent review mechanism for the assessment of potential adopters. Measures are also proposed to speed up the adoption process, with a range of powers to ensure local authority compliance.

In addition to significant changes in adoption practice, the Government also intends to change the law to align the Adoption Act 1976 with the Children Act 1989. It also proposes the setting up of specialised adoption court centres. Furthermore, it proposes the amendment of adoption forms so that agreement is stated to be in the best interests of the child being adopted. A particularly significant proposal is the introduction of a new form of child placement ('a special guardianship') which will provide permanence for children short of the legal separation involved in adoption. This new form of placement, the Government says, will be useful where children do not wish to be separated from their birth families, and where minority ethnic communities have religious and cultural difficulties with adoption. Long-term fostering will still remain available as an option, however.

In sum, the Government proposes 'to improve adoption services, put the child's needs at the centre of the process and ensure that adoption plays its proper role as part of an integrated service for meeting the needs and improving the life chances of some of society's most vulnerable children' (para. 3.7). Whether the Government's aims will be achieved in practice, remains to be seen.

Summary

1 Adoption severs the legal link between the birth parents and the child and creates a new legal link between the adopters and the child.
2 The law on adoption is laid down in the Adoption Act 1976.
3 A legal adoption can only be effected by an adoption order, which is irrevocable; it transfers parental responsibility from the birth parents to the adopters.
4 Only local authorities and approved voluntary adoption societies can run adoption agencies, which are responsible for the control and supervision of adoption placements.
5 The welfare of the child is the first consideration of the court and of any adoption agency when reaching a decision in relation to the adoption of the child (s.6).

6 A freeing order can be applied for under s.18 before an application is made for an adoption order. The court can make a freeing order only if the parent (other than the unmarried father without parental responsibility) or guardian consents to the adoption, or has had his or her agreement dispensed with. Only adoption agencies can make freeing applications. A freeing order can be revoked in some circumstances. A freeing order vests parental responsibility in the adoption agency.

7 A child under the age of 18 who is not, or has not been, married can be adopted.

8 Joint and sole applications for adoption can be made, but joint applications can only be made by married couples. A sole application cannot be made by a married person unless the other spouse has disappeared, the parties have permanently separated, or the other spouse is ill or disabled. Applicants for adoption must be over 21, but a birth parent applicant (in the case of a step-parent adoption) need be only 18.

9 Parental agreement to adoption is needed but can be dispensed with on certain grounds, the most common ground being that agreement is unreasonably withheld.

10 An adoption order can contain terms and conditions. In exceptional circumstances an adoption order can include a condition as to contact, or a person can apply for a contact order under the Children Act (see 12.3). In some cases, notably after adoption, an applicant needs the court's prior permission to seek a contact order (see 12.5).

11 Radical proposals for the reform of adoption law were made by the Conservative Government, but these were not implemented. However, as reform of adoption law is considered to be long overdue, the Labour Government has made proposals for change, which are expected to come into force in the near future.

Further Reading and References

Adoption – A Service for Children: Adoption Bill – A Consultative Document, Department of Health and Welsh Office, 1996.

Bainham, 'Gay survivors and lesbian parents' (1998) CLJ 42.

Barton, 'Adoption – the Prime Minister's Review' [2000] Fam Law 731.

Cooke, 'Dispensing with parental consent to adoption – a choice of welfare tests' [1997] CFLQ 259.

Lindley, 'Open adoption – is the door ajar?' [1997] CFLQ 115.

Lindley and Wyld, 'The Children Act and the draft Adoption Bill – diverging principles' [1996] CFLQ 327.

Lowe, 'The changing face of adoption – The gift/donation model versus the contract/services model' [1997] CFLQ.

Parker (ed.), *Adoption Now – Messages from Research,* 1999, Department of Health.

Pickford (eds), *Frontiers of Family Law* (2nd edn.), John Wiley, 1995, chap. 3.

Quinton, Selwyn, Ruston and Dance, 'Contact with birth parents – A response to Ryburn' [1998] CFLQ 349.

'*Re SC (A Minor)(Adoption: Freeing Order)* – Time for placement orders?' [1999] Fam Law 484.

Richards, 'It feels like someone keeps moving the goalposts – regulating post-adoption contact, *Re T (Adopted Children: Contact)*' [1996] CFLQ 175.

Richards, 'Relinquishment, freeing or abandonment' [1997] CFLQ 313.

Ryburn, 'Welfare and justice in post-adoption contact' [1997] Fam Law 28.

Ryburn, 'In whose best interest? – Post-adoption contact with the birth family' [1998] CFLQ 53.

Savas and Treece, '*Re M (Adoption or Residence Order)* – Adoption or residence? Too many parents ... ?' [1998] CFLQ 311.

Spon-Smith, 'The inherent jurisdiction and revocation of freeing orders' [2000] Fam Law 43.

Van Bueren, 'Children's access to adoption records – State discretion or an enforceable international right' (1995) 58 MLR 371.

Website

British Agencies for Fostering & Adoption (BAAF): www.baaf.org.uk/

Questions

1 Should the welfare of the child be the court's paramount consideration in adoption, not the first?
2 The Government proposes to introduce a new form of order which will provide permanence for children short of the legal separation involved in adoption (see 17.13). Is this a good idea? In what sorts of situations is it likely to be used? Can you foresee any problems?

Index